MORAL PANIC

Changing Concepts of the Child Molester

in Modern America

Philip Jenkins

YALE UNIVERSITY PRESS   NEW HAVEN AND LONDON

Designed by Rebecca Gibb

Set in type by The Composing Room of Michigan, Inc., Grand Rapids, Michigan

Printed in the United States of America by Vail-Ballou Press, Binghamton, New York

Library of Congress Cataloging-in-Publication Data

Jenkins, Philip, 1952–

Moral panic : changing concepts of the child molester in modern America / Philip Jenkins.

p.   cm.

Includes bibliographical references (p.   ) and index.

ISBN 0-300-07387-9 (alk. paper)

1. Child molesters—United States—Psychology.   2. Child sexual abuse—United States.   I. Title.

HV6570.2.J46   1998

364.15′554′019—dc21

98-14890

CIP

A catalogue record for this book is available from the British Library.

The paper in this book meets the guidelines for permanence and durability of the Committee on Production Guidelines for Book Longevity of the Council on Library Resources.

10 9 8 7 6 5 4 3 2 1

To Joel Best

Contents

Acknowledgments

It would be hopeless to attempt a comprehensive list of the individuals who have helped me complete this book, so I will confine myself to thanking my wife, Liz Jenkins, and my colleagues Michael Anesko, Deborah Clarke, Aminadav Dykman, Linda Ivanits, Gary Knoppers, William L. Petersen, and Stephen Suknaic.

I owe a special debt of gratitude to Kathryn Hume, who read and commented extensively on an early draft of the manuscript.

Note on Usage

Issues of language and usage are central to this book, which, in order to trace the complex history of attitudes toward the sexual maltreatment of children, examines the changing uses of terms like *pervert, pedophile, molester, defiler, psychopath,* and *predator*. None of these words or concepts is privileged in the sense of representing a universally accepted, objective reality, as each is rooted in the attitudes of a particular time, and each carries its ideological baggage. For instance, although the term *sexual abuse* has a long history, not until the mid-1970s did it acquire its present cultural and ideological significance, with all its connotations of betrayal of trust, hidden trauma, and denial; in discussions of earlier periods, it is anachronistic to apply these meanings to the term. In modern usage, on the other hand, it is inappropriate to use a largely obsolete term like *pervert,* except in quotation marks, and those who were called *sex psychopaths* in the 1940s would not be diagnosed as such by psychiatrists today.

A similar problem arises with terms that assume the factual accuracy of a statement that is not necessarily correct. Thousands of people claim to be "victims" or "survivors" of satanic or ritual abuse, although these claims would be regarded by many as highly suspect. Even where the reality of abuse itself is not in serious doubt, the use of the term *survivor* calls to mind aspects of the modern "incest survivor" movement. It seems impossible to write on this topic without using language that appears to accept the ideological interpretations of a particular school of thought, and in so doing forecloses the exploration of other avenues of interpretation.

Throughout the book, therefore, there are many instances where words should properly be qualified with quotation marks or even preceded by words like *so-called, alleged,* or *self-described,* but in practice this is scarcely possible. To use quotation marks for *abuse* and *victim* is not only pedantic; it incorrectly implies doubts about the reality of the phenomenon. Using quotation marks to bracket *pedophile* or *molester,* for example, can suggest that one is doubting the reality or culpability of the offense. In order to avoid misleading the reader or weighing down the text, therefore, I have generally avoided using quotation marks, italics, or qualifiers for words like *survivor, pervert, psychopath, pedophile, victim, abuse,* and *crisis,* even in cases where a word might have merited such qualification.

Creating Facts

This book concerns the creation of orthodoxies, of social facts so obvious that it seems incredible that they could ever have been ignored or doubted and yet which, in historical perspective, appear temporary and contingent.[1] Prominent among what are accepted as self-evident facts in contemporary America is the belief that children face a grave danger in the form of sexual abuse and molestation. This menace has certain well-known, stereotypical characteristics. Sexual abuse is pervasive, a problem of vast scope; molesters or abusers are compulsive individuals who commit their crimes frequently and whose pathologies resist rehabilitation or cure. Sexually deviant behavior often escalates to violence or murder. Sexual relations with adults invariably cause lasting damage to the children involved; a battery of psychological explanations exists to account for any failure by the victim to perceive harm from the abuse or to recognize its severity. Finally, sexual molestation results in what is called the cycle of abuse: molestation so disturbs the victim that he or she usually repeats the same act later against children of the next generation.

Any or all of these ideas may be objectively correct, but what is striking is how very recently they have been established and popularized; these were not social facts twenty-five years ago. In the sizable literature from the 1950s through the 1970s, one can easily find writers then regarded as leading experts making statements that are diametrically opposed to current beliefs and that would be roundly condemned if they were published today. A book from the 1960s, for example, would state what was then orthodoxy: molestation was a very infrequent offense unlikely to cause significant harm to the vast majority of subjects (the word *victims* seemed too harsh), and molesters were confused inadequates unlikely to repeat their offenses. Children were often regarded as seducers who provoked such offenses for their own psychological reasons. According to this perception, child molestation was as innocuous as it is injurious in the modern image. In turn, the benevolent view of these years was in sharp contrast to the more sinister notions of the 1940s and early 1950s, when many believed that children were under a vast social threat from predators who killed their victims or scarred them for life.

Images of the sex offender have changed dramatically and cyclically over time. Originating in the Progressive Era, the imagery of the malignant sex fiend reached new heights in the decade after World War II, only to be succeeded by a liberal model over the next quarter century. More recently, the pendulum has swung back to the predator model; sex offenders are now viewed as being little removed from the worst multiple killers and torturers. And in each era, the prevailing opinion was supported by what appeared at the time to be convincing objective research. One reality prevailed until it was succeeded by another.

The current formulation of the child abuse problem is sometimes presented as an evolutionary stage in social development: the contemporary package of beliefs is true, whereas its predecessors were not. Because one can argue that recent realizations have been made possible by both the steady accumulation of new knowledge and the rending of taboos that had restricted research in the past, the campaign to establish the new orthodoxy becomes a heroic struggle for truth against prejudice and obscurantism.[2] In this view, refusal to acknowledge the scale and danger of sexual threats is dismissed as *denial,* a term borrowed from psychology to suggest that one's opponents refuse to accept a reality that seems obvious to the speaker.

But the cyclical nature of public interest shows that we need a more subtle and complex explanation. Theories about sexual abuse have not evolved in a simple or linear way; rather, they have ebbed and flowed—we forget as well as learn. Public willingness to accept claims has also fluctuated over .time, and together these changes have affected how not only the mass media but also legislators, judges, medical experts, and criminal-justice professionals have approached the sexual abuse of children.

Constructing Problems

The child abuse problem is one of many that have varied enormously in the amount of attention they have received in different eras. Sometimes the degree of public concern may change for quite logical and comprehensible reasons. Sexually transmitted diseases, for example, which were a recurrent nightmare before 1910, were considered far less dangerous once medical science had them substantially under control by the middle of the twentieth century, but fears revived with the discovery of new incurable illnesses in the 1980s. In other instances, the perceived significance of a given problem grows or diminishes without any change in the real threat-potential of the condition itself. In the past decade, stalking, elder abuse, and sexual harassment have all become major social issues without any evidence that the behaviors themselves have increased, whereas other, once frightening issues like homosexuality, racially mixed marriages, and the eugenic decline of the race have all but disappeared as sources of alarm. And although there are far more people on the planet now than there were twenty or thirty years ago, overpopulation is no longer seen as the devastating "population bomb" that it was in those years. Another category of problem rises or falls according to an intermittent cycle that shapes public fears over, say, drugs, juvenile delinquency, or immoral music. Although a phenomenon may remain more or less unchanged over time, it can be seen as a problem or a social fact in one era but not another.[3]

We can see that the stereotypical sex offender who provided a nightmare image in the 1940s had become a semihumorous figure two or three decades later, but why did this change occur? How did the obvious facts of one generation become the arrant nonsense of the next, and vice versa? Many explanations are possible. The sexual revolution that began in the late 1950s increased tolerance for many once-stigmatized behaviors, while there was also a natural reaction, and perhaps overreaction, against earlier hysteria and hyperbole. But whichever theory proves most convincing, the change of attitudes can be explained without supposing that any one period has a monopoly on truth or falsehood. That an issue is approached through social and behavioral science does not exempt its interpretations from the influence of broader cultural and political trends.

Scholarly approaches to social problems usually fall under one of two broad headings. The first and more familiar view is objectivist, which accepts that something is a problem when it harms or disturbs a significant section of society. A social scientist aims to quantify that problem, to explore its roots, and to suggest possible ways of removing or solving it. The second view, constructionism, may or may not accept that the phenomenon exists or, if it does, that it is indeed harmful, but the central question is how the condition comes to be viewed as a problem in the first place. For constructionists, "our sense of what is or what is not a social problem is a product, something that has been produced or constructed through social activities."[4] It is impossible to define a problem in an objective or value-free way, since talking about a "problem" or "crisis" ipso facto implies that there is a solution, that change of some kind is necessary or desirable. If we ask how society can deal with the menace of sexual predators, we have already phrased the question in such a way as to preclude many possible approaches to the complex issues surrounding sexual offenses. To speak of a response to "sex offenders" without further definition implies what is far from clear: that anyone who violates one of the myriad statutes prohibiting sexual misconduct must be suffering from some kind of personality disorder.

In this book I contend that all concepts of sex offenders and sex offenses are socially constructed realities: all are equally subject to social, political, and ideological influences, and no particular framing of offenders represents a pristine objective reality. Each in its way is instructive for the light it casts on the concerns, prejudices, and fears of the society that thus defines its deviants and outsiders. The changing frames of the sex offender provide an index of shifting social attitudes to matters as diverse as the status of children, the structure of the family, the range of acceptable sexual behaviors, and tolerance of alternative sexual orientations. By definition, deviance supposes a norm: we can speak of what is odd or different only when we agree on what is normal. In order to understand changing notions of sexual deviancy, then, we must first understand fluctuating concepts of sexual normality. *Abuse* is meaningless without a standard of proper *use*.

Constructionism means more than simple debunking. Although a constructionist might challenge the factual claims used to support a particular cause, he or she does not argue that the problem itself has no basis in reality. Child molestation does occur and can cause severe physical and psychic damage; there are in fact human predators who rape, mutilate, and kill children. Similarly, a problem like drug abuse or drunk driving does have an objective basis. The questions are why issues are perceived as social problems in particular times and places but not in others and what methods are used by groups and individuals to make and establish their claims. In the case of child sexual abuse, the most important activist groups include therapists and psychiatrists, criminal-justice administrators, women's groups, sexual reformers and libertarians, and moral traditionalists and conservatives. A constructionist study examines the means by which their respective views were projected, whether through the news media and popular fiction or academic and professional sources. Also critical is the question of audience, of why people are prepared to accept one rather than another of the given models offered to them at different times.

The idea of applying a constructionist approach to successive sex crime crises is far from new. One of the most cited studies in social-problem literature, Edwin Sutherland's skeptical analysis of an earlier sex crime panic, was published in 1950, and Nicholas N. Kittrie's monumental *The Right to Be Different*, which critiqued the sex psychopath legislation passed in mid-century, appeared in 1971. Sex crime waves of the 1930s and 1940s have been discussed by cultural historians like George Chauncey, John D'Emilio, and Estelle Freedman, who all see the furor over the sex fiend as a veiled defense of particular concepts of masculine identity; each pays due attention to the changing roles of professional groups like psychiatrists and to the bureaucratic interests of law-enforcement agencies. David Finkelhor, one of the best-known advocates of the seriousness of the contemporary abuse problem, plausibly attributes the extreme claims of the 1940s to "moralists . . . campaigning against other kinds of progressive reforms, . . . e.g., sex education, humane treatment of sex offenders, end to censorship."[5]

Given this skeptical tradition, it is remarkable that when concern about child sexual abuse surged during the 1980s, so few scholars applied the same analytical approach to contemporary perceptions. We have masterly constructionist studies of the abuse issue and especially of the more bizarre fringes of that topic, but few have drawn historical analogies with the much maligned attitudes of the 1940s or the earlier crisis of the Progressive Era.[6] The consensus is that although earlier panics arose from ignorance, hysteria, and self-interest, contemporary formulations of child abuse are sober depictions of objective truth.

Meanwhile, the generation of scholars that grew up believing that sex psychopath laws were a catastrophic failure has scarcely responded to the effective revival of these measures across the United States during the 1990s. In neither our conceptualizing of the problem nor our devising of countermeasures is there much evidence of our having learned from history. Examining past crises over sex crimes shows us not only how claims tend to be exaggerated and distorted but also that policy responses exhibit the classic signs of panic legislation, namely, poor conception and drafting, overly broad scope, and inadequate consideration of likely side effects. Ideally, studying past failures would help us to avoid making the same mistakes in the new generation of sex law.

In this book I refer to *panics* over sex crime, a term derived from the moral panic theory formulated in the 1970s by British sociologists like Stanley Cohen and Stuart Hall. They argued that a wave of irrational public fear can be said to exist "when the official reaction to a person, groups of persons or series of events is out of all proportion to the actual threat offered, when 'experts' perceive the threat in all but identical terms, and appear to talk 'with one voice' of rates, diagnoses, prognoses and solutions, when the media representations universally stress 'sudden and dramatic' increases (in numbers involved or events) and 'novelty,' above and beyond that which a sober, realistic appraisal could sustain."[7] But what, in the context of child abuse, might be considered "a sober, realistic appraisal" of "the actual threat offered"? In the opening years of the twentieth century, social and medical investigators argued convincingly that American children were being molested and raped in numbers far higher than had been imagined in any earlier era, and this basic insight remains unchallenged. For all the caveats that can be raised about their methods and definitions, victimization surveys of the past two decades have consistently shown that millions of children are subjected to different forms of sexual maltreatment. The phenomenon demands public concern and an appropriate policy response. Why should we not panic?

The word *panic,* however, implies not only fear but fear that is wildly exaggerated and wrongly directed, and this is what can be observed quite spectacularly in eras like the late 1940s and the mid-1980s. At these times, concern over sexual abuse provides a basis for extravagant claims-making by professionals, the media, and assorted interest groups, who argue that the problem is quantitatively and qualitatively far more severe than anyone could reasonably suppose. Statements that in calmer years would mark the speaker as hyperbolic or paranoid suddenly acquire the status of incontestable fact, while skeptics are pitied for their callous denial. It comes to be believed that legions of sex fiends and homicidal predators stalk the land, that the number of active pedophiles runs into the millions, that tens of thousands of children are abducted and killed each year, that sinister cults have infiltrated preschools and kindergartens across the country, that incest affects one-fourth or even one-half of all young girls, that child pornography is an industry raking in billions of dollars and preying on hundreds of thousands of American youngsters every year. Ideas develop an organic life of their own, as one set of outlandish charges becomes the foundation for still more bizarre claims, and activists compete for the attention of a jaded mass media demanding ever-higher levels of shock value.[8] In response, lawmakers implement policies that may cause harm in areas having nothing to do with the original problem and that divert resources away from measures which might genuinely assist in protecting children. According to these criteria, the area of child molestation and sexual abuse has repeatedly produced panic responses during the past century or so.

Characteristic of such eras is the use of extreme language to portray the problem, to escalate the harmful and predatory quality of the behavior. The English language lacks an accepted value-neutral vocabulary for adults who engage in sexual acts with minors, and the commonly available terms make little distinction depending on whether the young person in question is a small child and or an older teenager. This is important, because public opinion draws a sharp distinction in the blame that can be attributed when the younger party is fifteen rather than five, and very different personality types are involved in each instance. What exactly should we call a man sexually interested in younger teenagers? The favored medical word, *ephebophilia*, is obscure, and the archaic *pederast* has virtually dropped out of common usage. Moreover, *pederast* usually applies only to man-boy interactions; no equivalent term exists for similar behavior between opposite sexes, because not until the twentieth century was this latter behavior regarded as pathological or illegal. Nor can we properly use a term like *boy-love, intergenerational intimacy,* or even *relationship,* which suggests elements of consent and mutuality unacceptable to the vast majority of observers. Although a *pedophile* is properly defined as someone sexually interested "in a prepubescent child (generally age thirteen years or younger)," the word is popularly extended to a man who carries out a sexual act with an adolescent, making him a "molester," a "baby-raper."[9]

No signifier used to describe sexual acts between adults and children represents a neutral consensus view, and most are either metaphors or reflect a discredited science. An adult man who has sex with a twelve-year-old girl or a fourteen-year-old boy is not literally a *fiend* or a *predator,* which are figurative terms designed to express horror at actions considered despicable or dangerous. In panic eras, the terminology of "objective" science is used, with the act being attributed to a *pervert,* a *degenerate,* a *defective,* or a *sex psychopath,* but in each case the word represents a scientific or medical worldview that is now obsolete. When technical terms enter general discourse and the mass media, their meanings become vastly aggravated through frequent retellings and come to imply compulsive violence and monstrous perversion directed against the youngest and most vulnerable. There is a constant cycle whereby experts introduce new and more objective words to describe sexual criminals, only to find that later the terms acquire the worst connotations; this is the fate that has befallen, in succession, *sex offender, molester,* and *pedophile.*

Problem construction is shaped by the activities of competing interest groups. Different groups perceive social problems differently, depending on how far a behavior or phenomenon contradicts their ideal of how the world should be and what values should predominate. When a group succeeds in convincing a broad section of society about the gravity of that problem, it is also disseminating a portion of its distinctive worldview. This is achieved either by raising awareness of a newly discovered issue or, more commonly, by imposing the group's particular interpretation of an already recognized problem. When multiple groups wish to co-opt the same issue for their various purposes, construction is negotiated through rhetorical and political conflict, as factions enter into transient coalitions in order to promote their goals.

The process of constructing a social problem begins with an event or condition that represents a serious challenge to accepted values. Different activists try to link that issue with other conditions that they believe to be harmful or threatening, so that the original incident is used to support a moral or political lesson and the narrative is embroidered with appropriate cultural cross-references. In the case of child molestation, genuine public horror is aroused by sexual attacks against children, but the problems constructed around these incidents address issues not immediately connected with sexual violence. Because child murder and forcible rape are already treated with the utmost gravity, claims-makers must turn their attention to behaviors that, while not obviously harmful in themselves, are cited as precursors of violence. Activists present minor sexual offenses as stepping-stones culminating in unacceptable violence and therefore deserving of our condemnation. Outrage at random violence is transformed into a largely symbolic crusade against the nonviolent and thus squanders resources on the mildly deviant.

This process is illustrated by the case of Westley Alan Dodd, who was hanged in 1993 for the sex murders of three young boys in Washington State. While societies vary in how seriously they treat particular acts of violence, it is difficult to imagine any community that would fail to view crimes of this sort as the gravest form of moral evil or social pathology. But not all communities agree in how prominent a role someone like Dodd should play in shaping social policy and criminal law: some societies view an act like his as an isolated expression of individual evil, whereas others place it in a broader context of moral, political, or societal failure which must be urgently remedied. In recent years, American policymakers and media have seen such crimes as developing inexorably from lesser sexual offenses, and association with so menacing a figure gives rhetorical urgency to the demand that these activities be curbed.

This approach is not new, as an "escalation theory" of sexual offenses has been the prevailing orthodoxy for most of the twentieth century. While the 1990s uses Westley Dodd, the 1930s and 1940s were haunted by the image of Albert Fish, who was executed in 1936 following a career of child homicide and extreme sexual perversion. The crimes of both men are taken to represent the predictable, if extreme, consequence of the conduct of the "ordinary" child molester. From this perspective, there is no such thing as a *minor* sexual offense, in that acts like exhibitionism, voyeurism, and sexual interference with children are potentially all symptoms of damaging pathological violence; homosexuals have repeatedly been stigmatized in this way. It is not obvious, however, that sex crimes are linked in a logical chain, and we do not have to go far back into history to find a time when the molester or child abuser was viewed very differently.

Child Murder

Because child-protection movements are commonly detonated by sex murders, it should be emphasized how extremely rare these incidents are. Using statistics to put such a phenomenon in context can invite charges that one is trivializing an utterly horrible event, that even a single case is far too many. Also, focusing on murder ignores grave crimes that injure but do not kill, like the act of rape and sexual mutilation, which provoked an upsurge of legislative activity against sex offenders in Washington State in the late 1980s. But a quantitative measure is useful in assessing the popular stereotype of the child molester as a man who repeatedly rapes and assaults children until finally he kills, perhaps claiming many victims. Although we can never know how many children are molested in a particular year, we can know with some certainty how many are murdered and in what circumstances, and the results are surprising.

Children are at very low risk from homicide, making nonsense of the claims, aired frequently in the 1980s, that many thousands were killed each year by serial murderers, pornographers, or pedophile rings. The proportion of children killed by strangers is small, as is the number killed in circumstances of sexual assault. Consider children below the age of twelve, the age-group of interest to pedophiles: between 1980 and 1994 in the United States, 13,600 such individuals were murdered—about 900 per year. Of these, more than 400 each year were infants under the age of one and were usually killed by their parents; indeed, 54 percent of all the child victims were killed by parents or other family members. In contrast, strangers accounted for the murders of just 6 percent of the annual total, or about 54 children per year, though some stranger homicides were also found in the "unknown relationship" category, 130 victims a year. But even the strangers were not necessarily sex killers. In only 3 percent of the crimes, or 27 cases each year, did "a sex offense either [occur] simultaneously with or preceded the murder of a child." One-fifth of these cases, about 5 victims per year, involved the murder of a child by a stranger in a sexual assault, the sort of crime carried out by a Westley Dodd; about 9 more deaths each year were attributed to neighbors or acquaintances. Examining cases of young people under the age of eighteen, a recent survey has estimated that about one hundred abduction murders annually can be attributed to strangers. These figures for sex killings can usefully be set alongside the hundreds of child murders caused each year by physical maltreatment, neglect, and torture, usually at the hands of parents or other family members or intimates. Framing the child abuse problem exclusively in sexual terms diverts attention and resources from this other lethal problem.[10]

Although recent debate about sex offenders has focused on child killers like Westley Alan Dodd and sex murders committed by strangers, like the men who killed Megan Kanka and Polly Klaas, these atrocious crimes represent a tiny proportion of homicide activity and of sexual offenses in general, and we should not use these cases as typical examples in shaping social policy toward sexual deviance.

The Cycle of Legislation

In the aftermath of these notorious crimes in the 1990s, nearly all states have undertaken a fundamental revision of their statutes concerning sex offenders, providing for harsher sentencing and long-term incapacitation for those seen as irredeemably dangerous. Other measures involve forms of community notification, mandating that released sex offenders be subject to close surveillance by police and be required to notify neighbors and community groups who might be affected by their presence.

Here, too, the historical record can offer a useful perspective, as these recent laws strongly recall the sex psychopath statutes that were passed with so much enthusiasm between about 1937 and 1957. In that era also, an offender could be designated as a sex psychopath, a judgment that could earn him (or, very rarely, her) an indefinite period of institutional confinement. A nuisance sex crime, even a misdemeanor, could in theory result in an accused person being incarcerated for many years, far longer than what would have been required for even a grave act of personal violence. These sex psychopath statutes echoed an even earlier wave of legislation passed to regulate those who were then called defective delinquents, a category that caused public panic between about 1908 and 1922. The modern rebirth of the sex psychopath laws powerfully illustrates the cyclical nature of concern about sex crime and the same popular tendency to seek legislative panaceas that also shape reactions to juvenile delinquency and substance abuse.[11]

In the sex offender laws of the 1910s, 1940s, and 1990s, each wave of legislation contained elements likely to invoke constitutional challenge.

The conditions that earned commitment under the respective statutes were very loosely defined, with the label *sex offender* often applied to those whose acts were not in themselves violent or predatory. Vague definitions gave authorities wide latitude in penalizing individuals guilty not of serious crime but of moral or sexual unorthodoxy, so that the impact was most sharply felt by minor offenders with little potential for violence. Procedural issues were also murky: deviants were subjected to a mixture of civil and criminal devices so that de facto criminal penalties were imposed without due process, and often retroactively. Finally, once enacted, these laws were so rarely invoked as to suggest that they did not fulfill a genuine social need.

What is remarkable about legislation beset with such difficulties is not that it ultimately fails but that it survives for any period in the first place, and the collapse of the sex psychopath laws in the 1960s might well presage the likely fate of legislation passed in the 1990s. Once the initial furor passed, numerous cases demonstrated the absurd or unjust effects of the laws. Mounting opposition from legal, judicial, and libertarian sources resulted in the acts being overturned or becoming inoperative. The panic atmosphere surrounding the passage of the laws itself produced a reaction, and rhetoric that once sounded plausible came to seem overblown and even ludicrous. While historical comparison is risky, the downfall of the earlier laws suggests that contemporary sex predator statutes are likely to meet a comparable fate and to achieve a similarly malodorous historical reputation.

Fathers and Predators

When it comes to the safety of children, societies vary not only in the degree of danger they perceive but also in the nature of the threat, and the modern emphasis on predators means that other forms of danger receive less notice or are neglected altogether. The idea of child protection as such is politically neutral, for the belief that children need defending says nothing about from whom or what. In the Middle Ages, many Europeans believed firmly that children were in constant peril of being abducted by Jews, who supposedly offered up children as victims in their ritual sacrifices, and also by witches and gypsies. In keeping with the religious ideology of the age, the absolute certainty of these perils was confirmed by the divine signs and miracles associated with missing and murdered children, who were venerated as saints.[12]

Today, while few would deny that millions of American children are vulnerable to sexual exploitation, there is much room for disagreement about the roots of the problem and the nature of the solutions. One central question is, does most of the danger come from within the family or from outside? Throughout the past century, identifying the offenders responsible for sex crime has been a perennial debate. In 1950, few doubted that the problem was one of outsiders, of sex fiends or sex psychopaths, near-demonic figures satisfying their baneful sexual urges at the expense of women and children unknown to them. This idea was found in the Progressive Era and again in the 1970s and 1980s, but in both these periods, predator imagery existed alongside rival interpretations that emphasized the distinct problem of incest or abuse by family members and acquaintances.[13]

The rival approaches differ vastly in their appeal and in the policy solutions implied: if the incest view lent support to far-reaching critiques of current social organization and gender roles, the stranger-molester concept was compatible with a conservative rhetoric of law and order, public decency, and moral reintegration. In the tumultuous controversy and claims-making of recent years, between about 1992 and 1995, American public opinion has shifted quite dramatically from the radical implications of a focus on incest back to an emphasis on "stranger danger," on the crimes of serial predators like Westley Dodd. The ascendancy of the predator theme involves major ideological compromise or concession by some child-protection advocates and a clear victory for moral conservatives. As so often in the past, the ever-flexible concept of the molester, the abuser, or the predator provides an invaluable gauge for the state of current social ideologies.

Saving the Children

Few people live their lives without engaging in some conduct that has been defined as either criminal or deviant in some context and (with surprising frequency) is so regarded in current American jurisdictions. At different times and places, the following acts have all been characterized as sexually deviant and often criminal: exhibitionism, voyeurism, abortion, bestiality, masturbation, contraception, consensual sadomasochistic activity, sexual relations with persons of a different race, homosexual relationships between consenting adults (male or female), heterosexual relationships between men and women not legally married to each other, and the practice of miscellaneous sexual positions or techniques, with even marriage providing no defense against prosecution for consensual oral or anal sex. The term *sodomy* has proved infinitely flexible in comprehending such acts. As recently as 1986, the U.S. Supreme Court upheld the principle of sodomy statutes; some twenty states still have enforceable laws, and half of them classify the behaviors as felonies. Adultery remains an offense in half of the states and a felony in Michigan, Massachusetts, Wisconsin, and elsewhere.[14] Nor has the blame for a deviant sexual act consistently been placed entirely on one or other party. For much of the twentieth century, in cases involving incest or molestation the child victim has been regarded as a sex delinquent quite as assuredly as the adult perpetrator was defined as a sex offender.

Sexually appropriate behavior is a socially constructed phenomenon, the definition and limits of which vary greatly among different societies, and this is especially true where children and young people are concerned. Perhaps a billion people alive today have been subjected as children to some form of genital mutilation or circumcision, which is demanded or approved by religious consensus, is virtually never regulated by secular law, and is never mentioned in literatures on sex crime or ritualistic abuse. Nor is there a natural age of sexual consent. Although a biological imperative dictates restrictions on the behavior of prepubescent children, no universal rule determines that sexual readiness properly begins at twelve or sixteen or twenty-one; before the 1880s, the age of consent for girls in most American jurisdictions stood at the alarmingly low figure of ten years.[15]

Anthropological literature shows huge disparities in attitudes toward sexual contacts between adults and children or adolescents, both in contemporary preliterate cultures and in the Christian societies of preindustrial Europe. European parents in the sixteenth and seventeenth centuries treated infants and toddlers with a playful sexual frankness that today would be not just wildly inappropriate but criminal. At the start of the seventeenth century, the child who later became King Louis XIII of France lived in a family environment in which adults frequently touched and played with his genitals.[16] After the age of seven, Louis was expected to conduct himself with greater sexual reticence, but he married, and consummated the marriage, at fourteen. Child-rearing practices in this case were unusual only in the detail with which they were recorded, and similar behaviors still prevail in many parts of the globe.

It is not self-evident that a sexual act between individuals of widely differing ages constitutes immoral or criminal behavior, that it causes grave harm to either participant, or that it involves a compulsive psychological condition. The selective nature of sex laws is suggested by the ancient double standard whereby relationships between an adult woman and an underage boy have always been regarded as far less reprehensible than those in which the gender roles were reversed. The young male faces no danger of becoming pregnant, nor does he risk the loss of honor or marriageability. For boys, such relationships are depicted as coming-of-age rituals rather than abuse, and these liaisons are fondly depicted in Western popular culture. Even with our heightened contemporary sensibility about exploitation, prosecutions of women who have had these encounters are still risky ventures for authorities.[17]

The fact that the notion of what constitutes sexual deviancy fluctuates over time is what makes the issue so useful as a means for understanding social attitudes. Chapter 2, "Constructing Sex Crime, 1890–1934," describes the history of American attitudes to sex offenders through the early twentieth century. The modern category of sex crime is little more than one hundred years old, and the idea that sexual misdeeds were symptoms of underlying sexual perversion owes much to the work of Richard von Krafft-Ebing in the 1880s: terms like *homosexual, pervert,* and *pedophile* entered the English language shortly afterward. The oldest American accounts of child molestation as a widespread social problem date from 1894, when we find the then-astonishing claim that "rape of children is the most frequent form of sexual crime."[18] In these same years, the national movement to raise the age of consent persuaded most state legislatures to enact America's first wave of statutes specifically aimed at defending children from sexual exploitation. Although it was scarcely noticed in America at the time, in 1896 Sigmund Freud formulated the epoch-making theory that many girls from respectable families had genuinely been traumatized by sexual abuse and incest. Concern about a pervasive sexual danger to children survived into the early 1920s, when it largely dissipated.

Chapter 2 also examines the earliest attempts to design special legislation against newly identified sex criminals. By 1910, social investigators were confirming the worst speculations about the prevalence of child sexual molestation, and panic about sex killers and perverts became acute about 1915. As in the 1970s, a proactive social work campaign against physical abuse uncovered numerous cases of sexual maltreatment, and as in the 1990s, a period of concern about children exploited within their families was followed by a new alarm about stranger predators. The response was the defective delinquent statutes, which provided the matrix for later measures against sex psychopaths and predators.

Although fears of sex crime reached a low ebb in the early 1930s, they swiftly revived around 1935. Chapter 3 describes the panic that ensued over the issue during the next two decades, when the phrase *sex offender* ceased to be a generic term for everyone who violated a sex law and came to signify sexually violent aggressors. Ideas of a public menace were initially nursed by the FBI and the newspapers and then popularized in books and magazine articles, in films and popular fiction. The intensity of public fears is all the more striking when set beside the number of other potent issues causing alarm in these years, including constant war scares, nuclear threats, and rumored domestic subversion. Claims struck a powerful chord among large sections of the population: the sexual menace focused ill-defined fears resulting from social upheavals at this time, which were causing a radical redefinition of gender roles and family obligations.

In reaction, sweeping sexual psychopath laws were passed by more than half the states, and these measures are studied in Chapter 4, "The Sex Psychopath Statutes." That the statutes were never applied to a large number of offenders suggests that their main function was symbolic rather than practical, but the laws did inspire acrimonious debate within the therapeutic community. Although some psychiatrists expressed wholehearted support for the underlying principles of the laws and the associated notion of the psychopath, others were more hostile, and complained about the misuse of psychiatric terminology.

In reaction to the sex crime panic, scholars and academics of the late 1950s and 1960s underplayed the scale and seriousness of the sex offender issue and urged a movement away from punitive public reactions. Molestation was seen as a nonthreatening symptom of sexual inadequacy, meriting therapy rather than punishment under an outdated legal system that harked back to more puritanical times. A sexual episode would cause little harm to a child, provided the police or courts did not "make an issue" of it. After the mid-1960s, liberal jurists reinforced this attitude by limiting the powers of forcible civil commitment and discretionary sentencing that had earlier been fundamental to official policies toward sexual deviants. Chapter 5, "The Liberal Era, 1958–1976," examines this libertarian attitude to forms of sexual expression once regarded as gravely deviant.

After the mid-1970s, public opinion moved in the opposite direction, with renewed perceptions of alleged threats to women and especially children. A new and unassailable social orthodoxy held that abuse was widespread and resulted in lasting damage. Between about 1976 and 1986, the casual attitude prevailing in the early 1970s changed so radically and swiftly as to constitute the "revolution" described in Chapter 6. Public opinion went far toward accepting what had recently been a distinctively feminist view: the most serious danger came not from strangers but from fathers and other family members. Responding to the new mood, legislators rushed to pass new measures protecting children from abuse and incest and reforming courtroom procedures. Although new techniques of interviewing children and presenting evidence were initially welcomed, they would soon have questionable consequences in the form of allegations that abuse was occurring in bizarre or ritualistic settings.

The child-protection issue appealed to moral conservatives as well as feminists, and some important claims-makers used the abuse threat to advance traditionalist viewpoints about moral decadence. As in the 1940s, homosexuals found themselves among the main targets of the new campaign against pedophiles and sex offenders, for it was suggested that homosexuality was closely aligned with predatory behaviors directed against children. Stigmatization of this sort was a common phenomenon in the framing of sexual offenses, as claims-makers drew attention to one issue because it symbolized another that could not be attacked directly. There have long been moralist groups who wished to denounce and stigmatize homosexuality, the sale of pornography, or the activities of fringe religious cults. They achieved little support for these views in the prevailing moral climate of the 1970s or 1980s, which emphasized adults' freedom to determine their private conduct. Shifting the focus to children's involvement fundamentally changed the moral and legal environment and made it impossible to claim that these actions were either victimless or consensual. In these years we find morality campaigns directed not against homosexuality but against pedophilia, less against pornography in general than against child pornography, not against cults and satanism but against ritual child abuse. In each case, claims-makers raised the stakes by arguing that real physical harm resulted from these offenses and that the perpetrators were conspiratorial gangs, sex rings, or devil-worshiping covens.

The success of these rhetorical strategies is illustrated by the moral debates of the 1980s, described in Chapter 7, "Child Pornography and Pedophile Rings." Notions about organized pedophilia enjoyed an ideological significance far beyond the real scale of any documented sex rings, relocating concern about molestation outside the nuclear family and diverting attention from incest to external predation. In contrast to earlier concepts of the molester as a species of defective, the newly reconceived pedophile possessed a dangerous criminal intellect, with access to the latest forms of technology, communication, and even behavior-modification techniques.

One popular version of the conspiracy idea appealed to religious and political conservatives because it blamed the abuse crisis literally on agents of the devil, that is, on satanic and ritualistic rings. Chapter 8, "The Road to Hell," examines the menace of pedophile rings said to be operating in America's preschools, a concept that became a reasonable facsimile of the medieval ritual murder threat. As before, allegations sprang from a coalition of interest groups, including therapists, feminists, religious and anticult groups, and theorists of political conspiracy. This abuse scare ultimately led to a setback for the child-protection movement, as growing incredulity about the charges and the techniques by which they had been produced resulted in unprecedented criticism of child advocates. Linked to this was the assault on the incest-survivor movement, particularly the idea that repressed memories of abuse could be recovered through therapy. In the new climate of the early 1990s, both adults' recovered memories of childhood and children's testimony concerning preschool diabolism were viewed with skepticism, and the entire survivor movement came to be seen as a pressing social problem in its own right.

While concern about sexual threats remained undiminished, doubts about abuse by parents and intimates led to a renewed emphasis on external predators. As Chapter 9 describes, in the 1990s molesters and pedophiles were again portrayed as alien and deviant, as monsters and predators. Fears found a novel focus in the Internet, which was viewed as means whereby pedophiles could stalk and seduce children on line, and the personal computer became a Trojan horse within the home. If molesters were so sophisticated in their methods and so compulsive in their behavior, they could be dealt with only by an emergency response, perhaps the lengthy preventive detention provided for by predator statutes.

Chapter 10 traces elements common to these successive panics and describes the complex interplay of the interest groups who defined and publicized the sex offender issue. Child protection is such a politically appealing theme that it is surprising to find eras when it is not at the forefront of public debate, and periods of panic can be accounted for more easily than can times of complacency like the 1920s or 1960s. The difference between eras is explained in terms of changes in the audience to whom activists are seeking to appeal. Fluctuations in public attitudes reflect demographic changes, which determine the assessment of social threats, and changing demographic patterns also decide how much latitude can properly be allowed to the young in their personal conduct. As we shall see, panics about sex offenders are closely related to other fears, from anxieties about youth crime to worries about drug abuse, a link that partly explains why concerns about sex crimes have so frequently acquired similar ideological directions, emphasizing external monster figures, psychopaths, and predators.

Constructing Sex Crime, 1890–1934

I was only eight years old;
And before I grew up and knew what it meant
I had no words for it, except
That I was frightened and told my Mother.

EDGAR LEE MASTERS, "NELLIE CLARK," FROM *THE SPOON RIVER ANTHOLOGY*

In 1926, psychiatrist Benjamin Karpman examined a man who in other eras would be variously termed a sex fiend, a defiler, a child molester, or a serial pedophile. Karpman quotes at length the words of the subject, Kenneth Elton, who emerges as a rounded historical figure rather than the monster of media stereotypes.[1] Born in Virginia in 1899, Elton claimed to have been raped by an adult woman, a neighbor, when he was seven, and this incident had a great influence on his later behavior. He began molesting younger girls when he was about fifteen. As often happens in such cases, there is disagreement about the ages of his victims: while authorities stressed his predilection for prepubescent children, Elton presented himself as merely a teenage boy with a taste for girls a little younger than himself. While working at an army camp during World War I, he associated with girls of thirteen or fourteen in preference to the "gold-digger" women frequented by soldiers, figuring that the youngsters were probably disease-free. In 1914, however, he was charged with the attempted rape of a girl aged between seven and ten. Pronounced feebleminded, he was consigned to a state hospital for the insane, but doctors there determined that he was not medically insane. In 1922, after approaching a young girl on the street, he received a one-year jail sentence; in 1925, after being caught performing cunnilingus on a girl of nine, he was committed to St. Elizabeth's Hospital in Washington, D.C. Elton was puzzled by the tough official reaction, and he minimized his offenses as "a kind of masturbation, just to get the gun off."

Elton's fate in the 1920s differed from what would have occurred a century or two earlier: rather than being viewed as acts of moral evil or lust, his misconduct was seen as a medical condition that merited treatment in a mental institution. Intervention was needed to interrupt a pattern of compulsive, "perverted" behavior unlikely to respond to simple deterrence. The gravity with which his acts were viewed suggests that Elton was seen as merely one manifestation of a larger problem, one that had acquired the name *sex crime*. Although he had not yet physically harmed his victims, authorities were aware of the chance that his misbehavior might escalate, and their awareness was based on the medically oriented views that permeated the criminal-justice and mental health systems by the early twentieth century. The new positivist criminology was founded upon the radical principle that deviant acts were symptoms indicating underlying medical or biological flaws in the offender, conditions that demanded treatment or incapacitation. This approach undermined traditional ideas of personal responsibility and legal guilt and placed a new emphasis on defending the community from the persistent wrongdoer.

Elton's case occurred at a time when the correct response to sexual offenses was being widely debated. Although all acknowledged the need to protect children, there were sharp differences of approach between advocates of social reform, slum clearance, and antipoverty programs, on one hand, and those who favored forceful action by police and courts, on the other. And as in later years, those who saw the problem in terms of stranger molesters influenced policymakers far more than did activists concerned with "insider" abuse and incest. In so many ways, the Progressive Era provides a distant mirror to contemporary debates over child abuse, a problem formulated for the first time in its modern sense between about 1908 and 1922. In a foretaste of the 1970s and 1980s, feminists allied with therapists, social workers, and moral reformers in order to defend children, and the new ideas were promulgated by a sensationalistic media. Also as in later years, the child-protection movement drew support from the bureaucracies of law enforcement and corrections, which gained new discretionary powers for controlling deviants.

Morality Laws

Although criminal laws regulating sexual behavior have existed since the oldest civilizations, the rationale for such legislation has changed substantially over time. In America the earliest colonial law codes contained lengthy lists of sexual offenses meriting punishment, with fornication, adultery, bestiality, and homosexuality all drawing severe physical penalties. These acts were forbidden because they were regarded as grave sins, and this religious consensus was reflected in the law of civil society.[2] Nineteenth- and twentieth-century concepts of perversion and sex crime were superimposed on legal codes founded on the very different concepts of sin and immorality.

One recurrent problem in studying the early laws is that deviant sexual behavior inspired such horror that cases are rarely described in detail, making it difficult for someone today to determine the exact nature of the original offenses: indictments in homosexuality cases, for example, sometimes refer only to "the crime not to be named among Christians." Although sodomy was universally condemned in the colonies and the early republic and could even receive the death penalty, there was much disagreement about what it entailed. Under common law, the offense involved sexual penetration that could not result in procreation, including intercourse between men, with animals, or with a prepubescent child of either sex. The specifications could be expanded, however, and in 1641 the Massachusetts Bay Colony faced a debate over a group of men who had sexually "abused," although not penetrated, two young sisters, Sara and Dorcas Humphrey. Some lawyers and divines argued that the behavior deserved the death penalty prescribed for sodomy, but the men escaped with a fine and whipping.[3]

Older morality statutes survived into the twentieth century. In 1934, the state of New York undertook a rare prosecution of a man for adultery with a married woman, but other cities were more enthusiastic: charges for fornication and adultery were regular events in Chicago's special Morals Court through the 1920s, while Boston recorded 242 arrests for adultery as late as 1948. Sodomy remained the generic label for numerous consensual acts, heterosexual or homosexual, including oral- or anal-genital contact as well as bestiality and necrophilia; the lack of definition provided some latitude, however, and early twentieth-century courts were not unanimous about whether fellatio was included. Until Illinois reformed its laws in 1961, all American jurisdictions enforced sodomy statutes, and penalties could be severe. In the 1940s, consensual sodomy with a person over eighteen years of age carried a maximum term of one year in New York but life imprisonment in Georgia and Nevada, and fifteen states provided maximum penalties of twenty years or more. Although male homosexuals usually bore the brunt of these savage penalties, they also applied to heterosexuals. In Wyoming and Indiana, sexual intercourse with a girl under twenty-one constituted fornication, which carried a penalty of several months in jail. If the man masturbated the girl but did not have sexual intercourse with her, then the charge was sodomy, with a maximum prison term of five years in Wyoming but fourteen years in Indiana.[4] California provided a fifteen-year sentence for "oral perversion."

The survival of older legal principles caused confusion as the sex offender problem came to be formulated, since it was impossible to analyze general information about sex crimes, which included a vast range of behaviors, forcible and consensual, grave and trivial. In Massachusetts, crime statistics from 1915 began to include a category of offenses "against chastity, morality and decency," but these included prostitution and pimping as well as adultery, bigamy, abortion, obscenity, polygamy, and cruelty to animals. Modern academic studies have been bedeviled by the abundance of violators guilty of technical breaches of archaic and arcane laws, but all of whom were technically sex offenders. Also, it has been difficult to identify truly dangerous or predatory offenders who should be subject to special sanctions. Efforts to draft a sex psychopath statute in the 1940s or 1950s required a list of specific acts which the person should have committed, and these catalogs all too often included sex offenses that in fact involved no force or violence. "An offender charged with carnal abuse may be one who has: forcibly raped an adult female; who has kissed or fondled a minor female; or who has had voluntary or forced intercourse with a minor female."[5] Even specifying that the individual should have committed a heinous or violent sex crime did not necessarily work, as indictments were phrased so as to make petty violations indistinguishable from extreme perversion.

These problems were acute in the area of offenses against children, as it was many years before medical and psychiatric professionals realized that an effective taxonomy of offenders would have to go well beyond existing legal categories. Through the sex crime panic of the mid-twentieth century, most writers stubbornly refused to recognize that many rapes and "offenses against children" in fact involved the statutory violation of laws based upon widely varying notions of the age of sexual consent. Although legally classified alongside an authentic molester like Kenneth Elton, many "child rapists" were boys or young men who had had consensual intercourse with teenage girls of roughly their own age.

The American colonies followed the common law principle that, before a certain age, a girl was too young to give valid consent to sexual activity. Most jurisdictions defined sexual intercourse with a girl younger than ten as rape or carnal abuse, while sexual interference short of intercourse would generally be classified as indecent liberties, "lewd and lascivious acts." Offenses were felonies if committed against children below the age of ten, but acts with slightly older girls were commonly misdemeanors. In 1885, the great majority of states still maintained the English age limit of ten years, while four enforced an age of twelve, but a widely popular social movement succeeded in raising these limits substantially over the next few years. In New York, for instance, a statute of 1787 established the age of sexual consent at ten years so that intercourse with a younger child constituted capital rape; the age of consent was raised from ten to sixteen in 1887 and to eighteen in 1895, at which it remained throughout the first half of the twentieth century.[6] By 1895, twenty-two states enforced as age of consent either sixteen or eighteen years, while ten more elected for fourteen years. Paradoxically, the average age at which youngsters experienced puberty fell steadily from the seventeenth through the nineteenth centuries, so that there was an increasing gap between biological maturity and the legal age for intercourse. By the early twentieth century, that interval was often five years or more, which hugely increased the potential for legal conflict.

The new principle of higher ages of consent did not win instant acceptance. Even after 1900, five southern states still set the age of consent at ten years, while several other jurisdictions maintained limits of twelve or thirteen; incredibly, Delaware's stood at seven years. In 1910, the United States recorded some fifteen thousand married girls who admitted to being fifteen or younger, but because overstating ages on marriage licenses was so commonplace a practice, this figure probably represents but a fraction of actual cases.

But the process of raising the age of consent continued in the next decades, leading to more than a few conflicts between law and practice. In 1934, for example, Tennessee law set the age of consent at twenty-one years, and a Tennessee court convicted a man of statutory rape for having sex with a twenty-year-old woman who had been previously married.[7] Some states took account of the man's age in each case, but most did not, even if he was younger than the girl. And while incest was prohibited in nearly every state, this offense was strictly defined as intercourse with penetration; other sexual acts could not be prosecuted under this law.

At midcentury, legal writers delighted in pointing out such anomalies as unreconstructed survivals of older social attitudes, but even today there is little agreement about the age of consent. In the United States, forty-one states enforce ages between sixteen and eighteen, but the remaining nine permit sexual activity by younger girls, in some cases as young as twelve or thirteen. (The Canadian age of consent is fourteen years.) States with higher ages will invariably have the larger numbers of violators of the law and thus apparently the highest concentration of sex offenders against children.[8] Age limits for adolescent boys having sex with men represent a murky legal area, but the issue may soon become urgent if states legalize same-sex marriage: if the same age limits are provided for both sexes, then the marriage of young teenage boys would be notionally legal in some states, however unacceptable to public opinion.

The moral rhetoric for regulating heterosexual behavior was reinforced by the pragmatic motive of preventing illegitimacy and reducing the burden on the public welfare system. The harm from which a young victim was to be protected was neither physical nor psychological but economic, because loss of virginity damaged a girl's marriageability; protection was extended as much to the girl's family as to her own prospects. In Edgar Lee Masters' *Spoon River Anthology* (1915), the father of eight-year-old Nellie Clark sets out to kill her molester because, with her virginity compromised, she is no longer marriageable within the community; although she later succeeds in marrying an outsider who is unaware of the incident, he abandons her when he discovers her true history. If a victimized girl were of legal age, her family would often try to force her to marry her molester, reinforcing their demand by violence or threats of ostracism. State laws reflected this "damaged goods" approach when they qualified the simple age limit by caveats about the girl's character. In mid-twentieth-century Pennsylvania, sex with a girl below the age of consent led to a reduced charge of fornication rather than rape if she was "not of good repute or was known to be previously unchaste." In North Carolina, sex with a girl between twelve and sixteen was rape only if she was a virgin, while in West Virginia, sex with a girl under sixteen was rape only if she was "of previous chaste character." In 1961, a sixty-year-old West Virginia man admitted to having committed sexual acts with a nine-year-old girl, but he was acquitted of statutory rape when the girl admitted to having previously had intercourse with a teenage boy.[9]

Defense of family honor was accompanied by concern about racial boundaries, and racial anxieties proved central in the enforcement of sex laws. Sexual incidents have often ignited racial violence in the United States, and the notion that white girls were threatened by black men was stoked by fictional works like the 1915 film *The Birth of a Nation*. Of the 4,259 lynchings that occurred throughout the United States between 1880 and 1920, rape, attempted rape, or molestation were the justifications cited in one-quarter of cases. Sex charges broadly defined accounted for roughly twenty-five lynchings each year in this period, and from the 1890s onward, 90 percent of all lynching victims were African Americans.[10] Whether by the action of the state or the mob, the death penalty was a frequent sanction for serious sex crime in these years.

Inventing the Pervert

Before the late nineteenth century, crimes involving sex were a commonplace part of the work of the justice system, but there was no sense of the sex criminal as a distinct or especially menacing category of malefactor. In colonial times, terms like *sodomy* or *carnal abuse* were reserved for actual behaviors rather than for inner tendencies, although the most scrupulous might speak of improper longings as "sodomy of the heart." In common usage, a sodomite was a person who *did* specific things rather than one predisposed to do so, just as a thief was one who stole and not just someone battling temptations to steal. After the late 1880s, American psychiatry and medicine were transformed by new perceptions of "sexual perversion," that is, a tendency to commit sexual acts that could not lead to procreation. Unlike the older notion of sodomy, perversion remained perversion, whether or not it was acted upon. This essentialist view caused a critical shift in the notion of sex crime and required new forms of official intervention.[11]

The framing of sex crime was part of a general reshaping of Western thought in the late nineteenth century, what Michel Foucault called a new episteme, a new means of assessing truth and knowledge. The dominant knowledge-system comprised ideas of evolutionary science, industrial progress, scientific racism, eugenics, and imperialism, and the accompanying social ideology found legitimacy by stereotyping and excluding the social categories that contradicted or defied these values. In the United States, the excluded shadow of progress included not just racial minorities but also criminal biological types and degenerates, homicidal sex fiends, and perverts, whose insidious effects on racial progress were symbolized by rampant venereal diseases, which became a pervasive nightmare for social reformers. And the new perspective, although convincingly dressed in the language of scientism, proved thoroughly compatible with contemporary notions of moral reform and sexual purity, which it was often employed to justify.

Among the varieties of perversion that came under scrutiny in America were pedophilia and homosexuality (the English term *homosexual* dates from 1892). Confirming the magnitude of the pervert danger was the evidence produced by Progressives and muckrakers about the vice districts of American cities, where gay and pederastic subcultures were apparent to any investigator. Case studies from these years sound quite familiar to a later audience: the "noted pederast" in Philadelphia who had given syphilis to a dozen of his victims; the "religious hypocrite" who "ruined a number of boys." In 1881, a Missouri case involving sodomy between an adult man and a thirteen-year-old boy was noted with the reproach that "this is a case which, however frequently committed, is rarely brought to the knowledge of the police." At the end of the century, social reformers venturing into the vice underworlds of American cities found evidence of child prostitution involving both girls and boys. In 1892, the Reverend Charles Parkhurst encountered a brothel where effeminate boy prostitutes engaged in "the worst vice that New York holds." Stephen Crane began a novel on the career of a boy of this type, a manuscript entitled "Flowers of Asphalt," before accepting his friends' advice that the topic made the work unsuitable for publication, even in a society growing used to literary muckraking. A vice investigation in Philadelphia in 1912 reported "the corruption of hundreds of young boys for the use of perverts. 'Numbers of boys in knee pants are commercializing themselves openly on our streets for the practice of perversion.' This use of boys from eight to fourteen has developed in the last five years to an appalling extent." In 1925, an account of Chicago's vice districts recorded "little boys as young even as ten years of age frequenting certain theatres for the purpose of soliciting men for homosexual practices. . . . We found them to be truants, runaways, defectives."[12]

The vast majority of such exposés addressed the exploitation of young girls. From the mid-1880s, American reformers were profoundly influenced by the activities of English moral crusaders Josephine Butler and W. T. Stead, who revealed the widespread vogue for underage girls in organized vice and who campaigned for a substantial increase in the legal age of consent and its more vigorous enforcement by police. American writers portrayed a pervasive threat to the safety and morality of young girls, who were effectively unprotected by a legal system that naively assumed a ten- or twelve-year-old could grant informed sexual consent. In 1893 Charlton Edholm's frequently reprinted tract *Traffic in Girls* cited supposedly typical cases of child exploitation: "When a big burly man fifty years of age is brought into a court of justice and confronted by the little ten year old victim of his lust, if he can prove that the child, for a paper of candy, consented to an act of which her childish mind is ignorant, that jury of twelve men— probably fathers of little girls themselves—will hold the child guilty and the man guiltless. If he cannot prove consent, still he may not be punished unless it is proved that the little child . . . resisted until exhaustion or death."

Such stories galvanized state legislatures to raise the age of consent, as feminists and religious groups combined to protest "the frightful indignities to which even little girls are subject." The national public campaigns surrounding these measures popularized the reformist view that a man who had sexual relations with children was not merely dissolute or hedonistic but a monster and pervert, a "moral leper" or "wild beast" who had committed a grave offense against both morality and racial well-being and who was as self-evidently dangerous as a carrier of smallpox. Edholm denounced "human gorillas, otherwise known as lecherous men."[13]

In the same years, medical writers were similarly arguing that sexual offenders posed an authentic threat to social and racial hygiene. Richard von Krafft-Ebing's *Psychopathia Sexualis* (1886) inspired an outpouring of writing on sexual conditions and complaints, as American scholars developed their own taxonomy of sex killers, pedophiles, and other sexually motivated offenders. In 1894 the widely read textbook *A System of Legal Medicine* included the pioneering account "Sexual Crimes," by Dr. Charles G. Chaddock, who the previous year had translated the first American edition of Krafft-Ebing's treatise. Chaddock's piece contained sections on rape, sexual abuse of children, sodomy (which included pederasty, bestiality, and tribadism), incest, exhibition and indecent exposure, and sexual perversion. In this authoritative survey, the first American work on the sexual abuse of children, Chaddock used European statistics to suggest that "rape of children is the most frequent form of sexual crime," amounting to perhaps 80 percent of rapes reported to the police. This frequency was easily explained, as children were weak and vulnerable, while men were always in search of novel sexual excitement. Also, a disastrous superstition said to flourish in Latin societies held that intercourse with a virgin could cure venereal diseases, and this association gave old-stock Americans yet another reason to attack the mores of new immigrant populations. Other forms of exploitation included sexual abuse, defined as "sexual manipulations which are unrelated to the normal sexual act," and pederasty was discussed in terms of anal intercourse. "Sexual perversion (erotic fetishism [sic]) might lead to an unnatural preference for children" and arose from "constitutional psychopathic deficiency."[14]

A *System of Legal Medicine* also contained a trailblazing piece entitled "Indecent Assault of Children," which was the first study to suggest the prevalence of incest and molestation in the United States. It was written by W. Travis Gibb, a young gynecologist who was the examining physician for the New York Society for the Prevention of Cruelty of Children (NYSPCC), a charity formed in 1874 to investigate physical maltreatment and neglect of the young. By 1910, the New York society had more than three hundred imitators across the country, and together they constituted a national movement for helping delinquent, neglected, or wayward children. The original goal of preventing cruelty evolved into wider schemes for remodeling the family structures of the poor in directions more in tune with middle-class models, partly through innovative devices like juvenile courts (1899). As child savers explored the life of the slums, they discovered other evils "besides . . . the constant presence of flagrant physical abuse of the type which led to this movement"—namely, "that girls, while mere children and before they know what they are doing, invite or are unwillingly subjected to horrible abuses from men" and are catching "loathsome diseases" as a result. As all the cases observed involved poor and often immigrant children, the problem was taken to reflect the non-Protestant values of city dwellers, leading Gibb to conclude that "the largest majority of cases . . . occur among the poorest and most depraved classes of people."[15]

Gibb's key insight was that molestation was a common crime, one that extended beyond the familiar image of men raping or seducing underage girls. Although Gibb had found "little or nothing in the medico-legal literature pertaining directly to the crime of indecent assault upon children," he concluded that the acts occurred "much more frequently than is generally supposed," were "usually committed in secret and without witnesses," and could be perpetrated by adult men against boys and by women against children of either sex. The NYSPCC noted "numerous instances" in which children were permitted or compelled to "perform an act of manustrupation" upon an adult man or woman. Gibb personally investigated an 1892 assault in which two men performed cunnilingus upon a girl of eleven. Assaults were perpetrated by "men who are insane, old men beyond the age of virility, men under the influence of liquor, and those suffering from some form of perversion of the sexual instinct which may be akin to insanity": this "pervert" category included men with an interest in cunnilingus or mutual "manustrupation." In their consequences these abusive acts varied enormously from case to case, often causing no harm "beyond the moral" but sometimes inflicting damage so extreme as to lead to death.[16]

Gibb cataloged the common forms of molestation, including cases in which children either performed masturbation or oral sex upon adults or were the recipients; this was a significant departure from the medical assumption of the day, which held that if a girl's hymen was found to be intact, she could not have been abused. Gibb struck a modern note when he advised doctors to be thorough in their physical examination of victims, observing symptoms of unusual genital abuse (including mutilation by foreign objects) and looking for evidence of discharges or sexually transmitted diseases. Less modern was his insistence that examinations be given without warning, so that false accusers would not have time to fake symptoms.

Gibb's observations would often be echoed by social investigators and moral crusaders, who cited sexual abuse as one of the evils arising from catastrophic poverty, poor education, and slum housing. Criminologist Henry Boies complained in 1893 that children "sporting promiscuously" in the streets, "where every foul nighthawk seeks its prey, lose the lovely innocence of childhood before they reach their teens." In 1913, an observer attacking the "inhuman herding in the tenements" remarked that "cases growing out of the defilement of innocent children by lodgers are common in the Children's Court," with attendant problems of pregnancy and syphilis; "in many of the houses were lodgers who came in tipsy at night, and there were young girls groping their way up those dark stairs too." Poor families depended for their economic survival on taking in lodgers, who generally shared rooms with children. In 1911, a committee on congestion in New York City advised that lodgers not be allowed to share rooms with children of the opposite sex over the age of twelve, although it apparently saw no dangers for younger children or children of the same gender. To some, the new urban America almost seemed designed to encourage the sexual exploitation of children. From about 1908, concern about the "unmentionable injuries" inflicted upon young girls became a priority for the cruelty agencies, and the report of the Massachusetts society remarked: "This is an abuse against which our communities have not yet learned to protect their children adequately. No city or town of any considerable size is free from this corruption."[17]

Reform efforts were directed at promoting both social purity (eliminating prostitution) and social hygiene (suppressing the venereal diseases that were a menace to the health of the race no less than to the wives of promiscuous men). As charity workers and doctors aggressively investigated the VD problem, they were horrified to discover just how many children were infected. In 1910, the president of the American Purity Alliance noted that "the social diseases . . . prevail to an alarming extent among school children, both boys and girls." In 1909, it was estimated that gonorrheal infections afflicted from eight hundred to one thousand girls in Baltimore alone, while a study of 262 young (prepubescent?) girls visiting one St. Louis hospital over a five-month period produced fourteen gonorrhea cases, or 5 percent of the total. Chicago's county hospital maintained a ward for children with venereal diseases, "one of the most pathetic sights" in the city, which over a twenty-seven-month period was used by six hundred youngsters under twelve years of age.

Medical experts varied in the realism with which they explained these troubling facts. In 1915, in a case study of sixty-six little girls diagnosed at the St. Louis clinic, researchers briefly considered the idea that infection might be spread by rape or sexual assault. But this possibility was seriously investigated in only four instances, none of which yielded confirmatory physical marks (which may mean that the researchers were considering only transmission by vaginal intercourse). Lacking other hypotheses, the writers of the article traced the contagion to badly designed toilet seats. But not everyone was so naive. A New York survey of sixty infected children some years later reported at least six cases of incest and two of rape. The cases at Chicago's county hospital were explained as follows: 60 percent contracted the disease "accidentally," 20 percent inherited it, and another 20 percent had been "criminally assaulted by diseased persons."[18] Even if we are skeptical about the large group that "accidentally" contracted the disease, the statement as it stands powerfully acknowledges the extent of sexual molestation.

Observers recognized the dangers of both incest and stranger molestation. Gibb's anecdotes recorded assaults by parents and acquaintances as well as by strangers, Progressive investigators amply confirmed the incest threat, and the cruelty societies regularly uncovered cases of intercourse between fathers and daughters.[19] Apart from charity workers and medical reformers, the new juvenile justice institutions also found copious evidence of abuse and incest. Young people who had been sexually active, often in circumstances that today would be described as molestation or incest, were commonly labeled as sex delinquents, partly from a sense that they had provoked the abusive behavior. In explaining gonorrheal infections among small children, one New York report noted that "of the eleven instances of sex delinquency, we find six cases of incest"; the sex delinquents were the infected children. One poignant case reported in 1931 involved an eleven-year-old girl brought before a juvenile court for her sex delinquency, which involved repeated intercourse with a sixty-year-old "boyfriend" who had picked her up in a park; the man was acquitted because the jury refused to send a man to prison "for a girl like that."[20] Obviously, the delinquent label offered a huge disincentive to reporting molestation.

However iniquitous the legal system, the existence of captive populations of delinquent youngsters provided a magnificent opportunity for social researchers, who easily corroborated claims about the extent of sexual maltreatment. In one classic study, Sophonisba Breckinridge and Edith Abbott examined the cases of delinquent girls who appeared before the Chicago juvenile courts from 1903 to 1908. Their research involved interviewing 254 girls about their first sexual "wrongdoing," which produced forty-six "unspeakably horrible cases in which the girls were victimized by members of their own family" as well as fifty other instances of "force or fraud." The case studies presented are littered with tales of incest and molestation: of a drunken father who "criminally abused two little daughters," of another who "criminally abused [the] girl when she was only seven." One girl was "criminally assaulted" by a drunken father when she was eleven, and he "also mis-

ask what harm these offenders actually did, the answer would have been readily available from the newspapers and the true-crime pamphlets: in extreme cases, perverts killed. As Dr. Chaddock noted, "All forms of sexual perversion may lead to criminal acts," and in extreme instances, perversion and "fetishism" culminated in lust-murder and mutilation.[25] In the last third of the nineteenth century, the American media reported numerous cases of fiends and maniacs motivated by uncontrollable sexual lust—what today would be called serial and mass murderers.

This was a startling new departure in the history of American crime. In 1874, the media pronounced sixteen-year-old Jesse Pomeroy a "boy fiend" when he sadistically murdered two small children in Boston, and the case became a sensation. A contemporary book pronounced it "the most remarkable case in the history of crime or criminal law," which may sound like hyperbole until we realize how very rarely sexual violence had been recorded in the United States before that time. Although such acts presumably had occurred, the police either did not identify the criminal or recognize sexual motivations, and a media well accustomed to sensational coverage rarely reported incidents of this sort. In 1868, a man already implicated in sex attacks on women and children was executed for the murder of a six-year-old Philadelphia girl. Although the offense sounds not unusual to modern ears, this was, astonishingly, "the only reported sexual assault on a murder victim of any age or sex" in the Philadelphia area between 1839 and 1901.[26]

The 1870s were marked by a wave of journalistic accounts of notorious sex crimes and serial killings. In some murder cases, the chief motivation was financial, but in others, the link to sexual perversion was unquestionable. This was clearly true of Jesse Pomeroy, and Thomas Piper raped several young girls in Boston between 1873 and 1875, killing at least two. Stephen Lee Richards, the Nebraska Fiend, killed nine people before being executed in 1879. But the notoriety of even these men was dwarfed by that of H. H. Holmes (Herman Webster Mudgett), who killed perhaps thirty people and targeted women visiting the Chicago World's Fair of 1893. His trial in 1895 was an international sensation. He was the subject of a half-dozen books, and like Pomeroy, Holmes has had a posthumous literary reputation that continues to this day. In addition to these domestic stories, in 1888 the American media took a lively interest in London's Jack the Ripper, the classic contemporary example of an insane sex killer. It was commonly believed that the man responsible had escaped to the United

States, where cases in the 1890s were associated with the legendary series of crimes. When newspapers reported during the next two decades that "Jack the Ripper" had killed and mutilated women in Cincinnati and Atlanta, they may have been suggesting that the same man who committed the atrocities in London was to blame for these crimes as well.[27]

Recurrent media imagery of fiends and demons reflected the extreme and irrational character of the acts committed, but the archaic nature of the terms further suggested that offenders were throwbacks to an earlier and more savage era. Holmes the archfiend, like the medieval Bluebeard, with whom he was often compared, operated from a "castle," and his proximity to the World's Fair permitted his sexual atrocities to be presented as a grotesquely subversive parody of the enlightenment and science being celebrated by the rest of the nation. Contemporary pamphlets used medieval and demonic terminology to describe the lives "sacrificed to the monstrous ogre's insatiable appetite." Although originating as metaphor, atavistic imagery found a powerful echo in the emerging criminological theory of Cesare Lombroso and his American followers, who similarly saw serious crime as the work of evolutionary throwbacks who defied the progress of the race.[28]

Recorded serial murders and sex killings accelerated in the early twentieth century, reaching a crescendo between 1908 and 1916. The apparent growth may reflect changes in media reporting or police detection, but an actual rise in crimes is plausible, given the new opportunities provided by the growing number of rootless immigrants and city dwellers, who often lacked the social networks necessary for drawing attention to disappearances. The *New York Times* reported seventeen serial murder cases for just the five-year period 1911–15, including separate series of murders in Colorado, Alabama, North Dakota, and Washington; in 1911 and 1912 alone, attacks on families in five Midwestern states claimed perhaps thirty victims. Between 1910 and 1912, Atlanta was brought to near hysteria following the "Ripper" murders of about forty women, which explains the savage public reaction when Leo Frank was accused of the sex murder of a thirteen-year-old girl in 1913. In a trial pervaded by anti-Semitic rhetoric, Frank was presented as a "lascivious pervert" with a long record of annoying women, and he was lynched two years later.[29]

New perceptions of sex killers are indicated by the response to the murders of two children, ages four and five, in New York City in 1915, probably the most intensively covered metropolitan story of that year. A Jack the

Ripper was blamed, and the police felt sufficiently familiar with the sex killer to remark confidently that "the ripper type . . . is one of the shrewdest and most elusive of criminals." Public alarm is suggested by reports of mobs attacking suspicious strangers: when an eight-year-old girl was molested on the Upper East Side shortly after the second killing, "residents . . . swarmed out into the streets with such weapons as they could pick up and surged up and down for some time, looking for suspicious characters." Two boys who saw a man "peeping" began a rumor that he was the killer: he was attacked by a crowd of fifty men and boys, and only determined police intervention saved his life. An "East Side Mother" warned that the time had come to cease tolerating minor sexual deviants and "evil-looking men hanging around the neighborhood. . . . The man who knows that an evil man lives in his neighborhood and goes on his daily round without ever trying to have that man apprehended is co-responsible with the degenerate."[30] Implicit in such accounts is the view that sex crimes must be the work of those outside the community, perhaps of easily identifiable dirty old men, rather than of relatives or acquaintances, neighbors or lodgers.

Police behaved in a strikingly modern fashion in these cases, exploring possible linkages among "serial" crimes. When Frank Hickey was arrested in 1912 for the sex killings of boys in New York and Massachusetts, police duly reconstructed his previous patterns of residence and employment in an attempt to connect him with unsolved murders in those areas. Also novel was the interpretation of these crimes as explicitly sexual acts. The Piper and Pomeroy cases had shown that children could be the objects of perverted violence, and this lesson was repeatedly reinforced. Both New York victims had been sexually mutilated, and another child of similar age was raped in what might have been a related crime. Police now paid much greater attention when girls reported that they had been approached or annoyed by an individual, presumably with sexual intent. They also investigated men found with suspicious collections of photographs of children, an early recognition that possession of indecent visual material might mark a pervert or a ripper.[31]

As in later panics, a murder series led to increased police intervention against those whom they believed to be part of the wider sex crime problem, which often meant homosexuals. The emphasis on fiends and sex criminals would be politically important in diverting blame for the problem of children's abuses away from incestuous fathers and toward dangerous outsiders like Kenneth Elton. This development was particularly important at a time when legal and psychiatric thought was raising doubts about the credibility of children's accounts of molestation within the home. In Massachusetts, the image of the dirty old man as child molester appears in the records of the state's cruelty society around 1910, at the height of the panic over sex killers, defective delinquents, and white slavers. The following year, Chicago's vice commission presented the classic stereotype of the "vicious and degenerate men" who "frequent the neighborhood of school houses and distribute obscene cards and literature. They go to public parks and take liberties with innocent children." They seduced children with dolls and toys, and at least one photographed his victims.[32]

The Borderland of Insanity

Responding to perverts required a new arsenal of criminal-justice responses and much greater use of medical or quasi-medical devices. A full-fledged sex fiend was simply imprisoned or executed, but it was more difficult to react to a person whose condition had not reached so extreme a stage. In the new perception, a sexual misdeed was a symptom of a serious medical condition, to be treated with the discretionary means available to doctors. Henry Maudsley, an English psychiatrist, observed in the 1870s, "Crime is on the borderland of insanity," and the crime-disease analogy revolutionized criminological theory in the late nineteenth century. In earlier ages, both the legal and the medical professions assumed that most people were responsible for their actions and could be punished for their conscious and rational decisions to violate the law. The law provided a special verdict for the small number of offenders judged not responsible, but insanity was a condition clearly reserved for people who suffered from gross delusions. After the early nineteenth century, however, pioneering psychiatrists like Isaac Ray explored aberrant mental states marked by odd or violent behavior but not by obvious delusions, psychosis, or abnormal intelligence. Various terms were proposed for the conditions, including *manie sans délire* and moral insanity, but the common term came to be *psychopathy*.[33]

Although a psychopath showed no obvious signs of insanity, he or she was capable of committing criminal acts without restraint or remorse, and the condition was often accompanied by sexual misbehavior. The sexual linkage may have been promoted by a popular misapprehension of the meaning of the word *psychopathic* as used in technical works like the *Psychopathia Sexualis*. For Krafft-Ebing and his followers, the term implied no more than mental disease or disturbance, but the very phrase *psychopathia sexualis* encouraged the idea that all sexual deviance was a type of compulsive or psychopathic condition. In the early twentieth century, much American writing on the psychopath concerned the sexually immoral woman, whose mental disorder rendered her incapable of controlling her lusts. When in 1920 Philadelphia's municipal court surveyed the mental condition of women arrested for prostitution, some 22 percent were diagnosed as "constitutional psychopathic inferiors," suggesting that psychopathic problems and defective heredity contributed to their activities as much as economic desperation did.[34]

Criminological writing in this era also focused on the mentally defective, or individuals of very low intelligence. The belief that defectives formed a substantial part of the deviant population was supported by the science of intelligence testing, which emerged early in the century and which for three decades consistently produced absurdly low estimates of the mental capacities of criminals, paupers, and other individuals of the lower classes. Walter Fernald declared that the feebleminded were "very frequently violators of women and little girls. . . . They frequently disseminate in a wholesale way the most loathsome and deadly diseases." In a daring intellectual leap, mental deficiency was linked to the moral deficiency of the psychopath, on the grounds that morality and intelligence were associated characteristics. For both the morally and the mentally defective, a lack of conventional inhibitions increased the tendency to lawbreaking. As the pioneering criminologist Arthur MacDonald wrote in 1890, "The want of power to resist criminal acts, and the want of feeling the wrong, together with having a clear knowledge of it at the same time, are the two main psychological characteristics of criminals."[35] By the end of the nineteenth century, controlling "defective delinquents" became the most important issue for those wishing to reduce the incidence of violence and sex crime, but this could be achieved only by a fundamental revision of the principles guiding the criminal-justice system and especially of traditional legal notions of responsibility.

Deterministic insights from social and behavioral science suggested that most compulsive repeat offenders acted not from rational calculation but under the pressure of external circumstances. This view was reinforced by new techniques of reliably identifying criminals, including photography and the Bertillon system, which allowed authorities to grasp just how extensive were the records of many offenders (the word *recidivism* appears in English in 1880). The influential Penitentiary Congress, which met in Cincinnati in 1870, was told that "a criminal is a man who has suffered under a disease evinced by the perpetration of a crime"; concepts of blame, responsibility, and punishment were outmoded. If accepted, the medical analogy would transform the whole practice of courts and prisons. Criminologist Enrico Ferri wrote in 1884, "As the sick person is kept in the hospital just as long a time as is necessary for his cure, and as the insane patient remains in the asylum all of his life until cured and leaves it when he is cured, so it should be with the delinquent." The main criteria of the new criminology were dangerousness and social defense, and the most unregenerate of criminals might never be released at all: "We would quarantine a man with smallpox; we do not wait until he has spread infection."[36] The positivist model applied with particular force to aberrant classes like perverts, psychopaths, and compulsive sex criminals.

Positivist and biocriminological ideas were introduced in the United States at exactly the same time that Europeans were formulating their ideas about perversion. In fact, the continuous history of American criminology dates from 1893, the same year that the translation of Krafft-Ebing's work appeared, and these theories were popularized by numerous scholarly and professional studies over the next quarter century. In 1909, John Henry Wigmore was the moving force behind the new American Institute of Criminal Law and Criminology, whose pioneering journal dates from the following year. Between 1911 and 1916, key European works on the new discipline reached an American audience in the volumes of the institute's Modern Criminal Science series, which included translations of Ferri and Lombroso.[37]

Between 1905 and 1915, most American states legislated some form of positivist penology, with a degree of indeterminate sentencing for all offenders. In most cases, this meant that ordinary criminals received open-ended sentences, such as "from five to ten years," but fully discretionary provisions were reserved for sentencing disturbed and dangerous offenders who fell short of the legal classification of insanity. In 1911, Massachusetts's Briggs Act against defective delinquents was one of the most aggressively positivist statutes of this era: thoroughly revamped and fully implemented in 1921, it became the basis for all later sexual psychopath laws. The act targeted habitual offenders, although in some cases a serious first offense could qualify for inclusion, and sexual misdeeds were particularly likely to be covered. Prosecutors and other officers from the correctional or mental health systems were to initiate proceedings, and two psychiatrists examined each suspect. Defectives were indefinitely committed to special and purportedly noncriminal institutions, potentially for the rest of their lives. The law involved a mixture of civil and criminal elements, requiring evidence of conviction of at least one criminal act and a diagnosis of defective status by two physicians, on the model of the civil commitment process used for the insane. The law became popular with authorities, with the number of cases examined as potential defectives rising from about sixty each year in the mid-1920s to seven or eight hundred annually by the early 1930s.[38]

The principle of the Massachusetts measure was widely imitated in other states. In 1915, an editorial in the *New York Times* claimed that the recent child murders were so horrible because they were preventable, providing a classic illustration of the identification between moral and mental deficiency: "It is always the crime of a mentally unbalanced, feeble-minded person. Moral degenerates are easily discoverable without waiting until acts of violence put them in the category of criminals." It was simply wrong to permit such men "to roam the State without any attempt to segregate them and to protect them from themselves and society. . . . It is high time that the state provide adequate places of custody for the feeble-minded where they may have treatment by skilled physicians." By 1921, New York law permitted mentally defective persons over sixteen years of age to be committed for life when convicted or accused of crime: they would be incarcerated in Napanoch prison, where the superintendent was a doctor rather than a prison warden.[39] As was often the case in later legislation, failure to require actual conviction on a specific charge reflected the therapeutic assumption that no real harm could come from merely being diagnosed or treated medically, and the social assumption that merely being charged demonstrated that a person was a troublemaker of some kind. The laws rarely recognized that police were quite capable of forcing confessions and forging evidence: Kenneth Elton claimed that his own 1925 confession had been obtained by third-degree methods.

Problems with the legislation soon became apparent. These laws mixed criminal and civil functions together in a confusing and perilous manner: was the person committed for penal or therapeutic ends, and was medical rhetoric being co-opted to justify penal incarceration? If the consequence was penal in nature, then the punishment was often far out of proportion to the act committed. Also, the means by which a person qualified for entry into this curious shadow world of law and therapy were poorly defined and capricious, leaving vast discretion for the agencies assigning the damaging label of defective delinquent. Although some protection against arbitrary imprisonment was provided by the involvement of medical professionals (usually two doctors), the horrible experience of the civil commitment system over the previous two centuries showed that physicians were all too willing to sign commitment papers for the convenience of authorities or the profit of the patient's relatives. Why should doctors be any more responsible when dealing with requests from police, prosecutors, or judges? With the study of defective states in its infancy, medical knowledge was inadequate to the task of confidently diagnosing conditions that would be treated with long-term incarceration. And although justified by humanitarian rhetoric, the therapeutic procedures were just as subject to abuse as their penal counterparts, and the defectives lacked even the meager due-process protections available to criminals.

Sterilization

The perils of legislating social defense were also evident in the other solution for combating defectives and psychopaths—namely, eugenic statutes. Since the 1870s, biological theorists had postulated that criminals and other deviants represented a kind of inferior type—an "imperfect, knotty, knurly, worm-eaten fruit of the race"—that might be rooted out through sterilization and selective breeding, and the word *eugenics* was coined in 1885. Perversion, like alcoholism, crime, epilepsy, and insanity, was a by-product of the "genetic rubbish" polluting the social gene pool and would stubbornly resist conventional legal solutions. In 1893, Dr. F. E. Daniel argued that castration was the appropriate treatment for perverts: "rape, sodomy, bestiality, pederasty and habitual masturbation" should involve the loss of all rights, including the right of procreation. Reacting to the New York Ripper murders, the "East Side Mother" urged that all perverts should be rounded up: "When eugenics is understood by the common people, when the press popularizes morality, immorality will be a very long way towards being ended."[40]

Laws permitting the sterilization of the unfit had been regularly proposed by American states since the 1890s, but measures passed with increasing frequency in the new century. Indiana enacted the first such statute in 1907, targeting "confirmed criminals, idiots, rapists and imbeciles," and eleven more states followed suit between 1909 and 1913. Ultimately thirty states would acquire these laws by 1937, and a handful used them with real enthusiasm: between 1909 and 1935, California carried out about ten thousand operations, almost as many as the rest of the states combined. Significantly, the proposed laws provided for sterilization rather than asexualization, showing that the goal was preventing the hereditary transmission of tendencies rather than incapacitation. Like the defective-delinquent laws, eugenic measures were passed with more zeal than wisdom: "Many of the sterilization statutes that were hurriedly passed were ill-founded because they were based on insufficient scientific knowledge. Rapists, those guilty of carnal knowledge, sexual perverts, syphilitics, drunkards, drug fiends, habitual criminals, lunatics, prostitutes, sodomists, are only some of the categories subject to legalized sterilization in the various states, because some legislature considered the condition hereditary."[41] Iowa's ambitious statute named a long list of categories that included rapists, drug fiends, and moral and sexual perverts. Sterilization was mandatory for anyone twice convicted of a felony or twice convicted of any sex offense, whether a felony or not; the only exception was white slaving, for which a single conviction earned mandatory sterilization. In California, groups eligible for the procedure included those convicted twice of rape, attempted rape, or seduction. Most states also listed "moral degenerates and sexual perverts," which usually encompassed homosexuals.

The U.S. Supreme Court struck down some of these laws on the grounds that they inflicted cruel and unusual punishment, and this fate befell Iowa's sweeping statute in 1914. But the *Buck v. Bell* decision of 1927 allowed compulsory sterilization in cases where it had proper eugenic goals and was not simply being used to augment criminal punishment. Not until the *Skinner* case of 1942, with the example of Nazi Germany in view, did the Court finally decide that a person's right to procreate was too precious to be sacrificed on the questionable grounds of "habitual criminality."[42]

Progressive Coalitions

The radicalism of Progressive Era measures is striking when we recall how fiercely traditional-minded judges and state legislators opposed moves toward discretionary and positivist justice, sometimes fighting a decades-long war of attrition against indeterminate sentencing and parole laws.[43] In both the defective-delinquent codes and the eugenics statutes, however, sweeping new laws were implemented with minimal criticism. The broad support they commanded must be explained in terms of the supposed gravity of the menace and of the complex constituencies that combined to favor the new legal responses.

The most obvious activists were the psychiatrists, who by the early twentieth century were evolving into a far more substantial and ambitious section of the broader medical community. No longer the despised asylum keepers of early Victorian times, doctors of the mind were now alienists who were receptive to the insights of European thinkers and who aspired to preventing insanity in addition to treating it. A movement to instill principles of mental hygiene into society at large was initiated by Adolf Meyer, who worked closely with William Healy and other pioneers in both criminology and social work.[44] For Progressive reformers, any effort at social reform had to include psychiatric and eugenic concerns. Similar ideas were disseminated by the academic lawyers and sociologists then in the process of forming the nascent profession of criminology, which found its public voice in Wigmore's American Institute of Criminal Law and Criminology.

Positivist reformers gained the crucial support of women's organizations, which were then at their height of mobilization in support of the twin causes of woman suffrage and temperance and which were closely linked to the child-saving societies. Since the 1870s, women's and temperance groups had supported discretionary penology as a move toward greater humanity in the justice system, and the concepts of social defense and social hygiene were presented in terms of protecting women and children against sexually depraved men. In the new century, these groups generally supported defective-delinquent laws and eugenic measures. The slogan "Votes for Women" was occasionally followed by "and Chastity for Men," an objective with obvious appeal for religious reformers. In the 1890s, the Women's Christian Temperance Union made the campaign for a higher age of consent one of its principal causes, and activists even used the legal age in a given state as an index of women's rights and status in that jurisdiction. Prominent in this movement were Charlton Edholm, Helen H. Gardener, and Frances E. Willard, all leading advocates of women's rights, and Edholm described woman suffrage as the only way to combat the organized traffic in young virgins "and its principal cause, the gin-mill." The interlinked movements against forced prostitution, white slavery, and venereal disease culminated in the federal Mann Act of 1910.[45]

The theme of sexual danger was trumpeted by the mass media, whose attitudes toward what was fit to print had been transformed by the Hearst and Pulitzer newspapers during the 1890s. Affecting the role of tribune of the people, the new press vastly increased its circulation by exposing the horrors of crime, moral degradation, and sexual deviance. As in later years, successive child-protection crises offered irresistible images, with the starkest possible contrast between psychopathic villainy and threatened innocence. Media-powered moral crusades were further fueled by criminal-justice agencies, who saw the potential to build their own powers and status. The history of American federal policing begins with the rudimentary powers granted to the "Bureau of Investigation" under the Mann Act, while under its new designation as the Federal Bureau of Investigation, the agency was further augmented by the kidnapping panic of the early 1930s.[46] Although founded on the rhetoric of science, medicine, and humanity, child-protection laws offered a rich appeal for the politics of law-and-order conservatism, a paradox that would shape all later movements against sex crime and sex offenders. The "progress" by which this era was defined included a substantial dose of sexual and moral repression.

The unstable tactical alliances on which the Progressive coalition was based disintegrated in the early 1920s, and earlier activism over sex crime subsided accordingly. This did not mean that the behaviors themselves necessarily diminished: the cruelty societies were still finding instances of incest and molestation, campaigners against VD continued to track the high incidence of infection among small children, and police were arresting deviants for the usual range of sex offenses. In the early 1930s, the New York Health Department recorded "a surprising number" of boys catching syphilis from older men but confessed puzzlement about the sources of widespread gonococcal infections among little girls. Indeed, the activism of the social welfare and social hygiene movements reached its finest flowering in 1935 in the remarkable work of Jacob and Rosamond Goldberg, whose study on child rape, molestation, and incest was by far the most detailed and perceptive account before the child abuse revolution of the 1970s. But the political climate of these years was not as friendly to strict moral enforcement as the earlier era had been. The women's movement achieved its greatest political success between 1918 and 1920 with the Eighteenth and Nineteenth Amendments to the Constitution, but political feminism then fragmented, and the disastrous consequences of Prohibition discredited moral activism. Prohibition also drove an enormous wedge between the attitudes of urban and rural America, and moral reformism came to be associated with fundamentalism and fanaticism. As the impulse toward social reform and child saving faded after 1917, the authoritarian elements within the child-protection movement came to the fore, and the mechanisms of "the cruelty" were increasingly viewed as middle-class busybodyism.[47] Despite the Goldbergs' achievement, the number of journal articles dealing frankly with the abuse histories of poor or delinquent children declined sharply after the early 1920s, suggesting that both social activism and research had lost their attraction.

Sensational sex crimes also lost their earlier power to fascinate when the media found more excitement in Prohibition gangsterism and the wave of bank robberies and kidnappings in the early 1930s, while, at least in major cities, homosexual underworlds were far more visible and more accepted than ever before. A kind of gay chic marked New York society in this era, a trend that created a broader tolerance for sexual unorthodoxy. The police usually realized that little public sympathy was to be gained by too sharp a repression of sexual deviancy, and arrest rates for minor violations fell to historic lows. In 1929, the number of prosecutions for offenses "against chastity, morality and decency" in Massachusetts represented the second lowest annual rate per capita since 1911.[48]

Although it is risky to argue from silence, a gauge of attitudes toward sex offenses is offered by the 1931 report of the National Commission on Law Observance and Enforcement, appointed by Attorney General George W. Wickersham. Drawing on the work of the leading criminologists and sociologists of the day, the Wickersham commission examined in enormous detail all the pressing problems of the criminal-justice system, including prohibition enforcement, juvenile delinquency, plea bargaining, racial discrimination, police corruption and brutality, and the state of corrections and parole. Barring a few illustrative cases involving rape, however, this comprehensive report said virtually nothing about sex crime, even though the section on crime causation was contributed by Morris Ploscowe, an authority on legal aspects of sexuality.[49] It is inconceivable that a detailed analysis of sexual offenses would not have been included in any comparable study of crime undertaken in 1915 (or 1950 or 1985), and the omission is difficult to explain unless fears about perverts were at a low ebb. If sex offenses were not exactly being ignored, then at least they were not being constructed as a serious problem.

Eugenic sterilization and the defective-delinquent laws represented a first wave of emergency measures intended to combat the perceived menace from compulsive sexual criminals "on the borderland of insanity." In fact, neither was used precisely according to its original specifications: sterilization of criminals was a rare event in most states possessing eugenic statutes, and those committed under the defective-delinquent laws often proved not to have the very low intelligence predicted by the measures' sponsors. Meanwhile, the ideas that gave rise to the statutes lost their edge: after 1920 the growing sophistication of the study of genetics made eugenics seem outdated, the end of mass immigration in 1924 reduced fears of rapid racial decline, and medical advances assuaged fears of venereal diseases. In the explanation of criminality, biocriminology was first challenged and then largely displaced by psychodynamic and sociological theories.[50] In the Wickersham reports, sociological analyses clearly took priority.

Even so, the new laws did contribute toward the medicalizing of responses to crime, and they familiarized legislators with policy devices (especially civil commitment) hitherto confined to the civil system and lunacy law. The belief that confirmed criminals were suffering from aberrant mental conditions was fostered by the increased practice of psychiatric evaluation following the Briggs Act and its imitators. Psychiatrists in courts and prisons were much more likely to label as psychopaths those who could be categorized as neither insane nor mentally defective, with the consequence that psychopathic diagnoses expanded in institutional populations. At Sing Sing State Prison, the director of the psychiatric clinic from 1915 was Bernard Glueck, one of the nation's leading authorities on crime and psychopathy, and Healy's *Individual Delinquent* established the American vision of the psychopath as a major source of criminality and, almost by definition, a sexual pervert. By the mid-1920s, surveys of state prisons were frequently suggesting that between 30 and 50 percent of inmates were psychopathic. The associated terminology was popularized through the sensational 1924 trial of child killers Leopold and Loeb, the first in American history in which the defense marshaled the leading psychiatrists and criminologists of the day. Both Glueck and Healy testified, as did William A. White, who has been called the father of criminal psychopathology in America.[51] By this point, psychopaths had clearly replaced the mentally defective as the category most likely to be blamed for crime. In 1914, Kenneth Elton was presumed to be feebleminded; ten or fifteen years later, he would have been diagnosed as a sex psychopath.[52]

Indeed, in 1951, psychiatrist Manfred S. Guttmacher drew a telling comparison between the legislation of the Progressive Era and the laws being passed to control psychopaths in his own day: in both eras legislators were quick to pass sweeping laws on matters about which medical science could draw only the most tentative conclusions.[53] Although his basic point was correct, he could have carried his analogy further. It was the Progressive Era that popularized and reframed the related notions of the psychopath and the defective delinquent, thus laying the foundation for the image of the sex psychopath, which would play so powerful a role in social mythology from the mid-1930s onward.

The Age of the Sex Psychopath, 1935–1957

For Heaven's sake catch me before I kill more. I cannot control myself.
WILLIAM HEIRENS, 1946

In 1934, a sixty-four-year-old man named Albert Fish was arrested in New York State for the murder, mutilation, and cannibalism of twelve-year-old Grace Budd. This gruesome crime was one episode in about three decades of violence and sexual molestation, a career that involved hundreds of assaults and perhaps fifteen murders of children. In addition to homicidal sadism, Fish had experimented with numerous perverse sexual activities, including self-mutilation and coprophagia, which he recorded in his terrifying diaries. Fish's trial in the spring of 1935 increased public awareness of the further reaches of sexual deviancy: his story remained in the headlines until his execution at Sing Sing State Prison in January 1936 and his enduring notoriety was ensured by the case history published by psychiatrist Fredric Wertham. Albert Fish represented the prototypical multiple killer in his day as definitively as Ted Bundy or Jeffrey Dahmer would in later years, and this case cemented the popular identification of the sex offender with the child killer.[1]

The Fish case suggested that dangerous perverts were wandering the country and threatening the nation's children and that they might operate for many years before their worst crimes were detected. But because their disorders did manifest symptoms that might be detected long before they actually killed, early intervention could save lives. Fish was an excellent advertisement for a positivist approach to crime: the fact that his case had been allowed to continue so long showed that authorities were neglecting defective-delinquent laws and other legal provisions at their disposal, which needed to be revived and brought into line with new psychiatric insights. His trial and execution formed a prelude to an era when sex criminals were viewed as a lethal public danger and even the most trivial sexual deviations were contextualized with offenses like serial rape and multiple homicide. Although some experts called for moderation, the popular consensus accepted the most extreme and threatening interpretations of the sex offender, and the debate focused on how best to combat this nightmarish danger: lives were at stake.

Discovering Sex Crime, 1935–1940

Fears of a criminal (though nonsexual) threat to children were aroused by the kidnapping wave that peaked with the Lindbergh case of 1932. Between 1934 and 1936, when Bruno Hauptmann was arrested, convicted, and executed for the kidnapping and murder of the Lindbergh baby, the story often shared front pages with accounts of Fish: Hauptmann's execution followed Fish's by three months. The juxtaposition may have encouraged readers to see the generalized danger to children in explicitly sexual terms. As in the Progressive Era, well-publicized multiple-murder cases contributed to shaping the public image of the sex criminal as a violent predator. In 1935, Alonzo Robinson was arrested for a series of murders in the Midwest, crimes that involved cannibalism, mutilation, and decapitation, and serial rapist Gerald Thompson was on trial in Chicago for the murder that was the culmination of his long career of sex attacks. Around 1934 began the most spectacular murder series of the period, the Cleveland Torso Killings, in which an individual mutilated up to seventeen victims. Just as this case was at its height in terms of media excitement, in the summer of 1938, the fourteen or so murders of Joe Ball were discovered in Texas, while a series of "lovers' lane" murders began in New Jersey. In 1941,

Jarvis Catoe was arrested for nine rape-murders in Washington, D.C., and New York City. Police and media agreed that these crimes were extreme forms of sexual violence: Alonzo Robinson "admitted that he was a sex pervert, which is considered to be the underlying cause for the crime," and like Fish, he had a penchant for sending obscene letters to women.[2]

In 1937, growing alarm found a focus in New York City, and as in 1915, the affair sprang from the sex murders of young children. Although the 1937 crimes were indeed horrible, the violent public reaction must be seen in the context of the Fish case and its extensive coverage in the metropolitan area, for the new cases were also committed by offenders with lengthy records of sexual misbehavior that should have been noted by authorities. In March, Salvatore Ossido killed a girl while he was on bail for a rape attempt; on July 31, eight-year-old Paula Magagna was killed by Laurence Marks, who had spent twenty-seven of his forty-nine years in prison, mainly for sex crimes. News coverage conditioned the public to expect that violent crimes would have perverted motives. When a four-year-old girl was murdered on August 12, this case was contextualized with the "wave" of sex murders, and the culprit was wrongly assumed to be a paroled sex criminal; his actual criminal record listed acts of drunkenness, physical assault, and wife beating. The final week of August brought reports of suspected molesters being threatened by mobs. Crimes by "murderous-minded perverts" provoked a torrent of denunciation by the press and political leaders, who advocated defensive measures like fingerprinting those who worked with children or enlisting the aid of deliverymen in reporting suspicious characters. A New York sheriff earned his moment of celebrity by recommending that child attackers be, not arrested, but shot on the spot. The fact that three little girls in southern California had been gruesomely mutilated and murdered in June ensured that the threat to children would be seen as not simply an East Coast problem: these "Pied Piper" murders were immediately, and mistakenly, blamed on a "degenerate" with a series of convictions for morals offenses against children.[3]

Perceptions of a crime wave were strengthened by the behavior of law-enforcement agencies. Under pressure to prove their competence in the face of this menace, police cracked down on minor offenders whom they normally tended to ignore. This was easy because in the cities, at least, mild sexual unorthodoxy was so common that agencies were obliged to exercise discretion, leaving large sections of the criminal code virtually unenforced. There were few bureaucratic rewards in relentlessly pursuing petty offenders, whose prosecution would simply clog the court system. Offenses were difficult to prove if the perpetrator made a determined effort to resist prosecution: it was not easy to prove the sexual intent of a subway *frotteur* or to show that a voyeur really intended to spy on neighbors. Official latitude extended not only to homosexuals but also to known child molesters, like the Boston man who was something of a local institution and was known by the telling nickname Tom the Cat; he remained at liberty throughout the 1930s, despite repeated protests to police by the local child-protection society and his young female victims. In "normal" years, such activity led to arrest only if it was blatant or if local citizens took the initiative and trapped a suspected molester.[4]

When a crackdown was needed, police had no difficulty in tracking down local perverts. Now the usual suspects were arrested rather than let off with a warning, and more serious charges were pressed. Prosecutors and magistrates pursued cases through to conviction and refused to accept the plea bargains that had been standard practice in such cases. In August 1937, a New York man who had assaulted two ten-year-old girls received what was then an exceptionally severe sentence: twenty-five years to life. The following day, police announced that they were compiling a list of known sex criminals and degenerates with a view to making periodic checks on their whereabouts and behavior. That more people were being arrested, and for graver crimes, created the impression that more offenses were being committed. In addition, newspapers were more likely to report local incidents and to contextualize them as part of a general problem. The role of New York City and Los Angeles as media markets ensured that concerns reached the national stage, so that by the fall of 1937 the sex offender crisis had become the subject of articles in the *Nation, Christian Century, Newsweek,* and *Literary Digest*. As Fredric Wertham remarked, "Public indignation has reached almost a mass hysteria which has affected not only the public but also official authorities."[5]

The Age of Sex Crime, 1945–1955

The 1937 panic marked a precedent that would often be repeated during the next two decades, with notable peaks in 1947–50 and 1953–54. The sex crime menace was regularly covered in magazines like *Time, Newsweek, Parents, Coronet,* and *Collier's*, reaching a crescendo in late 1949 and early 1950, when the topic also became the focus of radio documentaries. The atmosphere of the time is represented by a series of articles published by

Collier's, which reported that sex crime by "the rapist, the sex psychopath, the defiler of children" had "virtually gone out of control": "Rape has increased 200 percent in the past twenty years, the most phenomenal increase of any major category of crime. The hoodlum rapist lurks in the foliage of a dark street waiting for a woman to walk home from the bus-stop. . . . And rape-murders: nearly every city has its recent victims." There was also a vast dark figure of unreported crimes, "indecent exposure, following, accosting, and minor molestation": the reporting figure for forcible rapes might represent anywhere from 10 to 50 percent of the actual total. According to journalist Howard Whitman, women across the country were refusing to venture into the streets at night, and communities were organizing neighborhood crime patrols and warning systems. Cities were developing "no-woman's-lands" where females were afraid to go unprotected. "The shadow of the sex criminal lies across the doorstep of every home."[6]

The menace to the young was grave, Whitman continued: "Children in alarming numbers have been the victims of molesters, exhibitionists, perverts, and pedophiles. The sex hoodlum, hanging around schools with comic books and bubble gum to lure his victim, has imbued parents with a stark new fear." The nation faced "the grotesque, baffling problem of pedophilia": pedophiles were "roaming about, abusing, molesting, luring and perhaps one day killing." Indeed, certain conclusions seemed obvious: "As long as there is rampant day to day molestation and abuse of children, some of them are going to be killed." In every city, perverts were obsessed with the corruption of the young, and each might have molested dozens or hundreds of youngsters: even if the molester did not physically harm his victims, "he would have virtually destroyed them psychologically." Persons in positions of trust in churches or schools molested large numbers of their charges, raising the possibility that covert pedophiles had infiltrated the institutions.[7] It all sounds strikingly familiar.

Crime waves are strictly relative in nature, for what constitutes a crime wave depends on popular expectations of what is proper in terms of public order and safety. Although Whitman might have been accurately reporting social attitudes, his account of national terror was written during one of the safest eras in American urban history, when rates for all forms of violent crime were enviably low by the standards of later decades. In the late 1940s, for instance, both the media and the authorities in Los Angeles believed that the city was experiencing an unprecedented wave of sex crimes, an image that owed much to the 1947 "Black Dahlia" mutilation-murder. In 1949 the city's grand jury listed nine unsolved homicides committed since mid-decade, a "formidable roster of murdered women." In retrospect, it is remarkable that a metropolis of the size of Los Angeles would list so few unsolved cases for a four- or five-year period.[8]

Perceptions that crime was out of control were stimulated by reports of a handful of spectacularly brutal acts that were then reported at a regional or national level, thus creating an image of a systematic problem. Such cases occurred sporadically from the mid-1940s onward, culminating in the "Horror Week" of November 1949, when three young girls were murdered within the space of a few days. In Fresno, California, a seventeen-month-old toddler was raped and left to die, while in Burley, Idaho, a girl of seven was raped before being drowned in a drainage ditch. In Los Angeles, a six-year-old girl named Linda Joyce Glucoft was murdered by Fred Stroble, the elderly grandfather of her playmate. The media depicted Stroble as a symbol of unalloyed evil, referring to him as a sex fiend, a "weeping werewolf."[9] Reported nationally, these cases added fuel to local concerns in cities like Cleveland, which during the previous few years had experienced a number of rape-murders and sex murders of children as well as the notorious Cleveland Torso Killings mentioned earlier. By late 1949, "recurrent visitations of sex violence had given Cleveland a hair-trigger psychology. . . . When the flare-up came, the city would be thrown into a fright syndrome of mammoth proportions."[10] The precipitating incident came in December, when a woman was raped and stabbed. By this point, "the hysteria syndrome [was] mounting like jungle fever," and the *Cleveland News* ran the headline "City in Hysteria." Reports told of women arming themselves and taking judo classes, of men firing their guns at imaginary prowlers. Claiming that street attacks on women had reached "startling proportions," a grand jury demanded immediate countermeasures. Community, religious, and parents' groups formed ad hoc committees to press for intensified police action together with new legislation against sex criminals.

Cleveland's experience was not untypical. St. Louis was similarly determined to remedy its own problem of "scores upon scores of children led into alleys and molested on their way to school, the schoolyards turned into hunting grounds for pedophiles and perverts, . . . the tots of five and six coaxed into cellar-ways and obscenely handled, the children forced or defiled—in their ignorance—into acts of perversion." Led by the parents of a child who had fallen victim to a sex killer some years before, parent-teacher associations formed what were unashamedly described as vigilante patrols, and a children's protective association was formed. Women acted as block mothers to escort children on the streets, while children were instructed in the dangers awaiting them. California was equally agitated following the 1949 child murders. Mass meetings pushed the state legislature to form a special subcommittee on sex crimes, and by December Governor Earl Warren convened a conference, "Sex Crimes Against Children," for law-enforcement agencies. Fifteen states established commissions to study the sex offender problem, including New York, New Jersey, Michigan, and Pennsylvania. Official investigations kept the sex crime story firmly in the headlines at least through 1951, often through the active cultivation of the media by committee members and witnesses.[11]

Some agencies played an especially prominent role in promoting the crisis, above all the FBI and its director, J. Edgar Hoover. For Hoover, who popularized the image of sex offenders as predators, the enforcement of sexual morality had been a longtime concern: since the 1920s, a substantial share of the bureau's resources had been devoted to investigating Mann Act prostitution cases, which were termed "organized predatory crimes." The issue also promised a practical benefit: the decline of the bank robbery and kidnapping waves of the early 1930s had left the FBI without a high-profile cause, while a national drug scare in 1936–37 threatened to divert attention and resources to the rival Federal Bureau of Narcotics. Antidrug rhetoric painted terrifying images of uncontrollably violent drug fiends rampaging across the country, in a manner that uncannily foreshadowed the later images of violent sex fiends: the legendary films *Cocaine Fiends* and *Reefer Madness* both date from 1936. The FBI recouped visibility by generating stories about the "parole scandal," the supposed rash of crimes committed by men unwisely released from prisons. Hoover warned that parole boards were all too often guilty of "in effect, releasing a predatory animal," and in 1937, he claimed that the "sex fiend" was "most loathsome of all the vast army of crime."[12] If the FBN had the drug issue, then Hoover still had sex and violence, and he made the most of both. The FBI continued to invest heavily in its fight against sex fiends until it found a new justification for its existence with the Nazi spy scares of 1938–40.

After the war, Hoover returned to the sex-maniac theme with a widely quoted article in the *American Magazine*. In "How Safe Is Your Daughter?" Hoover (or his ghostwriters) asserted, "The most rapidly increasing type of crime is that perpetrated by degenerate sex offenders. . . . [It] is taking its toll at the rate of a criminal assault every forty-three minutes, day and night in the United States. . . . Depraved human beings, more savage than beasts, are permitted to rove America almost at will." Failure to confront degeneracy created "a situation which leaves maimed and murdered women lying in isolated areas, which leaves violated children in a state of hysteria." Throughout these years, newspapers repeatedly cited the FBI as a primary source for warnings that parents should protect their children by reporting suspicious characters. The agency distributed posters urging children to beware of "stranger danger": "Boys and girls, . . . for your protection, remember to turn down gifts from strangers, and refuse rides offered by strangers." In 1960, the bureau urged a national drive against molesters, and by 1962, Hoover was calling for teachers and other school employees to be fingerprinted so that accused molesters could be screened out.[13]

The sense of threat was reinforced by the mass media, especially the cinema. Although censorship made it impossible to deal overtly with perverts, rapists, or child molesters, the subject of warped killers did not fall under the same restrictions, as violence could be depicted even when sex was taboo. Fictional explorations of sex crime thus concentrated on the most serious aspect of the problem, namely the "maniac killer," whose sexual motivation could be subtly implied.[14] The best known portrayal was Peter Lorre's performance in the German film *M* (1931), which appeared in an American remake in 1951. Also influential was Alfred Hitchcock's version of the Jack the Ripper story in *The Lodger* (1926), which was remade in both 1932 and 1944. The number of treatments accelerated from 1937, the year in which *Night Must Fall* portrayed a deranged sex killer who carried the heads of his women victims as trophies. Later years brought *Stranger on the Third Floor* (1940), *Shadow of a Doubt* (1943), *The Brighton Strangler* (1945), *Spiral Staircase* (1946), *The Sniper* (1952), and *While the City Sleeps* (1956). There was even a humorous treatment in *Arsenic and Old Lace* (the play opened in 1938, and the film was released in 1944). The films depicted monstrous predators motivated by a perverted and compulsive sexuality, and the stories often directly borrowed from such real-life cases as those of Fish and William Heirens. Such works raised public sensitivity about sex criminals and at the same time disseminated the psychodynamic theories then in vogue in expert circles.

Similar themes appeared in novels by thriller writers like Robert Bloch and Jim Thompson, and Bloch's *The Scarf* (1947) was favorably reviewed by Fredric Wertham in a psychiatric journal. Charles Jackson's *Outer Edges* (1948) portrayed a convincing child killer, a mentally defective youth who rapes and mutilates two small girls who accept a ride in his car. These books showed an acute awareness of the media's role in manipulating public fears over sexual violence: In *The Scarf*, a sensationalistic journalist urges a colleague to write a book on the Cleveland Torso Killings: "People like to read about it. Look at the way those true detective magazines sell. Sex crimes. Blood. Everybody wants to know. . . . Ever hear about the ritual murders we had out here? The devil worshipers? They cut up a kid." *The Outer Edges* is less concerned with the unimpressive murderer himself than the means by which the media transform him into a fiend, generating polychromatic images that different consumers can regard with horror or admiration according to taste. As one journalist remarks, the case is "a beaut," and he has few illusions about his own role. "That's what he was here for: gore and bloodshed, rape, and if possible, mutilation, was what they wanted. It was his job to give it to them, even to stretching a point here and there if he thought of something good."[15] As the cliché still holds, "If it bleeds, it leads." In pulp fiction, maniac killers were a staple of the new genre of extreme horror comics like *Tales from the Crypt*, founded in 1950 at the height of the panic.

Changed perceptions of the "menace" can usefully be traced by means of the *Reader's Guide to Periodical Literature*, a standard source for research in American history. Although during the middle years of the century the *Reader's Guide* usually listed at most one entry per year on sex crimes or sex offenses, there were eleven items in 1937, sixteen between 1948 and 1950, and ten in 1953–54. A similar picture emerges from other indexes covering a comparably lengthy time span, especially the annual index to the *New York Times*. Also, index categories changed to reflect popular usage: if a newspaper reported a sexual act involving a child, the classification of this deed and the significance that it was accorded varied according to the era in which it occurred. From the early years of the century to 1936, sexual misdeeds were submerged under the general heading of "assaults" or "robberies and assaults," where they made up a tiny proportion of the hundreds of stories each year about physical violence, muggings, and gang fights. Indecent acts rarely appeared unless they involved some additional element which made them sensational or newsworthy. "Sex crimes" appear as a separate index category in *Reader's Guide* and the *New York Times* only during the 1937 panic. Once the *Times* began its "sex crimes" heading, this general term covered actions ranging from rape, child molestation, and sex murder through voyeurism, homosexuality, abortion, indecent exposure, and pornography, and throughout the 1940s, all were seen as culpable, damaging, and presumably derived from a similar etiology. The act of naming the menace was crucial to assimilating these diverse types of conduct into a single problem and, moreover, as a threat directed at children.

The Sex Psychopath

The national threat was seen as one posed by *sex fiends* or *sex psychopaths*, terms that were used interchangeably. Most quantitative estimates drew no distinction between violent or predatory sex crimes and minor or consensual acts. If the latter were included, then the nation had many thousands or even millions of sex criminals, but these numbers were then presented as if they referred to individuals like Albert Fish. The *Saturday Evening Post* asserted: "Most of the sex killers are psychopathic personalities. No one knows, or can even closely estimate, how many tens of thousands of them are loose in the country today."[16]

The image of the compulsive sex fiend was reinforced by notorious cases of child killers like Fred Stroble and Laurence Marks. Apparently a classic example of predictable dangerousness, Marks had several insane relatives and a lengthy record of sexual violence in his own background. Before he committed murder in 1937, he had twice been convicted of sexual acts against little girls and had served two lengthy prison terms. In the words of Bertram Pollens, who headed the sex clinic at the prison on New York City's Rikers Island, "It is obvious that he was a mere marionette, propelled by blind forces and instinctive cravings which his intellect was powerless to stem." In 1946 the case of William Heirens fostered the identification of sex offenders and sex psychopaths. Heirens had committed several hundred burglaries and three murders, including that of a six-year-old girl whom he dismembered, as well as hundreds of petty sex crimes like the theft of women's underwear. He left at one murder scene a note that read, "For Heaven's sake catch me before I kill more. I cannot control myself," which was apparently a model of the psychodynamic theory of crime.[17] Heirens was only seventeen when he was arrested; his case, like Jesse Pomeroy's, seemed to show that monsters were formed at an early age and that, if they were not detected, their criminal careers might last for a very long time.

Even before the outbreak of the sex crime panic, the psychodynamic origin of criminality was a critical area of research for American psychiatrists, and the sex psychopath issue became a major focus of concern in the professional literature. Between 1937 and 1946, articles on sex crime appeared in all the major scholarly psychiatric journals, and in 1938, Karl Bowman and others contributed to a special symposium in *Mental Hygiene*. Concern peaked once more between 1948 and 1952: this period brought coverage in *Diseases of the Nervous System* and the *American Journal of Psychiatry* as well as an important symposium in *Federal Probation*.[18]

The contemporary portrait of the psychopath resembled nineteenth-century doctrines about moral insanity. In 1949, Philadelphia child murderer Seymour Levin was seen as a classic psychopath who recognized the difference between right and wrong but who was "not willing or able to exert inhibitions against anti-social behavior as strong and effective as those which can be exerted by the average person." The doctrine was viewed as simplistic by many professionals in psychiatric practice, but it found distinguished supporters. Perhaps the best-known authority for some forty years was Benjamin Karpman, who wrote in 1951 that "sexual psychopathy involves a type of sexual behavior characterized by socially prohibited aggressiveness, by lack of regard for the unwilling participant; by being compulsive and irresistible in character; and by being committed under the influence of an exceptionally strong overwhelming urge, the tension of which is released by the particular behavior." Accounts of "compulsive and irresistible" behaviors pervaded the reports that now guided official reaction to sex crime. New Hampshire's 1949 investigation declared: "The sexual psychopath is interested only in the immediate satisfaction of his instinctive drive, irrespective of the manner of attainment or of consequences. His action is usually directed toward the innocent and the unsuspecting or helpless members of the opposite sex. The victim is attacked in a lonely location, the assault is accompanied by force, brutality or violence, even sufficient to cause death. Elaborate plans are usually made for a quick escape and against the possibility of recognition. This cunning is invariably present and marks the sexual psychopath."[19]

Although experts did agree that psychopaths existed, they could not agree about exactly how these deviants might be recognized or even characterized. Karpman himself agreed that "there is no consensus concerning the meaning of the word psychopath: it is a loosely-conceived entity regarding which psychiatrists disagree. The broadness of definition allows its interpretation to include homosexuals, adolescents and young children." As one institutional psychiatrist claimed, "I have lived with the criminal for 24 years, and I know there is the psychopathic individual, but I just cannot describe him." Another therapist summarized the criteria as "anyone who is a queer guy, the fellow that does not fit, he is a psychopath." Remarks of this kind made nonsense of the *Saturday Evening Post*'s assertion that the "psychopathic personality can easily be detected early in life by any psychiatrist" and of the corollary that preventive legislation could be drafted easily.[20]

If identifying the psychopath was so difficult, then it was impossible to trace the developmental stages of the condition. The general public, however, saw no such obstacles: the sex *offender* and the sex *psychopath* differed only in the degree of the threat. Criminologist Edwin Sutherland argued that popular views of sex offenses were pervaded by outrageous myths, "that most sex crimes are committed by sexual degenerates, sex fiends or sexual psychopaths, and that these persons persist in their sexual crimes throughout life; that they always give warning that they are dangerous by first committing minor offenses; that any psychiatrist can diagnose them with a high degree of precision at an early age."[21]

Sutherland was accurately summarizing the general opinion that offenses progressed from minor misdeeds to severe violence. Although an exhibitionist caused no direct or immediate harm, the pleasure that he obtained by exposing himself was sadistic and might escalate: "This sadistic urge may no longer remain satisfied merely from the look of horror on women's faces . . . but may translate itself into stronger and more potent sadistic drives such as rape, assault or murder." Whitman agreed, "The exhibitionist may become a molester, the molester may become a rapist, the rapist may become a killer." As Pollens wrote in 1938, "The misdemeanants of today may be the rapists and murderers of tomorrow." Hoover argued, "With few exceptions, long before a sex criminal reaches his eventual crime of violence, there is ample evidence of his tendencies."[22]

The perception that all sex offenses were ultimately linked was crucial for policy and legislation. There *were* no minor sex offenses, and contemporary authors regularly place quotation marks around the word *minor* in this context. In 1948, the psychiatrist brought in to train St. Louis police in how to respond to child molestation offered instruction in supposedly related behaviors like "transvestism, fetishism, exhibitionism, sadism, masochism, pedophilia, and the whole gamut of sex psychopathy."[23] The 1952 film *The Sniper* shows police investigating a sex murder by holding a "showoff," in which an array of known offenders is put on parade, to the hilarity of a police audience; the implication is that a serial killer would be drawn from the ranks of these "rapists, defilers, peeping toms," and so on.

The escalation idea found equivocal support from Karpman, whose 1954 text *The Sexual Offender and His Offenses* went through nine printings over the next decade. Karpman himself occasionally sounds relativist in his approach, noting the opinion that "sex offenses are behavior that offends a particular society in a particular culture." Like most psychiatric experts, he acknowledges that sex offenses are committed by a wide variety of types: at least in some instances, proper intervention and treatment could ensure that a single act would not be repeated and need not be a stepping-stone to a lifetime career. On the other hand, there were true sex fiends like Heirens and Marks and the murderer whose case Karpman discusses, "a constitutional psychopathic inferior, doomed from birth to be a menace." One might think that Karpman of all people would therefore deny that the sex offender is automatically a sex psychopath, and yet this is precisely what he does claim, accepting a sweeping definition of the problem: "A sexual offense is sexual behavior that offends the particular society in which the offender lives. . . . The majority of sexual crimes, but not all, are the result of sexual deviation. The sexually deviated person is commonly known as a sexual psychopath."[24] It is this last leap of logic that is most startling.

The view that sexual deviation was closely related to aggressive sexual crime had bleak implications for homosexuals, who faced the most immediate collateral damage from the movement against psychopathy.[25] Some observers saw homosexuals as ipso facto dangerous, but even the most benevolent writers discussed homosexuality alongside other pernicious behaviors and conditions, so that a stigma was certain to be acquired.

The ambiguous psychiatric attitude was represented by Karpman, whose views were quite liberal for the mid-1950s. He was happy to imagine homosexuals becoming "normal perverts," and he offered case studies of homosexuals in stable "married" relationships, for "to the extent that the pervert . . . is moral, he is also normal." Yet Karpman had no hesitation in including homosexuality in his list of sexual offenses: the mere fact of having homosexual desires constitutes a deviation in its own right, while fulfilling those desires through intercourse invokes the offense of "sodomy and pederasty." In his text, homosexuality stands alongside grievous acts like rape, necrophilia, fetishism, exhibitionism, and bestiality, and the condition was in close psychic proximity to sadomasochism, pedophilia, and incest. In a telling juxtaposition, Karpman noted that "of 270 cases of sexual psychopathy studied in an army hospital, the great majority were cases of homosexuality." Walter Bromberg's discussion of this topic began with the phrase, "homosexuality, a variant of sexual psychopathy."[26]

Prevailing therapeutic orthodoxy viewed homosexuality as a form of arrested psychosexual development, one likely to be associated with an unnatural attraction toward children. As Freud had pronounced, "Perverted sexuality is nothing but infantile sexuality magnified and separated into its component parts." In 1951, an editorial in *Psychiatric Quarterly* asserted, "The adult homosexual . . . is in a stage of arrested psychosexual development; he is not far above the child level. . . . If most homosexual adults are attracted chiefly to other adults—which is debatable—many are still attracted to children; and more still are attracted to adolescents. The impulse to seduce is, like homosexuality itself, characteristic of arrested development." Bromberg remarked of homosexuality that, "in this group, the criminal action varies from relations between adults who openly avow their inclination, to homosexual activity with young boys or adolescents under threat or though the use of trickery."[27] Midcentury dictionaries and medical texts defined *pederast* in terms of both "boy-love" and anal sex and gave *sodomite* as a synonym, so that English usage thoroughly supported the identification of homosexuals and pedophiles.

Tolerance for homosexual lifestyles was inversely proportionate to the degree of popular concern over sex crimes and threats to children. When public fears were at their height, homosexuals were most vulnerable to vice purges and mob vigilantism, to incarceration and medical intervention. In southern California, the rumored molestation of a young boy in the fevered atmosphere of 1936 led to an attack on local homosexuals by the vigilante White Legion. In 1955, the city of Boise, Idaho, began a purge of its gay underworld, a phenomenon that gained celebrity when it was depicted as a twentieth-century witch-hunt in the book *The Boys of Boise*. Originating in a power struggle between rival factions in the state's business and political establishment, the vice campaign was explicitly justified on child-protection grounds. As *Time* reported, "A widespread homosexual underworld that involved some of Boise's most prominent men . . . had preyed on hundreds of teenage boys for the past decade."[28]

Predatory themes permeate Whitman's *Terror in the Streets* (1951), which describes men who commit sexual acts against small girls as "pedophiles" but men who molest boys as "homosexuals," suggesting an equivalence between the two terms. One Pittsburgh sex offender "murdered an eleven year old boy during the forceful commission of a homosexual act," after having earlier been "brought to court for molesting little girls": the contrast is evident, in that crimes against little girls did not involve a "heterosexual act." Even homosexual activities between adults are couched in the language of criminality: "Detroit, like most big cities, is plagued by the homosexual prowler. . . . He makes a flagrant display of himself in the public lavatories; he infests the most beautiful public parks, making them repugnant and fearsome to decent citizens. Police know that such men are dangerous—that when trapped, they may kill." The term *prowler* connotes predatory criminal activity, but here it is employed for men engaged in urban cruising, seeking consensual sex partners. Lesbians are also so characterized: "actual female prowlers who accost women and try to proselyte [*sic*] girls quite as vilely as men prowl after other men, and with quite the same possibilities of violence and murder."[29]

The word *proselyte* creates an image of homosexuality as an evangelistic cult as well as a communicable condition, a foretaste of the modern speculation that pedophile rings are literally cultlike or ritualistic. The metaphor dated back to the turn of the century, and in 1925, raids on a pioneering gay rights organization in Chicago led to newspaper headlines on the theme of "Strange Sex Cult Exposed." Whitman implies that homosexuals, male or female, convert the victims they molest and thereby create a new generation of perverts. The language of evangelism recurs throughout the literature: in 1943, Lewis Doshay's cohort of "boy sex offenders" included an Italian teenager who "became involved with a vicious group of adults who conditioned him to all the practices and ceremonials of homosexualism." Cult imagery appears in Whitman's case study of Detroit murderer Theodore Hilles, who in 1949 killed a six-year-old boy. Hilles's career of perversion and homicide is blamed on his having been exploited by a series of older homosexual men during his several years as a male prostitute; he himself became drawn to younger boys, whom he abused in turn, "and the vicious circle of proselytism was completed."[30]

Homosexuals were therefore seen as a serious social danger. In 1949, former Los Angeles prosecutor Eugene D. Williams warned: "The sex pervert, in his more innocuous form, is too frequently regarded as merely a 'queer' individual who never hurts anyone but himself. All too often we lose sight of the fact that the homosexual is an inveterate seducer of the young of both sexes, and is ever seeking for younger victims." Popular tolerance continues until "the mangled form of some child or woman directs the attention of the world to the fact that sex perverts do exist." A Los Angeles police psychiatrist wrote, "The homosexual will murder his victim during an act of sexual frenzy and afterwards rob him." *Coronet* magazine cautioned that homosexuals "descend through perversion to other forms of depravity, such as drug addiction, burglary, sadism and even murder."[31]

Desultory enforcement of laws against homosexual activity permitted law enforcement to exercise wide discretion, often in exchange for bribes, but laxity ended suddenly during a sex crime panic. Sodomy arrests in New York City reached an all-time high in the late 1930s, with more than 180 cases in both 1936 and 1938, each more than double the figure for 1932.[32] Arrests for homosexual activity in New York's subway lavatories ran at 707 in 1940 and 1,072 in 1944, but 3,289 in the "crime wave" year of 1948. Waves of antigay panic followed in other cities in the late 1940s, when writers on sex crime urged police vice squads to work "tirelessly tracking down every instance of perversion, however slight." In Pittsburgh, "the prowling of sex deviates around movie houses, public lavatories and a downtown shopping arcade became so blatant in 1948 that the citizens rose up in arms. They told the Bureau of Police that their town virtually was being taken over."[33] In response, the morals squad began a campaign against "the blatant prowlers, the ones who made quagmires out of public parks, the proselytizers of youth," making almost five hundred "homosexual arrests" during a twenty-month period.

The "queer threat" was now taken up by other activists. In February 1950, Senator Joseph McCarthy warned of the hordes of Communists who had infiltrated the State Department, and the twin dangers from Reds and perverts were soon assimilated. According to contemporary mythology, the danger of Communist blackmail was severe: Hitler "is alleged to have had a list of homosexuals in high posts all over the world. This list is supposed to have fallen into the hands of the Russians." In 1951, the FBI launched what became a vast program against sex deviates, set up to purge highly placed homosexuals, and the ensuing inquisition forced hundreds to resign from their official positions. Karpman denounced the attack on homosexuals as "hysteria, . . . an orgy of intolerant and sadistic hatred, a means of releasing free-floating hostility"; but the psychiatric profession as a whole

Table 3.1 Sex Crimes in New York City, 1930–1939

	Number Indicted	Percentage Convicted of Felony
Felony		
abduction	63	54
carnal abuse	333	42
forcible rape	418	66
incest	98	74
seduction	21	62
sodomy	414	51
statutory rape	1,948	20
TOTAL	3,295	35
Misdemeanor		
indecent exposure	1,063	
impairing morals of a minor	1,463	
TOTAL	2,526	
Total	5,821	

Source: *Report and Analysis of Sex Crimes in the City of New York for the Ten-Year Period 1930–1939* (New York: Mayor's Committee for the Study of Sex Offenses, 1940), p. 42.

in the next decade, and 9 of these were acquitted or discharged. "Sporadic with some, sex crime is a single episode in the lives of many."[39] The observation may be flawed, for perhaps the police simply did not catch the habitual offender again or bother to arrest him when they did; even so, the committee's perception would have repercussions throughout the 1950s.

The Diversity of Sex Offenses

That the acts making someone a sex offender were often trivial is illustrated by Doshay's study of 256 sex offenders, boys ages seven to sixteen, who were being treated at the New York City Children's Court clinics between 1928 and 1933. Doshay's conclusion, enlightened for the time, was that early apprehension for a sex offense need not lead to a subsequent career of sexual deviancy: "Given the benefit of proper court and clinic treatment, juvenile sex delinquency tends to become automatically self-curing."[40]

The conclusion is not surprising when we consider the acts by which boys came to the attention of authorities (Table 3.2). Most of the delinquency was harmless or consensual (see Chapter 2). Many boys were included because of homosexual acts, commonly with others of the same age though also through prostitution with older men. Acts of fellatio, mutual masturbation, or sodomy with another boy accounted for about a quarter of all offenses.

A number of offenses were remarkably trivial. Doshay's account of offenses begins with the "excessive masturbation" found in one-fifth of the acts. Fourteen percent of offenses involved speaking or writing obscenity, presumably including graffiti. "Group affairs with girls" meant acts of "the mild petting and inspecting nature, and occurred in a group of children on a roof adjoining a school."[41] "Heterosexual experiences" simply meant relations with a girl of a similar age. Only a dozen or so of the 350 recorded offenses could be classed as serious crime, exemplified by the fifteen-year-old boy who carried out a near-fatal sex assault on a woman. The proportion of offenders who went on to commit further offenses was also trivial, including only ten sex violations for the whole cohort (mainly sexual interference with young girls). It is in this tiny subgroup that we find the rare case histories of authentic sex criminals like "Harold," a Bronx boy who was repeatedly arrested for various acts, including exhibitionism, molestation, and harming a girl with a lighted match. His later career involved convictions for burglary, and in 1939, when he was twenty-one, a group of men found him molesting a young girl. He was killed while allegedly jumping from the roof to escape.[42] A predator like Harold stands out sharply from the pathetic cohort of so-called sex offenders.

By the late 1940s, a great deal of quantitative evidence was available to challenge the outrageous charges made by the media about the scale of the sex crime problem. Various state-level inquiries denied that sex crimes were surging, as the FBI claimed, and showed that rates might even be dropping.[43] This material provided the basis for two well-known criminologists' attacks on the construction of the psychopath problem. The first was Edwin Sutherland, a sociologist who played a critical role in the development of criminological thought; he was a pioneer in the study of what he dubbed "white-collar crime." In two important articles published in 1950, Sutherland analyzed 324 reported murders of women and children, found that only 5 percent involved rape or suspicion of rape, and concluded that

Table 3.2   Sex Offenses Among 256 Boys
in New York City, 1928–1933

Offense	Number
masturbation, excessive	71
masturbation, mutual	9
exhibitionism	25
peeping	9
speaking or writing obscenity	47
fellatio active	25
fellatio passive	22
sodomy with father or older siblings	14
sodomy with other adult	50
sodomy with same age boy	26
sodomy with younger boy	7
sodomy with girl	7
sodomy with younger siblings	4
"all types of perversion"	23
group affairs with girls	3
sex attempts with little girl	25
heterosexual experiences	23
touching little girls' parts	26
touching sister's parts	5
touching woman's parts	18
incest with sisters	13
attempted incest with mother	1
sadism	7
violent sex assault on woman	1

Source: Based on Lewis J. Doshay, The Boy Sex Offender and
His Later Career (1943; reprint, Montclair, N.J.: Patterson
Smith, 1969), p. 72.

killings by sex fiends were far rarer than popular opinion might suggest. This estimate was compatible with modern homicide statistics, which indicate that between 1 and 2 percent of all homicides are committed in the course of sexual attacks, while the vast majority of murders are the work of intimates or family members. If indeed sex fiends by the thousands were roving across the country, most of them were causing extraordinarily little damage. Those who believed that sex crime was a serious problem criticized Sutherland for taking his accounts of murders from the sober *New York Times* rather than other papers with a more avid interest in sensational crime, but even if he was understating the issue, he was not doing so to any significant degree.[44]

Another critic was Sutherland's long-standing rival Paul Tappan, who in 1950 was the technical consultant for a report by New Jersey's Commission on the Habitual Sex Offender, which largely replicated the findings of the mayor's committee. This gave Tappan a platform from which to attack the sex psychopath problem, allowing him to list "myths about the sex offender": "That tens of thousands of homicidal sex fiends stalk the land, . . . that the victims of sex attack are 'ruined for life,' . . . that sex offenders are usually recidivists, . . . that sex psychopathy or sex deviation is a clinical entity." Current concern was wildly distorted, he claimed: "The vast majority of the sex deviates are minor offenders. . . . Most of the persons adjudicated are minor deviates, rarely if ever sex fiends." At most 5 percent of convicted sex offenders were dangerous in the sense of using force or inflicting injury. Most offenders were "immature and underdeveloped emotionally and sexually," with sex drives well below rather than above the normal range.[45] Far from being persistent and unstoppable, "sex offenders have one of the lowest rates as repeaters of all types of crime," and only homicide offenders were less likely to repeat their crimes: the New Jersey study found that only 7 percent of sex offenders had previously been arrested for similar offenses in the past. Moreover, many of the offenses were harmless or consensual acts like homosexuality and exhibitionism.

Tappan drew ammunition from the recently published research by Alfred Kinsey into human sexual behavior. However questionable their methodologies, the Kinsey reports showed convincingly that "deviant," "perverted," or "unnatural" acts were remarkably common: far more people said that they had engaged in homosexual acts than any previous study had indicated, and many heterosexuals regularly engaged in behavior that technically qualified as felony sodomy. As Tappan noted, "A very large number of the male population of New Jersey has engaged in practices coming within the enumerations of our present abnormal sex offender law, on the basis of which they might be committed to one of our state mental hospitals. . . . The number of cases that could be held under the statute in the future is virtually unlimited." As Ploscowe noted in 1951, if Kinsey was right, then each year there might be 6 million acts of sodomy and deviant sex for every twenty convictions. A Pennsylvania legislative commission cited Kinsey's estimate that two-thirds of the total male population had engaged in perverse sexual behavior. If true, Pennsylvania had some 2.3 million male sexual deviates, with only two hundred psychiatrists to deal with them all. Karpman noted, "According to Kinsey, 85 percent of the younger male population could be convicted as sex offenders if laws were strictly enforced": "sex offenders are a very large portion of the population." Albert Ellis asked, skeptically, if every man who had ever had a same-sex contact should be labeled a sex psychopath.[46] If nearly everyone was a deviant, then there was no norm from which one could be said to deviate.

Paradox

In the first phase of the sex crime panic, between 1937 and 1940, special legislation against sex offenders emerged as an ad hoc response to the menace portrayed by the media and law enforcement, but the prescriptions were without any detailed theoretical foundation. After 1945, steadily accumulating technical and social scientific evidence should have suggested a need for caution about the sex psychopath problem and about the connection between such individuals and lesser offenders.[47] Moreover, the pitfalls in any proposed statutes were obvious to most experts, as predictable as the stages of a mathematical proof: confining petty sex offenders for preventive purposes would impose a disproportionate burden on minor deviants while diverting attention from the truly threatening cases, and there would be massive overdiagnosis of sex psychopaths. But the faster the criticisms accumulated in the late 1940s, the more enthusiastically legislatures passed new sex offender legislation. By 1960, a majority of American states had acquired sex psychopath statutes founded on exactly the principles that the medico-legal experts derided.

The simplest explanation for this paradox was that social and demographic trends created constituencies with a powerful interest in demanding official protection from the perceived menace. One aspect of this was the sense of risk among women whose husbands were in the armed services. The war years of 1941–45 and 1950–53 disrupted traditional family structures, removing millions of adult men and bringing large numbers of women into the workforce to replace them. Between 1940 and 1944, the proportion of women in the workforce grew from 27 to an unprecedented

35 percent, and 3 million women were employed in war production. Many women felt themselves to be without the protection of their husbands, and the need for day care left children separated from nuclear family units.[48] The ascendancy of the sex criminal as a media villain reinforced the sense of a threat to women alone during wartime. A spate of thrillers like *Gaslight* and *Experiment Perilous* depicted isolated women threatened by sex fiends and psychopaths or other homicidal menfolk, and *The Seventh Victim* pioneered the image of women pursued by a homicidal satanic cult. When American men returned from the forces in vast numbers after 1945, the process of their wives resuming their "proper" roles in the home was greatly facilitated by the comforting knowledge that the renunciation of paid work contributed to protecting children from the legion of sex fiends. This message was reiterated over the next decade by women's magazines and religious and family publications alike.

Although the end of war in 1953 restored a more normal gender balance to American society, it was also around this time that the baby boom was peaking, and the emphasis of sexual fears decisively focused on the danger to children. Precisely then, the phrase "child molesting" became nearly synonymous with sex crime in media usage: whereas J. Edgar Hoover in 1947 had rhetorically asked the American public "How Safe Is Your Daughter?" the title of his 1955 article was "How Safe Is Your Youngster?" In *Reader's Guide* the phrase *child molesting* first appeared in 1953, in an article in *Better Homes and Gardens,* and family-oriented magazines began serving as the chief vehicles for coverage of the molestation issue, from *Parents, Ladies' Home Journal,* and *National Parent Teacher* magazine to *Redbook* and *Good Housekeeping,* with their regular stories on the lines of "How to Protect Your Children Against Perverts." Self-help and community child-protection schemes became a flourishing subgenre within the family magazines, peaking in 1957.[49] Thereafter, molestation stories fell to one or two a year, remaining at that level till the new explosion in the late 1970s.

Lawmakers and police faced overwhelming pressure to do something about sex crime, and special legislation directed against sex psychopaths was the natural quick fix. In the desperate public mood of 1937 or 1949, it would have taken suicidal courage to oppose or even question a bill ostensibly intended to protect the innocent from sex fiends, even if a legislator knew perfectly well that the measure would be worse than useless. (In the late 1940s, a third of Americans surveyed believed that "prison is too good for sex criminals. They should be publicly whipped or worse.")[50] Legal action to defend women and children was politically profitable or even essential, and the possibility of injustice against minor offenders was scarcely worth considering.

Also, although psychiatric opinion about the psychopath problem was by no means united, this period was marked by sharp growth in the therapeutic profession (in both numbers and prestige) and in their influence in policymaking. Stimulated by major grants from private concerns like the Rockefeller Foundation, medical schools and universities devoted far greater attention to psychiatric research from the 1930s, especially in the area of crime and violence, and research centers developed in several cities. The raw numbers are impressive: the American Psychological Association grew from 2,739 members in 1940 to 30,839 by 1970; the American Psychiatric Association expanded from 2,423 members to 18,407 in the same period. As George Chauncey notes, psychiatrists gained status during wartime through "the crucial role they had played in screening and managing the millions of people mobilized for military service."[51] After 1945, psychiatrists and psychologists dominated the investigative commissions charged with formulating responses to the sex crime problem, and their language and assumptions heavily influenced representatives from other professional groups, including lawyers, judges, police, and clergy. The ability to define the sex psychopath menace as lying within the purview of psychiatry conveyed a prestige that carried over into many areas of life and behavior. Psychiatrists would thereafter occupy a key role in the educational system as the source of advice for parents and teachers seeking to protect the children in their care and to prevent the nurture of new psychopaths and delinquents.

Accepting the popular notion of psychopathy also meant a great expansion in the use of medical concepts and terminology in the criminal-justice system. During the late 1940s, police agencies imported psychiatric experts and academics to provide orientation on the whole world of sexual perversion and crime, and there were calls to institutionalize this contact. As Whitman warned picturesquely in 1951, "A police academy without a psychiatrist is like a gun without sights." The increased role for psychiatrists and psychologists sometimes led to the creation of a whole range of therapeutic institutions midway between prisons and mental hospitals. Chauncey remarks that "in the name of protecting women and children from sex deviates, the [Michigan] Commission's psychiatrists urged the

73

public to support the expansion of existing psychiatric institutions and the development of new ones, even if they were only peripherally related to the problem of sex crime."[52] State investigative commissions of these years advocated a thorough revamping of criminal justice to transfer powers from lawyers and correctional administrators to psychiatrists and therapists. All this was not solely a question of professional self-interest, as many psychiatrists sincerely wished to promote therapeutic intervention as a benevolent alternative to the punitive assumptions of the prevailing system. With whatever qualms, enough psychiatrists supported the new legislative arrangements to permit the establishment of the new regime for defining and restraining sex psychopaths.

The Sex Psychopath Statutes

"He's in prison now, being punished; and the trial doesn't even begin till next Wednesday; and of course the crime comes last of all." "Suppose he never commits the crime?" said Alice. "That would be all the better, wouldn't it?" the Queen said.

—LEWIS CARROLL, *THROUGH THE LOOKING GLASS*

His sexual life, for example, was entirely regulated by the two words *sexcrime* (sexual immorality) and *goodsex* (chastity). *Sexcrime* covered all sexual misdeeds whatever. It covered fornication, adultery, homosexuality and other perversions and in addition, normal intercourse practised for its own sake. There was no need to enumerate them separately since they were all equally culpable and in principle, all punishable by death. . . . He knew what was meant by *goodsex*—that is to say normal intercourse between man and wife for the sole purpose of begetting children and without physical pleasure on the part of the woman; all else was *sexcrime*.

—GEORGE ORWELL, 1984

The problem of the compulsive sex offender was given fictional form in the 1952 film *The Sniper,* in which a didactic prologue declares that "high among police problems is that of the sex criminal, responsible last year alone for offenses which victimized 31,175 women. Adequate and understanding laws do not exist. Law enforcement is helpless. Here in terms of one case is the story of a man whose enemy was womankind." The story depicts a rooftop sniper who attacks women in a symbolic attempt to kill his mother, and like the real-life Heirens, he leaves a note urging the police to catch him before he strikes again. According to the film's critique, disturbed offenders receive a series of short spells of incarceration, only to be released before they can receive adequate therapy, with the consequence that truly dangerous offenders are out on the streets. Even after so many years, so many lurid stories, the example that the film cites to prove this point is still Albert Fish, here credited with sixteen murders.

Sniper was a manifesto for the positivist view of petty sexual deviancy as a symptom of a potentially lethal pathology, requiring treatment for the overall condition rather than punishment for a particular crime. The psychiatrist who represents the voice of reason in the film urges officials not to "strike out blindly but to act with reason" and demands a new law: "Let every socially dangerous sex offender as soon as he is caught, for his first offense, be committed to a mental institution. . . . Those who can be cured will be cured. Those who can't—well, at least they'll never get out to try it again."

Working from a rationale of social defense and community protection, most American states were at just this time passing laws to stem the supposed tide of violence perpetrated by sex psychopaths, and these measures were usually upheld by courts. The laws marked an ambitious experiment in the integration of therapeutic and criminal responses to deviancy, but their operation demonstrated the pernicious dangers of such a combination and therefore offer instructive parallels to modern laws against sex predators. Put simply, the laws were far too likely to target minor violators of public morality, while there is no evidence that they fulfilled their advertised function of preventing atrocious violence.

The Revolving Door

There was widespread agreement in the 1930s and 1940s that the existing justice system was failing miserably to confront sex crimes. The vast majority of offenses were simply not recorded, and even when they were, there was no certainty that a report would lead to an arrest, nor that arrest would be followed by conviction. Then as now, overloaded courts and overworked prosecutors were forced to plea-bargain, reducing serious sex offenses to a felony of lesser degree or converting a felony to a misdemeanor.[1] The records of sex offenders often contained such vague charges as "impairing morals," which covered an incredibly broad range of activities, from sexual molestation to nonsexual behaviors like gambling (Table 4.1). Suspects pled guilty to this crime rather than face the graver charges which, had the prosecution been so inclined, could have been pursued as felony rape, carnal abuse, or sodomy. "This is especially serious because it is in the

Table 4.1   Impairing Morals Cases, New York City, 1930–1939

Specific Behavior	Number of Cases	Percentage of Total
attempted intercourse	322	23
intercourse	226	16
fondling	205	14
finger in female organs	163	12
exposure to female child	103	7
masturbation of offender by victim	96	7
anal copulation	90	6
masturbation of victim by offender	69	5
oral copulation	57	4
intercourse in presence of child	38	3
sleeping in room with female child	28	2
other	19	2
Total	**1,416**	

Source: Report and Analysis of Sex Crimes in the City of New York for the Ten-Year Period 1930–1939 (New York: Mayor's Committee for the Study of Sex Offenses, 1940), pp. 54–55.
Note: Victims in all cases were under sixteen years of age. Due to rounding error, sum of percentages exceeds 100 percent.

impairing morals group that many of the abnormal sex offenders who have a penchant for sex play with small children are found."[2] Vagaries of prosecutorial practice made it difficult to use criminal charges to assess a person's actual conduct.

Rape offered a similar picture, though this legal category includes both forcible and statutory offenses. In New York City during the 1930s, rape charges often resulted in convictions of assault in the second or third degree, while no fewer than 80 percent of statutory rape cases were converted to misdemeanor charges. Over half the men arrested for rape in New York State during 1948 were acquitted or had their cases dismissed, and only one-tenth of the original total were finally convicted of felony rape. In 1948, New York State recorded 1,674 arrests for sex felonies: 776 were acquitted or had charges dismissed, and 561 more pled down to misdemeanors or minor charges. Only one-fifth of those arrested were ultimately convicted of the felony for which they had been arrested.[3]

Those charged with lesser offenses might well drop out of the system altogether. During the 1930s, one-third of all arraignments for indecent exposure in New York City led to acquittal or DOR, discharge on the defendant's own recognizance (which reflected a decision not to pursue the case further). Offenses against children were particularly likely to be dropped. Of the decade's three thousand arraignments for impairing the morals of a minor, over half resulted in acquittal or DOR. This high rate reflected defendants' reluctance to make plea bargains that would admit guilt, thus demanding that prosecutors either pursue the case through a trial or else give up at an early stage. Prosecutors often chose not to proceed rather than face the difficulties of seeking corroboration and using children's testimony, as cases of this sort were chancy at best and could be suicide missions.[4]

The difficulties of using child witnesses were all too familiar. When, in 1936, the American Bar Association appointed a commission to examine the issue of evidence in cases of incest and molestation, the chairman was none other than John Henry Wigmore, who since the turn of the century had been arguing against the credibility of children, especially young girls, in sex cases. The commission's report concluded with a stark warning about accepting testimony arising from "the erotic imagination of an abnormal child of attractive appearance" and cited "thousands of observed cases" of false charges. In 1938, Bertram Pollens attacked public hysteria over sex crime on the grounds that lurid coverage stimulated the fantasies of children, who might report their imaginings as authentic crimes and falsely accuse innocent adults. A decade later, Kinsey remarked that "not a few older men serve time in penal institutions" because they had been accused of wrongdoing by small girls who shared the "public hysteria over being touched by a strange person."[5]

Hostile legal attitudes could have parlous results for child witnesses in the courts. Howard Whitman described how "a clever lawyer can make mince-meat of their testimony. It is possible to confuse children on the witness stand, to frighten them, to get them tangled up, to explode their credibility by showing how children 'imagine things' and are influenced by their elders." In the Fred Stroble case of 1949, doubts about the reliability of child witnesses permitted an offender charged with multiple counts of sexual abuse to plead only to "suspicion of indecent exposure and child molestation." Even though Stroble's was "as obvious a case of pedophilia as could be found," he was freed on bail, only to be rearrested several months later for killing a first-grade girl.[6]

Individuals actually convicted of serious sex offenses were generally those who lacked the connections or legal representation to arrange benevolent deals; at the same time, some serious and persistent offenders obtained relatively mild outcomes, being convicted of misdemeanors whose designations were not even explicitly sexual. For those who adhered to the escalation theory of sex offenses, this was a dangerous situation. Compulsive or psychopathic offenders were committing numerous acts of increasing severity that either were not noted or did not lead to substantial sentences, until the sequence culminated in a homicidal outbreak. The case of Albert Fish had provided abundant early warnings in the form of multiple arrests, some for theft but others for sexually oriented offenses like writing obscene letters. In 1930, psychiatrists had determined that although Fish did have a "psychopathic personality" of the "sexual type," he was not insane, and he was released after only a few months. The following year, when Fish was arrested for mailing obscene letters, investigators discovered a cat-o'-nine-tails that he regularly used upon himself, but another brief spell of psychiatric observation was followed by early release. A similar history could be traced for Salvatore Ossido, the Brooklyn man who committed the 1937 child murder. He had several convictions and arrests for sexual acts against young girls; the first offense resulted in imprisonment, but subsequent ones resulted in trivial fines or plea bargains, and he was out on bail when he murdered the girl. In cases like Fish's and Ossido's, behaviors like annoying a girl or impairing morals genuinely were precursors to worse offenses. The danger was compounded if the offenders had records in several jurisdictions, since the records were never collated by any central agency. "The repeatedly arrested but released sex offender is a special bogey."[7]

A need for prolonged incarceration was suggested by cases like that of the fifty-three-year-old man described by Pollens in 1938. The offender's known criminal record began in 1910 with a prison sentence for indecent assault and carnal abuse of a child. He was arrested again in 1921, 1925, and 1936, on each occasion serving a prison sentence and being paroled, only to reoffend; his current sentence would keep him imprisoned until about 1941, when he was eligible for parole again. As Pollens writes, the man "is dangerous when at large, and . . . needs to be confined to an institution for an indefinite period." Whitman reports the similarly obsessive case of a man who received a year's imprisonment in 1942 for indecent exposure to two young girls. Released in 1943, he soon received thirty days in prison for exhibitionism. The year 1944 brought probation for molesting a five-year-old girl and then another year in jail for indecent exposure to more little girls. The man was rearrested again each year from 1946 through 1949, when he was finally committed indefinitely as a sex psychopath. One man with a penchant for fondling young girls' genitals received six-month jail terms in 1923 and 1931, but his third offense in 1937 led to only a fifty-dollar fine.[8]

Other studies produced evidence of compulsively dangerous offenders. In 1948, a psychiatric team led by David Abrahamsen assessed the potential dangerousness of 102 sex offenders in New York's Sing Sing Prison, finding that eighteen of the sample "are of such psychological makeup that they are predisposed to commit crimes of violence and are likely to commit new acts of violence if released." They could not under current law be detained past the term of their sentence, however, and several of them had already been released by the time the team's report was published in 1951. Protection of the public demanded earlier recognition and intervention, even if this meant drastic changes in conventional principles of criminal sentencing. The revolving door through which offenders passed so regularly needed to be firmly closed. As a New York City judge remarked when sentencing a child molester in 1937, "Sex perverts are baneful enemies of society who should be segregated for the longest possible time in order to protect our little ones." In 1949, the *St. Louis Post-Dispatch* therefore argued for a special law for the state of Missouri: "Strenuous efforts are made to detect tuberculosis, cancer and other diseases early. Should not equally strenuous efforts be made to detect and treat cases of dangerous sex perversion before they have a chance to announce themselves in their own dreadful terms?"[9]

The Sex Psychopath Laws, 1937–1940

New legislation to confront sex crime had its roots in the panic of 1937, when judges, police, and legislators vied with one another in finding the most effective way to stop perverts. Some advocated moralistic solutions like enforcing bans on obscene or indecent literature; others supported castration and sterilization. Chicago and New York both created central "sex bureaux," registries for keeping track of sex offenders against children. The New York mayor's committee proposed that all accused sex offenders be thoroughly investigated before being granted a misdemeanor plea in a given case, so that minor dispositions would not be granted to offenders with a strong tendency to commit sexual offenses. And the committee also explored stricter measures against the small category of persistent offenders, some of whom might be potential killers: "One is particularly likely to encounter such individuals among defendants charged with the more aberrant types of sexual activity such as carnal abuse of children, sodomy and incest," the committee noted in its report, in a remarkable statement given the grab bag of miscellaneous acts comprehended under the term *sodomy*. The committee recommended a sexual psychopath law "which would make it possible to retain convicted sex offenders who are not reasonably safe to be at large, in institutional confinement even after the expiration of sentence. This would make it possible to retain custody over abnormal sex offenders who are neither mentally defective nor insane, but who because of constitutional penchants for abnormal methods of satisfying sexual passions are dangerous to be at large."[10]

As implemented, sex psychopath legislation built on the positivist precedent of the defective delinquent laws, which meant observing sex offenders in order to determine their mental condition and dangerousness and, where appropriate, committing perverts indefinitely to a special institution for dangerous defectives. The new system emerged on an ad hoc basis during 1937. In New York City, Mayor La Guardia ordered a psychiatric examination for all men sentenced under charges of indecent exposure, impairing the morals of a minor, sodomy, and attempted rape. Upon release, each man would be taken before a magistrate and then sent to the psychopathic ward of Bellevue Hospital for further observation, with the possibility of commitment to an institution for the insane or mentally defective.[11] This emergency measure was based on the view that a single criminal act could be a symptom of sex psychopathy and, as such, justified long-term commitment.

States began applying the same principles in legislation modeled on Michigan's pioneering law of 1937. Under this statute, a person convicted of a sex crime could be identified as a "sex degenerate or pervert or [as suffering] from [a] mental disorder with marked sex deviation and tendencies dangerous to the public safety." The court examined the individual with the assistance of two physicians, and the diagnosed psychopath would be indefinitely committed to a mental hospital. The following year, this measure was declared unconstitutional by the state supreme court: the *Frontczak* decision found that, although the psychopathy hearing took the form of a criminal proceeding, it lacked the essential protections of a jury trial and violated the double-jeopardy principle, two limitations that have often been cited in such cases up to the present day.[12] Duly warned, Illinois passed the first enduring statute in 1938, avoiding constitutional traps by ensuring that committal could occur without a criminal conviction and drawing more heavily on the procedures of an insanity hearing rather than on those of a criminal trial. However, a person committed to a mental institution as a psychopath would still, on release, face criminal charges for the act that had originally brought him to the notice of the authorities. Once the statute was judged constitutionally sound, it was widely imitated in other states.

In 1940, the U.S. Supreme Court heard the case of Charles E. Pearson, who had been identified as a psychopathic personality under Minnesota's 1939 sex psychopath law.[13] Pearson complained that the proceedings violated due process and that the law's definitions of psychopathy were capricious or subjective. There were signs of judicial nervousness about due-process safeguards, but the Court agreed with the state's contention that the psychopathic personality was properly defined, for the statute was careful to list "underlying conditions, calling for evidence of past conduct pointing to probable consequences . . . as susceptible to proof as many of the criteria constantly applied in prosecutions for crime." The constitutionality of the laws was not challenged again for another quarter century.

Expansion, 1945–1957

More legislative endeavors followed after World War II. Sex psychopath laws were passed in Massachusetts and Washington in 1947, and six more states followed in 1949. By 1950, laws were in place in fifteen states and the District of Columbia, and further measures were under consideration in Maryland (enacted 1951), Pennsylvania (1952), and elsewhere. Ultimately, twenty-nine states would pass laws targeting psychopaths under various names, including *sexually dangerous persons, mentally disturbed sex offenders,* and *defective delinquents.*[14] New laws were sometimes superimposed on the older defective delinquent statutes, creating uncertainty about proper jurisdiction.

Laws were generally passed in response to public panic, like the "mass hysteria" that occurred in Indiana following a series of murders there in 1947. "The newspapers and radio kept the public fully informed through lurid and sometimes sensational accounts of the killings, providing the impression that sex fiends lurked in every doorway." Initially, the governor suspended the paroles of all habitual criminals who were second offenders. Long-term measures included barring plea bargains with sex offenders in order to avoid their premature release, using indeterminate sentences and pretrial detention for such offenders, and granting a greater role to psychiatrists examining "persons suspected of being sexually maladjusted." By 1949, Indiana acquired its Criminal Sexual Psychopath Law. A similar sequence occurred in Missouri in 1948–49. Child advocates in St. Louis formed a committee to press for a special law to control sex psychopaths, and this campaign moved to the state capitol, where a law was enacted in 1949. In Washington, D.C., the movement began in 1946, at a point when "sex crimes were turning the national capital into a bog of horror" and the *Washington Post* was claiming that the district had become "a haven for sexual degenerates." The Miller Law, passed in 1948, provided for sex psychopaths to be committed for treatment at St. Elizabeth's Hospital until "sufficiently recovered so as not to be dangerous to other persons."[15]

The New York law of 1950 gave judges the discretion to impose fully indeterminate sentences in cases involving "rape or sodomy involving the use of force and violence, or against small children, or . . . felonious assault involving a sexual purpose." Individuals were "quarantined," a word that again suggested the medical model on which the measure was based. The law established clinics to study and treat inmates confined under these terms; a psychiatric examination was required before a sentence could be imposed, and although further examinations were given every two years thereafter to see if release might be warranted, commitment could in theory be lifelong. In Pennsylvania, the 1951 legislative commission recommended the immediate establishment of a diagnostic center and the segregation of sex offenders. A new sex offender statute was the first law in the state's history to authorize a sentence of "one day to life."[16]

Child protection was often the motive cited to justify such laws. In Massachusetts in 1957, the incentive for legislation came when two boys were assaulted and murdered by a man released from prison after serving time for a sexual offense. The legislature immediately responded with a comprehensive sex offender law that required a person accused of a sex crime to be observed by psychiatrists for sixty days. An offender judged a "sexually dangerous person" was remanded to a special treatment facility at Bridgewater, where he would remain from one day to life, or until found to be no longer "sexually dangerous." As late as 1963, Oregon passed an innovative statute that tried to solve the well-known difficulties of using children's testimony in court. A person found to be sexually dangerous to children could be civilly committed on an indeterminate basis, and a special facility for offenders was constructed at the Oregon State Hospital, the first of its kind in the country.[17]

The upsurge of custodial solutions was very much in line with other practices of the era, when the mentally disturbed and deviant were commonly confined against their consent in special hospitals or asylums. The population of state mental hospitals rose from 160,000 in 1910 to 270,000 by 1930 and reached a peak of about 550,000 in the mid-1950s, a rate of growth far higher than that of the population at large. This increase was made possible by lax commitment standards, and police and doctors exceeded their authority in order to incarcerate those who were troublesome or inconvenient rather than dangerous. Courts rarely intervened, trusting in the discretion and integrity of the medical professionals involved; this was scarcely an area where the language of rights could be applied. Limitations on the powers of the hospitals and psychiatrists were attempted only in the aftermath of occasional journalistic exposés, like the campaign that followed the 1948 film *The Snakepit*.[18] If so little care was devoted to protecting the civil rights of the innocent insane, it was unlikely that sex criminals would receive any more consideration.

Although individual statutes varied, all were based on the principle of the compulsive nature of psychopathy and the escalation theory of sexual offenses. As a medical problem, the issue needed to be met with the principles of civil commitment. In several states, no criminal charge was necessary for commitment: a complainant would initiate a charge with the prosecutor, alleging that a given person was a sexual psychopath; if the court agreed, the accused would be committed to an institution until pronounced cured. It was usually not necessary to find the person guilty of the specific crime charged.

The laws used similar language to define psychopathy. In Illinois, the person was "not mentally ill or feebleminded to an extent making him criminally irresponsible" but was predisposed to "the commission of sexual offenses," was "lacking in power to control his sexual impulses." In Massachusetts and the District of Columbia, "the sexual psychopath must have demonstrated repeated misconduct in sexual matters, evidencing lack of power to control sexual impulses and a likelihood of attacking or otherwise inflicting injury, loss, pain or other evil on the objects of his desire." Wisconsin typically defined a psychopath as "irresponsible for sexual conduct and thereby dangerous to himself and others because of, (1) emotional instability; or, (2) impulsiveness of behavior; or, (3) lack of customary standards of good judgment; or, (4) failure to appreciate consequences of acts; or, (5) combination of the above." Although most states explicitly identified sexual misbehavior in their descriptions of who would be considered offenders, some cast a wider net: Maryland, for example, targeted "persistent aggravated antisocial or criminal behavior." Vermont required incarceration "of persons who because of psychopathic personality violate the criminal laws of the state or are guilty of gross immoral conduct."[19]

The standards applied in assessing the psychopathic condition recalled the loose criteria for defining defectives and candidates for sterilization. What acts were considered psychopathic varied from state to state, but they generally comprised "rape, aggravated rape, indecent liberties, sodomy, certain sexual acts with minors, incest, or attempts to commit some of these acts." The acts did not even have to be felonies. New Jersey's Sex Offender Act of 1949 was ambitious, requiring a psychiatric examination for any individual convicted of "rape, sodomy, incest, lewdness, indecent exposure, uttering or exposing obscene literature or pictures, indecent communications to females of any nature whatsoever, or carnal abuse, or an attempt to commit any of the aforementioned offenses." This list was curtailed the following year to "rape, carnal abuse, sodomy or impairing the morals of a minor," or attempts to commit the same.[20]

The lengthy catalog of acts in the original New Jersey statute indicated the wide trawl of this kind of legislation. Of three hundred inmates examined in the first year after the 1949 law was enacted, only a few had been involved in violent or coercive crimes, and many had been arrested for consensual acts (Table 4.2). When Michigan appointed a commission to investigate "sex offenders" between 1949 and 1951, the term applied not just to sex murderers but also to sadomasochists, homosexuals, pedophiles, rapists, exhibitionists, voyeurs, and conceivably anyone too "immature" to fulfill expected social and sexual norms. The legal descriptions of the offenses make it difficult to know whether sexual relations with a minor necessarily involved what later generations would call child abuse, since age ranges are given for neither offenders nor victims. The Ohio and New Hampshire statutes applied to rapists without distinguishing between forcible and statutory rape, while sodomy was included regardless of the age of the other participant.[21]

Table 4.2   Charges Against the First Individuals Examined Under the New Jersey Sex Offender Act of 1949

	Number	Percent of Total
sexual assault	21	7
forcible rape	8	3
statutory rape	61	20
incestuous relations	11	4
noncoital sex relations with a minor	51	17
exhibitory sex acts	89	29
distributing obscene material	8	3
homosexual relations	49	16
other sex offenses	2	1
Total	300	100

Source: Albert Ellis and Ralph Brancale, The Psychology of Sex Offenders (Springfield, Ill.: Charles C. Thomas, 1956), p. 11.

Not every individual assessed under the laws was committed as a sex criminal, but even the acts that led to commitment included many consensual or minor offenses (Table 4.3).[22] In Indiana, 160 individuals were committed between 1949 and 1956 under the state's criminal sexual psychopath law. Sixty of these had committed offenses that could be classified as "crimes of violence against persons," a category including assault and battery, rape, molesting, and kidnapping, but many other offenses were far less threatening (Table 4.4). Sundry "immoral" acts accounted for almost two-thirds of total commitments and over half of the incidents involving children. Although some "psychopaths" may have been involved in violence, there is no suggestion that their detention was doing anything to keep rapists or child killers off the streets.

Indiana was typical in labeling as sex psychopaths countless individuals whose dangerousness was minimal. In one state, the first batch of sex psychopaths in the 1940s included the following cases: "public masturbation (without indecent exposure), . . . the following of a white female by a Negro (no assault or approach to 'victim'), . . . a non-aggressive homosexual convicted of passing bad checks, . . . three men who engaged in homosexuality with young males (including fellatio and sodomy), . . . sex relations

Table 4.3 Charges Against Sex Offender Inmates at New Jersey
State Prison, Trenton, May 31, 1950

	Number	Percent of Total
sexual assault	35	10
forcible rape	83	23
statutory rape	8	2
incestuous relations	24	7
noncoital sex relations with a minor	113	32
exhibitory sex acts	36	10
distributing obscene material	1	0
homosexual relations	50	14
other sex offenses	9	2
Total	**359**	**100**

Source: Albert Ellis and Ralph Brancale, *The Psychology of Sex Offenders* (Springfield, Ill.: Charles C. Thomas, 1956), p. 11.

with (experienced) juvenile females." In Michigan in the 1940s, a man who committed the misdemeanor offense of indecent exposure was petitioning the courts for release after seven years' incarceration. Nicholas N. Kittrie aptly summarizes this definition of the psychopath or defective delinquent as "a recidivist with a propensity to habitual crime (with emphasis upon sexual offenses)."[23]

Homosexuals all too easily qualified for inclusion under the new legislation because of the inclusion of sodomy in the lists of offenses meriting psychopath status. As critics of the laws noted, "If the primary function of these laws is to segregate the dangerous, their objective is not being achieved for some of the most dangerous men are those rejected as sexual psychopaths merely because they are not amenable to treatment, while some of the least dangerous (e.g., homosexual offenders vs. adults) are retained." In 1942, a Michigan man carried out a homosexual act with another consenting male. Because he was unlikely to desist from his deviant "career" if left at liberty, he was committed "until fully and permanently recovered" from his criminal tendencies, a condition that made commitment a virtual life sentence.[24]

One redeeming feature of the statutes was that, for all the fanfare with

Table 4.4   Morals Offenses Attributed
to "Criminal Sexual Psychopaths" in
Indiana, 1949–1956

sodomy	60
public indecency	23
contributing to the delinquency of minors	13
peeping in windows	7
incest	3
disorderly conduct	1
unnatural acts with wife	1

Source: quoted in Fred Cohen, ed., The Law of Deprivation of
Liberty (St. Paul, Minn: West Publishing, 1980), pp. 676–77.

which they were passed, they were little used.[25] Between 1949 and 1956,
Indiana committed about twenty-three individuals each year, which was
high in comparison with other jurisdictions. Minnesota committed about
thirty-five people each year immediately following passage of its statute in
1939, but this number fell to around ten a year by the end of the 1940s. Illinois committed only sixteen during the entire decade of the 1940s. Only
California retained its initial enthusiasm, committing 435 defendants in
the first decade of the act's operation, or an average of forty or so cases each
year, and the statute remained in full operation into the 1970s. Across the
whole nation, the total number of "psychopaths" committed annually during the 1950s would rarely have exceeded a couple of hundred.

Those deemed to be psychopaths tended disproportionately to be
white. Obviously, this did not mean that black sex offenders were ignored
or treated leniently, but their relative absence from the rosters of sex psychopaths may suggest that wealthier offenders used these laws as a means
of securing more lenient treatment regimes. Or it may mean that police
were more sensitive to offenses involving white women and children, pay-
ing little attention to acts of molestation or exhibitionism committed by
black offenders against black victims. Whatever the reason, the racial im-
balance was consistent, and surprising in view of black overrepresentation
in the prison population at large. In the early 1970s, of the child molesters
studied at California's Atascadero State Hospital, only 5 percent were

black, while 3 percent were Hispanic and 7 percent were American Indian; 85 percent of the inmates were white.[26]

Sex offender legislation stressed incapacitation; as one Wisconsin administrator summarized that state's law, "The sexual psychopath gets locked up, and that's the end of it." Although the civil procedures used for this purpose implied that offenders would be treated, therapy was not generally available. In 1958, a Michigan court noted that "a person committed under this remedial and corrective legislation is in fact serving potentially a life sentence in our biggest state prison, treated in all respects similarly to other criminals therein confined." In the early years, failure to provide treatment opened one of the few legal avenues for challenging the acts. In 1953, a U.S. Court of Appeals decided that a sexual psychopath could not simply be held "without treatment in a ward for the hopelessly insane."[27]

With these limitations, some jurisdictions did make well-intentioned efforts to treat sex criminals. In 1951, Wisconsin initiated a special sex offender facility at Waupun, and the unit claimed a high success rate in rehabilitation, using techniques like intensive group therapy. Similar efforts were in progress in Massachusetts, Washington, and California, all of which hoped to use their special institutions to study offenders in order to develop policies of prevention. New York offered group therapy and individual psychotherapy within the walls of Sing Sing, and in 1950, New Jersey opened its showcase research facility at Menlo Park.

California's experience was on a completely different order. As it had been with regard to sterilization, the state emerged as a national leader in experimental penology. Atascadero State Hospital, which California opened in 1954, was explicitly designed for the confinement and treatment of "mentally disordered sex offenders," and like Waupun, the "hospital" claimed significant successes. Between 1954 and 1957, almost two-thirds of the 1,414 sexual psychopaths treated at the institution had been discharged, for they were seen as no longer representing a threat to others. While on probation, most released offenders succeeded in avoiding rearrest on further sex charges, supporting claims of their successful rehabilitation. By the early 1970s, Atascadero housed five hundred offenders, of whom perhaps 10 percent were child molesters.[28] For its advocates, Atascadero represented the highest form of therapeutic penology and the most optimistic model.

The demand for treatment was fueled by liberal and humanitarian activists, although in retrospect we might wonder whether the therapeutic practices of the day offered the prospect of doing harm rather than good. From the 1930s, psychiatric practice experimented with interventionist and poorly understood strategies in treating mental patients and the sexually deviant, including electroshock and psychosurgery. While most incarcerated psychopaths never received the questionable benefits of medical intervention, many homosexuals did receive such attention, including chemotherapy and electroshock treatment, and some were castrated or sterilized. In 1950, a conference on sex offenders was told of successes at a school for mental defectives in Kansas, where treatment for some deviants included castration: "Many of these individuals so treated were very vicious homosexuals and very brutal in attacks on small children. They were very unstable and would create a disturbance at every opportunity. After castration they become stabilized and those who cannot be paroled are good useful citizens in the institution. They have lost their excessive sex urge."[29]

Critics

Sex psychopath legislation could be attacked from several quite distinct and mutually contradictory directions. Legal and political conservatives saw the laws as a violation of traditional principles of justice and as an ominous intrusion of psychiatric or psychological justifications into accepted standards of guilt and responsibility. The statutes could also provide a way for dangerous criminals to evade proper penal sanctions. Law-and-order concerns might explain why legislation was less popular in the South and West: only five of the eleven states of the former Confederacy had passed statutes by the 1960s. This is an important commentary on the political constituencies favoring the reform of sex crime laws, which were often initiated by the more socially progressive jurisdictions of the Midwest and by the more industrial and urban states. Although later attacked as repressive, the laws were seen at the time as a desirable advance in employing humane principles of therapy and medicine in the treatment of offenders.

Psychiatrists themselves criticized the unsatisfactory blending of civil and criminal principles in the statutes, which effected a curious sort of forced therapy. In the District of Columbia, failure to cooperate with a therapist for the purpose of diagnosis was counted as contempt of court. The psychiatric examinations upon which psychopathy was determined often showed little understanding of proper diagnostic techniques, usually consisting of psychiatrists' impressionistic conclusions based on their conversations with accused individuals. Psychiatrists retained by police or prisons were notorious for giving their employers what they wanted, usually offering boilerplate reports rather than detailed, individualized commentaries. When a suspect denied or questioned the alleged facts in a given case, psychiatrists tended to see this as decisive evidence of psychopathic tendencies, as showing that the accused was a compulsive liar with a weak grip on reality. They rarely considered the possibility that a suspect had in fact been railroaded through a forced confession or a third degree, which was especially likely when a man was accused of rape or child murder. If the diagnosis was so subjective, then the cure could scarcely be objectively assessed, although many statutes required that inmates show proof that they had "recovered" from their psychopathy before they could be released.[30]

Some therapists were alarmed by the prostitution of medical terminology and the use of half-comprehended psychiatric language as the basis for social policy. Reacting to Benjamin Karpman, psychoanalyst Melitta Schmideberg attacked the tendency to call "every sexual offender a psychopath, and I believe there is growing opposition to the general use of this name from many other competent physicians." Her colleague Emil Gutheil agreed, saying that the terms *sexual psychopath* and *sexual psychopathy,* which were of popular origin, had "no legitimate place in any psychiatric and scientific classification." When Abrahamsen analyzed the "psychopathic" sex offenders in Sing Sing prison, he concluded that most should properly be described as suffering from neuroses, psychoses, or alcoholism: "The diagnosis of psychopathy can only be reached after excluding all other psychiatric conditions," and not by the rough-and-ready assessments offered by the courts' tame doctors. The escalation theory was also being questioned, and Manfred S. Guttmacher was among those who denied that "serious criminal sexual behavior evolves progressively from less serious sexual offenses." Guttmacher thought that grave sexual violence was more likely to be presaged by burglary than by the "pathetic instances of individual maladjustment" like homosexuality, voyeurism, exhibitionism, and transvestism. In fact, proposed Abrahamsen, robbery and burglary might well be sublimated sex offenses: "Robbery may be considered symbolic of rape and vice versa."[31] The extensive criminal record of William Heirens consisted entirely of "nonsexual" acts like burglary and weapons possession.

Although a handful of psychiatrists protested that the legislation ignored the insights of behavioral science, others could make the equally plausible case that individual rights were being sacrificed to therapeutic fads and jargon. Nor did the statutes provide customary legal protections for individuals facing ill-defined charges: only in Illinois did procedures involve juries, and that to the scorn of psychiatrists. But the dangers were manifest. What, other than the subjective opinions of police and courts, decided what constituted "misconduct in sexual matters" or "lack of customary standards of good judgment"? Did the same customs and standards apply to all classes, regions, and races? Some statutes mentioned the psychopath's "likelihood of . . . inflicting injury, loss, pain or other evil on the objects of his desire," but what was considered "other evil"? Did harsh language that caused emotional pain count? In 1947, Governor Thomas Dewey of New York vetoed a sex psychopath statute on the grounds that the law's specifications for sex crimes were too vague and would allow due-process rights to be trampled. Edwin Sutherland argued, "The concept of the sexual psychopath is so vague that it cannot be used for judicial and administrative purposes without the danger that the law may injure the society more than do the sex crimes which it is designed to correct." Paul Tappan agreed: "Sex psychopathy . . . is not a sufficiently clear diagnostic entity to justify legislation. . . . Some extremely dangerous precedents have been established for adjudicating individuals without ordinary due process." Tappan wrote of "the tendency of prosecutors to consider the statutes merely as an useful tool to be employed or avoided in accordance with their own convenience." As a result, the laws were inoperative in most of the states that had them: they were "completely nullified" in four states and "completely ineffective" in six more.[32]

Unlike some later critics, Tappan was not criticizing the use of psychiatric intervention as such. What he was protesting was the improper confounding of civil and criminal procedures within the legislation and the misuse of psychiatric labels in order to achieve quasi-penal consequences. The sex psychopath laws represented not an unwonted intrusion of psychiatry into criminal justice but an inadequate acceptance of psychiatric insights and methodologies. In fact, he proposed moving the sex crime problem into the therapeutic realm entirely: "The psychiatrically deviated sex offender should be regarded as suffering with a mental disorder and . . . the procedure of disposition be by indeterminate commitment as provided by the law for persons with mental illness. It is clear that the identification of the psychiatrically deviated sex offender and the estimate of his danger to the community are functions of which the responsibility rests largely on the psychiatric expert."[33]

As a technical consultant for the New Jersey Commission on the Habitual Sex Offender, Tappan greatly influenced the ideas disseminated via the commission's 1950 report, which was freely cited by legislative bodies and professionals. The Pennsylvania legislative commission that investigated the "sex crime problem" concluded that specific sex offender laws had generally been unsuccessful not only because the laws were framed in ill-defined terms and the facilities for diagnosing and treating offenders were inadequate but also because such legislation posed inherent dangers to individuals' civil liberties: "Any statute which restricts a citizen because he does not conform constitutes an impingement of his civil liberties and an abrogation of constitutional guarantees." Morris Ploscowe agreed that the laws "start with vague and elusive criteria of mental abnormality. What is worse is that they do not clearly define the sexual misbehavior to which the laws are applicable." The acts offered inadequate safeguards against improper commitment, while treatment facilities were lacking. Incarceration for life should be considered only for a very small cadre of extremely dangerous violent rapists and sex sadists as well as for compulsive pedophiles: "It is from these two groups of individuals that potential sex killers are drawn."[34]

Although these flaws in the legislation had become clearly apparent by about 1949, new laws continued to be passed well into the 1960s. But the arguments of the critics retained a strong foothold in the scholarly and professional literature, and in time they achieved the status of a new orthodoxy during the very different social and political circumstances of the late 1960s. By that point, not only would the psychopath statutes be abrogated, but they would become a byword for incompetently drafted panic legislation. For many years the sex psychopath laws were cited as a model example of failed legislation called forth by politicians pandering to ill-focused public fears but that had done nothing to reduce crime or detain the truly dangerous.

The Liberal Era, 1958–1976

All laws which can be violated without doing any one an injury are laughed at. . . . He who tries to do everything by law will foment crime rather than lessen it.

—BARUCH SPINOZA

In reaction to the panic of the 1940s and early 1950s, psychiatrists and scholars of the next two decades underplayed the scale and seriousness of the sex offender issue. In the professional literature, the real problem was described as lying not in the aberrant sexual behaviors themselves but in the public hysteria surrounding them. Liberal therapists and academics aimed to quiet popular concern by debunking claims about rape, incest, and sexual violence, while the most heavily consulted textbooks and manuals of the period argued that sex crime laws were disproportionately invoked against racial minorities. These experts acknowledged that sex offenses were symptoms of troubled personalities, but they dismissed the stereotype of the lethal sex criminal as a product of a sensationalistic press aided and abetted by cynical law-enforcement bureaucrats. From the mid-1960s, jurists and legislators reinforced this attitude by sharply limiting the powers of forcible civil commitment and discretionary sentencing that had earlier been the foundation of official policies toward sexual deviants. This was part of a general social and intellectual movement that was reflected in voguish concepts like decriminalization, decarceration, and deinstitutionalization. By 1975, the rehabilitative thinking that had once guided correctional ideology was utterly discredited, one of many orthodoxies that perished in the social upheavals of these years. Even if a war on sex crime was thought to be worth waging, the legal means to do so were now quite lacking.

Sex Crime as Lynch Law

At first glance, the newspapers and magazines of this period seem to have reported sex crimes with the same avid fascination that they had in earlier years, but the continuing volume of news reports masks a real change in content and a dramatic reduction of concern about sexual threats to women and children. The emphasis had shifted to allegations of racism in the prosecution of sex crimes, a development that would be critical in shaping perceptions of offenders both north and south.

In any typical year from the 1920s through the 1950s, a substantial proportion of sex offenses recorded in major newspapers involved black offenders and white victims, generally in a southern state, so that "assault by a Negro" became almost a journalistic formula. In early years, the racial danger seemed self-evident. In 1921, a black man in West Virginia accused of assaulting an eight-year-old white girl was indicted, tried, and sentenced by the end of the day after the attack, in a case reported by the *New York Times* as a striking example of the efficiency of the court system; the triumphant headline proclaimed, "Negro Gets Quick Justice." Northern sensibilities changed after the "Scottsboro Boys" case of 1931, in which nine African-American youths in Alabama were falsely accused of raping two white girls.[1] All but one of the accused were sentenced to death, despite testimony by doctors who examined the women that no rape had occurred and despite procedural irregularities that caused the U.S. Supreme Court, in two historic decisions, to overturn the sentences. After Scottsboro, liberal opinion was deeply skeptical about the fairness of charges of interracial sexual assault, and the idea that false accusations were made by neurotic or malignant white women was popularized by Harper Lee's novel *To Kill a Mockingbird* (1960) and the film that it inspired. Even in cases where black men were justly convicted, the severe punishments that they received reflected white southern society's extreme sensitivity to blacks' transgressions of sexual taboos. "Negro Convicted by All-White Jury" came to be a headline quite as standard as "Negro Attacks Girl" had once been.

The consequences of conviction were often lethal, for southern states regularly executed rapists until the legal suspension of capital punishment in the mid-1960s. Between 1920 and 1960, rape charges alone accounted for 445 legal executions, or 10 percent of all executions in the United States, and the severest punishments for sexual attacks were usually meted out in the South. In the 1940s, almost 15 percent of all executions resulted from this offense, and rape charges led to fifty military executions in the 1940s and 1950s. Also between 1920 and 1960, 142 individuals, most of them black, were lynched in cases involving real or alleged sex offenses.[2] On average, for each year from the 1920s through the 1950s, sixteen men were executed in the United States for sex crimes, whether legally or otherwise; the great majority were African Americans, and most of them perished in the South.

Northern revulsion at southern justice reached new heights in the late 1940s and early 1950s, when a number of notorious cases prompted publication of a lively literature about past and present horrors. In the four years from 1949 through 1952, the *New York Times* index listed 233 entries under the heading "sex crime," but 100 of these, or 43 percent, derived from cases in just six southern states, usually instances in which black men were accused of sexual attacks on white women; 87 derived from a handful of controversial cases in Mississippi, Florida, and Virginia. In one Florida affair, four African Americans accused of raping a white woman were threatened with lynching by a mob, who actually killed one of the suspects. In 1951, seven black men were executed for raping a white woman in Martinsville, Virginia. Other infamous cases included that of Willie J. McGee, executed for rape in 1951, and the 1952 conviction of a North Carolina man for "leering" at a white girl.[3]

The judicial misdeeds of the American South were held up for obloquy not just by the northern liberal media but also by the press from around the world. Significantly, these reports coincided with the height of the sex psychopath panic in the rest of the nation: southern sex offenses were treated as qualitatively different, not least in their tendency to attract international criticism and to discredit American prestige in the new nation-states in Africa and Asia. Fears of global stigma reinforced liberal calls to end injustices and contributed to the desegregation movement ordered by the federal courts from 1954 onward. During the next decade, when the national media covered cases of sex crime, most of the trials reported were in the South. In the *New York Times,* thirty-two of forty-nine reports for the year 1959 concerned cases in states of the former Confederacy, and the emphasis of the reporting was on the innocence of the accused and the attempts to save them from the death penalty. In 1961, the figure was nine stories out of fifteen.[4]

Not all judicial scandals were confined to the South. In 1952, one of the original Scottsboro boys was tried in Albany, New York, for assaulting a thirteen-year-old girl. But whatever the actual circumstances of individual incidents, there was a strong perception that such prosecutions arose from official malice. These interpretations were regularly presented by defense attorneys provided by the NAACP and were often given credence by courts of appeal. Sustaining skepticism about sexual allegations was the number of cases in which accusers ultimately recanted their charges or whose charges were dismissed as imaginary. In 1954, two men in New York City were cleared of rape charges after five months' detention in jail, following the discrediting of the main witness and an embarrassing police scandal.[5] And most people thought that, even if proven, an offense like rape was certainly not serious enough to deserve death: throughout the 1950s, one of the longest-running causes célèbres in the justice system involved Caryl Chessman, who had been arrested in 1948 for a series of brutal robbery-rapes. A classic "sex psychopath," he received a death sentence, which was eventually carried out in 1960. In the intervening years, however, the public mood changed radically, and his articulate efforts to resist execution won him wide support.[6] Thus at least one sex fiend lived long enough to be viewed as a martyr to the institutional savagery of the justice system.

Media coverage of sex offenses overwhelmingly stressed themes of official overreaction and injustice. For the ten years between 1954 and 1963, the *New York Times* offered a total of 234 sex crime stories, but 61 of these addressed themes of unjust conviction and racial bias in the South. Omitting southern cases and overseas news leaves 135 stories for the ten-year period, or an average of just over one per month. Reports of authentic sexual threats to children were a rarity in the newspaper in these years: only eighteen stories from the entire decade directly concerned the sexual abuse of minors, and several of these cases involved girls in their midteens, often where there was an element of consent. One 1960 case involved a fourteen-year-old girl and a number of male students at Yale University;

the following year's reports of sex crimes included that of a seventeen-year-old girl who made a pornographic film. Little here supported notions of a sex crime "problem," still less an epidemic. A typical criminological text noted in 1959 that "the most serious [of sex crimes] are associated with rape, particularly forcible rape, or with assaults on young girls or elderly women. But contrary to public opinion, there are few outright cases of this type. Most of the rape cases deal with statutory rape. . . . So far as forcible rape is concerned, it has been much overrated. In many cases the female has offered little resistance, and in others she has 'framed' the male. In other cases the female has reported the man only after he has jilted or abandoned her."[7] Such a trivializing dismissal of the causes and consequences of sexual assault is of course utterly at odds with modern interpretations and may seem shocking, but the view is typical of this era.

Inventing the Child Molester

These were also the years when the terms *child molestation* or *molesting* evolved to suggest minor sexual interference rather than acts of force or violence. The term was useful because it permitted the media to differentiate between acts seen as relatively harmless and those genuinely harmful or violent offenses which retained the designation of sex crimes. Molestation was only tenuously connected with the spectrum of sex crime and obviously did not lead to violence or murder.

In the *Reader's Guide to Periodical Literature*, the word *molester* first occurs with any regularity from about 1955, and over the next two decades it is chiefly found in magazines oriented toward parents and female audiences. The word was originally a euphemism considered fit for the ears of ladies, as "molestation" referred to annoyance or disturbance, though without the specificity or violence of rape or even sexual assault. In 1950, Sutherland remarked contemptuously that "molestation is a weasel word and can refer to anything from rape to whistling at a girl."[8] By the late 1960s, this weasel word came to be the standard term for most nonviolent sexual acts between adults and children. Between 1937 and 1960, *Reader's Guide* indexed articles concerning sexual offenses against children as sex crimes, but the heading "child molestation/molesting" appeared in 1963–64 and was detached from the old category. For a few years, molestation was subsumed under "children and strangers," before the term eventually assumed independent existence about 1969. Originally small entries containing one or two items a year, stories about molesters grew in volume over the next decade, while sex crimes shrank proportionately. Between 1971 and 1975, only six stories appeared under the rubric of "sex crimes," as against four under "child molesting." The nature of the articles under the heading of sex crimes now changed to focus on very serious acts of rape and multiple sexual homicide: in 1973, both entries on this theme described the gruesome Houston serial killings committed by Dean Corll. Sex crimes were serious; molestation was not.

In the *New York Times*, too, the "sex crimes" category fragmented in the 1960s. The old heading had included not just rape and molestation but also prosecutions for abortion, homosexuality, indecent literature, and even contraceptive use. Support for legalizing such conduct was growing rapidly, and it seemed ridiculous to describe all with a blanket term as severe as "sex crimes." It was plausible that, apart from acts as self-evidently dangerous as sex murder, most of the other types of sexual deviancy would soon come to be seen as far less pernicious than they were in an unenlightened past. Portraying mere molesters as sex criminals was as hyperbolic as applying the label to homosexuals or abortion providers.

The word *pedophile* also shifted in meaning. The term initially gained popular currency during the sex crime panic of the 1930s, when public and media alike believed that pedophiles were deeply dangerous and potentially homicidal and *Time* listed recent sex murders as "appalling examples of pedophilia." Even a critic of the psychopath legislation like Morris Ploscowe had justified the long-term incarceration of "compulsive pedophiles" in order to protect lives. It was by no means obvious, however, that all molesters should be labeled as pedophiles or should be contextualized with the notorious sex criminals. One lesson of the Kinsey reports was that a sexually deviant episode was not automatically a symptom of a fundamental pathological condition: if not every man who had sex with another man was necessarily a homosexual, then perhaps a man who interfered with a child was not necessarily a confirmed pedophile. In *Sex Offenders: An Analysis of Types,* published in 1965, Paul Gebhard and his colleagues claimed that only about a quarter of their sample of heterosexual offenders against children could be classified as true pedophiles, as opposed to casual offenders.[9] A growing number of therapists argued for a milder view of molestation, and their views gradually gained support. By the early 1960s, few scholars would disagree with these benevolent theses about the nature of child molestation: that the offense was a sign of immaturity or confusion; it was unlikely to lead to worse acts; violence or compulsion were very infrequent elements of the crime, which was usually an isolated, one-time occurrence; offenders could be treated successfully, after which recidivism was infrequent. Although they might be sex psychopaths, molesters were among the more innocuous of the breed.

And even in cases where molesters could clearly be considered pedophiles, how dangerous were they? Krafft-Ebing had first popularized the term *pedophile,* attributing the behavior to "acquired mental weakness" resulting from "senile dementia, chronic alcoholism, paralysis, mental debility due to epilepsy, injuries to the head, apoplexy and syphilis," and most successors emphasized mental weakness and senility. Havelock Ellis remarked that "the chief contingent [of pedophiles] before old age is furnished by the weak-minded," and William Healy stressed the role of "senile delinquency" in causing sex offenses against the young. David Abrahamsen felt that "the greatest number of sex offenders are those who are impotent, old or senile. . . . Pedophilia . . . is carried out by impotent men, usually older ones." For Bromberg, "pedophilia, when scrutinized, is less an abhorrent sexual lust than a sign of serious neurotic conflict in the offender."[10] Supposed sex fiends came from the ranks of the immature, the feebleminded, and the senile, and even then they were rare.

Although references to pedophiles are scattered through the psychiatric literature, their rarity suggests that the condition was regarded as uncommon. The encyclopedic Karpman did offer a dozen case studies of the behavior, but in the 1960s Johann W. Mohr and his colleagues searched the standard psychiatric works and found that they either omitted the subject altogether or dismissed it in a paragraph or two: "A number of accounts which discuss even such rare phenomena as zoophilia, coprophilia and necrophilia do not even mention pedophilia." Bromberg's survey of psychiatric criminology (1948) devoted only two pages to the condition, and even by 1960, there was still no book solely devoted to pedophilia, and only one each covered the topics of incest and exhibitionism. Albert Hess's classic book *Die Kinderschändung* (The Ravishing of Children) was briefly noted in American journals on its German publication in 1934 but never translated into English.[11] As late as the mid-1970s, standard psychiatric textbooks rarely mentioned pedophiles.

Scholarly neglect was reflected by the crudity of definitions. Only in the mid-1950s did the literature create a taxonomy for the diverse types of adults who were sexually interested in children, distinguishing between exhibitionists and active molesters. Age was another area of uncertainty, and academic studies of the 1950s varied greatly in their definitions of pedophilia: did it involve activity with youngsters under twelve, under sixteen, or even under twenty? The standard police text, *The Sexual Criminal*, described pedophilia as sexual activity with "a child or adolescent," not even specifying that the offender be older than the victim. Many alleged instances involved minimal age differences between the parties, in interactions better regarded as juvenile sexual intimacy or sex play rather than deviation. Only in 1955 did B. D. Glueck propose the term *hebephilia* (later *ephebophilia*) to differentiate between adults interested in teenagers as opposed to prepubescent youngsters. By the 1960s, scholars were requiring that there should be a minimum number of years in the age difference between participants to qualify a sex act as deviant: the modern definition demands that "the individual with pedophilia must be age sixteen years or older and at least five years older than the child."[12]

Although detailed case studies of pedophiles were rare, those we do possess differ totally from modern commonplaces about the condition, its threat-potential, and the chance of successful treatment. Manfred Guttmacher describes a sixteen-year-old Baltimore boy who sexually interfered with a five-year-old girl, an act that the psychiatrist viewed as a form of adolescent experimentation. Through his urging, the offender was treated leniently and, in Guttmacher's view, became a reformed character leading a productive life. The worst outcome for both offender and victim would have been to prosecute the affair vigorously in the courts, which would have destroyed the teenager's life and future prospects and would have traumatized the girl. Noting the prevalence of older molesters, men in their sixties and seventies, Guttmacher remarked: "Most of the child murders that are not the work of sadistic psychopaths must be committed by men who are really psychotic. They are not the acts of men undergoing simple senile change, . . . who are so often essentially passive, non-aggressive individuals, who can be dealt with leniently with minimal supervision."[13]

Guttmacher's claim that his patient had responded readily to treatment was typical for the age. Other studies also claimed excellent results with a variety of therapies, including group therapy and brief psychoanalysis, which in one experiment was believed to have cured seven out of eight pedophiles: after criminal careers dating back twenty years or more, they were now "free of their former compulsions . . . to use children as sex objects." Successful psychotherapy was even claimed for a man who had at knifepoint forced a seven-year-old girl to perform fellatio upon him but who had escaped criminal punishment. Both remission and cure were confidently reported in the literature, where recidivism in sexual offenses was described as "low in general," with the lowest rates being found among heterosexual pedophiles, and where these cases were seen to illustrate "the futility of sentencing sex offenders to prison." Similarly, "exhibitionism is not a progressively dangerous sexual offense." For many, the idea that molestation or exhibitionism could degenerate into violent behaviors was so absurd as to be hardly worth considering.[14]

Although it is perilous to argue from silence, the scarcity of the calculating, compulsive, or sadistic pedophile in the professional literature suggests that the type was either unknown or regarded as a myth of the sensationalistic media. Nor was any kind of organization or sex ring activity even considered. Comic books and magazine articles were wrong to portray the molester as "a stranger who attacks unsuspecting children in lonely places," and even presenting this image could "have a substantial harmful effect in instilling a paranoid attitude in a child."[15]

Mere Molestation

If offenders were to be pitied rather than punished, then one could not properly speak of their *victims*, a word that frequently appeared in quotation marks. Because pedophiles suffered from arrested development, their misdeeds resembled sex play between small children and involved fondling, petting, or manipulating. "Sexual intercourse is not common among pedophilic offenses," stated one group of researchers. "Penetration and intravaginal acts are rare among sexual acts with children." Another group concluded, "The great majority of the offenders against children are not physically dangerous since they did not use force and since they seldom attempted coitus." These observations are in sharp contrast to the findings of researchers from the Progressive Era, whose writings about the prevalence of venereal diseases among child victims had been virtually forgotten. In addition, advances in the treatment of sexually transmitted diseases since the early twentieth century meant that this aspect of the problem now attracted less attention.[16]

Although medical opinion was divided over the degree of real or lasting trauma resulting from molestation, there was general skepticism about the effects of a single incident of fondling or exhibitionism. When the New York City Mayor's Committee for the Study of Sex Offenses assessed the effects of rape on a sample of nearly three thousand victims, they classified damage under the categories "injuries," "disease," and "pregnancy," but where none of these conditions could be observed, as was the case for 60 percent of the victims, the category was "no effects," implying that only tangible physical harm merited attention. If rapists did so little harm, then no worse could be expected from exhibitionists, *frotteurs,* or voyeurs: "These individuals are generally not assaultive or dangerous, however much their behavior may annoy, frighten or shock women and children who observe it or are subject to it."[17] New views of the effects of sexual interference on children explain the disappearance of the emotive word *defiler* from the popular vocabulary after the early 1950s. In every way, scholarship of this era presented the plight of the abuse victim in language that seems stunningly callous to modern ears.

Paul Tappan rejected the view "that the victims of sex attack are 'ruined for life'" as one of the pernicious myths diverting social policy. He argued that little lasting harm *need* be caused by the experience of "rape, carnal abuse, defloration, incest, homosexuality or indecent exposure": "In some instances the individual does carry psychic scars after such an experience. Characteristically the damage is done far more, however, by the well intentioned associates of the victim or by public authorities than by the aggressor. This is not to condone the offense, but merely to emphasize that its implicit danger has been grossly exaggerated, and that the possible traumatizing of the individual is almost always a product of cultural and individual responses to the experience rather than because of the intrinsic value of that experience itself. . . . The young individual in our own society who has not been exposed to an excess of parental and community hysteria about sex can absorb the experience of a socially disapproved sexual assault without untoward consequences." The Kinsey researchers agreed: "The emotional reactions of parents, police officers and other adults who discover that the child has had such a contact may disturb the child more seriously than the sexual contacts themselves," and the danger was all the worse given "the current hysteria over sex offenders."[18]

There were even doubts about the potential harm arising from incest. That the effects of this behavior could be devastating and lifelong was familiar from literary works like Scott Fitzgerald's *Tender Is the Night* (1934), but incest was considered so extraordinarily rare as scarcely to deserve study. In 1955, Samuel Weinberg's standard account stated that "incest is very rare in all types of societies," and the few cases that did occur were believed to be largely confined to bizarre and isolated subcultures. As to the question of harm, Wardell Pomeroy, one of the original Kinsey team, argued that incest between adults and children could be "a satisfying and enriching experience," giving rise to "many beautifully and mutually satisfying relationships between fathers and daughters. . . . They have no harmful effects." One reason that incest appeared so rarely in the public record was that "the female is too guilty or too fond of the offender to bring charges."[19]

Although molested children might seem to be disturbed, this condition preceded and even contributed to the molestation rather than followed it as its visible consequence. In 1964, Mohr and his coauthors concluded, "If one excludes cases of violence or force which are fortunately rare, the amount of damage—if any—would depend primarily on the child's emotional status and his security in his environment." Excessive official intervention could provoke evil consequences, and interrogation and cross-examination in court could wreak more harm than the actual offense. This tradition dominated the professional literature through the 1970s. In 1975, a book seeking to demolish myths about homosexuality specifically challenged the idea that molestation converted children to a homosexual lifestyle: "Child seduction, though it can be traumatic when parents make an issue of it, is virtually powerless to start a sexual pattern."[20]

In their 1978 text on child abuse, Ruth S. Kempe and C. Henry Kempe argued, "A single molestation by a stranger, particularly of a nonviolent kind, appears to do little harm to normal children living with secure and reassuring parents"; this was powerful testimony, for Henry Kempe was one of the principal authorities in constructing modern concepts of child abuse. Another standard text stated that "early sexual contacts do not appear to have harmful effects on many children unless the family, legal authorities or society reacts negatively." The implication is that balanced and mature families have a duty to raise children who are sufficiently well-informed not to be disturbed by sexual assault, while responsible parents know better than to risk their child's well-being by dragging the incident to the attention of police and courts: the danger lay in making an issue of mere molestation. "Irrationality about sex led to the original offense; it is important that parents and other adults keep their own irrationalities from doing any further damage to the child."[21]

Further minimizing the harm done by molestation was the common view that youngsters contributed to sexual contacts with adults. The report by the New York City mayor's committee commented, "Generally there is to be found something in the personality, the environmental background or the family situation of the victim of the sex crime which predisposes her to participation in sex delinquency." The limited professional literature on child victims argued that many were actively seeking "affection, attention and approval from the offender, accompanied by the feeling that their own parents did not fully appreciate them." Mohr and others believed the literature showed "predisposing factors in many victims which make them prone to participate in sexual acts with adults, by way of passive toleration up to active seduction."[22] Again, this was in stark contrast to the Progressive literature, which had portrayed urban children at constant risk from indiscriminate assault by their elders, but it could be argued that improved social conditions and housing had so fundamentally changed most families' living environments that victims could more plausibly be blamed for failing to take appropriate precautions and in some cases even inviting attack.

More than one researcher wrote that seductive or flirtatious children should not be presented as exploited victims irrevocably tarnished by a sexual encounter. In 1960, Abrahamsen wrote of rape: "The victim herself unconsciously . . . may tempt the offender. . . . Often a woman unconsciously wishes to be taken by force. . . . We sometimes find this seductive inclination even in young girls, in their being flirtatious or seeking out rather dangerous or unusual spots where they can be picked up, thus exposing themselves more or less unconsciously to sexual attacks." Writing of underage victims, Karpman opined: "Generally the fact that a particular girl is the victim is no accident; there is something in her background, personality or family situation that predisposes her to participation. Frequently victims are victims in the legal sense only; the attitude that the child is an unwilling victim is not always true; in some cases the child is the aggressor. In some cases parents have abnormally stimulated sex urges." "Certain children, even at early ages, incite elders to sex experience even as elders incite them," and deliberate incitements by wayward girls constituted a "widespread problem." In 1974, a psychiatric textbook cited the "well-known" fact that "a nine year old girl may be capable of seduction." Boys were no better: one 1975 study of man-boy sexual contacts around the time of puberty suggested how often "the 'victim' was the provocateur." An Australian study of the relationships between a pederast and his hundreds of sexual contacts found a vast range of interactions and degrees of seduction.[23]

The Youth Revolution

Reaction to earlier concern about adult-child sexuality was influenced by new attitudes both by and toward the young, as the large baby boom cohort entered its teenage years. In the 1960s, a youth culture already alienated from the assumptions of its parents was radicalized by political protest, extensive drug use, and dramatic sexual experimentation. This social environment was hostile to traditional controls on the young, and liberal opinion favored a general relaxation of restraints in areas like drug use and sexual conduct. The young consequently became more sexually aware and active at a much earlier age, and by the early 1970s, the limits of acceptable sexual behavior had become less strict and attitudes more tolerant than they had ever been in American history.

These attitudes extended to the age of sexual consent and to sex acts between adults and children. Technically, a sexual act between a twenty-year-old man and a fifteen-year-old girl constituted statutory rape in most states, but by contemporary standards it scarcely seemed a gross moral violation. Also, the spread of a gay liberation movement after 1969 massively reduced the stigma of acts involving teenage boys. The age of sexual consent became a very soft boundary that corresponded poorly to social or psychological reality: if one granted that eighteen made little sense as the age at which all people everywhere could be declared sexually mature, by how much could the figure be reduced? Was even the age of puberty an appropriate legal limit? From the late 1960s, states tried to come to terms with the new situation by lowering the age of sexual majority and easing laws on statutory rape. Such measures were taken in New York, Pennsylvania, Wisconsin, and Illinois, while in the 1970s New Jersey debated lowering its age of consent to thirteen. The recognition that children could be sexually active in their own right confirmed the notion found in the professional literature: young people sexually involved with adults should often be seen as willing and knowing participants rather than victims.

In popular culture, sexual activity by those in their midteens was regarded as customary and acceptable, and adult-child relationships were not necessarily to be condemned. The trend can be traced to the appearance of Nabokov's 1955 novel *Lolita*, which concerned an adult man's obsession with a seductive twelve-year-old girl, and sexual and pederastic underworlds were explored in the novels of writers like William S. Burroughs.[24] In the cinema, the 1956 film *Baby Doll* depicted a sexy child bride, while *Town Without Pity* (1961) portrayed a sixteen-year-old girl whose provocative behavior results in gang rape. *Lolita* itself was filmed in 1962, with a fourteen-year-old star. Such treatments proved tame in comparison to the films and novels that emerged at the height of the social and sexual revolution of the late 1960s. In 1969, Arlo Guthrie's film *Alice's Restaurant* featured Reenie, a teenybopper whose main interest in life is scoring sexual experiences with rock musicians. She is "fifteen, going on fourteen," but the film does not suggest that the hero would be committing a serious moral breach if he succumbed to her temptations. Reflecting the relaxed censorship standards of these years, Reenie appears topless for most of her on-screen appearance. Teenyboppers and underage girls also featured in countless rock songs of these years: the Grateful Dead recorded "Good Morning, Little Schoolgirl," and the protagonist of the group's "Mexicali Blues" found himself in a cantina with a fourteen-year-old girl. Magazines of the alternative culture frequently ran explicit nude shots of young teenage girls, and the rock supergroup Blind Faith reproduced a photograph of a topless pubescent girl on the cover of their 1969 debut album.

During the 1970s, sexually precocious girls below the age of consent appeared regularly in mainstream cinema, featuring in films like *Night Moves* (1975) and *Taxi Driver* (1976). *The Exorcist* (1973) depicted a demonically possessed young girl urinating and masturbating. Teenage actresses like Brooke Shields and Jodie Foster became stars by portraying sexually active young women at a far younger age than would have been thought acceptable in either earlier or later epochs. Sometimes they were depicted in states of semi- or total undress. In 1970, the Australian film *Walkabout* depicted a young teenage girl bathing nude in a pond, and a young Melanie Griffith appeared seminude in *Night Moves*. *Pretty Baby* (1978) starred Brooke Shields as a twelve-year-old New Orleans prostitute.

Although films in this period never ventured to offer a fully sympathetic portrait of a child molester, characterizations were far removed from the utter evil that would have been obligatory in later years. British cinema led the way with a series of explorations of fringe sexuality which were often well-received in the United States; the best-known was the pioneering drama *Victim,* with its theme of homosexuality (1961). The same era produced accounts of sex offenders: *Never Take Sweets from a Stranger* (1960) was an account of an elderly child molester who unintentionally causes the death of a child whom he is pursuing, and *Serious Charge* (1959) concerned a false accusation of sexual misconduct between a man and a teenaged boy. The Oscar-nominated film *The Mark* (1961) sympathetically portrayed a man trying to reconstruct his life after serving prison time for sexual misconduct with a young girl. Rehabilitation is viewed as possible and desirable, if it is not derailed by the malice of an ill-informed public goaded by a sensationalist press.

The molester was again a scapegoat in the British film *Chariot of Fire* (1970), scripted by Tony Parker, who had published serious criminological studies of offenders.[25] This film examined a woman's tragic relationship with a man who had spent twenty years in prison for offenses against boys. The script suggested that children in these cases suffered far more from the misplaced outrage of puritanical parents and authorities than they ever could from the sexual contact itself, while molesters were manipulated emotionally by the child objects of their affections. *The Naked Civil Servant* (1975) featured a group of young boys attempting to extort money from an elderly, effeminate homosexual; if he does not pay up, they threaten, then they will make a false molestation complaint to police. The concept of the molester as victim seemed especially valid in the context of the justice system. The plot of Sidney Lumet's *The Offence* (1973) revolved around the killing of a child molester beaten to death by an indignant police detective. The plight of sex offenders within the correctional population was highlighted by Miguel Pinero's 1975 play *Short Eyes* (filmed in 1977), which showed how the most savage and unregenerate of "normal" criminals justified their own moral righteousness and machismo by vindictively persecuting a molester.

Another liberal, even favorable, portrayal was found in Sam Peckinpah's 1971 film *Straw Dogs*, which featured "dirty pervert" Henry Niles, a shambling, childlike figure closely modeled on Lenny in *Of Mice and Men*. Henry has long enjoyed a reputation as a molester, and he cannot be deterred from "hanging around the girls." By no means an idealized figure, he is sufficiently dangerous to kill a girl accidentally in a misguided attempt to protect her (his last words to her are "No, they might hurt you!"). Although in some sense a sex killer, he is a far more sympathetic figure than the village people who ostracize him, and the plot turns upon the hero's attempt to defend Henry from vigilante violence by the thuggish locals. For all their rhetoric about defending children, Henry's persecutors emerge as the true criminals, implicated in rape, murder, and burglary. Moreover, the incident precipitating the final crisis arises from the girl's attempt to seduce Henry after she is rejected by a more attractive older man. *Straw Dogs* depicts the molester as essentially harmless unless provoked or enticed by flirtatious neighbors.

Later portrayals were less subtle, but their humorous quality suggests the trivial nature of the threat posed by molesters. The Who's rock opera *Tommy* (1969) featured an obsessive but generally comic molester in wicked Uncle Ernie, who "fiddled about" sexually on the body of the deaf and dumb hero; when the album became the basis of a film in 1975, Ernie evolved into a ludicrous comic-book villain visually resembling Chester the Molester, the farcically demonic antihero of cartoons appearing in *Hustler* magazine.[26] In the popular comedy *Airplane* (1980), an airline pilot engages in explicit conversation with a prepubescent boy, constantly bringing the conversation around to homoerotic themes: although the scene shows the seduction of a young boy, the audience is meant to view it as entirely comic. Against this cultural background, it was difficult to view the molester as a serious peril worthy of draconian legislation.

The Legal Environment

Between 1965 and 1975, racial and political crises raised fundamental questions about the legitimacy of the American state and its right to make and enforce law. The academic disciplines of sociology and criminology were radicalized by doctrines holding that a label signifying deviancy, be it *mental patient, addict,* or *sex offender,* had little to do with any inherent qualities of the individual so described but rather reflected the values and interests of the social groups possessing the power to apply the label. Ideas like deviancy theory, interactionism, labeling, and the entire approach called new criminology undermined traditional concepts of the objective nature of crime and illness. To quote the title of a radical criminology text, *Whose Law? What Order?*[27]

A thriving academic literature now emerged on the question of victimless crimes, a term suggesting that acts should not be considered offenses unless they threatened harm to persons other than those voluntarily and pleasurably committing them. In 1967, Sanford Kadish published his influential article, "The Crisis of Overcriminalization," while in 1970, the Presidential Commission on Obscenity rejected charges that pornographic materials caused significant harm. Historical prohibitions of drink and drugs provided the basis for radical analyses of the American tendency to pass laws that stigmatized substances and the groups who used them.[28] Such studies lent support to wide-ranging decriminalization, and even if laws were not actually repealed, there was a general tendency to regard them as essentially unenforceable. Activities like smoking marijuana or underage sex were widely viewed as only formally illegal, in the technical sense that permitted the survival of largely unenforced statutes against adultery, homosexuality, fornication, or the enjoyment of pornography.

Both court decisions and academic works depicted existing sex laws as relics of the prudery of an earlier generation that had stigmatized many consensual activities: overturning penal laws against nonviolent molesters, exhibitionists, and other deviants proceeded alongside the liberalization of other puritanical morality codes. The ascendancy of a libertarian rhetoric was evident in the activism of the Supreme Court and the federal courts, which between 1957 and 1975 oversaw a general relaxation of the laws relating to personal behavior and sexual morality. In 1957, the *Roth* case expanded freedom of speech to include material previously regarded as criminally obscene and in the process permitted the American media greater latitude in exploring sexual themes. In 1965, *Griswold* overturned a Connecticut statute prohibiting contraception on the basis of a constitutional right of privacy that certainly extended to other sexual matters. In the 1973 case *Roe v. Wade,* the notion of privacy was cited to justify abortion rights.

Liberal legal thought was skeptical of official claims to objective expertise exercised in the best interests of the suspect or inmate. This doubt grew from perceived injustices against minority defendants during the years of the civil rights revolution, for many egregious cases of official abuse had involved poor black defendants in southern courts and police precincts, especially in instances of alleged sexual misconduct. Racial injustice provided an essential intellectual context for the due-process cases of the 1960s, which formed the sequel to the great desegregation decisions. In a series of celebrated cases, the Supreme Court declared that police who failed to respect the rights of suspects and defendants ran the risk of forfeiting evidence critical to a prosecution. The celebrated *Miranda* case of 1966 involved a classic sex offender, a man with a record of sexual assaults and peeping and who now faced charges of rape and kidnapping.

Aware of the abuse of discretion, courts in these years asserted the need for due-process protections in those areas which the positivist tradition had classified as therapeutic and medical in nature, rather than punitive. In juvenile justice, the fundamental principle throughout the first half of the century was that young offenders did not require due-process protections because they were not being treated as adult criminals. In consequence, a nuisance offense that would not lead to anything worse than a small fine if committed by an adult could lead to prolonged incarceration in a reform school if committed by a teenager. The informal proceedings in juvenile cases lacked all the safeguards available to a criminal defendant, including legal representation, the right to confront witnesses, protection against self-incrimination, and the crucial right to a jury of one's peers. The 1967 *Gault* case challenged virtually all the existing practices of the juvenile court, as the Supreme Court demanded the application of appropriate protections for an accused, who could no longer be disguised as a client or a patient. (This case incidentally concerned a boy labeled as a budding sex offender on the strength of his obscene phone calls to a neighbor). Over the next decade, federal and state courts asserted the need for due-process safeguards to be applied to all offenders on the borderland of insanity. As Kittrie remarked in 1971, "After floundering in semantics for nearly half a century, the courts are finally casting off the false rationale that a non-criminal and non-punitive label justifies the denial of procedural safeguards."[29]

The courts now undermined the entire legal foundation on which the mental health system had operated for over a century, and the sex offender statutes fell victim to this wider onslaught. In 1971, a U.S. district court decided in *Lessard v. Schmidt* that a person threatened with involuntary commitment to a mental institution was entitled to extensive procedural protections, including the right to counsel, the right to a jury trial, and the right to know who would testify against him or her. Characterizing a hearing as civil did not permit a court to admit hearsay testimony or to void the right against self-incrimination. This case applied the criterion that institutionalization should be avoided where possible and that the authorities must always employ "the least drastic alternative" available. In 1975, the Supreme Court held that "there is still no constitutional basis for confining [mental patients] involuntarily if they are dangerous to no one and can safely live in freedom."[30] In the wake of such decisions, extended involuntary commitment became difficult to impose except where individuals posed a grave and immediate danger to themselves or the community.

Legal activism reflected increasing popular hostility to psychiatric abuses, and an influential antipsychiatric school attacked therapeutic assumptions as ultimately ideological and self-interested. Radical critics challenged the historic reliance on institutional responses to deviancy, whether for mental patients, convicts, or the poor. Even if inspired by humane motives, asylums invariably became repressive institutions operated for the convenience or profit of their administrators, and they should never be regarded as an acceptable long-term solution for social dysfunctions. A decline of faith in the therapeutic professions coincided with the transformation in psychiatric practice wrought by new drugs for treating mental disorders, which in time permitted the release of many thousands of mental patients. Between 1955 and 1981, the number of inmates in state mental hospitals fell from 560,000 to 138,000 and to 116,000 by 1984.[31]

Critical perspectives toward psychiatry entered popular culture through best-selling books (and films) like Richard Condon's *Manchurian Candidate*, Ken Kesey's *One Flew over the Cuckoo's Nest*, and Anthony Burgess's *Clockwork Orange*. The Kesey and Burgess works suggested how psychiatry had acquired immense powers to alter human personality in the interests of the group or government sponsoring the behavior-modification activity. All three stories further showed that psychiatric techniques could potentially be used to cause unimaginable pain and suffering. In whose interests would such powers be exercised, and how could they properly be reconciled with the principles of law and constitutionality? The *Clockwork Orange* image of behavior modification was all the more powerful because, despite its Orwellian trappings, it corresponded to actual trends within the correctional world. In 1970, an article in *Psychology Today*, which ran under the headline "Criminals Can Be Brainwashed—Now," noted how therapists could combine "sensory deprivation with drugs, hypnosis and astute manipulation of reward and punishment to gain almost absolute control over an individual's behavior." By 1973–74, behavioral experiments had entered the domain of national politics, when Watergate-era exposés showed that the CIA and other U.S. government agencies had explored the possibility of mind control and behavior modification.[32] These revelations fueled conspiracy speculations, and programmed assassins became a staple of popular fiction: in 1974, the film *The Parallax View* depicted a clandestine intelligence group using behavior-modification techniques to train disturbed individuals and sex offenders as political assassins.

As with psychiatry, American prisons entered a period of grave crisis in the decade following 1965. Many believed that the rehabilitation of criminals was a myth and that the means used in this endeavor were useless at best, brutal at worst. The therapeutic ideal had been founded upon the optimistic notion that deviant individuals could be corrected or reformed according to the standards of the normal and law-abiding, but in the era of the Vietnam War and the urban riots, distinctions between normal and deviant, legal and criminal, were more disputed and tenuous than they had ever been in the nation's history. Racial tensions turned the prisons into battlegrounds, with the worst bloodshed occurring at New York's Attica facility in 1971. The media exposed the abuses endemic within prison walls, including racial and religious persecution and a culture of prisoner rape. Courts played an interventionist role in attacking these problems, to the point of declaring that the prison systems of entire states represented cruel and unusual punishment. A series of devastating studies emphasized the repressive aspects of the rehabilitative or correctional model. Books like *Struggle for Justice* and Jessica Mitford's *Kind and Usual Punishment* emphasized the biases of ostensibly objective administrators and demanded the ending of indeterminate sentencing and forced treatment. In 1974, an extensive study of correctional treatment and rehabilitation programs was quoted as finding that "nothing works": the study found no documented evidence of any program that had achieved convincing results in reforming criminals. A new orthodoxy espoused by conservatives and liberals alike emphasized just deserts, determinate sentencing, and limiting official discretion.[33] Cumulatively, these attacks all but killed the rehabilitative ideal as a respectable component of American social policy.

Overturning the Sex Psychopath Laws

It was unthinkable that the sex psychopath statutes should fare better than other aspects of the positivist program, and in 1970, the influential book *The Honest Politician's Guide to Crime Control* cited these laws to illustrate the bankruptcy of the rehabilitative ideal.[34] The courts now found the sex psychopath legislation wanting on various grounds, including its lack of due-process rights and protections. In addition, recent cases on involuntary commitment raised doubts about whether an individual could legally be incarcerated for many years, without the prospect of release, if proper treatment were not available. The issue then arose of whether any potential treatment even existed for a medically tenuous condition like psychopathy.

In 1967, the same year as *Gault*, the Supreme Court heard the case of *Specht v. Patterson*, involving a Colorado man convicted of indecent liberties with a child. The defendant faced a criminal sentence of ten years for this act, but the state invoked its sex offenders act, under which he could be sentenced for "one day to life." The judicial decision depended on a psychiatric evaluation, which, despite its weighty consequences, did not give the defendant the right to confront witnesses or access to counsel. The court rejected the state's optimistic view that the psychiatrist was an objective professional with everyone's best interests at heart rather than a hostile accuser: "The commitment proceedings whether denominated civil or criminal are subject both to the Equal Protection Clause of the Fourteenth Amendment . . . and to the Due Process Clause." Imposing a new indeterminate sentence would require "a new finding of fact [that the person convicted constitutes a threat of bodily harm to the public] that was not an ingredient of the offense charged." As a U.S. court of appeals held in a case on Pennsylvania's sex psychopath procedure: "At such a hearing, the requirements of due process cannot be satisfied by partial or niggardly procedural protections. A defendant . . . is entitled to the full panoply of the relevant protections which due process guarantees in state criminal proceedings, . . . including the right to confront and cross-examine the witnesses against him."[35]

The *Potter* case of the same year concerned an Illinois man charged with public indecency and repeated exhibitionism. In a psychiatric examination, the defendant talked freely of his deviant tendencies and admitted to the acts charged as well as others, so medical experts duly reported that he was a sexually dangerous person liable to indefinite commitment. But before his conversation with the psychiatrists, the defendant had not received the kind of warning about his rights that would have been required in a police interrogation following recent cases like *Miranda*. A federal appeals court decided that the psychiatric examination, because it was an integral part of the process that led a person to receive a penalty, must be surrounded with appropriate protections, and *Miranda* thus entered the psychiatrist's office.[36]

An acute example of the conflict between legal and therapeutic standards came in Maryland, which in 1951 had passed an ambitious measure against defective delinquents and sex criminals. The state operated a model treatment facility at Patuxent, where the large custodial staff included psychiatrists, psychologists, and social workers.[37] The institution was a "total therapeutic milieu" in which each inmate's life-style depended entirely on his or her cooperation with and progress in treatment. The average number of "patients" rose from 186 in 1956 to nearly 500 in 1968, but the times were perilous for even this shining example of the therapeutic ideal. The final crisis was initiated by Edward McNeil, who in 1966 was sentenced to five years' imprisonment for assault on a police officer and assault with intent to rape. He was sent to Patuxent for evaluation as a possible defective delinquent, but as he denied both offenses, he militantly refused to cooperate with therapists. A noncooperator could make no progress within the institutional hierarchy of rewards and privileges, and until he was diagnosed he could not be treated, so release seemed impossible. Even so, when McNeil's formal criminal sentence expired, he petitioned for release from Patuxent, which the Supreme Court granted in 1972 in a decision that undermined the state's whole defective delinquent law. Although not rejecting the idea of compulsory clinical observation, the Court warned that this must not provide an excuse for the indefinite warehousing of a troublesome individual.

After several years of subversion, the sex psychopath statutes received a lethal blow with the *Davy v. Sullivan* case of 1973, when a U.S. district court struck down Alabama's statute on the grounds that it set an impossibly high standard for release, demanding "full and permanent recovery" from psychopathy. The Court showed, moreover, that it would be willing to entertain any one of a number of possible challenges to any existing or future sex psychopath law. The decision criticized the statute's overly broad and unscientific definitions and its mixing of civil and criminal elements: "As a criminal statute imposing punishment on convicted sex offenders, [the] statute is unconstitutional in that it either subjects a person to two criminal proceedings and possibly to two criminal sentences for a single statutory crime, or if not for a single offense, then in one of the two proceedings for the mere crime of having a mental disorder."[38]

Legal decisions of these years shifted the focus of judicial concern toward the sufferings and injustices of the criminals or patients involved in sexual misdeeds and away from the victims who had provided the rationale for the original statutes. In 1968, federal judge David Bazelon determined in *Millard v. Harris* that a compulsive exhibitionist could not be confined on grounds of public safety, as the behavior would affect only "unusually sensitive adult women and small children": exhibitionism or nonpenetrative molestation need cause no grave or long-term damage. The same impression emerges from psychiatric studies that attempted to assess the dangerousness of criminal offenders. In 1974, federal litigation resulted in a review of inmates confined in an Ohio hospital for the criminally insane; the goal was to ascertain how many had been correctly diagnosed as a sig-

nificant danger to themselves and the public. Although psychiatric professionals differed on the definitions and manifestations of dangerousness,
there was particular disagreement on the issue of sex offenses: "most commonly, . . . sexual assaults that were not accompanied by serious physical
injury were not to be categorized as dangerous." One evaluation argued
that a particular inmate had "the capability of repeating almost immediately the sexual offenses for which he was charged," namely, the molestation of young girls, "but he is not considered to be dangerously assaultive
in that it is not felt that he would be likely to kill"; therefore, it determined,
"this patient is not in need of continued hospitalization in a maximum security facility."[39] From the point of view of the 1940s or the 1990s, such remarks seem remarkably cold-blooded.

The sex psychopath laws had assumed that transgressors needed to be
treated by appropriate experts, but the 1960s and 1970s witnessed increasing criticism of the entire therapeutic regime in these institutions, especially the intrusive procedures popular in some facilities. These included
electroconvulsive therapy, so horrifyingly depicted as a form of torture in
One Flew over the Cuckoo's Nest, the antihero of which was incarcerated
for statutory rape. Other aversive therapies involved subjecting patients to
unpleasant chemical or electrical stimuli while they watched images of antisocial behavior. In this *Clockwork Orange* model, the subject is conditioned to associate that behavior with the reactions of pain or fear suffered
during therapy and thus to avoid the violent or sexual stimuli that evoked
the undesirable response. In 1968, a scholarly article reported how painful
electrical stimuli had been used to condition a homosexual pedophile to
replace his penchant for boys between six and twelve with a sexual preference for adult men. Although the idea had plausible medical foundations,
it involved subjecting prisoners to severe pain of a kind that would be
legally unthinkable without the justification of therapy.[40]

In the new legal environment, "conditioning" was commonly viewed as
cruel and unusual punishment, if not torture. In the 1973 case of *Knecht
v. Gillman,* a U.S. court of appeals heard that inmates of a prison medical
facility in Iowa were given doses of the drug apomorphine as a means of
curing disciplinary problems like lying, swearing, and disobedience; although ostensibly given in order to condition prisoners to behave accept-
ably, the drug induced vomiting and other unpleasant side effects. The
court, however, applied the now-familiar rule that "the mere characterization of an act as treatment does not insulate it from Eighth Amendment

scrutiny," and the prison's practice was condemned. Also in 1973, a Michigan state court forbade the use of psychosurgery to regulate a prisoner's violent impulses, even though, in this case, the inmate himself had consented to the procedure; the judges questioned whether a prisoner in these coercive circumstances could ever give valid consent. In 1975, convicted molesters in Connecticut successfully sued to end the rule that they could achieve parole only if they underwent painful aversion therapy involving electric shocks to their genitals. Although nominally voluntary, the therapy was linked to release and thus obligatory in practice.[41]

Such decisions undermined or invalidated the procedures of facilities for defective delinquents and other treatment institutions in penal systems throughout the country, leaving the entire system of therapeutic facilities and practices in a legal limbo. Under assault from so many different directions, existing sex psychopath laws and treatment facilities were overwhelmed. Some laws were repealed, others recognized as legally moribund.

By the early 1970s, it was the legislation concerning sex offenders that was portrayed as the pressing social problem, not the offenders themselves. Because the laws reflected outmoded sexual prejudices, they were both unrealistic and repressive. A common perception was that many charges were false (and often motivated by racial bias) while the prevailing penalties were excessively severe. Where authentic molesters or abusers were found, they were docile individuals who did not merit great public or official concern. They certainly did not deserve the vicious physical tortures visited upon them in the name of therapy, and their actions did not justify the existence of harsh legislation. In fact, special legislation was inherently suspect, for it enhanced official discretion within the criminal-justice system, and that discretion had repeatedly been abused. Administrators could not and should not be trusted with vast discretionary powers for dealing with even dangerously violent criminals and obviously not for merely inconvenient offenders like child molesters.

The Child Abuse Revolution, 1976–1986

The sexual abuse of female children is a process of education that prepares them
to become the wives and mothers of America.
— FLORENCE RUSH, 1971

If you have been sexually abused, you are not alone. One out of three girls and one out of
seven boys are sexually abused by the time they reach the age of eighteen. Sexual abuse
happens to children of every class, culture, race, religion, and gender.
— ELLEN BASS AND LAURA DAVIS, 1988

By 1974, the federal courts were reflecting a broad consensus that child
molestation was not a significant problem, but at just this point, other social developments were heralding another reversal of the pendulum. In
1974, feminists were engaged in a national campaign to raise concern about
the prevalence of rape, while professionals in the fields of medicine and social welfare had successfully drawn attention to the menace of child battering or physical abuse. Initially, neither issue was necessarily connected
to the theme of molestation, but within a few years, concerns over sexual
exploitation and domestic maltreatment combined to create a perception
that all American children were sexually at risk. From about 1977, the
nascent problem called *child sexual abuse* gradually appropriated the
generic term *child abuse,* and a cascade of works about abuse, incest, and
sexual exploitation reached flood proportions by 1984. Child protection

became a national social orthodoxy, a package of basic beliefs and assumptions that weighted discourse on a variety of seemingly unrelated issues. Shifting attitudes toward child abuse constituted a revolutionary and perhaps irrevocable change in American culture.

The fact that millions of Americans were indeed reporting that they had been subjected to unwanted sexual experiences during their early years means that the new construction of the problem cannot be described as a groundless panic. But these claims were embellished by statistics suggesting an incredible frequency not just of molestation but of the most extreme forms of rape and incest, a process of inflation accomplished by the familiar midcentury device of expansive definition and of assimilating all minor forms of deviancy with the most threatening acts of sexual predation. In 1984 as in 1950, a "minor molestation" was considered an oxymoron, a despicable trivialization of a national crisis. Moreover, the reframing of the abuse problem was fueled by lurid stories of organized pedophile rings, child pornography, and serial murderers of children. All these phenomena existed on a limited scale, but all were now treated as if they were commonplace and represented a natural stage in the sequence of molestation. Although the new problem recalled the Progressive Era in its view of abuse as an issue of families and communities, it also harked back to the midcentury panic in its revived vision of predatory molesters.

Formulating Child Abuse

The libertarian era of the 1960s and early 1970s was not congenial to new claims about supposed sexual dangers, and concerns about child welfare initially focused on other aspects of the problem. Modern concepts of child abuse grew out of the recognition, from about 1962, of "baby battering," or violence inflicted on children in their homes, usually by members of their families.[1] Professionals came to see physical abuse as a common phenomenon affecting families of all social strata and posing a lethal danger to the young. By the mid-1970s, these perceptions had been disseminated in the media, demanding a prompt official response. Politically the issue had wide appeal: all political persuasions could agree that measures to protect vulnerable children were a good idea, and liberals were sympathetic to a campaign that addressed the evils of authoritarian structures within the patriarchal family. In 1974, Walter Mondale sponsored the federal Child Abuse Prevention and Treatment Act, which mandated the reporting and investigation of abuse allegations and promised matching funds for states that identified abused children and prosecuted abusers.

The federal measure was crucial for later developments, for it justified the creation of state and local agencies whose sole raison d'être was the investigation of child maltreatment. Mandatory reporting swelled abuse statistics, while the practice of basing investigations on confidential and anonymous reports opened the way to a high volume of groundless or malicious charges.[2] In contrast to earlier periods, the fact that reporting now applied regardless of class opened the way to the discovery of child maltreatment in middle- and upper-class households. Concern was institutionalized through a number of public and private agencies. The National Center on Child Abuse and Neglect (NCCAN) was founded as a section of the Department of Health and Human Services in 1974, and private groups formed between 1970 and 1975 included the Children's Defense Fund, the National Committee for the Prevention of Child Abuse, Parents Anonymous, Parents United, and the Society for Young Victims.

The discovery of the *physical* abuse of children was the essential prerequisite for popularizing the concept of sexual abuse. Discussions of violence against children repeatedly emphasized the same themes: this was an enormous problem that could threaten any child in any type of home; the statistics, however troubling, represented only the tip of the iceberg, while solutions to the problem were thwarted by a general refusal to acknowledge that such appalling acts could occur; the hidden epidemic could be cured only by creating specialized groups or agencies with both the will and the power to intervene. These same ideas were gradually applied to the phenomenon of sexual acts committed against children, a linkage first suggested in the late 1960s by the American Humane Association, which published some influential studies of sex crimes against children. Warning that "for too long, the needs of sexually abused children have been ignored," the association cited "an enormous national incidence many times larger than the reported incidence of physical abuse of children." The vocabulary for describing child sexual abuse also reverted to an old phrase: *sexual abuse* was the prosecutor's traditional term for interference with a child short of penetration, but in the new era, the term migrated from the legal lexicon to enter general speech.[3]

The new ideas achieved the status of a mass social movement following the activism of a coalition of disparate interest groups. Although feminists and humanitarian groups did much to reformulate popular notions about sex crime and child abuse, these ideas also appealed to conservative and traditional-minded groups who were on other issues deeply unsympathetic to the women's movement. Both feminists and conservatives found themselves in hearty agreement on the dangers posed by unrestrained sexual license and on the need to combat threats against children.

The Politics of Morality

Moral conservatism gained rapidly in vigor and public support from about 1975 and reached its apogee when Ronald Reagan was elected president in 1980. Renewed interest in child exploitation coincided with an irresistible political trend to reaffirm traditional values and discipline, through law if necessary, and to stigmatize immoral behaviors. For moral traditionalists, a campaign against sex crime provided an effective weapon for combating what they saw as a slide toward decadence, which had been unchecked since about 1965 and which was symbolized by the tolerance of divorce, abortion, homosexuality, drugs, and sexual promiscuity. Legal restraints on sexual behavior had steadily withered, as had controls on media depictions of formerly taboo subjects. Sexually explicit topics now appeared in mainstream cinema, while hard-core sexual materials were available to the general public. Liberalization brought a backlash: a series of obscenity prosecutions during 1976 illustrated concern about moral laxity, and federal law enforcement began undercover investigations of organized crime activity in the pornography industry.[4]

The campaign against vice and illicit sexuality gained national visibility with its emphasis on child pornography. Libertarians had normally defended sexually explicit material on the grounds that it was both made and used by consenting adults whose actions affected no outside party. Child pornography subverted these arguments because children could not meaningfully consent to their participation, and the mere manufacture of the material therefore constituted harmful and criminal behavior. As activist Judianne Densen-Gerber remarked, "There is no such thing as a child consenting to be photographed sexually: it is an act fundamentally of exploitation." Moral campaigners and child welfare advocates found an area in which there was heavy public support for legal intervention, and libertarians could offer few plausible defenses. Similar arguments also applied to child prostitution, although with somewhat less force, as most offenders were teenagers rather than small children; but here, too, child protection offered a politically popular rationale for mobilizing against vice. During the early twentieth century, attacks on vice focused on abducted women who were compelled to serve as white slaves, while in the 1970s the emphasis shifted to young people below the age of consent, but in both cases the goal was to minimize arguments that commercial sex could be a mutual and consensual transaction. Not coincidentally, the enduring fable of the literally homicidal genre of snuff pornography was also born at about this time.[5]

A public campaign against child pornography and prostitution was led by Densen-Gerber, who had earned celebrity through her work at New York City's Odyssey House, a narcotics rehabilitation facility for young people. Her attention was drawn to sexual dangers by the book *For Money or Love,* in which investigative reporter Robin Lloyd sounded an alarm about commercialized sex operations. With support from other activists, including social workers, religious leaders, and community improvement groups, Densen-Gerber pressured the New York City mayor's office and police department. In early 1977, police responded with a crackdown on the freewheeling vice culture that had emerged around Times Square, where child pornography films and magazines were readily available in adult stores and where an underground manufacturing industry employed as models the numerous runaways and street hustlers of the area. The New York campaign was imitated in other cities, and Odyssey supporters organized demonstrations against child-oriented pornography in Chicago and Philadelphia.[6]

Claims makers successfully presented their views on the national stage. After April 1977, the child pornography issue was widely reported throughout the news media, on television programs like *60 Minutes* (May 15, 1977) and in print sources like *Redbook* and *Parents, Newsweek* and *U.S. News and World Report, Ms.* and *Time,* and in most major newspapers. In April, *Time* noted with horror the plots of some of the most extreme pornographic items said to be in circulation: "An 8mm movie shows a ten-year-old girl and her eight-year-old brother in fellatio and intercourse. . . . Members of a bike gang break into a church during First Communion service and rape six little girls." The following month, a news report on NBC stated extravagantly, "It's been estimated that as many as 2 million American youngsters are involved in the fast-growing, multimillion-dollar child pornography business." Also in May, a series in the *Chicago Tribune* detailed the whole subculture associated with child pornography and prostitution, introducing many readers to argot terms like *chicken hawks* and alerted mainstream readers that special areas of vice districts were catering to men seeking children and young teenagers. The manufacture of child pornography was said to involve up to 100,000 children at any given time, a figure that had no known basis, and the issue was contextualized with the seduction and abuse of runaway children and youth: "Child pornography is a nationwide multi-million-dollar racket that is luring thousands of juveniles into lives of prostitution." According to Densen-Gerber, the child models were "emotionally and spiritually murdered."[7]

Political action followed swiftly. That spring, the Kildee-Murphy bill proposed that the manufacture, distribution, and possession of child pornography be prohibited, and congressional hearings on the sexual exploitation of children followed in May and June. Witnesses included child-protection activists like Densen-Gerber, Kenneth Wooden, and Lloyd Martin, from the Los Angeles Police Department's new unit on sexually exploited children. Pornography opponents found a regional base in Michigan, the home of representatives Dale Kildee and John Conyers, who led congressional action in the cause; also from Michigan was prosecutor Robert F. Leonard, whose testimony warned of national conspiracies of pedophiles and child pornographers. As president-elect of the National District Attorneys Association, Leonard was able to project his concerns and to encourage other prosecutors to become active in the cause. This core of child advocates, especially Martin and Densen-Gerber, were the experts most often quoted in the swath of stories about child pornography and exploitation that became almost obligatory for major media outlets in these months.[8]

The hearings provided excellent media copy, and they hit hardest when citing the titles and subject matter of pornographic magazines and films, the mere existence of which shocked the great majority of viewers and listeners. Witnesses were offered a rostrum from which to describe the vast scale of the enterprises in child pornography and its ties both to organized crime and to pedophilia. Witnesses linked the commercial sexual exploitation of children to child sexual abuse in the family setting, an argument supported by the ambitious statistics then emanating from the antirape movement. Martin claimed, "A child who has been sexually abused will frequently turn to prostitution, pornography, narcotics or other criminal activity."[9] This linkage explains why the movement attracted near-unanimous support, not just from moral conservatives but also from feminists and liberals. Criticisms of the proposed new law came only from the American Civil Liberties Union, who protested its overly broad language, and from adult magazine publisher Larry Flynt. The bill passed in the House of Representatives by a vote margin of 401 to 0.

As in the late 1940s, the child-protection movement was fueled by antihomosexual sentiment, although in a significantly different legal environment. The gay movement attained public visibility following the Stonewall riot of 1969 and achieved major political victories during the next decade, while media images of homosexuals became far more benevolent.[10] Between 1971 and 1976, sixteen states repealed their sodomy statutes, and by 1980 six more had either undertaken repeal of these laws or had them declared unconstitutional. In several other states, sodomy laws remained notionally in effect but were subject to court decisions that made it unlikely that they would ever be enforced. The American Psychiatric Association reflected the new mood in 1973 when it removed homosexuality from its diagnostic manual of mental illnesses and ended its approval of attempts to "cure" homosexuals. Although the gay movement could count many advances, a series of political events between 1976 and 1978 threatened to revive the older homophobic stereotype. The attack on child exploitation coincided with the most significant conservative campaign yet launched to reverse the social and political progress made by homosexuals, and the two movements inevitably contributed to each other.

By the mid-1970s, several jurisdictions proposed to extend gay rights further by prohibiting discrimination on the grounds of sexual preference, but antigay and religious activists used referendum campaigns to mobilize public opposition. The 1977 vote that overturned a gay rights ordinance in Dade County, Florida, was followed over the next three years by electoral battles in Minnesota, Kansas, and elsewhere, while a California ballot measure sought to prohibit the advocacy of homosexuality in public schools. Conservatives like Anita Bryant stressed the threat to children, and her umbrella organization was called Save Our Children and later renamed Protect America's Children. Although ostensibly intending to save children from generalized moral decay, the organization's approach revealed a subtext: its assumption that homosexuals would corrupt children by sexually molesting them, transforming victims into fellow perverts in the process once described as proselytizing. A slogan that apparently originated with Bryant herself asserted, "Homosexuals can't reproduce, so they have to recruit."[11]

Bryant stressed homosexuals' alleged predilection for child pornography and involvement in organized pedophile rings. Save Our Children declared, "The Los Angeles Police Department recently reported that 25,000 boys seventeen years old or younger in that city alone have been recruited into a homosexual ring to provide sex for adult male customers." Other statements claimed that antidiscrimination laws would end the exclusion of homosexuals from Big Brothers organizations, exposing ever more children to molestation. This "pedophile agenda" was especially apparent in the California debate. In the 1977 congressional hearings, Robert Leonard reported a case of several men who recruited runaway teenage boys as "male prostitutes to serve wealthy homosexuals." The *Chicago Tribune* tracked "a nationwide homosexual ring with headquarters in Chicago [which] has been trafficking in young boys." It was scarcely surprising that, as Kenneth Wooden noted, "most agree that child sex and pornography is basically a boy-man phenomenon."[12]

The effects of Bryant's movement were far-reaching. Ironically, one consequence was to give a powerful stimulus to gay political activism, which found a visible symbol in the historic march on Washington, D.C., in 1979. On the conservative side, the Bryant campaign proved a crucial step in the creation of the religious-based Moral Majority, which was founded in 1979, and further gave an enormous boost to political activism by Christian fundamentalists. Pedophilia was central to antigay rhetoric until the mid-1980s, when it was largely replaced by the still more effective terror weapon of AIDS.[13]

The Politics of Rape

While conservatives contributed significantly to new concerns over sexual deviance, also critical were feminists with radically divergent opinions on matters like abortion, sexuality, and the virtues of the traditional nuclear family. For feminists, the movement against child abuse in these years was a direct outgrowth of the campaign against rape, which formulated the concepts and vocabulary that would become integral to child-protection ideology.

As early as 1965, rape victim Gladys Shultz published in *How Many More Victims?* a protest against the contemporary trivialization of sex crime. She argued that offenses like rape were more widespread than was popularly believed, that sex crime caused grave physical and psychic injury (including long-term mental trauma), and that victims often included children as well as women. Shultz used contemporary stories of authentic sex fiends to defend J. Edgar Hoover's 1947 article "How Safe Is Your Daughter?" which by this time had come to be seen as an almost humorous example of panic mongering.[14]

Shultz's argument went against the popular current at the time her book was published, but it would enter the mainstream in the next decade. Developing from the ferment of social radicalism in the late 1960s, the women's movement acquired a forceful public voice, and concern about sexual violence grew apace: Women Against Rape (WAR) groups appeared about 1972, and in 1973 the National Organization for Women (NOW) created a rape task force. The issue brought the feminist movement into sharp conflict with the hedonistic and libertarian values of the alternative Left culture from which it had originated. For other radicals, sexual liberation was an unqualified good that advanced the revolutionary transformation of society. For feminists, however, sexual hedonism led to rape and exploitation and contributed directly to social oppression; with regard to pornography and underage sexuality, sexual expression must be regulated in order to defend the powerless.

In the feminist view, rape was sexual terrorism directed against women as a collective group, much as lynching had historically been employed to subjugate an entire race. Rape and sexual assault were far more frequent than official figures would suggest, but in the face of this structural crisis, the police, the media, and the public were so unsympathetic as to actually encourage the crime. Public attitudes suggested that women regularly invented false charges, were "asking for it" by behaving irresponsibly, and suffered little real harm from attacks. Victims who reported their rapes to police were subjected to embarrassing delays in precinct houses while awaiting the doctors who would take the samples essential to proving cases. In court, victims found themselves subjected to intrusive questions about their sexual histories, the aim being to prove their bad character and sexual irresponsibility. Reluctant to risk the ordeal of a "second rape," many women refused to file complaints.[15]

A series of books on the rape issue revived earlier ideas about the seriousness and prevalence of sex crime and the dangerousness of the offenders. One provocative title from 1974 was *The Politics of Rape: The Victim's Perspective,* by Diana E. H. Russell: the idea that a crime like rape might be a political phenomenon was integral to feminist ideology, but this book represented a major departure in public views of sex crime. Also in contrast to the writings of the 1940s was the emphasis on the victim, in terms of both her personal suffering and her mobilization with other victims as a means of achieving social change. Feminist themes were popularized by national and local pressure groups and by the rape crisis centers that appeared in most metropolitan areas.[16]

Antirape activists secured significant changes in both law and police practice, promoting reforms that assumed the truthfulness of women complainants. Between 1971 and 1975, many states changed their laws to end requirements for physical corroboration in rape cases and to reduce the defense's ability to introduce evidence about a woman's prior sexual history; specialized police units for handling rape cases were created in major cities. Courts also expanded their definition of rape to include nonconsensual intercourse inflicted by boyfriends or husbands.[17] Reformers created a new environment in which victims would be more prepared to report crimes and press complaints, raising the probability that cases would be pursued to conviction: the number of rapes reported annually in the United States rose from 22,467 in 1965 to 55,400 in 1974 and to more than 76,000 in 1979; by 1990, the figure exceeded 100,000.

Child Sexual Abuse

The rape issue was crucial for the rediscovery of the issue of sexual offenses against children. In 1971, Florence Rush made a historic presentation to the Rape Conference of the New York Radical Feminists, in which she declared that these crimes were far more common than was supposed. Abuse "is permitted because it is an unspoken but prominent factor in socializing and preparing the female to accept a subordinate role: to feel guilty, ashamed, and to tolerate, through fear, the power exercised over her by men." Rush was a pivotal figure: older than most of the new women activists (she was born in 1918), she had lived through the earlier sex crime wave and the Kinsey era and had acted as a bridge from that time into the 1970s.[18] Her work with the Society for the Prevention of Cruelty to Children made her a conduit from the social work tradition to the new feminism, which may explain why the new movement tended to revive the term *abuse* in the sexual context. This may also have been the first recorded occasion in which a presentation on sexual abuse began with a recounting of a personal history of victimization. For several years, Rush's much-quoted remarks were the most readily available feminist analysis of the molestation issue, making her presentation as epoch-defining in her time as Travis Gibb's paper had been in the 1890s.

In response partly to observations at women's shelters and rape crisis centers and partly to the intense publicity surrounding child pornography and prostitution, feminist activism and research from the mid-1970s focused attention on younger victims. Theorists like Diana Russell and Ann Burgess extended their research interests from the rape of adult women to the victimization of minors, and for Judith Herman, father-daughter incest became "a paradigm of female sexual victimization." By the end of the decade, a substantial literature on child sexual abuse was appearing, just as works on rape had mushroomed a few years earlier: in 1977, few books on child sexual abuse had been published by either professionals or activists, but an explosion of research and publishing soon followed. Between 1978 and 1981, a number of path-breaking books appeared, among them *The Sexual Assault of Children and Adolescents, Sexually Victimized Children, Betrayal of Innocence, The Best-Kept Secret,* and *Father-Daughter Incest.* By the mid-1980s, a vast literature discussed once ignored or underplayed issues like the effects of abuse on victims, their treatment and rehabilitation, and the creation of effective programs of prevention and deterrence. A growing literature on the molester or pedophile reemphasized the compulsive and dangerous quality of the behavior.[19]

The new sensibility reflected changing emphases within the therapeutic professions, and an institutional foundation for the study of child maltreatment arose in specialized clinics and in some university departments dealing with social work and social problems. Something approaching a freestanding child abuse profession developed out of existing traditions in social work, therapy, and counseling, and the associated societies, conferences, and journals soon emerged. In 1976, an international congress laid the foundation for the new International Society for the Prevention of Child Abuse and Neglect, and its journal, *Child Abuse and Neglect,* dates from 1977; both society and journal owed much to the sponsorship of C. Henry Kempe, who had been the leading figure in the discovery of baby battering. The year 1979 marked America's first national conference devoted to the theme of child sexual abuse.[20]

Research was funded by new official agencies, and Russell's research on the incidence of rape and incest was funded by both NCCAN and the National Institute of Mental Health. Federal support intensified under the Reagan administration, suggesting once again the congruence between conservative agendas and the child-protection cause. In 1984, the newly operational National Center for Missing and Exploited Children (NCMEC) became a leading force in disseminating extreme claims about

Questions of definition are always central. For example, among a random sample of 930 San Francisco women interviewed in 1978, Russell found 647 cases of "child sexual abuse," but she defined the behavior very broadly. "Incestuous" abuse was "any kind of exploitive sexual contact or attempted sexual contact that occurred between relatives, no matter how distant the relationship, before the victim turned eighteen years old." "Extrafamilial" abuse was "one or more unwanted sexual experiences with persons unrelated by blood or marriage, ranging from attempted petting (touching of breasts or genitals or attempts at such touching) to rape, before the victim turned fourteen years, and completed or attempted forcible rape experiences from the ages of 14 to 17 years (inclusive)." Conclusions rested on subjective perceptions about what constituted "attempted" or "exploitive" behavior: though many of the actions involved might have been trivial or debatable, Russell's data were quoted, wrongly, to suggest that 40 percent of children were subjected to rape and the most devastating kinds of sexual violence and that one-sixth had suffered incest.[26] Moreover, the survey occurred in a city that at the time had a level of feminist consciousness paralleled in few areas, with a sample population singularly prepared to interpret actions as abusive.

These caveats received little notice when Russell's survey findings were reported and found their way into popular culture. One recent book claims that incest is a "very ordinary part of many children's lives: one out of three girls, one out of seven boys." The figure is obtained by classifying all forms of questionable sexual activity within the family as *incest,* a term that in general usage still signifies intercourse. NCMEC states: "Many kinds of child sexual exploitation—rape, molestation, prostitution, pornography—pervade our society. At least 22 percent of Americans report having been sexually assaulted in some way as children—by such means as sexual intercourse, fondling, sodomy, or confrontation by an exhibitionist."[27] The figure of 22 percent accurately refers to the number of Americans who in one survey reported having experienced some form of loosely defined abuse, yet the context implies that this is the proportion of people victimized by rape or sodomy.

Whatever their flaws, these quantitative claims gained credibility from the precedent of physical abuse. Once it would have been angrily denied that tens of thousands of children were targets of violence within their homes, but now that fact was broadly accepted. Similar denial might initially impede acceptance of the hazards of sexual abuse, but here too the problem would be confirmed. The practical consequences were stunning. If 30 or 40 percent of all children were abused, then this figure should apply to the population coming to the attention of any teacher, doctor, or psychologist, and of course no institution was finding anything like this rate. For some, this meant that professionals were not being sufficiently proactive in seeking out abuse and that countless victims were concealing the crime, both to the outside world and to themselves; a remedy for this all-encompassing denial was to develop techniques of investigation and therapy that validated the quantitative claims.

Missing and Murdered

From the late 1970s, scandals and news stories buttressed the idea of a general danger not only to children's moral well-being but to their very lives. Between 1979 and 1981, the media gave prominent attention to the long-running case of the child murders in Atlanta, the abductions and murders of young Adam Walsh and Etan Patz, and the sexual homicides of children and teenagers by notorious serial killers like John Wayne Gacy and Randy Kraft. These last cases became prominent in antigay polemics, as focusing on "gay serial killers" tended to confound homosexuals with pedophiles and child killers. Fears about child homicide merged with a general panic over missing and abducted children, in which it was alleged that many thousands of children fell victim to kidnappers in any given year. In 1985, the director of the NCMEC stated that "at least twenty to fifty thousand kids are abducted each year in the United States and are never seen again," though other estimates placed the figure closer to 1.5 million. In 1982, the U.S. Senate designated May 25 as National Missing Children's Day. The impact of a constant diet of horror stories is suggested by the dramatic peak of news reports during 1982 concerning alleged incidents of Halloween sadism, in which children's treats were said to have been poisoned or tampered with.[28]

Inflated figures achieved credence through the efforts of child advocates who often testified before official hearings. Among the main activists were John Walsh, Adam Walsh's father; Florida senator Paula Hawkins, who divulged that she had been molested as a child; and Kenneth Wooden, who in 1977 produced the pioneering exposé, "Kiddie Porn," on 60 Minutes. Over the next decade, Wooden's role as a producer on news shows like 60 Minutes and 20/20 gave him a uniquely powerful platform from which to issue warnings about child murderers and abductors.[29] With the support of powerful senators like Paul Simon of Illinois and Arlen Specter of Pennsylvania, these individuals became visible spokesmen for legislation to protect children from murder and molestation by expanding the federal role in the search for missing and exploited children.

Between 1981 and 1985, federal hearings exposed the supposedly intertwined issues of child pornography and pedophilia, serial murder, and missing children (Table 6.1). Walsh related the issue of missing children to that of serial sex killers: "We found that the number of random unsolved murders of women and children in this country rose from 600 in 1966 to 4,500 in 1981." (In the popular myth that soon arose, serial killers accounted for four or five thousand victims each year, a figure that inflated the real phenomenon at least tenfold.) Every hour, Walsh stated, 205 children in the United States were reported missing (a figure that represented 1.8 million cases per annum), and many would be found murdered. Wooden told his congressional audience, memorably: "Children in America are treated like garbage. Raped and killed, their young bodies are disposed of in plastic bags, in trash trucks, and left in city dumps." Specter concurred, "The molestation of children has now reached epidemic proportions." Charges were self-feeding: the parade of witnesses provided frequent good copy for the media, which raised public awareness of the problem and in turn enhanced political and bureaucratic rewards for individuals and agencies making the claims. After a decade of bitter hostility to expanded federal powers in policing, the Justice Department now won support for a more powerful interstate role in fighting the menace from serial killers and potentially from perpetrators of "rape, child molestation, arson and bombing."[30]

Although Specter's own Senate judiciary subcommittee was the usual venue for charges, other committees and investigators followed suit, and claims were aired before the special investigation of pornography sponsored by Attorney General Edwin Meese in 1985. By this point, very high estimates of the scale of child kidnapping, abuse, and serial murder were cited in the news media on an almost daily basis. Only gradually did journalists and scholars begin to challenge these statistics, often reducing claims to a tiny fraction of their original scale. In retrospect, a well-informed FBI expert remarked, earlier claims could be traced to "the media, profiteers, and well-intentioned zealots."[31]

Table 6.1 Official Investigations of Threats to Children, 1981–1984

1981

November — Hearings of the Missing Children's Act before the House Committee on Civil and Constitutional Rights.

1982

April–December — Hearings on missing and exploited children before the Juvenile Justice Subcommittee of the Senate Judiciary Committee; chairman, Arlen Specter. Witnesses include Paula Hawkins and John Walsh.

1983

February — Hearing on child kidnapping before the Specter subcommittee.

July — Hearings on serial murder before the Specter subcommittee. Witnesses include John Walsh and Paula Hawkins.

September — First arrest at the McMartin preschool in Manhattan Beach, California. Mass child abuse case begins in Jordan, Minnesota.

October — Justice Department publicizes view that serial murder is a serious and growing danger.

1984

February–March — Hearings on the Missing Children's Assistance Act before the Specter subcommittee.

March — National publicity follows arrests in the McMartin preschool case.

March — Kenneth Wooden's reports on ABC's *20/20* focus on the murder and disappearances of children.

Spring–Summer — National attention focuses on the Jordan mass abuse investigation.

April — John Walsh and Kenneth Wooden testify, before the House Committee on Human Resources, on the Missing Children Assistance Act.

May — Hearings on child sexual abuse victims in the courts before the Specter subcommittee. Witnesses include Kee MacFarlane and Lael Rubin, both involved in the investigation of the McMartin case, and Paula Hawkins.

August — Specter subcommittee begins hearings on pornography, child abuse, child molestation, and problems of conduct against women.

October — Missing Children's Assistance Act passed; creates National Center for Missing and Exploited Children.

November — Hearings on child pornography and pedophilia before the Senate Permanent Subcommittee on Investigations.

Father Rape

Although few doubted the basic truth of the remarkable statistics of sexual exploitation, there was disagreement over the identity of the perpetrators. Congressional hearings directed their ire toward strangers—molesters and abductors, sex killers and pedophile rings—and these were the targets identified by both conservative activists and law-enforcement agencies. The professional literature, however, changed the focus of concern from strangers to family members, the most common setting for attacks from deserted parks and public restrooms to the family home. The problem was incest, not stranger rape. Perceptions of an intimate danger had already emerged in the professional literature during the 1960s, when Gebhard and his colleagues had remarked, "Contrary to general opinion and to parental fears, it seems that the immature female is more vulnerable to adult friends and acquaintances than to mythical strangers lurking in concealment." As American Humane Association studies confirmed, molesters were neighbors or family acquaintances, whose acts reflected opportunism rather than sophisticated planning or stalking.[32]

Feminists made this doctrine of intimate danger central to their analysis of sexual offenses. In 1975, Susan Brownmiller's classic study of rape, *Against Our Will*, included a section on the frequency of "father rape" as part of "the absolute dictatorship of father rule," and during the 1977 child porn crisis, *Ms.* magazine published an article entitled "Incest: Sexual Abuse Begins at Home." The devastating consequences of incest were examined by the 1979 book *Betrayal of Innocence* and also by a spate of articles in magazines like the *Ladies' Home Journal*. Around this time, 16 percent of Russell's sample reported incestuous abuse before the age of eighteen—4.5 percent of the total by fathers, the remainder mainly by uncles, brothers, and male first cousins. In the 1980s, abuse literature increasingly noted activity by symbolic fathers, including clergymen and other male authority figures close to the family. By 1984, "incest survivor" Katherine Brady could tell Specter's committee, "There is an incest epidemic in America. . . . One out of four girls, before she reaches thirteen in America, she is sexually molested by fathers, stepfathers, uncles."[33]

Feminist works on rape had drawn on autobiography as a means of permitting women to discuss their experiences and to assist others who had suffered similarly, and this genre of survivor writings was taken up by the rising movement against incest and child abuse. Louise Armstrong's *Kiss Daddy Goodnight* (1978) was a pioneering "Speakout on Incest," and it appeared the same year as the bleak account of physical abuse and emotional neglect in Cristina Crawford's *Mommie Dearest*, which was filmed in 1981. Both books stressed the presence of child maltreatment in middle- or upper-class environments, where it was rarely noted by child-protection agencies. Memoirs that recounted incest now proliferated, among them Katherine Brady's *Father's Days* (1979) and the collection of essays *I Never Told Anyone* (1983). These writings confirmed the feminist view of the patriarchal family as the scene of gender conflict and exploitation, a setting for sexual assault and domestic violence.[34]

If an unimaginably vast epidemic of sexual abuse within the family had remained unnoticed before the late 1970s, the feminist movement was authentically revolutionary in its attack on the pervasive secrecy of patriarchal society. The imagery of secrecy and exposé was reflected in the titles of the books that now began to pour forth from publishers: Florence Rush's *Best-Kept Secret* (1980), Sandra Butler's *Conspiracy of Silence* (1978), Diana Russell's *Secret Trauma* (1986), Robert Geiser's *Hidden Victims* (1979).[35] For activists, "denial" was a public scandal little less appalling than the sexual abuse itself.

Claims about proliferating sexual violence echoed the ideas of the late 1940s, but there were significant differences between the two eras. Although an observer from the earlier period would have had no difficulty in comprehending a sex psychopath like John Wayne Gacy, much of the modern literature on sex crime emphasized the activity not of singularly evil beings but of quite ordinary men who were often quite literally part of the family.

Concepts of the motivation of sex offenders were transformed. In earlier years, rapists and molesters were believed to possess not only abnormally high sex drives but also low social status and poor interpersonal skills, which prevented them from gratifying their desires through consensual interactions. Even in the 1940s, a few writers had seen rape and abuse as a matter of power, aggression, and violence, but this was strictly a minority view until the 1970s, when feminists stressed that offenders scarcely differed from ordinary men in their sexual urges. Activists denied that rape was a sex crime. Given the appropriate circumstances, any man subjected to the constant barrage of sexual and misogynist messages from society and the media could become an exploiter of the most brutal kind. For feminists, sex crimes occurred not because of abnormalities in pathological individuals but because of the patriarchal ideologies of the society as a whole, and it was unacceptable to suggest any degree of connivance or provocation by the victim. In Russell's view, the prevalence of violent crime "points to a critical problem in the collective male psyche that is proving lethal to women and to men alike. . . . This culture's notion of masculinity—particularly as it is applied to male sexuality—predisposes men to violence, to rape, to sexually harass, and to sexually abuse children." Indeed, "males are socialized with a predatory approach to obtaining sexual gratification."[36]

In 1951, Howard Whitman's jeremiad had depicted women and children as facing a pandemic threat from sex criminals, but none of the dozens of specific cases that he described involved assaults by intimates: virtually every instance was blamed on a drifter or a stranger who was a pedophile or psychopath. In the new view, women and girls were most at risk from men whom they not only knew but probably had close relationships with. The sour perception that "every man is a potential rapist" was validated when Brownmiller showed how randomly chosen men became sexual exploiters when the opportunity arose (in her study, during wartime or while confined in prison). By 1991, the *New York Times* was reporting as accepted fact the view that "few [rapists] are sexual renegades driven by hate; most are ordinary men acting on impulse." The question about recorded sex offenses was not so much why they occurred but why so very few of the millions that took place resulted in a formal report, arrest, and conviction. By 1986, Shirley O'Brien could write, "By conservative estimate, there are four million child molesters within the United States population today." This estimate expands the meaning of the term *molester* from its customary sense of a man who repeatedly assaults children to include any man who has ever performed such an act; other authorities broadened this definition still further. Dr. Gene Abel, an expert on the treatment of sex offenders, opined that "pedophiles make up one percent of the population; this works out to 1.8 million pedophiles in the United States."[37] Sex fiends were far more commonplace than even J. Edgar Hoover had dreamed.

Opinions about the potential harm wrought by sexual abuse changed quite as dramatically as the estimates of incidence had. While the common pattern of molestation went far beyond mere exposure or fondling and might involve anal or genital rape, even the lesser types of contact were seen as ruinous. Dismissive earlier comments like those of Tappan now appeared callous, as the new view asserted the devastating and lifelong consequences of even brief or isolated sexual impropriety committed against minors, even though researchers were far from unanimous that such acts caused the extreme, long-term harm implied by activists. Again, the roots of this change could be found in the 1969 AHA report, which argued that even where victims had allegedly contributed to molestation, there were still signs of grave long-term effects.[38]

The change of attitude is suggested by the term *survivor* as applied to victims of rape, incest, or sexual abuse, with the implication that they had passed through an ordeal comparable to that of a natural disaster or homicidal attack and that the experience would define much of the rest of their lives; hitherto, the term had been most commonly used in the context of cancer survivors, those who had overcome bouts with the disease. The rhetoric of survival disarmed potential criticism of the victim and demanded public sympathy; also, describing an individual as a survivor implies that others had not been lucky enough to retain their lives. After the mid-1980s, in what can almost be seen as a second wave of the movement against sexual abuse, offering treatment for incest survivors was seen as a major responsibility of the therapeutic professions.

Belief in the lasting damage caused by abuse contributed to raising public and political awareness of the issue and the sense of urgency in finding remedies. Abuse victims were believed to be at high risk to become juvenile delinquents or adult violent criminals. Therapists argued that abused children often grew up to become child abusers themselves or the wives of abusers, conniving in crimes against a new generation of children. The notion of the abused become abuser acquired the name of the "vampire" theory, an example of the imagery of monstrosity and contagious evil so often found in the literature on sexual offenses.[39] When this image was linked to the assessment that serial molesters assaulted large numbers of victims in their careers, the implications were terrifying.

Momentum

The ferment of ideas in the professional and activist literatures was popularized through numerous articles in the news media at a time when media values were in rapid transition. There was a shift toward sensationalist coverage in many news sources: the major television networks began offering news programs modeled on the tabloid press, talk shows that featured prurient topics, and true-crime documentaries that blurred the lines between fact and fiction, and local news stations followed the lead offered by network programming. In 1984, NBC's highly rated documentary *Silent*

Shame presented an apocalyptic exposé of the hazards of child abuse and child pornography and prostitution, and the show was praised in congressional hearings for raising public awareness of the problems.[40]

Made-for-television movies offer a useful index of changing perceptions of social problems and menaces. To a higher degree than cinema productions, these films are often tailored to currently fashionable concerns, and the gap between a specific incident or outrage and the release of the television movie responding to it can be only a few months. Although critical response to these films is mixed, with slighting references to their slavish treatment of the "victim of the month," the vast audiences they sometimes win suggest that producers are accurately judging public tastes. In the 1970s, popular television movies reflected contemporary fears over both rape (*A Case of Rape,* 1974) and child battering (*Mary Jane Harper Cried Last Night,* 1977).

In various mutations, the child abuse issue would be a perennial of this genre over the next decade. The Emmy-nominated *Fallen Angel* (1981) set the tone for later productions with its account of a seemingly benevolent family friend who proves to be a covert pedophile and child pornographer. In October 1983, NBC's *Adam* dramatized the case of Adam Walsh and emphasized the relevance of the study by a linked feature on the plight of missing children. In early 1984, *Something About Amelia* studied incest in an outwardly respectable middle-class family, a theme reprised in *Kids Don't Tell* (1985). Public response to these presentations was overwhelming, especially to *Amelia,* which precipitated thousands of telephone calls reporting experiences of abuse.[41] Sensing a winning streak, the networks persisted in abuse-related topics: *The Atlanta Child Murders* (1985) reminded the audience of the perils of serial child murder, and the sexual exploitation of runaway children was the subject of *Children of the Night* (1985), *Children of Times Square* (1986), and *South Bronx Heroes* (1986). Efforts to detect and apprehend pedophiles were the subject of the 1986 films *When the Bough Breaks* and *A Child's Cry*. Neither of these works, incidentally, drew its hero from the traditional cast of police or detective characters: child abuse was exposed in the two works by, respectively, a child psychologist and a social worker. In movie theaters, a popular feature of 1984 was *Nightmare on Elm Street,* which featured the demonic figure of Freddie Krueger, a child molester murdered by a group of vigilante mothers but who returned from the grave to take his revenge on the living.

Changed perceptions of the problem are indicated by the words used to report sexual offenses against children. By the late 1960s, the *Reader's Guide* listed sexual acts against children under "child molestation," while the term "child abuse" signified physical violence and was cross-referenced to "cruelty to children." The category of child abuse swelled dramatically in 1977 and simultaneously acquired a distinctly sexual theme. Over the next decade, the volume of coverage of abuse and molestation grew dramatically. The years 1984–86 produced 164 entries on child abuse and child molesting, compared to only three or four in a comparable period of the mid-1970s. Characteristic titles from 1984 alone included "The Cruelest Crime" (*Life*), "An Epidemic of Child Abuse" and "A Hidden Epidemic" (both *Newsweek*), "The Chilling Facts About Sexual Abuse" (*Glamour*), and "Child Molesting: The Sad New Facts of Life" (*Reader's Digest*).[42] In the *New York Times,* the index heading of "child abuse" appeared as a separate subcategory of "children and youth" in the early 1970s and swelled after the pivotal year 1977. In 1983, child abuse became a separate topic in its own right, with a column and a half of entries in the newspaper's annual index. The following year, this entry ran to nine columns— over three pages of densely packed references. By this point, child sexual abuse was one of the leading social issues reported in the mass media, and the level of interest has been more or less sustained up to the present day.

Child abuse was widely discussed in educational programs, and popular magazines now reinvented the once popular 1950s genre of advising parents how to protect children from molesters. Pamphlets and self-help books were aimed at both children and parents, with titles like *No More Secrets, It's MY Body, It's OK to Say No,* and *Please Tell!* In 1985, the peak year for these efforts, the hugely popular children's authors Stan and Jan Berenstain produced *The Berenstain Bears Learn About Strangers,* and Winnie the Pooh encountered suspicious outsiders in the Disney cartoon *Too Smart for Strangers.* Kenneth Wooden's *Child Lures* purported to reveal the tactics commonly used by molesters and abductors, the title suggesting the potent image of children as potential prey requiring protection from hunters. Pamphlets and reports flowed from official agencies like the NCMEC, which placed photographs of missing children on milk cartons. This constant barrage of materials could not but sensitize parents to threats. By the mid-1980s, opinion surveys were showing vastly heightened awareness of threats to children, whether from sexual molestation, kidnapping, or child pornography.[43]

Presuming Guilt

A revolutionary shift in social attitudes inevitably had legal implications. The new assumption was that abuse charges were never made falsely and that accusations were almost invariably justified; the movement came close to demanding a presumption of a defendant's guilt where sex crime was concerned. In the late 1980s, for instance, legal controversies surrounded women involved in custody disputes who claimed that their former husbands had abused their children and who thus refused to permit the men to exercise court-granted visitation rights. In one case, a doctor named Elizabeth Morgan was jailed for several years for contempt of court when she refused to reveal the whereabouts of her daughter. The media largely portrayed Morgan as a heroine defending her child, a feminist prisoner of conscience. Also lionized was Faye Yager, whose Children of the Underground organized safe houses for children escaping from the custody of allegedly abusive fathers and was characterized as a modern-day Underground Railroad.[44] Such cases illustrated a now-familiar theme: courts and law-enforcement agencies had failed to appreciate the scale of child abuse, partly because of their patriarchal biases and assumptions, and the inadequate legal system must be reformed or, in extreme cases, resisted in pursuit of the higher goal of child protection.

At the height of the abuse panic of the mid-1980s, new legislation poured forth at both federal and state levels, with measures to protect missing or abused children, register sex offenders, and investigate day care centers. These laws reflected the view that a war on child abuse necessitated extreme measures and perhaps the sacrifice of liberties, especially in the courtroom. Children's testimony was pivotal to most molestation cases, but the courts were historically suspicious of their reliability as witnesses. As had often been noted in earlier decades, young children were deemed unfit to testify, while older ones were liable to cross-examination in hostile and potentially traumatizing circumstances, which could be seen as a "second molestation." Following the collapse of the Jordan mass abuse case during the mid-1980s (Chapter 8), this unsympathetic environment was seen as a major obstacle to the successful prosecution of molesters, and the *New York Times* carried disturbing coverage of "the jeopardy of children on the stand."[45]

At the same time, it became an article of faith among child abuse experts and child advocates that children's testimony was almost invariably truthful. Research on the capacity of children to report truthfully at different developmental stages was believed to show that children virtually never lied when making allegations of sexual abuse and that charges were all the more plausible when very young children, who lacked knowledge about sexuality, offered detailed testimony about the actions of an accused molester. The younger the child, however, the greater the need for expert assistance to elicit his or her evidence. A whole new professional field of therapists specialized in the detection and treatment of sexual abuse, and these individuals developed an unprecedented role in producing and presenting a child's testimony.[46]

In the 1980s, new state laws removed the obligation that child witnesses confront the individuals against whom they were testifying. Some permitted children to give testimony from behind screens or through the medium of closed-circuit television, and a few sought to reduce the ability of counsel to undertake hostile interrogation or cross-examination.[47] Although intended to assist child victims, these special conditions could not fail to raise questions about exactly why children needed to be protected from defendants, whose guilt was self-evident. Laws offering protections to "victims" assume that victimization really has occurred, which is usually a point to be determined by a jury. In the Jordan cases, which attracted so much unfavorable publicity, defense attorneys were performing their proper task in attacking a prosecution now widely agreed to have been false in almost every particular. Equally controversial was evidence drawn from a child with the assistance of therapists, who often used tactics like play therapy, at best a novel approach in the legal environment, and leading questions were regularly employed in such sessions. Could testimony be presented by the child with the direct assistance of the therapist? Or, as some reformers advocated, could the therapist present testimony at secondhand, without bringing the child into the courtroom at all? From one point of view, the reforms provided safeguards for brutally abused children; from another, the legal maneuvers destroyed the protections of innocent people charged by cynical prosecutors on the evidence of elaborately coached toddlers.

Reforms received a mixed reception from a divided Supreme Court, but enough of the new laws withstood challenge to alter substantially the legal environment of child abuse cases. In 1988, the Court heard the case of *Coy v. Iowa,* in which a man accused of molesting two thirteen-year-old girls was tried under a law that permitted child victims to testify from behind screens. A majority of justices agreed that this provision violated the Sixth

Amendment to the Constitution, which requires that defendants be confronted with witnesses against them. Justice Antonin Scalia agreed that
face-to-face confrontation might be a difficult experience for crime victims, "but by the same token, it may confound and undo the false accuser
or reveal the child coached by a malevolent adult." Doubts about victim
shield laws were overcome in the 1990 decision in *Maryland v. Craig*. Sandra Craig was convicted of abusing a six-year-old girl, following a trial in
which the girl testified from outside the courtroom by means of closed-circuit television and was examined in the same location by both prosecution
and defense. Craig based her appeal on the Sixth Amendment grounds that
had been successful in *Coy*, but the Supreme Court held that the right to
confrontation was not absolute and was qualified by the "state's interest in
the . . . well-being of child abuse victims." The decision emerged from a
sharply divided court (which split five to four), with the minority arguing
that granting an exception to constitutional protections was a perilous
precedent. Two years later, the emphasis shifted yet again, when *Coy v.
White* found once more that although a child might suffer trauma in judicial proceedings, this consequence did not outweigh the necessity for a fair
trial.[48] These fluctuating divisions reflected a fundamental conflict over
the perceived threat of child exploitation and how far the interests of child
witnesses and victims should override legal principles.

The child-protection movement was immensely successful in establishing
its views as a component of social orthodoxy and winning acceptance from
virtually all ideological camps. The events of 1977 had shown that no policy would be seen as too severe in combating a vast and unqualified evil like
child abuse, or any issue that could be plausibly related to it, while no political benefit was to be found in opposing or questioning such measures.
If anything, concern became even more intense during the next decade.
The new environment raised opportunities for diverse interest groups,
who were able to employ this solid consensus as a basis for making claims
about other social issues. Other forms of behavior could be stigmatized and
legislated against by being mapped together with the phenomenon of child
abuse and molestation, whether that other activity was homosexuality,
pornography, or sex education. Each was contextualized within the frame-
work of the now established problem of child abuse. Traditionalist groups
believed that growing tolerance for homosexuality would increase the incidence of pedophilia, just as feminists and antipornography activists be-

lieved that explicit sexual material would provoke men to assault children. Guilt by association with child abuse was not a cynical rhetorical tactic, but in practical terms these linkages made threats to children a foundation for intense activism during the next two decades. Debates over such dangers as child pornography, pedophile rings, and ritual or satanic abuse would always have these pervasive moral and political subtexts.

Child Pornography and Pedophile Rings

Sex before eight or it's too late.

—SLOGAN OF THE RENÉ GUYON SOCIETY

I can only imagine that all that had happened to her must have seemed utterly hideous,
a deathlike horror.

—STAVROGIN'S CONFESSION IN DOSTOYEVSKY'S *THE DEVILS*, 1871

The child pornography issue was critical to redefining views of abuse and molestation. This material escalated the perceived threat from molesters, who could no longer be depicted as confused individuals succumbing to a warped impulse: that they were photographing or filming children in sexual contexts suggested the deliberate, repetitive, and premeditated quality of the activity.[1] The commercial gain obtained from the ventures showed that molesters were dehumanizing children, treating them as commodities to be bought and sold: so much for boasts of "boy-love" and "intergenerational intimacy." Beginning in the late 1970s, child pornography was depicted as such an unqualified social threat that its mere possession was harshly penalized, a stigma hitherto reserved for the most dangerous addictive drugs. The changing scope of the laws criminalized an ever-increasing number of individuals, permitting police and media to portray an ongoing crime wave. In reality, child porn was never manufactured domestically on any large scale after the 1970s, and continuing arrests and seizures could be sustained only by steadily expanding the definitions of what was illegal and by emphasizing the role of pornography consumers rather than only the makers or distributors. This expansion assimilated anyone connected with the use of child pornography, however tenuously, with the predatory activity of actual pedophiles and child sex rings.

The assumption was that photographs and videos would be shared or sold through widespread vice networks. The phenomenon of pornography rings became linked in the public mind with the idea of the pedophile as an organized career criminal, a violent predator who was potentially capable of abduction and serial homicide and who usually hunted in packs. The scandals of the early 1980s led law-enforcement agencies and the media to suggest that child pornography was often the work of organized pedophiles and that pedophiles, individually and in rings, molested large numbers of children, sometimes abducting their victims. Although a new departure in the stereotype of the molester, the sex ring idea developed immense force and retained a grasp on the public imagination long after the most extreme charges concerning these operations were discredited.

Obscene or indecent pictures of children have been taken virtually since the invention of photography. In the early 1970s, pornographic pictures and films of children became widely available in the United States: much was imported from Europe, especially from the Netherlands and Scandinavia, but some was manufactured domestically, often disguised as imports to evade the attentions of law-enforcement agencies. The market was divided between pictures of "moppets" (young children between the ages of three and eleven) and "lolitas" (aged roughly nine to fourteen): although most depicted nudity and genital display, some showed children engaged in sexual acts, both with each other and with adults. By mid-decade, typical publications available in larger cities included titles like *Children-Love, Lollitots,* and *Nudist Moppets.*[2]

Following the initial exposés in 1977, attacks on child pornography remained a media staple through the next decade. The financial element augmented the sensational appeal of notorious cases like that of the McMartin preschool (see Chapter 8) and added a motive that was more comprehensible for a public still reluctant to believe that adults could exploit children sexually. About child porn the media presented startling claims and statis-

tics, many of them derived from guesses or vague estimates by child advocates. One of the most powerful stemmed from Robin Lloyd's assertion
that 300,000 boys in the United States were involved in selling sex; Judianne Densen-Gerber extrapolated that a like number of underage girls
were probably involved in prostitution or pornography, creating a victim
population of at least 600,000 nationwide. Local activists produced still
more implausible figures, claiming that 120,000 children in the New York
City area were "involved in some type of sexual activity for money." Lloyd
Martin claimed "that 3,000 children under age 14 and more than 25,000 in
the 14 to 17 age group are being exploited sexually by at least 17,000 adults
in the Los Angeles area," figures that grew vastly in subsequent retellings.
Martin also spoke of a clandestine form of child pornography in which victims were murdered, and he suggested that recently discovered bodies
might be the results of child snuff films.[3]

These speculative ideas gained visibility from frequent citation within
the same small group of child advocates, and they would often be mis-
quoted in the antipornography literature. In 1985, an exposé of "the shame
of the nation" in a family magazine noted "a dramatic increase in child sexual abuse over the past five years in this country, at least half of them involving children compelled to participate in the making of pornography.
According to one Los Angeles Police Department estimate, at least
300,000 children under the age of 16 are involved in the nationwide child
pornography racket." This problem was connected with "even more dramatic increases in the number of missing children" and "ever-widening
child pornography distribution rings that are making unprecedented profits." In 1986, antipornography crusader Donald Wildmon claimed that
"each year, fifty thousand missing children are victims of pornography.
Most are kidnapped, raped, abused, filmed for porno magazines and
movies and, more often than not, murdered." In 1988, supporters of a National Pornography Awareness Week announced that "300,000 children
are sexually abused each year to produce child pornography." In 1988, the
authors of *The Courage to Heal* used Densen-Gerber's figures to assert that
"between 500,000 and one million children are involved in prostitution and
pornography in this country; a high percentage of them are victims of incest." An investigative series in the *Christian Science Monitor* claimed that
between 100,000 and 300,000 children were working as prostitutes in
North America.[4]

Activists gave extremely high estimates for the scale of the child porn industry, and Lloyd's estimate that there were 264 child pornography magazine titles available was retold years after the figure had ceased to approximate reality; in some accounts, it became a claim that 264 child porn magazines were being published each and every month. Another recurrent legend held that child pornography was an industry with annual revenues of $5 billion. Even in the mid-1970s, child pornography activity would more properly be characterized as at most a multimillion-dollar industry, but the figure claiming revenues in the billions circulated until the next decade, when it was derided by the FBI's leading expert in this area.[5]

True or not, such statistics had a horrifying power that sustained public fury, offering a compelling rhetorical weapon to morality campaigners who juxtaposed claims about child pornography with attacks on other forms of explicit literature. In the 1985 hearings of the Meese commission, statements about "the special horror of child pornography" were followed by claims about how "regular" adult pornography contributed to sex crimes, molestation, and child prostitution. One witness reported how his own obsessions with obscene material led him to molest two fourteen-year-old girls. Adapting these claims, one antipornography advertisement declared that "police records show that pornography is directly involved or specifically imitated in 41 percent of sex crimes investigated. . . . In communities where pornography has been eliminated, incidents of rape and assault have decreased as much as 83 percent." Another averred that 77 percent of child molesters of boys and 87 percent of child molesters of girls "admit imitating sexual behavior seen in pornography." Supported by visible activists like Father Bruce Ritter of New York's Covenant House, moral conservatives of the Reagan era tried to portray "the greatest needs of disenfranchised youth" not as confronting poverty or poor education but as moral enforcement and "stronger antipornography legislation."[6]

The belief that child pornography represented both the direct product and the immediate cause of criminality made it easy to enlist support for suppression, and legislation passed in these years had broad implications for public attitudes to other forms of indecency and obscenity. During the 1970s, the availability of sexually explicit material became a major source of grievance for moral conservatives, while feminists campaigned against pornography on the grounds that it degraded women. In the mid-1980s, feminists and traditionalists formed an unlikely coalition to pass antipornography ordinances in several cities.[7] The Meese Pornography Commission aired opinions about the demoralization and physical harm caused by the material, including the idea that "pornography is the theory, rape is the practice." The courts, however, remained unsympathetic to attempts to pass stringent legislation and drew a vital distinction between merely indecent or offensive material, which was constitutionally protected, and obscene items, which could be prosecuted. In practice, juries proved hard to convince that specific examples of adult sexual material were in fact obscene, and depictions of nudity, intercourse, and many types of sexual "perversion" therefore continued to circulate freely.

But tolerance by courts and the general public ended where children were concerned, and most favored the repression of items that would have been deemed merely indecent or even just suggestive had they depicted adult subjects. The debate over child pornography largely supported the decency campaigners' assertion that this material directly caused criminal acts—that the images stimulated consumers to reproduce acts with other children and possibly to use pornographic pictures in order to entice youngsters. The protection of children justified the revival and expansion of antiobscenity laws that otherwise might have fallen into disuse. Realizing the political potential of this cause, antipornography campaigners throughout the 1980s systematically enhanced the scope of child-protection legislation as a means of attacking the "mainstream" sex industry. As Catherine MacKinnon asked, if child pornography "speech" could be subject to penal sanction under the First Amendment, why should the same rule not apply to all adult pornography?[8] If we concede that one is the actual cause of criminality, why not the other?

The legal environment concerning sexual imagery of children became progressively harsher. The initial Protection of Children Against Sexual Exploitation Act of 1978 prohibited the manufacture or commercial distribution of obscene material involving subjects under sixteen years of age. Several later acts increased penalties and expanded the powers of law-enforcement agencies to seek out and suppress this material. In 1984, Senator Arlen Specter sponsored the radical Child Protection Act: publicized by sensational hearings before his subcommittee, the act removed the requirement that a given image depict a child actually participating in sexual activity, opening the way to prosecuting material that was merely indecent, rather than obscene, and virtually removing the whole category from First Amendment protection. It also raised the age of a minor for these purposes from sixteen to eighteen, at a stroke extending the status of child to about 7 million American adolescents. The courts upheld the progressive expansion of the child pornography label: in 1982, the key Supreme Court decision in *New York v. Ferber* rejected constitutional challenges to the special standards of indecency applied in child pornography cases and agreed that the government had "compelling" and "surpassing" interests in the protection of children. By the 1990s, child pornography was defined as "visual depiction . . . of a minor engaging in sexually explicit conduct," including "lascivious exhibition of the genitals or pubic area of any person," a characterization that, where adults were concerned, would result only in a charge of indecency.[9]

Although sexual material involving adults implicated only the manufacturers or distributors, the net of liability was cast much more widely where performers were minors. A crime was committed by anyone who "knowingly receives or distributes" or "knowingly possesses" images, in addition to anyone who made or sold them. In the 1990 case of *Osborne v. Ohio*, the Supreme Court agreed that private possession in the home, in this instance of a photograph of a "nude male adolescent," should be criminalized. Although a precedent defended the private possession of obscene matter, conviction was justified in order to protect "the victims of child pornography" and to destroy "a market for the exploitative use of children"; the decision was widely criticized for its troubling implications for privacy rights.[10] As in the *Craig* case of that year, the decision accepted the radical notion that child protection took precedence over older constitutional assumptions.

If child pornography as such was indefensible, the only means of protest or criticism concerned not the laws themselves but their procedural flaws or their overreach into matters only tangentially connected with the protection of children. One controversy concerned the defendant's knowledge that pornographic images in his possession were images of a minor—in legal terms, whether intent or *mens rea* was required to prove commission of a criminal act. No doubts applied where subjects were toddlers or infants, of course, but when a subject was closer to the cutoff age of eighteen years, it could be hard to determine whether possessing a given picture was legal or not. One of the most popular porn stars of the 1980s was Traci Lords, who later revealed that she had begun her career at the age of fifteen; at that moment her early work suddenly became child pornography, and the retroactive reclassification resulted in the conviction of one of the distributors of her films. But in 1992, a federal appeals court overturned laws that failed to require proof of guilty knowledge concerning age. Although the Supreme Court salvaged most of the legislation, the justices agreed that the government had to prove that a defendant knew he was dealing with underage materials.[11] Equally troubling for the question of intent was a 1996 law that defined child pornography in terms of sexual images of what was *or what appeared to be* a child, a response to computer techniques that synthesized images of multiple individuals to create a "virtual child." But appeared to whom? This element of subjective definition gave enormous discretion to prosecutors.

And if "children" were hard to define for criminal purposes, so was pornography, and there were recurrent debates over portrayals of young people in artistic or educational contexts. An early casualty of the laws was the popular 1970s sex education manual *Show Me!* which had to be withdrawn by its publisher because of its pictures of nude children. In 1990, successful family photographer Jock Sturges became the target of an investigation of his images of naked children and families. Not only were Sturges's images made without obscene or lascivious intent, but they were no more revealing or more provocative than those found in the long tradition of western painting or sculpture or, more recently, in much advertising copy, and official action in this case raised the danger that authorities might prohibit virtually any suspect image of a young person. The French winemaker Mouton Rothschild withdrew from the American market a label featuring a drawing of a nude ten-year-old girl. The remarkable discovery that pornography could extend to clothed subjects led to *Knox v. United States* (1993), in which a man was imprisoned for possessing suggestive videotapes depicting scantily clad young girls, with the camera focusing on "lascivious exhibition" of their genital areas. When the Justice Department suggested that the videos were not in fact prohibited under existing laws, a political firestorm developed, with conservatives protesting that the administration of President Bill Clinton was defending child pornography. Desperate to avoid the appearance of being lax on the issue, the president launched a personal campaign for strict enforcement even in this marginal area. In 1995, Calvin Klein advertisements depicting clothed young people in suggestive poses were threatened with prosecution as child pornography. By 1997, attention shifted once more to the Sturges images, as morality protesters tore pages out of copies of his books on store shelves and demanded that Barnes and Noble and other retailers be prosecuted for distributing child pornography.[12]

Publishers, booksellers, and libraries encountered a nightmare situation. As a legal critic noted following the *Knox* decision, "There are in mainstream bookstores and libraries around the country thousands and thousands of images of clothed children that some people might consider pornographic, erotic, or suggestive."[13] *Show Me!* is still available in hundreds of libraries, though its possession theoretically opens the institutions to prosecution subject to the whim of any decency group or police officer. Nor did artistic merit or intent offer the defense that it would with adult obscenity, and in a notorious 1997 case, local police purged Oklahoma City's video stores of all copies of the Oscar-winning film *The Tin Drum*. The prohibition against visual images might even extend to mail-order catalogs with photographs showing children in underwear. Arguably, every parent who has ever taken photographs of his or her naked infant is liable under the laws.

The legal status of child pornography created a favorable environment for investigators and prosecutors: because the behavior was all but universally detested, action against it earned praise from superiors and the media, while excesses would be tolerated. Capitalizing on this public mood in 1990, the Justice Department's embattled obscenity unit changed its name to a more politically popular one: the Child Exploitation and Obscenity Section. Prosecutions were far more likely to succeed here than in the near-impossible area of adult obscenity, since all that was required after 1984 was to show that an individual knowingly possessed indecent or explicit material involving minors. Moreover, the existence of one contraband item opened the way for a search warrant that might well produce further illegal material.

Several federal agencies became proactive in investigating cases, notably the U.S. Customs Service and the Postal Service. The number of investigations undertaken by the Customs Service's Child Pornography and Protection Unit rose from twelve in all of 1983 to 220 during the first eight months of 1986. In 1996, the Postal Inspection Service could announce that, since 1984, "postal Inspectors have conducted over 2,600 investigations, resulting in the arrests and conviction of more than 2,200 individuals for trafficking in child pornography through the U.S. Mail." Agencies boasted of cases in which the pursuit of indecent material prevented the actual molestation of children, and a special Customs campaign in 1988, Operation Borderline, was touted as leading to the arrest of twenty-four molesters.[14]

Methods employed by federal agencies often came perilously close to entrapment. In 1992, the Supreme Court overturned the conviction of Nebraska farmer Keith Jacobson, who had ordered adult homosexual-oriented materials through the mails. Guessing that he would be likely to purchase child pornography, undercover Postal Service agents bombarded him with invitations to buy such articles; when he finally succumbed, he was charged with illegal possession. In this case, not only was federal action judged to be entrapment, but Jacobson was even the subject of sympathetic coverage on *60 Minutes* and in the *Washington Post,* and a *New York Times* editorial discussed his case in a piece entitled "Entrapment Out of Control."[15]

The latitude granted to law enforcement is important for our understanding of the degree of criminal organization actually involved in the child pornography trade, for had sophisticated or corporate-style enterprises existed, they would certainly have been detected by these task forces and special units. Despite all the individual cases uncovered in these years, however, little evidence emerged of large-scale networks, and most cases involved strictly domestic productions by local entrepreneurs, often just one or two adults. One rare exception was an enterprise run by a Los Angeles woman arrested in 1982—a case that was often cited in antipornography literature for years afterwards In 1985, a U.S. Senate committee found that "what commercial child pornography does exist in the United States constitutes a small portion of the overall pornography market and is deeply underground." Even the most vociferous antismut campaigners concurred that "it's the underground industry—the cottage industry—that accounts for the vast bulk of child pornography today." In the mid-1990s, the largest syndicate uncovered by federal authorities had an annual turnover of around half a million dollars, a paltry sum by the standards of gambling or narcotics operations.[16]

Despite all this, those reporting on child pornography cases continued to exaggerate the involvement of criminal syndicates, indiscriminately using terms like *pedophile rings* and *child pornography rings* even when participants were not charged with any direct contact with children. Moreover, police and media spoke of "rings" when dealing with a nebulous grouping of men whose only common activity involved correspondence or sharing indecent materials, purchasing from one supplier, or patronizing the same group of underage prostitutes. This is illustrated by one of the larger federal investigations of recent years, which originated when a man entering the United States from Mexico was arrested for carrying child pornography videos. Although the firm organizing the business was broken up, postal inspectors used its mailing list to send out two thousand solicitations offering videos featuring children between seven and eleven years old. Some of those solicited ordered videos; if they accepted delivery of the tapes, authorities then obtained warrants to search their premises for child pornography. This single investigation led to forty-five arrests in what a headline in the *New York Times* characterized as a "Nationwide Child Pornography Ring," even though most members of the group had never met one another and their only association was having responded to the same mail-order solicitation.[17]

Partly because law-enforcement officials were eager to justify the real harmfulness of the child pornography trade, references to "rings" became steadily more common in the decade after 1977, advancing the idea of the molester as a member of a gang or syndicate. In fact, the best-known academic treatment of this subject is entitled *Child Pornography and Sex Rings,* as if the two phenomena were interchangeable or at the least indissolubly linked. Evidence of organization and commercialization initially grew out of the 1970s investigations of metropolitan networks of underage prostitutes and the chicken hawks who patronized them. Young prostitutes operated through pimps and occasionally served as models for the making of pornography. To the extent that illegal services and materials were disseminated through clandestine networks of clients, both suppliers and consumers of underage sexuality were participating in a financially driven ring, but these networks were very different from the later images of pedophile rings. Underage sex operations exposed in the 1970s employed young people who were participating of their own volition, so there was no question of child abduction or coercion.[18] In addition, such rings grew out of preexisting organized crime activity in prostitution and pornography; operations were not initiated by pedophiles themselves, whose role was that of consumers and customers.

From the late 1970s, claims about child sex rings placed a new emphasis on the pedophiles themselves taking the initiative in syndication. In 1977, the *Chicago Tribune* suggested that kiddie porn was organized through "child sex rackets" which "operate on a national and international scale involving thousands of adult perverts often working with one another and exchanging child victims." Congressional hearings permitted child advocates to cite alleged examples of organized molestation. Lloyd Martin reported a national pedophile ring, which was based in New Orleans, had correspondents throughout the country, and was responsible for "widespread infiltration of adult suspects into all types of national youth groups and youth-oriented organizations: there is nationwide mobility, interaction and communication among adults involved in child exploitation." Michigan prosecutor Robert Leonard concurred with Martin: "The tentacles of this illegal activity form an underground network stretching from New York to California and Michigan to Louisiana. Prosecutors in cities across the country have uncovered and compiled information pointing to a high degree of exchange and communication among those who prey on our children. Seemingly isolated cases of such deviancy reveal a frightening set of sophisticated intercommunications upon closer scrutiny." Summer camps, educational foundations, and churches were said to serve as covers for pornography and molestation.[19]

In the early 1980s, claims about organized molestation were boosted by the support of Ted Gunderson, a former FBI agent who was much cited by writers exploring the world of sex rings. Partly through his influence, child-protection activists described syndicated networks characterized by a hierarchy of organization and a division of labor among those undertaking various tasks from intelligence gathering, victim recruitment, and photography to pimping and perhaps kidnapping and murder. Groups might operate partly for financial motives, with the profits from child pornography, prostitution, and blackmail serving to finance other operations and to bribe law-enforcement officials. If authentic, an organized network of this sort would represent a formidable challenge to social order and an enormous threat to children, who could be targeted, abducted, and enslaved by an powerful conspiracy. In policy terms, it is vastly easier to mobilize resources against a threat portrayed in such terms than against isolated inadequates.

In fiction, the image of pedophiles as well organized and highly placed was reflected by authors like Jonathan Kellerman, Robert Campbell, James N. Frey, and especially Andrew Vachss. Kellerman's *When the Bough Breaks* featured the Gentlemen's Brigade, a voluntary social work group that concealed a network of elite child molesters and "closet sickos." Ron Handberg's *Savage Justice* had as its villain a judge who used pornographic videos to seduce pubescent boys and whose extensive connections enabled him to escape detection and to silence critics, by murder if necessary. The idea entered mainstream literature in Leslie Marmon Silko's *Almanac of the Dead,* which depicted networks of perverts and pedophiles among Anglo whites in a southwestern city's law-enforcement bureaucracy.[20]

Perceptions of a danger from organized pedophiles owed much to the furor inspired by the North American Man-Boy Love Association (NAMBLA), an authentic pressure group that sought to lower or even eliminate the age of consent, permitting sex between men and boys. This grew out of an informal preexisting "pederast underground," and in fact "boy-love" is a literal translation of the Greek term that became the English *pederast*. The decision to create a formalized movement seems remarkable in view of the inevitable violence of the public response, but this should be placed in its historical context. Other movements had been successful in securing the legalization of sexual behaviors that only a few decades earlier would have seemed too indecent even to be raised in public discussion, a process illustrated by public acceptance of abortion, sexually explicit visual or literary materials, contraception, and homosexuality. There was no prima facie reason why a campaign to reduce or eliminate the age of sexual consent should be less successful, especially considering the fact that the argument could be presented in terms of gender equality: several states already permitted girls well below the age of sixteen to be sexually active. When the pioneering gay rights organization known as the Mattachine Society was founded in 1948, at the height of an earlier "pervert panic," its members too seemed to be engaged in a futile and perilous venture. Perhaps time would similarly vindicate those who now sought to legalize "man-boy love" and who would explicitly cite the Mattachine precedent. The legalization of gay sex had seemed quite as unthinkable in 1956 as the tolerance of pedophilia did in 1976: why should one campaign fail where the other succeeded? There were also European precedents for a boy-love movement, notably in the Netherlands and Great Britain.[21]

Formal organization in the United States was a direct response to police efforts to suppress child pornography, which produced a cyclical process of intervention and protest. Under pressure from organizations advocating child protection and public decency, authorities sought out the networks believed responsible for child pornography. The campaign in turn sparked mobilization by pederast-oriented groups, who gained greater public visibility, leading to enhanced public concern and police vigilance. The coincidence of timing in the campaigns against homosexual rights and child pornography in 1977 made it possible to contextualize le-

link the group with other kidnappings and disappearances of small children, including that of a twelve-year-old Iowa boy named Johny Gosch, who had been abducted while on his newspaper delivery route. NAMBLA was depicted as "a group of child kidnappers, pornographers and pimps," and perhaps of child killers, with an "international sex ring" lurking behind the quasi-legitimate front of the civil rights organization. The idea was not ludicrous per se (in both England and Belgium, well-documented pedophile rings active in child abduction, pornography, and murder have recently come to light), but in NAMBLA's case, the evidence was very weak.[26]

Although NAMBLA held a news conference to rebut all charges, the stigma now attached to the group was devastating. Reporting the return of one boy said to have been abducted, *Time* described "the systematic exploitation of the weak and immature by the powerful and disturbed." In March 1983, the FBI and other agencies formed a task force to investigate "the kidnapping and selling of children and their use in porn films, the murder of children and adolescents by kidnappers." The Gosch kidnapping and its alleged link to "organized pedophilia operations" received national publicity during hearings before Arlen Specter's Senate subcommittee. Seeking to show that pedophile groups were active in child abduction, Gosch's family and supporters produced newsletters and interviews from NAMBLA and the René Guyon Society, a tiny and semimythical group that has served as the lightning rod for protests against pedophilia. The Meese Commission urged the creation of a national task force to examine "possible links between sex rings, child pornography and organized crime . . . [and] possible linkages between multi-victim, multi-perpetrator child sex rings throughout the United States."[27]

Although no link was established to high-profile abduction cases, pederast groups were tarnished by suspicions of violence and rape as well as their alleged infiltration of organizations like the Boy Scouts. In 1985, a media exposé of child pornography laid the blame for manufacture on "a thriving underground cottage industry, run mostly by so-called 'sexual freedom' groups that openly advocate sex between adults and children. These groups operate an extensive exchange and classified ad service that circulates child pornography among their members." Once again, NAMBLA and the René Guyon Society were named as culprits. Even the FBI's Kenneth Lanning, a restrained and skeptical commentator, described NAMBLA as "the most dangerous organization of pedophiles in the U.S."

The group was periodically exposed thereafter, though accounts by hostile moles leave the impression of a group with security arrangements so lax that they are difficult to reconcile with charges of serious criminal conspiracy. Conspiratorial themes were however popularized in fictional works like Andrew Vachss's 1985 novel *Flood,* which featured a pedophile villain who had raped a child in a day-care center and was active in the manufacture and sale of child pornography. The book is set in a sordid and violent underworld of teenage prostitution and illegal pornography containing scenes of actual torture and murder. One scene features the fictitious Boundaries Society, which exists to discuss "Intergenerational Sex, the new euphemism for child molesting."[28]

In retrospect, the creation of a formal organization of pederasts or pedophiles was an utterly counterproductive move on its members' part, for the very existence of NAMBLA gave concrete form to the public's most lurid fears about the extent of organized molestation. During the next decade, the group became even more isolated on the radical fringe of sexual and political activism, and its ideas were considered to mark a dangerous extreme with which no reputable group or activist could afford to be associated. Of course, the group attracted the fury of the conservative right, for whom it represented the natural culmination of gay social aspirations. Through these years, conservatives often cited NAMBLA's purported slogan "Sex before eight or it's too late," although in fact this phrase originated with the René Guyon Society. Campaigns against gay rights made extensive use of the supposed association with child molestation and pornography, often quoting and misquoting NAMBLA statements. And polemical material vastly exaggerated the scale of such organizations, claiming a preposterous figure—ten thousand members—for the René Guyon Society.[29]

The link between gays and pedophiles, which proved so rhetorically powerful in the late 1970s, often reemerged in subsequent attempts to weaken or abolish gay rights legislation, especially in state referenda of the early 1990s. In 1993, Christian evangelicals circulated a polemical anti-homosexual film called *The Gay Agenda,* which reported the most bizarre and provocative of the homosexual parades and public statements, and NAMBLA's presence in gay pride marches was used to stigmatize the entire movement. In Louisville, Kentucky, in 1995, antigay television commercials produced by the American Family Association depicted pedophile activists marching with the "sex before eight" slogan on their

the Stonewall protest, a historic event commemorated by parades and public gatherings, but gay and lesbian activists strenuously opposed NAMBLA's participation either in its own right or as a component of the ILGA. Also in 1994, NAMBLA received another devastating, though self-inflicted, blow when pederasts were shown frankly discussing their sexual conquests in the documentary film *Chicken Hawk: Men Who Love Boys,* which received largely negative reviews in both gay and mainstream publications.[34]

Politically, the twin dangers of pedophilia and child pornography provided powerful ammunition for conservative interests, who could focus public concern about child endangerment on these forms of stranger danger, the outside menace, rather than the subversive doctrine of mass intrafamilial abuse. Successive laws passed to regulate child pornography also advanced conservative notions of obscenity and indecency, using these concepts to harass an adult sex industry that seemed immune to other legal challenges. Although these endeavors produced sweeping legal changes, resistance was difficult because of the broad consensus that they commanded in the media and among the public at large. This posed difficulties for libertarians as well as for gay rights groups, none of whom wished to be associated, however distantly or implausibly, with the loathed pedophiles and child pornographers. By constructing an enemy that was literally indefensible, the most conservative wing of the child-protection movement thus secured an ideological victory that resonates to this day.

The Road to Hell

RITUAL ABUSE AND RECOVERED MEMORY

And we also pray that we may be considered candidly and aright by the living sufferers as being then under the power of a strong and general delusion, utterly unacquainted with and not experienced in matters of that nature.

—APOLOGY OF THE SALEM JURORS, 1697

Who is stalking your children for Satan?

—PAT PULLING, 1989

The media's linkage of child pornography and organized abuse escalated the perception of not only the threat posed by pedophiles but also the urgency of devising effective law-enforcement strategies. And while child-protection advocates initially benefited ideologically from the exposure of organized molestation, the credibility of their ideas suffered when it was found that the existence of many pedophile rings had been postulated on the basis of weak evidence and were subsequently disproved.

In recent years, this fate has befallen a whole subset of claims about pedophile rings engaged in "satanic and ritualistic abuse," or SRA. In the late 1970s, investigators became willing to accept children's testimony as objectively accurate, even when it was elicited by questionable investigative techniques. Reluctance to doubt victim testimony induced investigators to accept as authentic outlandish stories of bizarre abuse and torture and to make sense of them in the only way that seemed possible—by presuming that the atrocities were the work of ritualistic cults. Other evidence of sinister practices arose from memories that adult survivors of abuse recovered during therapy, and here, too, the fantastic accounts seemed explicable only within the larger narrative of cult rituals.

The difficulty was that charges of ritual abuse would ultimately be tested in a legal environment, with its radically different attitudes about what constitutes convincing evidence. Within a few years, advocates of the reality of SRA and the validity of recovered memories were faltering on every front, raising fears that the debacle would destroy public credibility in the child sexual abuse problem as it had been defined since the late 1970s. In the early 1990s, the media continued to report abuse stories with as much enthusiasm as they had a decade before, but now with a major change of perception. In the new genre, the therapist investigating a case was no longer depicted as a selfless crusader against child exploitation but as a fanatical witch-hunter, irresponsibly inventing wild charges that set child against parent and that persecuted the innocent.

The years 1993 and 1994 marked by far the sharpest criticisms of how the issue of child sexual abuse had been defined and approached since the mid-1970s. The stage was set for a reformulation of the abuse problem, one still recognizing that children were vulnerable to molestation but now reconceiving the perpetrators as outsiders and predators.

Creating Ritual Abuse

The ritual abuse phenomenon grew out of two powerful trends in the child abuse movement, namely, the quest for pedophile rings and new methods of interrogating child witnesses. A 1982 case in Bakersfield, California, began when one man was accused of sexually abusing his two daughters, but the affair grew until it was alleged that the family was part of a network of adults who exchanged children for sexual purposes, including the making of child pornography. The charges were duly proved by intense questioning of several young "victims," showing that in certain circumstances, children could be induced to agree that abuse had occurred and to invent details sufficiently convincing to appeal to a jury. Within two years it was alleged that seven more child sex rings had been operating in Bakersfield, and the allegations included florid stories of satanic rituals and murdered children. Some commentators later compared these trials to witch-hunts, and here it is ironic that the panic in Bakersfield subsided for precisely the same reason that it had in Salem in 1692: when the children ran out of adults whom they could plausibly accuse, they began directing charges at the investigators themselves, police and social workers.[1]

Fears about pedophile rings were in the air in the early 1980s, but so were beliefs about the therapeutic means of combating the apparent threat. The problem was that children could produce tales that sounded so improbable that the stories must be either rejected or contextualized in some novel way. This dilemma emerged in acute form in a case that erupted in 1983, when a delusional woman alleged that her son had been molested at the McMartin preschool in Manhattan Beach, California, and local police investigated a teacher named Raymond Buckey. Police relayed the allegations to the parents of other children at the preschool, urging them to take their children to be examined at a local therapeutic institution. Panicked families then heard that hundreds of children were recounting appalling tales of molestation involving the mutilation and killing of animals, and one ten-year-old child told a court that he and other children had been taken to a church where "adults wearing masks and black robes danced and moaned." Buckey and six female colleagues were arrested in 1984. Investigators explored charges that children had been taken to other locations, in some instances by plane, which suggested that this "pedophile ring" was well connected. That the group was active in child pornography as well as prostitution was implied by children's claims that they had been filmed and by therapists' reports that mentioned a game called Naked Movie Star. These charges came to light only a few months after the NAMBLA affair, which had similarly combined molestation charges with accounts of child trafficking, pornography, and violence. The Meese Commission cited ritualistic preschool cases in its analysis of child pornography, claiming that the absence of obscene photographs proved the cleverness of the perpetrators rather than the weakness of the evidence against them.[2]

Noting the extraordinary ritualistic conduct, other activists asserted that the sex ring had been a satanic cult and that perhaps the school had been designed from its inception as a place for recruiting and exploiting children. This interpretation owed much to a sensationalistic 1980 book that would have great impact on attitudes to child abuse in the coming decade: in *Michelle Remembers,* a psychiatrist describes how a woman recalled, during therapy sessions, the ritualistic sexual abuse that she suffered as a child in Vancouver during the mid-1950s; eventually she described a clandestine cult that caged, molested, and tortured children and sacrificed animals. Parallels between this much-criticized book and the tales from the McMartin therapy sessions suggested that similar cults were still operating and continued to violate childhood innocence for diabolical purposes. One ring had been detected; how many others were still operating behind the cloak of other schools and day care centers?[3]

In retrospect, examinations of the McMartin fiasco have demonstrated how this volume of evidence was produced. Therapists were accustomed to dealing with cases of clear and known abuse in which traumatized children refused to acknowledge that molestation had occurred and needed subtly encouraging treatment techniques in order to overcome their denial.[4] This might involve relentless questioning and perhaps the use of psychological pressure to persuade children that admitting abuse would gain approval from adults and peers. The danger was that admissions would still be forthcoming in cases where no molestation had occurred, as suggestible small children (often four or five years old) would seek adult approval by agreeing to hints about supposed events. Lacking knowledge of sexual matters, they concocted the most shocking acts available to their imaginations, which would explain why interrogations often produced tales of teachers forcing pupils to engage in or observe toilet functions. As therapists became familiar with accounts of stars, circles, and robes, they incorporated these and other "ritualistic" elements into subsequent questions, whereupon the suggestions were readily confirmed. Psychological findings seemed corroborated by speculative types of pediatric examination, which were believed to prove that many child witnesses had been subjected to anal and genital rape. Unfortunately, these techniques are also likely to produce large numbers of false positives, on the strength of symptoms that have quite normal and noncriminal interpretations. Flawed therapeutic evidence was then taken over wholesale by local prosecutors, who characterized it as a correct account drawn forth by skilled behavioral-science investigators and used the material as the basis for their florid indictments.

Allegations were leaked to local media, who viewed the matter as too serious and too sensational to permit a presumption of innocence. In the national press, the McMartin indictments produced high-profile news stories throughout 1984, none doubting that a ruthless criminal organization had been at work at "California's nightmare nursery." *Time* offered the simple headline "Brutalized," and the *New York Times* quoted a Los Angeles detective who explained how pedophile rings commonly used preschools and day care centers: "They use the children, . . . not only for personal gratification, but often share them, often for a fee, with other pedophiles. Often, videotapes or still photographs are made of the children, which are sold or given free to other pedophiles."[5]

Despite initial enthusiasm, the McMartin prosecution soon careened to disaster. When a new district attorney took office in 1986, his office critically reexamined all the allegations and dropped the charges against all but two of the original defendants. Two sensational trials culminating in 1990 produced only deadlock over some charges and acquittals in others. By this time, the media had become more skeptical: CBS's *60 Minutes* twice offered accounts sympathetic to the McMartin defendants, and the *New York Times* ran headlines like "Swept Away in a Vortex of Panic" and "System Run Amuck." Although some activists continue to offer "proofs" of even the most bizarre allegations (including secret tunnels under the school), the McMartin case has become a byword for incompetent investigation and yellow journalism.[6]

The McMartin affair was followed by dozens of comparable cases in all parts of the country, all involving bizarre or ritualistic methods of abuse and all sharing similar backgrounds. Whether in Bakersfield (California), Jordan (Minnesota), Edenton (North Carolina), Martensville (Canada), or Wenatchee (Washington), the affair generally began with a limited, plausible allegation: that a small number of children had been abused, often in a preschool or kindergarten setting. In the ensuing investigation, interrogation of child "victims" produced evidence that far more abuse had occurred than originally thought, and ultimately the compounding reports and rumors would implicate dozens of local residents in what could only be called sex rings or cults. Supposed victims were questioned, until they confirmed the charges and offered their own creative embellishments.

Already sensational charges became further inflated, and soon widespread ritual murder was being postulated. In late 1984, abuse investigators in Jordan, Minnesota, turned their attention to unsubstantiated charges of occult rituals and human sacrifice, and over the next year, there were frequent journalistic investigations into the homicidal operations of imagined rings or cults. Growing police interest in occult topics is suggested by the number of related stories in the professional press from the mid-decade as well as the proliferation of training seminars, while Ted Gunderson became a recognized spokesman on the danger of sacrificial cults. By 1988, extravagant charges of ritualized child abuse and murder were given national visibility in a network television program hosted by

**Table 8.1   Newspaper Stories About
Ritual or Satanic Abuse, 1983–1995**

Items Combining the Word *Abuse* with the Words:

	Ritual	*Satanic*
1983	1	2
1984	4	1
1985	6	4
1986	11	5
1987	16	27
1988	14	12
1989	32	36
1990	171	173
1991	345	175
1992	202	153
1993	274	213
1994	364	352
1995	293	270

Source: Lexis-Nexis "ALLNEWS" database, searching for word
abuse within five words of the term *ritual* or *satanic*.

Geraldo Rivera and entitled *Devil Worship: Exposing Satan's Underground,* which was produced by Kenneth Wooden and broadcast, appropriately, near Halloween. Tales of human sacrifice were popularized in books like Maury Terry's *Ultimate Evil,* Larry Kahaner's *Cults That Kill,* and Carl Raschke's *Painted Black.*[7] For several years, belief in the existence of satanic cults and ritual murder achieved wider credence in the United States than it had in any other society since that of sixteenth-century Europe. The number of news stories concerning satanic and ritual abuse grew dramatically, as is suggested, however crudely, by Table 8.1. Outside the United States, the explosion of reports in 1990–91 reflects the spread of concern to other countries, including Great Britain, Canada, the Netherlands, Australia, New Zealand, and South Africa.[8]

By the end of the decade, the topic of SRA had a prodigious presence in the media. Books on the theme continued to proliferate, most of them fervently embracing the reality of the problem. Many purported to contain survivors' recollections of satanic abuse and child exploitation; many were self-published ventures, but not a few were published by major commercial houses. By 1994, ritual abuse survivors had access to a self-help manual, *Safe Passage to Healing,* and the solid publishing firm Routledge presented a collection of essays in an authoritative, professional style, *Treating Survivors of Satanist Abuse*. Ritual abuse was discussed in articles in popular periodicals as diverse as *Ms., Vanity Fair,* and *Christianity Today,* and the topic earned extensive coverage in theme issues of the *Journal of Child and Youth Care* (1990), *Child Abuse and Neglect* (1991), *Treating Abuse Today* (1991), the *Journal of Psychology and Theology* (1992), and the *Journal of Psychohistory* (1994). Occasional papers also appeared in respected psychiatric journals, often with titles that assumed the objective existence of the SRA phenomenon. Official task forces on ritual abuse were formed in Los Angeles, San Diego, and other cities.[9] Especially active were self-help groups like VOICES in Action (Victims of Incest Can Emerge Survivors), Believe the Children, Incest Survivors Anonymous, SurvivorShip, and SOAR (Survivors of Abusive Rituals), which offered pamphlets, newsletters, and videos to a national audience through the mails and later the Internet. There were even self-help books for children, on the model established by the abuse prevention programs of the 1980s. Resources included "a therapeutic comic for ritual abuse survivors" and *Don't Make Me Go Back, Mommy,* "a child's book about satanic ritual abuse."[10]

During the mid-1980s, the SRA phenomenon was treated respectfully on news programs like ABC's *20/20* and NBC's *1986*. Celebrated mass or ritual cases were fictionalized in television movies like *Do You Know the Muffin Man?* an account of a preschool prosecution broadcast shortly before Halloween 1989, during the final stages of the McMartin trial. Three months later, as the McMartin case reached its conclusion, the film *Unspeakable Acts* reported an earlier and successful prosecution of a day care predator. Both treatments enjoyed lengthy afterlives in reruns, which continued long after the initial panic had subsided. The topic was also featured in best-selling fiction. Andrew Vachss' *Sacrifice* (1991) depicted a boy transformed by cult abuse into "Satan's child," a programmed assassin suffering from multiple personality disorder (MPD), while the hero kills satanic cult members in the middle of a child sacrifice ceremony. Andrew Greeley's *Fall from Grace* (1993) similarly linked ritual abuse with human sacrifice: the villain is a Catholic priest, a pedophile, and a cryptosatanist;

a satanic pedophile priest also appears in Malachi Martin's novel *Windswept House* (1996).[11]

Roots of a Panic

By about 1989, the idea that ritual abuse was quite common had almost acquired the status of social fact, and this remarkable assumption requires explanation. Responding to the sensational coverage of the original McMartin case, parents were suddenly alerted to the dangers that lurked in what they had regarded as the safe environments of preschools and day care centers. As families became sensitized to any hint of institutional abuse, a host of preschools and kindergartens experienced scandals on the strength of rumors that once would have been dismissed as ridiculous. The incidents seemed to enhance the probability that any adult who worked with small children might be guilty of abuse, and the supposition encouraged investigators to seek evidence of accomplices in organized molestation as well as child pornography.

The Manhattan Beach case had a major impact on the therapeutic professions. If cabals of satanists were systematically abusing children and terrifying them into compliant silence, then it was hopeless to expect reports to come from children or parents so that conventional police investigations could be launched. Cases of this sort would emerge from incidental symptoms coming to the attention of teachers, doctors, or psychologists, who must be trained and required to report their suspicions to the authorities. An investigation must be undertaken by behavioral experts, who would understand the special forms of interviewing, symbolic communication, and play therapy required to draw the truth from very young victims, and during the mid-1980s, numerous training courses and seminars instructed therapists and social workers in the new methods.

The changing attitudes in the therapeutic professions transformed the standards employed to assess abuse allegations. Before the 1980s, prosecutors were reluctant to proceed with cases involving small children, whose readiness to tell incredible stories showed their inability to recount unadorned facts. This view should perhaps have been vindicated by the amazing incidents reported throughout these years—impossible accounts of meeting cartoon characters, tales of hidden tunnels and flying machines (McMartin), of being barbecued in microwave ovens or dangled over alligator pools (Edenton).[12] Other children reported assaults and stabbings that should have left serious wounds, although no trauma was found by detailed medical examinations. That what were obviously fantasies were not considered sufficient to discredit the cases reflected a new determination to believe victim testimony at all costs.

The refusal to disbelieve owed much to the precedent of the antirape campaign, which had effectively criticized the insensitivity of police and courts to adult victims. The professionals in the new field of child abuse asserted, by extension, that children never lied about matters of sexual abuse and that once children admitted to being abused, this fact must be accepted and affirmed with tenacity. Therapists were haunted by the example of Sigmund Freud, who had withdrawn his early claims about the widespread and damaging nature of childhood sexual abuse, later saying that the allegations were fantasized. Freud's shameful *Assault on Truth* provided an awful warning of the dangers of compromising professional principles.[13] The truth of abuse must be believed. Falsehoods might be harmless frills, irrelevant to the substance of the accusation, but the nonsensical quality of the tales could indicate that ingenious molesters were deliberately committing their crimes in fantastic settings in order to discredit children's accounts. An abuser might tell a child that his name was Fred Flintstone or Bill Clinton or simulate an incident involving a fake microwave oven; indeed, claimed some, the more fantastic the story, the more likely it was to indicate the reality of serious and systematic abuse. The ideology of "Believe the Children" contributed to a readiness to accept apparently outrageous stories of ritualistic abuse. To express skepticism, on the other hand, was to signal not only denial of the reality of victimization but also tacit acquiescence.

The coalition fighting to expose SRA found adherents among "social workers, therapists, physicians, victimology researchers, police, criminal prosecutors, fundamentalist Christians, ambitious politicians, anti-pornography activists, feminists, and the media." It also had roots in the anticult movement, which emerged in the United States in the 1970s and which combated fringe religious groups like the Children of God and the Unification Church. The mass suicides of the People's Temple followers in Jonestown, Guyana, drew attention to cult violence as well as to the sexual and physical abuse said to have been inflicted on children there. By the early 1980s, anticult writers were formulating a mythology claiming that the most dangerous fringe movements were clandestine satanic groups who undertook human sacrifice, and these ideas gained immense force from the McMartin allegations. These theories appealed particularly to

evangelical Christian groups, for whom an upsurge of contemporary satanism would confirm their pessimistic theology about the imminence of
the Last Times and the Apocalypse.[14] Between 1984 and 1992, the danger
from satanism and ritual crime was a central theme in the writings of the
evangelical Right, as evidenced by the sizable sections labeled "Cults" in
most Christian bookstores. The SRA phenomenon gave new force to fundamentalist attacks on other "diabolical" phenomena seducing the young,
including New Age religion, rock and roll, fantasy role-playing games, and
the celebration of Halloween. It also validated the growing interest in "spiritual warfare," with its revival of exorcism and spiritual healing.

Anticult charges exercised a potent appeal for sections of the psychiatric
profession, particularly for therapists interested in the long-term impact of
traumatic experiences and the related themes of repressed memory and
MPD. By the late 1980s, thousands of patients were reporting recollections
of abuse that could be understood only in the context of the sort of ritualistic, cultlike groups described in *Michelle Remembers* or seen in the ongoing mass abuse cases, and the claim was that early maltreatment had
long-term consequences in the form of psychic fragmentation. These
claims were questionable, for the allegations derived from therapy were
rarely subjected to any kind of factual verification, while the explosion of
MPD diagnoses raised suspicions about faddism. The diagnosis of MPD
had been extremely rare and usually tentative before the much-publicized
1973 book *Sybil* (filmed 1976), but by the late 1980s, thousands of instances
were being claimed each year, often with a degree of fragmentation that
beggared belief. Patients were said to have dozens or hundreds of separate
personalities, some claiming knowledge and linguistic skills that the conscious personality could never have acquired, some ostensibly drawing on
experiences from previous incarnations. MPD was beginning to look more
like demonic possession than an authentic personality disorder, with "alters" appearing and vanishing in a manner similar to that of the demons described in ancient stories of exorcism.[15] But while the allegations seemed
fantastic, the same credibility extended to children was felt to be appropriately extended to adult survivors.

Personality fragmentation was initially seen as a defense mechanism by
which the abused child staved off a terrifying reality, but other explanations
soon developed. MPD theorists proposed that the condition was deliberately created as a means of mind control or mental programming, by which
subjects could be brainwashed into serving the goals of a cult, perhaps as

programmed slaves or killers. The mind-control idea owed much to the conspiracy speculations of the 1960s and 1970s, when clandestine government agencies were accused of employing programmed assassins on the model portrayed in *The Manchurian Candidate*. A lively if ludicrous folklore described the sinister work of "Dr. Green," a Jew who had collaborated with the Nazis and later transmitted German mind-control experiments to the CIA and the U.S. intelligence community. Meanwhile, the anticult movement proposed that members of fringe religious cults were converted by a form of brainwashing or programming.

During the 1980s, the themes of MPD, deprogramming, and conspiracy theories interacted in the campaign against ritual abuse, and this odd concatenation explains the otherwise puzzling presence in SRA bibliographies of works concerning CIA experiments with brainwashing through drugs and hypnosis.[16] (In an ironic reversal, behavioral technologies once considered as appropriate treatment for child molesters were now viewed as a powerful tactic deployed by the abusers themselves.) Among the varieties of conspiracy theory advanced by some works on the fringes of the sex ring literature, one idea claimed that the organized pedophiles might be sufficiently well connected to evade punishment for their actions. This was confirmed by tales of McMartin children being transported to locations where they would be molested by persons unknown, presumably wealthy pederasts. But such allegations reached their richest flowering in a Nebraska scandal that became a major political event in that state between 1988 and 1991. This affair began with the collapse of the Franklin Savings and Loan, when investigations of fraud and political manipulation evolved to produce allegations that some of the state's most prominent citizens were implicated in a child sex ring active in narcotics trafficking, pornography, and prostitution. Participants were said to include figures in Nebraska's Republican party as well as leaders in business, banking, government, and media. Children were reportedly flown to neighboring cities to be abused by local magnates as well as by members of NAMBLA. The operation was said to have intelligence dimensions, involving CIA arms dealing and blackmail. Rumored networks of homosexual prostitution implicated officials of the Bush administration, but the central organization was a cult of devil worshipers involved in the mutilation, sacrifice, and cannibalism of numerous children.

The Nebraska scandal attracted interest from the regular conspiracy theorists, but the story also won the sympathy of child-protection leaders like Judianne Densen-Gerber; and activists received national attention in 1988, when they appeared on the notorious television exposé, *Satan's Underground,* hosted by Geraldo Rivera. Despite years of rumors, none of the charges involving either sexual abuses or satanic rituals could be substantiated in the slightest degree. A grand jury ultimately reported that the ornate Nebraska affair rested on a "carefully crafted hoax," and in 1991, the woman who had been a major source for the abuse stories was convicted of perjury.[17]

The Great (Dis)simulation

The ritual abuse mythology was tenacious. Even if the allegations of widespread abuse in the nation's day care centers were disproved, this still left the corpus of "recollected" testimony describing similar atrocities in bygone years. Much smoke seemed to prove the existence of at least a little fire. During the early 1990s, however, public skepticism became so intense that the entire edifice of charges was undermined, raising questions about any evidence that rested on similar foundations.

Stories about ritual abuse had attracted critics since their first appearance following the McMartin case, as the charges presupposed a far-reaching conspiratorial network. Advocates were suggesting that child sacrifice was a daily event in North America; that a clandestine alternative religion existed undetected and that its agents had infiltrated schools, kindergartens, churches, and police departments; that satanic rituals were commonplace in day care institutions; that women regularly bore babies for sacrifice; and that all these phenomena had occurred systematically in American society for decades, perhaps back to the seventeenth century. A typical survivor claimed that as a child she had been the victim of a cult led by civic leaders, businesspeople, and church officials in "an upper-middle-class town in the Midwest" in the mid- or late 1930s. The pseudonymous Annette was "abused in rituals that included sexual abuse, torture, murder, photography and systematic brainwashing through drugs and electric shock." By the age of twelve, she was a "breeder," bearing children for the cult to sacrifice.[18] Although her account was published as nonfiction in the enormously popular recovery text *The Courage to Heal,* the bible of the incest-survivor movement, the story stretches credibility to the limit and beyond.

Despite the flagrancy of these satanic misdeeds, the authorities had never uncovered any signs of the ugly reality before 1983. It was plausible that unenlightened police forces might have failed to appreciate the significance of animal bones, robes, and ritual fires, but it was ludicrous to suggest that they would have ignored traces of human sacrifice. Equally implausible were a number of other assumptions: that no defector had ever violated the secrecy of the cult; that no local police chief, prosecutor, or newspaper editor had ever tried to make a career by exposing what must have been powerful suggestions of local cult activity; and that satanist abusers had achieved a success beyond the capability of other powerful groups participating in organized crime, espionage, narcotics trafficking, contract murder, and terrorism. This hermetic silence could have been preserved only if the satanists were deeply entrenched in local businesses, official agencies, news media—if suspicious deaths were concealed by satanic funeral directors and coroners, for example, and if investigations were perverted by diabolistic detectives and prosecutors. It was all wildly improbable.

Another flaw was that, in order to be believable, stories of ritual abuse in bygone decades required actual cultists or satanists, and culprits were all but impossible to find before the occult boom of the late 1960s. Although *Michelle* and its imitators portrayed satanic cults in the early 1950s, no corroboration exists for the existence of such groups at that time. In tracing the history of the problem, ritual abuse advocates were reduced to drawing on the most spurious anticult and anti-Catholic tracts of earlier days. Chrystine Oksana, author of *Safe Passage to Healing*, cites as a precedent the "cult that bred babies for sacrifice," which was described (along with a prototype of the tunnels supposedly dug under the McMartin preschool) in the nineteenth-century text *Maria Monk*; Oksana does not acknowledge that this alleged cult was in fact a regular Roman Catholic convent, and the whole story of Maria Monk has been regarded as false, and its author as probably deranged, since the 1830s. Other theorists draw deeply from the tainted well of American paranoid theory, attributing ritualistic crimes to groups like the Illuminati, Masons, and Jews. When they portray satanic rituals, they report dates and events that do not correspond with the experience of real occult groups and that are drawn undiluted from medieval witch-hunting manuals like the *Malleus maleficarum*. In its origins the contemporary literature on ritual abuse resembles speculations about the Jewish ritual murder of Christian children and is precisely as worthless.[19]

The "satanism" portrayed in the anticult mythology is in fact a literary and synthetic concoction, one largely taken from thrillers written in the

1930s by English writer Dennis Wheatley, who was the first to integrate the genuine traditions of ritual magic with the fantasies of the European witch-hunters. *Michelle Remembers* contributed a few other elements from folktales of the colonial era in West Africa, when groups called the Leopard Men allegedly abducted, tortured, caged, and killed children. A series of exposés has demolished the claims of most of the individuals claiming to be survivors or defectors from such groups.[20] In the absence of actual satanic or ritual abusers, it is difficult to speak convincingly of their supposed crimes—strictly speaking, it is not possible to prove a negative. But where claims demand so massive a revision of consensus reality, the burden of proof is on those making the assertions, and confirmation of any kind has been woefully lacking. The SRA movement represents an eerily postmodern dominance of created illusion over supposedly objective reality—what Baudrillard would term the stage of pure simulation.

Most day care and preschool prosecutions resulted in either the acquittal of the accused or the conviction of some individuals on counts that involved neither satanic nor ritualistic elements. Even these convictions were often overturned when appeals courts examined the means by which testimony had been elicited from children. In one New Jersey case, kindergarten teacher Kelly Michaels was accused of "licking peanut butter off [children's] genitals, playing a piano while naked, forc[ing] the children to drink urine and eat feces; assaulting them with silverware, a sword and Lego blocks; forcing them to play the 'cat game' where they all got naked and licked each other; amputating children's penises; putting a real car and tree on top of one of them." Although these nonsensical charges were unconfirmed by medical evidence, in 1988 Michaels was convicted of 115 counts of child abuse and sentenced to forty-seven years in prison. Two true-crime books portrayed her as the incarnation of pathological evil, and journalist Anna Quindlen used the case as a model of why the public should "believe the children" in abuse cases. On appeal, the defense showed how children had been induced to give damning testimony and were rewarded or blamed depending on whether their reports meshed with the picture sought by the prosecution. The conviction was reversed, but only after Michaels had served several years of her sentence. Hers was one of many cases to collapse in these years, when it was shown how far overeager prosecutors and therapists had gone in drawing forth fantastic stories from preschoolers.[21]

Despite years of allegation and investigation, no cases validating the ritual abuse menace had been produced by the early 1990s, raising questions about the whole portrayal of the supposed menace. Crucially, the FBI's leading investigator of sex ring cases, Kenneth Lanning, remained severely skeptical of allegations about "occult crime," and those exploring the validity of such charges would soon encounter this hostile, or at least critical, source. In 1994, a NCCAN-sponsored study of allegations of ritualistic crimes discredited virtually all charges. In a wide-ranging survey of psychologists, social workers, prosecutors, and police departments, researchers found a very few cases where "lone perpetrators or couples" had used ritualistic trappings to intimidate children and perhaps to add a bizarre thrill to sexual activities. In not one out of twelve thousand incidents investigated, however, was there the slightest hint of "a well-organized intergenerational Satanic cult who sexually molested and tortured children in their homes or schools for years and committed a series of murders."[22]

The failure of the McMartin trials in 1990 initiated a general media reaction against ritual abuse cases as well as mass abuse cases that lacked overt ritualistic elements. Between 1990 and 1994, debunking pieces appeared in magazines as varied as the *New Yorker, Harper's, National Review, Vanity Fair, Redbook, Mother Jones, Village Voice,* and *Playboy.* And while publishers continued to issue the sculpted fantasies of ritual abuse "survivors," they also released critical studies like *Abuse of Innocence* (a survey of the McMartin case), *Satanic Panic,* and *Satan's Silence* (a comprehensive demolition of the SRA movement). The visual media were equally hostile. After about 1987, most network news programs and newsmagazines turned decisively against credulous coverage of satanism and child abuse, partly in embarrassed reaction to the extravagance of tabloid documentaries and talk shows. Throughout the early 1990s, mass abuse prosecutions were attacked in segments on CBS's *60 Minutes* and *48 Hours,* ABC's *Primetime Live* and *20/20,* and documentaries on PBS's *Frontline.* By 1995, similar criticisms reached a mass audience through the television docudrama *Indictment,* which attacked the prosecutorial work and the media hysteria in the McMartin case.[23]

A media consensus now viewed the McMartin case and its clones as "witch-hunts," a peculiarly apt term given the occult nature of many of the charges. The term gained popularity from Arthur Miller's play *The Crucible,* which explored how those prosecuted as witches in Salem became scapegoats for the fears and repressions of the entire community. Also implied in the usage was the networking mechanism by which charges were disseminated: a presupposition of guilt permitted flimsy or ludicrous charges to adhere to one suspect, proving that grave evil was present in the community. In this paranoid environment, the slightest unorthodoxy or misbehavior was taken as a sign of membership in the conspiracy, and proof of guilt was readily forthcoming from witnesses whose credibility would not normally be entertained, including children and the mentally unstable; even dreams and spirit visitations became acceptable evidence of wrong-doing. Originating among isolated critics of the mass abuse prosecutions during the mid-1980s, the densely packed rhetorical terms "witch-hunt" and "Salem" now become a commonplace description of such affairs and were freely applied to cases like that of Kelly Michaels.[24]

The ascendancy of new attitudes became clear during 1994, when a Pentecostal minister and his wife were accused of abusing children in We-natchee, Washington. Authorities suggested that as many as one hundred other individuals might be involved in child sex rings that had been oper-ating in the community for several years. According to investigators of the alleged orgies and rapes of entire groups of children, "There were so many children they had to stand and wait their turn to begin sex acts with adults." Although the affair began on a note reminiscent of the McMartin and Jor-dan disasters, media expectations were utterly different on this occasion, and the press began using such words as *witch-hunt* at an early stage of the proceedings. The sources used to contextualize the Wenatchee events were not the anticult theorists who might have appeared some years ear-lier, but skeptical investigative reporters like Debbie Nathan and Dorothy Rabinowitz. From the time the affair reached national attention in the fall of 1995, it was assumed that the allegations probably reflected the malice or incompetence of investigators; these perceptions were found in mod-erate media outlets like *Time,* and *Reader's Digest* ran a story entitled "Witch-Hunt in Wenatchee." The *Wall Street Journal* made the affair a cause célèbre, suggesting that the case was "a concoction of incredible charges and runaway prosecutions." A CNN report summarized the opin-ion of local residents, who felt that "a rogue police officer and obsessed so-cial workers created an atmosphere of sexual hysteria in which adults were bullied into confessions and children coaxed into accusations, in part, through questionable 'recovered memory' therapy."[25] The revised media atmosphere could not but affect the decisions of future prosecutors con-templating how to proceed with similar charges. Nobody wanted to risk bearing the stigma of pursuing "another McMartin" or now, perhaps, "another Wenatchee."

Significantly, Wenatchee was depicted as a throwback to another era, to the "hysteria" or witch-hunt atmosphere of the dark days of the 1980s. Typical of the new historical consensus was a documentary broadcast in 1996 on ABC's *Turning Point*, which reported the case of two Bakersfield children whose testimony had sent their parents to prison in 1984 but who years afterward reported the grossly improper means by which their evidence of abuse had been obtained. Reviews of the program reflected the emerging commonplaces of historical retrospect: "hysteria, . . . vindictive accusers, credulous social workers, zealous investigators and prosecutors, and juries ready to believe the most bizarre tales from the mouths of children, . . . highly improbable or even impossible goings on, drawn from easily manipulated youngsters."[26] The program contextualized the case alongside the McMartin and Michaels affairs, noting that hundreds of people had been falsely convicted in such incidents.

Recovered Memory and False Memory

In 1996, a commentary in the *San Francisco Chronicle* discussed the "witch-hunt" that had caused the jailing of George Franklin on murder charges subsequently overturned on appeal. At first glance, the Franklin case seemed to have little in common with the pursuit of literal witches and occultists in the ritual abuse inquiries. Many years after the alleged fact, he was accused of murdering a small girl and was tried for the crime; the charges were brought when his adult daughter claimed to recall memories of the event. But the prosecution was weak, for the daughter could provide no evidence that could not have been obtained from contemporary newspaper accounts.[27] That the designation "witch-hunt" was applied to the Franklin case suggests how intimately the issue of recovered memories had become linked to the ritual abuse debate, in that both depended on how much credence could be placed in accounts recalled in therapy. If a person was convicted of a crime on the basis of "recollections," whether of an adult or a child, was this any more just or reliable than the spectral evidence used with deadly effect in seventeenth-century Salem?

Belief in recovered memory originally had nothing to do with claims of satanism. The idea had its roots in core Freudian beliefs about the power of infantile experiences connected with sexuality and the repression of memories in later life. These assumptions became part of a powerful therapeutic trend in the early 1980s, when failings and anxieties encountered by adult patients were traced to forgotten instances of early abuse—memories that the therapist recovered through hypnosis or suggestion. In 1987, Judith Herman published what would become the classic text in the field, a study of a group of women who, while in therapy, recovered memories of childhood sexual abuse. Once identified as incest survivors, such patients could confront their problems and begin a process of healing their "inner child," usually through self-help groups of other survivors, following the familiar model of Alcoholics Anonymous. This vision was publicized in books like *The Courage to Heal,* by Ellen Bass and Laura Davis. Already well filled, the shelves of the recovery sections in bookstores expanded to meet the needs of "secret survivors" of incest, the victims of "toxic parents." Although initially directed toward women, books in this genre later assured male survivors that they too need be "victims no longer."[28]

These therapists believed that abuse had very likely occurred even though they had no corroborating evidence, except for ill-defined symptoms that others might identify as accidental personality traits. *The Courage to Heal* assured readers: "If you are unable to remember any specific instances . . . but still have a feeling that something abusive happened to you, it probably did. . . . If you think you were abused and your life shows the symptoms, then you were." Denial is the factor here: "Survivors go to great lengths to deny their memories. One women convinced herself it was all a dream." Skepticism was discouraged: as E. Sue Blume wrote, "if you doubt you were abused, minimize the abuse, or think 'Maybe it's my imagination,' these are symptoms of post-incest syndrome." That patients believed that horrible acts had been done to them was in itself a fact of enormous significance, while skepticism on the part of the therapist would violate the trusting relationship believed essential for successful treatment. Counselors were instructed in the cardinal doctrines of recovery: "Be willing to believe the unbelievable. . . . No one fantasizes abuse. . . . Believe the survivor." Partly because SRA had become so integral to the therapeutic culture of the mid-1980s, elements from that mythology influenced the tales that therapists now drew forth from their cooperative subjects, and the imagined reality of this era was therefore projected back onto earlier decades to form a nightmare pseudohistory. *The Courage to Heal* included an influential section on ritual abuse and murder, with confirmatory citations of *Michelle Remembers* and *The Ultimate Evil.*[29]

Although expressed in the psychological terms of self-help, the recovery movement owed its strength and resilience to its pervasive ideological and even religious quality. The treatment of incest survivors relies on ancient themes like the loss of primal innocence through sexual sin and the recovery of an untarnished childlike state. Equally familiar to the evangelical tradition, this restoration often occurs in a sudden emotional moment of realization, which is essentially a conversion experience. The analogy is not perfect, for the survivor is realizing, not her own lost and sinful state, but rather the evil visited upon her by a victimizer, but the underlying structure of loss, regeneration, and redemption is accurate. Also recalling religious systems is the emphasis on faith, of belief in the testimony of others, even if it directly contradicts common sense: the children, external or internal, must be believed at all costs. As with many religions, survivorship implies a worldview impervious to disproof or even challenge by conventional standards of evidence or rationality.

The number of therapists active in memory-recovery treatment grew dramatically from the late 1980s. Acceptance of these ideas was encouraged when celebrities like Roseanne Barr and Oprah Winfrey declared themselves incest survivors, providing a newsworthy tag that resulted in articles in popular magazines like *Cosmopolitan* and *Lear's*. Winfrey sponsored a television documentary, entitled *Scared Silent: Exposing and Ending Child Abuse,* which was broadcast on all networks in September 1992, and massive public reaction reportedly led to 150,000 viewers seeking help from the National Childhelp Child-Abuse Hotline. As in the 1970s, concern about child abuse mirrored broader anxiety about sexual violence against women, a topic regularly featured in the news media in the early 1990s, often in the context of women being "stalked" by disturbed men.[30] Awareness of pervasive sexual harassment was raised to unprecedented heights by the twin scandals of Clarence Thomas's confirmation hearings as a justice for the Supreme Court and the Tailhook affair, in which male naval aviators assaulted female colleagues. By 1991–92, sexual violence was at the forefront of American gender politics.

The idea of recalling repressed memories was familiarized through television movies and talk shows as well as through depictions in novels like Jane Smiley's *Thousand Acres.* The Ellen Franklin story was favorably reported even on *60 Minutes,* a program normally hostile to therapeutic claims in the area of abuse. Several other cases used recovered memories to convict individuals of serious crimes, including murder, while memories of victimization provided the basis for civil actions, offering a fertile field for attorneys. Legislatures were sympathetic: in 1990, California was the first state to extend the statute of limitations in abuse cases from the age of nineteen to twenty-six and also to permit actions to be brought within three years after the time that a person of any age *recalled* an offense, a lead followed by more than twenty states in the next two years. This reform greatly expanded the potential for civil litigation, and during the next three years, several hundred suits followed, most involving adult women suing members of their family. In 1992, "pedophile priest" James Porter was successfully prosecuted following the recovery of abuse memories by several former victims.[31]

Some academics and psychologists had long been dubious about the potential for recovering supposedly lost memories, suspicious both of the techniques employed in therapy and of the chance that recollections would accurately reflect events that had genuinely occurred. These criticisms were reinforced by pressure groups composed of people who complained that they had suffered as a result of wrongful abuse prosecutions. VOCAL (Victims of Child Abuse Laws) grew out of the Jordan trials of 1984–85, and the False Memory Syndrome Foundation (FMSF), founded in 1992, claimed several thousand members by the mid-1990s. After 1992, the mass media became increasingly active in their attacks on recovered memory. The charge was that concern over sex abuse had led to the creation of a therapeutic industry with a vested interest in the identification of sexual trauma, while dubious therapies were giving rise to false accusations.

The recovery movement was attacked in magazine articles and syndicated stories and in visible outlets like *Time* and *Newsweek;* in 1993, the *New York Times* denounced "the incest survivor machine." Again, television news programs from *20/20* and *60 Minutes* to *Primetime Live* were in the vanguard of critical reporting, demonstrating the skepticism that they had learned during SRA debates. The stories that appeared on such programs usually followed a well-established pattern. Generally, a woman or teenage girl would consult a therapist for a personal problem like an eating disorder, only to be convinced after some weeks or months that her real problem could be traced to an early history of ritual abuse in which her parents had participated. The "victim" would sever connections with her family, who were depicted in the reports as confused elderly innocents lacking the slightest comprehension of the charges to which they were now subjected. There was never any question that the memories were consciously or otherwise fabricated during therapist-patient interactions and were implanted during the workings of the "memory mills."[32]

The dual attack on ritual abuse and recovered memory reached impressive dimensions between 1993 and 1995. There was soon a growing scholarly literature on the debate over memory and false memory syndrome. Hostile critiques were publicized in books with titles like *The Myth of Repressed Memory* or *Making Monsters: False Memories, Psychotherapy, and Sexual Hysteria,* while the title *Victims of Memory* epitomized the theme that therapeutic zeal to protect children had damaged innocent lives. An attack on false memories became almost an obligatory feature for all major media outlets. These often took as their text the academic findings of psychologist Stephen Ceci, who showed how repeated questioning of children over lengthy periods would generate false but plausible-sounding memories, which subjects would report with conviction as objective reality: in the right circumstances, the question became the answer. The press had reported this research in respectful terms since about 1990, but the stories became far more frequent during the critical years of 1993–94, earning front-page coverage in the *New York Times*. Ceci's findings provided the basis for a story on *20/20*, which emphasized the inability of experts to distinguish between accounts of authentic and artificially generated memories. ABC's *Primetime Live* suggested that therapists were creating false memories of ritual abuse in adult patients, a theme also argued in a CNN news special.[33] At the same time, the news media in mid-1993 were reporting extensively on the collapse of the Michaels case and other miscarriages of justice in abuse trials.

One bizarre case in the news at this time involved two women who claimed to recall being ritually abused by their father, Paul Ingram, who confessed but then recanted. The Ingram saga was reported at length in the *New Yorker* before forming the basis of a book, and in 1996 reached a mass audience in the form of the made-for-television movie *Forgotten Sins*. Still more influential was the case of Stephen Cook, who in late 1993 testified that he had been sexually victimized by two Catholic priests in the mid-1970s: one was Joseph Bernardin, who had since gone on to become the immensely popular cardinal of Chicago.[34] Although the charges received national publicity, Cook soon withdrew them, recognizing that his "memories" had been distorted during therapy. The Bernardin case aroused public anger about media credulity in reporting unsubstantiated and fantastic tales.

Against the survivor, skeptical commentators counterposed the "retractor," the person (again, usually a woman) who came to realize that her allegations did not reflect objective reality. A new hostility to therapy was exhibited in legal cases in which wrongly accused parents successfully sued therapists who had produced such charges, on the grounds of malpractice or slander. Doubts about abuse accusations were enhanced by well-reported instances in which abuse charges were cynically employed as weapons in child custody cases, an issue that had aroused concern since the late 1980s.[35] Following the era of legal reform based on the principle of no-fault divorce, abuse allegations provided a potent means of reintroducing the concept of blame and securing an advantage in negotiations.

The new atmosphere was suggested by two lengthy treatments of the issue: both were broadcast on PBS's prestigious documentary series *Frontline* in 1995 and were directed by Ofrah Bikel, who had earlier reported critically on the Edenton cases. One program explored tales of recollected satanic abuse and showed therapists moving with remarkable speed to assume a given case had cultlike elements: on minimal evidence, an eight-year-old boy was diagnosed as a programmed cult assassin requiring prolonged psychiatric incarceration. The program revealed the remarkable profitability of this treatment, in which insurance companies paid several million dollars for the commitment and treatment of patients. One psychologist noted that MPD diagnoses were particularly likely for patients with rich benefit plans.[36]

Perhaps the final blow to the memory industry was the growing number of patients who, while under therapy, produced accounts of abuse and abduction by alien beings and UFOs, an experience that simply could not have happened as an objective event; yet these reports were buttressed by exactly the same arguments as accounts of childhood abuse. For abductees, as for SRA survivors, the same stories were reported across the nation and indeed around the world, and both types of subject reported remarkably similar types of experience, even to the same alleged scars or physical traces of abuse.[37] If UFO events had not literally occurred, why should any credence be placed in reported memories of ritual abuse or abuse of any kind? Belief in SRA already demanded an acceptance of real-life sorcerers and witches: must one also believe in demons from other worlds? The line between psychiatry and necromancy was wearing thin.

Backlash

In 1994, a collection of essays was published under the title *The Backlash: Child Protection Under Fire*. At first sight, the phrase may seem strange, for the current American president was more explicitly committed to the rhetoric of children's rights and interests than any of his predecessors, and there had been no diminution in the activity of child welfare agencies and child protective services. While there may have been no backlash against the notion of child protection as such, it was not fanciful to see a reaction against elements of recent campaigns and a growing skepticism resulting from far-fetched claims about ritual abuse and recovered memory. The shift could not fail to raise questions about the investigation of abuse within the family setting. With so many reports of parents and intimates being falsely accused, the feminist idea about the ubiquitous quality of incest no longer commanded the consensus that it had briefly achieved in the 1980s. On the defensive, child-protection activists found themselves forced to deny that child abuse was a witch-hunt, and Anna Quindlen challenged what she saw as the popular idea "that there is a national hysteria about the sexual abuse of children."[38]

The new public mood harmed the image of the therapeutic profession, which had benefited so substantially from the child-protection movement, and the SRA idea had gained the support of prestigious exponents of the "Believe the Children" idea like David Finkelhor and Roland Summit. Gloria Steinem had offered support to therapists treating the multiple personality conditions of survivors of ritual abuse, and gave financial support to the project to excavate the McMartin "tunnels." Although children's advocate Faye Yager had been a media heroine in the late 1980s, by 1992 she herself was on trial, facing criminal charges of child maltreatment. Among other things, it was alleged that she had "bullied . . . children into alleging that their father sexually abused them and worshiped the devil." Ultimately Yager was acquitted, but the media showed a novel hostility to activists, and *People Weekly* commented on the "trial of a child abuse vigilante."[39]

Media denunciations of memory therapy customarily included a disclaimer that no doubt was being cast on the truthfulness of the majority of abuse complaints and indeed that false allegations were pernicious because they might lead to unjustified skepticism about authentic complaints. But allegations of improper proceedings and false charges lent support to claims that suspects that suspects had been unjustly caught up in witch-hunts. Accounts of wrongful charges now became more common in popular culture. This was the theme of Jane Hamilton's novel *A Map of the World* as well as articles in magazines like *Newsweek*. As the subtitle of one newspaper article summarized most of these tales, "A false report of child abuse: scared children, a zealous social worker, and a lawsuit." This perception contributed to the courts' new tendency to rein in the sweeping powers claimed by law-enforcement and social service agencies during the 1980s.[40] Between 1992 and 1994, federal appeals courts even decided some cases in which child pornography investigations were judged to have violated defendants' rights.

When in 1993 a Massachusetts abuse case resulted in the conviction of an elderly couple, the Souzas, the public response was in marked contrast to what might have been expected five or ten years earlier, when the accused would have been presented as the epitome of evil and there might have been speculation about wider networks or cult involvement. *Newsweek* pictured the couple on the cover of a special issue devoted to the misuse of children's testimony, under the title "Rush to Judgment." The couple appeared on the Phil Donahue Show and the *Today Show,* in each case presented as victims of a child abuse witch-hunt, and the story was told alongside other miscarriages of justice like the Michaels case. In 1977, the media decided with one voice that child sexual abuse was an evil so pervasive that no measure was too extreme to combat it; in 1993, the same sources discovered that a war on child abuse could involve atrocities on both sides, and caused serious injury to innocent bystanders.[41]

Child-protection advocates were alarmed. The 1994 edition of *The Courage to Heal* included a counterblast against the insidious effects of the backlash, entitled "Honoring the Truth"; but even in this book, SRA has now become "sadistic ritual abuse," perhaps reflecting embarrassment about Satanic claims. Commenting on the attack on memory therapy, Judith Herman complained, "We're back where we were twenty years ago. This is a mobilization of accused perpetrators and their defenders to take the spotlight off perpetrators of crimes and put it back on victims and issues of their credibility." Skeptical articles like those which appeared in profusion during 1993 were denounced as "a backlash against survivors," an attempt "to go back to square one in our understanding of incest." Herman was one of many advocates to charge that "pedophile advocates" were themselves influencing the false memory debate in order to conceal their own misdeeds, a charge usually accompanied by a vast exaggeration of the ability of groups like VOCAL and FMSF to influence the media. Andrew

Vachss's novel *False Allegations* depicts a professional "debunker" of child abuse allegations who is shocked to find a case in which a pedophile ring has genuinely been engaged in atrocities over many years.[42] But a forced retraction by one of his key witnesses is ballyhooed by a hostile media, who paint the case as a Salem witch-hunt orchestrated by a malevolent "feminist psychologist." "Salem" thus becomes a canard to divert public attention from real crimes against children, part of the rhetorical arsenal of the molesters themselves.

Such fears proved excessive, in that both law-enforcement agencies and the media demonstrated a sympathy to child abuse allegations that would have been inconceivable before the 1970s, but Herman and Vachss were right to detect a new skepticism about abuse and especially to pinpoint incest as the concept most damaged by this debacle. For the foreseeable future, charges of abuse within the family and the immediate community were likely to be viewed with skepticism, especially if they suggested any degree of wider organization among parents, neighbors, and teachers or if evidence was obtained by means other than familiar reactive policing. Intervention by social workers or therapists was all too likely to lead to charges of that this was another Salem or a witch-hunt. In contrast, no such skepticism was forthcoming in exactly these years when law-enforcement agencies made far-reaching claims about itinerant child killers and abductors. While the issue of child abuse as such still resonated powerfully, it achieved its greatest power when it was framed in terms of molesters and pedophiles who attacked from outside the home and family, of what now came to be known as sexual predators. Half a century later, in modernized and technological guise, the sex fiend returned to haunt American public life.

Full Circle

Chronic sexual predators have crossed an osmotic membrane. They can't step back to the other side—our side. And they don't want to. If we don't kill them or release them, we have but one choice. Call them monsters and isolate them. . . . I've spoken to many predators over the years. They always exhibit amazement that we do not hunt them. And that when we capture them, we eventually let them go. Our attitude is a deliberate interference with Darwinism—an endangerment of our species.

—ANDREW VACHSS

Distrust all in whom the impulse to punish is strong.

—FRIEDRICH NIETZSCHE

After the late 1980s, child molesters were viewed as being extremely persistent in their deviant careers, having sexual contact with very large numbers of children over many years. They were virtually unstoppable, either by repeated incarceration or by prolonged programs of treatment or therapy, because their acts arose not from any temporary or reversible weakness of character but from a deep-rooted sickness or moral taint. And now, many believed, sex offenders were mobilizing the latest technology in their remorseless quest for victims, so that cyberspace had become a potential hunting ground quite as perilous as the lonely park or field. Concerns that pedophiles were using the medium of the Internet to seduce children and to distribute obscene materials led to the creation of a whole lexicon—*cyberporn, cyberstalkers,* and so on. This eruption of fear, which led to new federal legislation in 1995–96, is notable testimony to the protean quality of the child abuse idea and its ability to adapt to changing political and technological environments. Today's sex crime panic is as fierce as that of the late 1940s, and it has given the predator a role in the national demonology that is quite as pronounced as that of his psychopathic predecessor. We have truly come full circle.

Pedophiles Revisited

During the 1980s, legislatures and criminal-justice agencies began treating sexual offenses as a far higher priority than they had before, and changes in courtroom procedures made it easier to gain convictions. Not surprisingly, therefore, the number of offenders prosecuted rose substantially. There were about 58,000 sex offenders in the nation's prisons in 1988; by 1990 that number had increased to 85,000, a 47 percent increase in just three years, and sex offenders (however defined) composed one-sixth of all inmates in federal and state institutions. Among the highest proportions nationwide were the states of Washington (30 percent) and Colorado (27 percent). By 1993, California had 16,000 imprisoned for sexual offenses, Texas, 10,000. At mid-decade, correctional authorities were supervising 234,000 sex offenders, 60 percent of whom were on parole or probation. Although the upsurge in the numbers of known and convicted offenders resulted largely from the reorientation in law-enforcement priorities, it lent credence to claims that the sexual abuse of children was an epidemic out of control.[1]

Studies now emphasized the role of the repeat offender, the career sex criminal. The recidivism figures were troubling enough, but interviews with incarcerated molesters suggested that the arrest records were telling only a very small part of the story. In extreme cases, convicted pedophiles were reporting careers in which they had abused several hundred children, mostly without legal consequences. The validity of such confessions was open to debate, as imprisoned offenders of any sort are notorious for their tendency to recount the histories that they know their counselors and therapists expect to hear, but, even so, it no longer seemed reasonable to repeat the view that molestation was a one-time offense. The new perceptions were reflected in the language used by both expert and popular opinion, in which the term *pedophile* described virtually anyone who had been sexually involved with a minor and contained ever more sinister connotations of obsession and violence. The more an act of molestation was a symptom of an inherent personality disorder, the less amenable was the offender either to deterrence or to reform. These meanings were especially attached to the term *serial pedophile* or *serial molester*, which became common in the late 1980s under the influence of the well-known phrase *serial killer*.[2] The term is technically accurate in that a person who commits the same sort of crime repeatedly does indeed engage in a series of offenses, but in practice *serial* implies compulsivity and extreme dangerousness.

Predators

In the 1980s, Washington State became a pioneer in evolving legal devices for combating sex criminals, especially in King County, Seattle, where specialized units attracted both praise and criticism for their vigorously proactive pursuit of child abuse cases. The institutionalization of the child-protection movement provided a context for the furious public response to a gruesome series of crimes, a reaction that culminated in the sexual predator statute passed there in 1990. The most sensational case concerned Earl K. Shriner, who in May 1989 assaulted a seven-year-old boy, mutilating his genitals and leaving him for dead. Shriner had been assembling a spectacular criminal record since the mid-1960s, when he was hospitalized after allegedly killing a male classmate; afterward he received sentences for molestation in 1977, 1987, and 1988. In prison, Shriner had designed a van that he reportedly proposed to use for abducting, torturing, and killing children, and corrections officials knew this. Nevertheless, he was released. The question was why an offender was released into the community when so much evidence showed that he was both able and eager to do further harm.[3]

Washington's legislature was under overwhelming public pressure to do something about sex offenders, to increase penalties and intensify incarceration and supervision of criminals for whom treatment was futile. A legislative panel now proposed the long-term incarceration of serious sex offenders, who would be punished as much for their predicted future dangerousness as for the specific act that brought them into contact with the criminal-justice system, and a law passed in 1990 provided for community notification and prolonged, even indeterminate incarceration. Dangerous sex offenders were required to register with police when they moved into neighborhoods so that neighbors, including schools, day care centers, and women's refuges, could be duly warned. The law's second component allowed for special detention: after a sex offender served his sentence for a given criminal act, the state was empowered to detain him past his release date pending a hearing on civil commitment, when a finding of future dangerousness could lead to indefinite confinement in a high-security special commitment center.[4]

Following the precedent of the sexual psychopath legislation, the new measure combined civil and criminal procedures in a law that reflected the best of both worlds, or at least the elements most advantageous for prosecutors. Used alone, civil commitment offers the possibility of indefinite incarceration, but it is risky, for psychiatric institutions sometimes release individuals far earlier than would have been the case had they been serving criminal sentences. In the 1980s, several jurisdictions passed laws permitting lengthy confinement for sexual predators, and in 1986 the Supreme Court approved an Illinois measure that allowed prosecutors to choose whether they wished to proceed civilly or criminally against a given defendant. Washington built upon this principle with a law that offered a de facto criminal sanction, but one justified in terms of a civil medical matter. Nevertheless, the net effect was summarized in a *New York Times* headline: in Washington, "Strategy on Sex Crimes Is Prison, Then Prison."[5]

Critics suggested that the law was not only harsh but also unconstitutionally retroactive. It was applied to offenders who were released after the act came into effect but who had been convicted before its passage: in other words, a man convicted of an act in 1985 would be indefinitely detained under provisions that did not exist at the time he committed his offense. It also had elements of double jeopardy, in that diagnosis as a dangerous predator was proved before a court using evidence from the person's past offenses. This might involve, for example, hearing testimony from women who had been raped by a man who had already been tried and convicted for these criminal offenses. In theory, the witnesses had come back to court for the completely different purpose of assessing the defendant's future dangerousness, but it looked very much as if earlier acts were being retried. Despite some observers' doubts about its constitutionality, the Washington law attracted interest from other jurisdictions and was cited when other states or cities experienced a sensational crime involving a sexual predator.[6] By 1995, similar statutes had been passed in Arizona, California, Kansas, Minnesota, and Wisconsin, and forty other states were considering comparable measures, assuming legal difficulties were resolved.

The diffusion of predator laws was assisted by other notorious crimes during the next two or three years and most spectacularly by another case

of ritual abuse or recovered memory: one type of threat progressively gained in media acceptability as the other declined. In 1992, the media described the case of Eddie Savitz, who lured hundreds of boys to his Philadelphia apartment, an affair made even worse by the fact that "Uncle Eddie" had AIDS. In reality, the fetishistic acts that Savitz enjoyed carried no risk that the disease would be transmitted, but the presence of AIDS greatly enhanced the potential damage of abuse. In another highly visible case, David Lee Thompson confessed to molesting numerous small girls in at least five states in the early 1990s, and although his acts did not involve violence, his fantasy scenarios involved child murder. In contrast, the Lewis Lent case of early 1994 did entail the authentic abduction and murder of children in New England and New York. The depth of public feeling over sex offenders was shown when Californian Ellie Nesler became a popular heroine after she killed the man accused of molesting her young son. Initially depicted in terms of a mother seeking justice against a vicious abuser coddled by the law, the story was reported by all major television news programs and talk shows and inspired bumper stickers celebrating "L. E. Law," that is, "Ellie Law."[10] The years 1992 and 1993 witnessed the height of public concern about sexual abuse by clergy, some instances of which involved genuine serial pedophiles, like Massachusetts priest James Porter. In reality, though, the vast majority of compromised clergy were involved with adolescents rather than small children, and the popularity of the phrase *pedophile priests* is powerful testimony to how far the word *pedophile* had come in representing a generic term for any adult sexually active with minors. In actuality, let it be said once more, *pedophilia* refers only to sexual misconduct with prepubescent children.

The child abuse theme had been entrenched in popular culture since the late 1970s, but now depictions tended to focus more sharply on the lone predator, commonly a pedophile, who was painted in the darkest possible terms. One early example was seen in the 1989 television movie *I Know My First Name Is Steven*, which was based on the true story of a young boy who had been abducted and retained for several years in the 1970s; *Bump in the Night* (1991) was the tale of a boy kidnapped by a pornographer. For the first time in the genre, serial molesters and pedophiles now became the subject of several true-crime books, while cases dating back a decade or more were revived to accommodate the new public mood. In 1991, the Gacy murder case of the late 1970s became the theme of the TV movie *To Catch a Killer*. Extreme cases of clergy sexual abuse were treated in the television movies *Judgment* (1990) and *The Boys of St. Vincent* (1994) as well as magazine articles and television documentaries. Predatory imagery found stark expression in the sadistic villain of the 1991 film *Cape Fear,* a "psychopath" who had been jailed for raping a young girl.[11]

Through these years, news and documentary programs reported on predators with all the zeal that they had earlier addressed to exposing incest and child abuse in preschools. On the show *48 Hours,* the single year of 1991 included lengthy items on Westley Dodd ("Serial Killer," May), rape and rapists ("Crime in the Dark," September), and Washington's sex offender legislation ("Predators," November). The story of Lewis Lent was covered in an episode bearing the frightening title "Child Hunter." The stress on pedophiles gave vigorous new life to the fear of child abduction, and in 1994, the New York legislature required that all public schools in the state provide kindergarteners through eighth graders with lessons imparting "awareness skills, information, self-confidence and support to aid in the prevention of child abduction." Child abuse prevention programs, which in the 1980s had stressed that any adult could be involved in offering "bad touches," now reemphasized the role of strangers, giving lessons in escaping and evading abductors.[12]

"America's Child"

In 1993, a shocking criminal case uniquely dramatized the peril from itinerant sex criminals. The Polly Klaas story began in October 1993, when the twelve-year-old girl was having a slumber party with friends at her house in Petaluma, California. A man broke in and abducted Polly at knifepoint; after a massive search her body was found, and it became apparent that she had been murdered shortly after her disappearance. Random violence had intruded into apparently safe surroundings—into a household setting with which any middle-class family could identify—and in fact Petaluma *had* represented the archetypal American community in films like *American Graffiti.* "An angel named Polly" was in no way to blame for her tragic end, and "the murder of America's child" was widely covered in television and newspapers, with several lengthy articles in the best-selling *People Weekly* as well as pieces in *Time, Newsweek, McCall's,* and *Redbook.* The perpetrator was Richard Allen Davis, a criminal who had a lengthy record dating back to his teens and who had been imprisoned for fourteen of the previous twenty years. Despite his multiple convictions for offenses like kidnapping, sexual assault, burglary, and weapons offenses, he was "the man who kept going free." In January 1994, ABC's *Primetime Live* enumerated the many occasions on which Davis could have been sentenced to prolonged imprisonment, a story of "how the system failed society—and a little girl named Polly Klaas."[13]

Juxtaposed images of the savage killer and the innocent victim made a potent combination. A campaign for severity against repeat offenders found a figurehead in Polly's father, Marc Klaas, who regularly appeared in the media throughout 1994, arguing that children were "crying for protection." The Polly Klaas Foundation was organized to assist in searches for missing children and lobbied for California's Polly Klaas Memorial Habitual Offenders Bill, which proposed that sentences for violent criminals be increased. A California ballot initiative that year overwhelmingly approved the California "three strikes" law, under which multiple convictions for serious or violent felony would result in prolonged and possibly lifelong incarceration. Another scandal developed in early 1994, when it became known that a convicted serial rapist was to be paroled to the San Francisco Bay area. Communities systematically refused to receive him, and the issue became a major one in state politics. Shortly afterward, the release of another sex offender was delayed when state officials intervened with prison authorities. A solution was found when the man, Christopher Hubbart, had his parole revoked on the grounds of his "severe paraphilia," an action that copied the Washington principle of civilly confining offenders after their criminal sentences were completed.[14] The Hubbart case was cited by Governor Pete Wilson in sponsoring the state's new Sexually Violent Predators (SVP) Act, a measure that would potentially affect the roughly four hundred individuals released each month.

The year after the Klaas murder brought another horror story with enormous legal and political implications. This time the offender was Jesse K. Timmendequas, who had been convicted in attacks on children in 1979 and 1981 and who was described by a judge as a "compulsive, repetitive sexual offender." He was nevertheless released after serving seven years in New Jersey's sex offender facility at Avenel, and, along with two other sex offenders, he took up residence in a suburban neighborhood. In July 1994, he raped and strangled seven-year-old Megan Kanka. The outcry following the case went far beyond criticism of any one agency, and New Jersey legislators introduced a series of bills within a month of the murder, "rushing to vote without first holding customary hearings or even working out some details."[15]

New Jersey passed a statute modeled on the Washington law, under which the state would register and track convicted sex offenders for a ten-year period after release and a second sexual offense would lead to mandatory life imprisonment. The centerpiece of the new law was community notification, under which authorities notified neighbors and schools of the presence of high-risk offenders in a community. This came to be known as "Megan's Law," a term canonized by its inclusion in recently published dictionaries. Even if a legislator had qualms about voting in favor of the statute, it would have taken foolhardy courage to question a bill personalized by close association with the martyred child. While the state assembly debated the measure, a placard featured photographs of other murdered children, with such headlines as "Free to Rape," "Protecting Our Children from Violent Predators," and "Sex Offender Charged in Girl's Strangulation." The bill gained force from passionate personal campaigning by Megan's mother, Maureen Kanka.[16]

The community-notification idea quickly acquired the status of a national movement. By mid-1996, the principle had become legislation in thirty-five states and was under consideration in most of the remaining jurisdictions, and convicted offenders were required to register with the police in all states except Massachusetts. States were divided between those requiring "active" notification, in which police notified relevant groups considered to be at risk, and "passive" notification, in which private citizens must take the initiative to seek information about offenders: twenty-four states adopted active policies, eleven adopted passive ones. Notification acquired federal status in a crime bill signed into law in 1996, in effect a national Megan's Law, requiring states to warn communities when convicted sex offenders moved in.[17]

Federal activism in this area reflected a consistent political trend. Although the cause of child protection clearly stood high among President Clinton's ideological priorities, it also became politically essential. During his first two years in office, Clinton was much criticized by conservative advocates of traditional morality and family values, and the president countered rhetorically by defending the interests of children. This debate became sensitive in 1993, when Clinton struggled to achieve the admission of gays to the U.S. military while fending off charges that the administration was supporting perverts and predators.[18] The president's determination not to be outflanked on children's issues partly explains his fervent activism during late 1993, when the Justice Department seemed to relax the severity of the child pornography laws. Following the 1994 elections, which were disastrous for his party, Clinton was still more eager to present himself as sound on issues like family, morality, and values, and during the next two years the White House became a staunch supporter of measures like sexual predator statutes and laws to protect children on the Internet.

President Clinton placed himself at the forefront of the movement against sex predators. In January 1994, he referred to the Polly Klaas incident in his State of the Union address—a moment that, as one news commentator claimed, "tugged at the heartstrings of every parent in this country." By 1996 the president was campaigning for a national registry of sex offenders and child molesters, as outlined in a bipartisan bill co-sponsored by Senators Joe Biden and Phil Gramm. Under this law, police throughout the country would be able to access a database providing information on all offenders, regardless of the jurisdiction in which they committed their crimes—the sort of federal facility envisaged by the Specter committee's hearings a decade earlier. Clinton's aspiration was that "the police officer in Cleveland should be able to get information on all known sex offenders in Cleveland whether they committed their crimes in New York or Los Angeles. . . . There is no greater right than a parent's right to raise a child in safety and love. That's why the law should follow those who prey on America's children wherever they go, state to state, town to town." In a radio address, the president declared, "Deadly criminals don't stay within state lines, so neither should law enforcement's tools to stop them." During the 1996 election campaign, the Democrats ran a television commercial in which Marc Klaas used home videos to tell Polly's story and then praised Clinton's activism: "When it came to protecting children, the president had the courage to make a difference."[19]

Megan's Law involved public participation in the supervision of sex offenders—one of the most ambitious and perhaps alarming aspects of the get-tough attitude. Before, proposals to keep ex-convicts under surveillance had given police departments or other agencies the responsibility of keeping records of their locations and ensuring that they reported periodically. In the 1990s, anticrime activists enlisted the public at large to maintain offenders under a kind of community surveillance that had few precedents in Anglo-American law, at least not since the days when thieves, adulterers, and blasphemers were branded or otherwise mutilated in order that they be identifiable by their crimes. The departure was seen as justified by the extreme harm caused by offenders, their immunity to reform or treatment, and the ubiquitous danger posed to the nation's children. A sex offender, however nonviolent his crime, was felt to cause a far more immediate menace than the mugger, robber, murderer, confidence trickster, or corporate polluter, who were not subject to like restrictions.

The idea of warning the public originated in an ad hoc way by the quirky decisions of local courts through the 1980s. When a twice-convicted child molester was sentenced to prison in Oregon in 1987, his parole conditions required him to move to a new house in a different neighborhood, where he would place a sign on his front door stating "Dangerous Sex Offender—No Children Allowed." The local American Civil Liberties Union drew a predictable analogy with Nathaniel Hawthorne's *Scarlet Letter,* but stigmatizing practices later acquired statutory force. Under Louisiana's "scarlet letter" bill, a released sex offender was required to personally notify neighbors of his record; in urban areas this meant mailing details about himself and his offense to everyone within a three-block area. Ex-convicts were required to wear special clothing and to indicate their status by signs on their houses or special bumper stickers on their cars. Some pressure groups consciously sought a more precise revival of the scarlet letter, proposing that predators be physically tagged or branded and calling for automatic lifetime surveillance of all sex offenders.[20]

The scarlet letter was primitive when set beside the new technologies made available in the next decade in the form of computers and the Internet. In 1994, Indiana adopted Zachary's Law, named for a child victim named Zachary Snider; this required child sex offenders to register with all local law-enforcement authorities in the communities where they lived for ten years following their release, and a Web site posted a statewide registry of convicted offenders. Other jurisdictions saw this as exemplary. A contemporary Web-based "magazine" exposed "the names, mug-shots and offense information for every sex offender known to authorities beginning with the state of Minnesota, including those scheduled to be released from prisons each month and those who change their name or gender. . . . There are nearly 350 mug-shots of sex offenders who were released from Minnesota prison facilities in 1995." The state of California now offers a CD-ROM containing the names and records of sixty-four thousand sex offenders.

Although the notification idea was popular, legal concerns now shifted the emphasis of anticrime militants to more passive ways of sharing information. As originally envisaged, police officers or members of other groups would visit the appropriate houses in a community, informing them that their new neighbor was a sex offender. Under the revised model, information would not be given out freely but would still be available to anyone who cared to inquire, either by visiting an office, accessing a computer database, or calling a phone number for information about the record of a given individual. New York's Megan's Law permitted the names and addresses of convicted sex offenders to be released through local police departments and by means of phone numbers in order to preserve children from "dangerous pedophiles and sexual deviants." But a federal judge prevented the implementation of such notification procedures, which would have publicized the whereabouts of some five thousand offenders on parole or probation in the state.[21]

Community notification was controversial, for it incited vigilantism and made rehabilitation virtually impossible. Nor could these problems be dismissed as unexpected, as they had been thoroughly foreshadowed during previous eras. The Fred Stroble case of 1949 led the California legislature to implement severe measures requiring all sex offenders to register with county sheriffs. The remarks of journalist Howard Whitman are worth quoting, especially as he himself believed firmly in the gravity of the sex crime menace: "It was the old idea of the brand all over again, though it took the form of this blacklist file instead of the old scarlet letter of New England. There was little thought of doing anything to rehabilitate these people—or even to protect society from them. The emphasis was merely on having them branded and filed, Gestapo style, so that they could be hounded and cracked down upon when the public mood so demanded. . . . Why not burn them at the stake? Saves transportation." These words still carry an echo. As an attorney defending Louisiana offenders remarked: "What you're doing is setting these people up for complete failure. Nobody can live in a house with a sign out front that says 'Hi! I raped a child.'" Ex-offenders in Washington State "have been harassed, evicted, fired from jobs, and in one case, burned out by frightened neighbors." When one molester was released, "friends and families of his victims used the information and photographs from police to make thousands of fliers warning of his release, then posting them and handing them out at schools and at ferry terminals. Local news programs showed a picture of the . . . man on their evening broadcasts, and students were sent home with emergency notices warning their parents about him."[22]

What Is a Sex Offender?

As in the 1940s, much debate is possible about exactly what constitutes a "dangerous" sex offender, and authorities err on the side of caution in stigmatizing minor sexual deviants. Early examples of the New Jersey legislation included one case in which a twelve-year-old boy admitted to sexually fondling his eight-year-old step-brother while they were taking a bath—an incident that most jurisdictions would not contemplate prosecuting as a criminal matter. The child received a three-year probation term, but on its completion, he was required to register and be tracked as a sex offender for the next fifteen years. In New York State, individuals qualified as sex offenders by committing any one of thirty separate crimes, seven of which were misdemeanors. The first man thus labeled in the state had committed statutory rape with a sixteen-year-old girl, which brought a sentence of sixty days' house arrest; it was his only sexual offense. Although not a pedophile, serial or otherwise, and fitting no one's definition of sexual dangerousness, the man was required to register so that his whereabouts could be tracked by local communities.[23] He was forced to leave his home, which was located near an elementary school—a prohibition reflecting the law's principle that all sex offenders constituted a danger to children.

The only defense for this system was that minor sexual charges were predictors for larger problems, but would even so broad a trawl catch potentially dangerous offenders? As had been noted in the 1940s, a criminal record did not necessarily give an accurate guide to a person's real character. When Megan's assailant had been tried in 1981 for choking and assaulting a seven-year-old girl, initial charges included five felonies, including kidnapping and attempted murder, but these were reduced to the far less serious "attempted sexual contact and attempting to cause serious bodily injury." This reduction occurred because of the difficulty of using child witnesses and the family's desire to avoid placing their child in a courtroom situation. Because the man was convicted of only these lesser offenses, even if a predator law had been in effect at the time of his trial, it is not obvious that he would have qualified for inclusion. Special offender laws threatened to persecute relatively minor offenders while allowing the truly dangerous slip through. *Plus ça change* . . .

Legal challenges accumulated. The original Washington State law was criticized for mingling the approaches of civil and criminal justice: although using the language of civil commitment, the statute's criteria for labeling a "sexual predator" differed significantly from general civil commitment laws, which required a specific finding of mental illness. All that was needed was proof that the person had been "convicted or charged with a crime of sexual violence" and had suffered from "a mental abnormality or personality disorder which makes the person likely to engage in predatory acts of sexual violence." Using a mere charge, rather than a conviction, to justify penalties involves assumptions far different from those of normal criminal procedure. California's SVP statute was likewise attacked for confusing civil and criminal procedures: "In order to accomplish its goal, the statute permits indefinite confinement on the basis of disorders which do not rise to the level of a mental illness. It applies its provisions if a fact-finder believes a defendant is likely to reoffend at any point in time, without requiring any present dangerousness. It allows for lifetime confinement even if treatment offers no potential for success." In Canada, legal doubts overcame early enthusiasm for special legislation, which similarly arose when a boy was murdered by a paroled molester, but a proposed law was withdrawn as probably unconstitutional.[24]

The new statutes appeared to violate *ex post facto* principles by imposing penalties that were not in legal effect at the time a crime was committed, in some cases demanding the registration of offenders whose acts had been committed years or decades before. Other courts were sensitive to complaints that double penalties were imposed for the same offense. In August 1995, a federal judge overturned the Washington statute on the grounds that community notification involved additional punishment imposed after the offender had completed his or her sentence, and courts in New Jersey, Alaska, and New York reached the same conclusion. A federal judge in New Jersey remarked that, further, "even without considering the potential to incite vigilante activity, dissemination of this information could severely disrupt the lives of the [offenders] and reduce their ability to maintain gainful employment."[25]

By mid-decade, measures passed across the United States were in a state of thorough legal confusion. In both Wisconsin and Washington, predator statutes were upheld by state supreme courts, but the Washington law was ruled unconstitutional by a U.S. district court. Also controversial was Kansas's Sexually Violent Predator Act of 1994, under which a sex offender who had served his sentence was subject to a separate, civil jury trial to determine if he were still dangerous and suffering from a "mental abnormality" that caused his criminal behavior; if these conditions were found to exist, he would then be civilly confined in a mental hospital and reevaluated each year, with the potential for lifetime commitment. The law was struck down by the state supreme court in 1996 on the grounds that "mental abnormality" had no psychiatric basis and that people who were not mentally ill could be unconstitutionally confined. The defendant involved, Leroy Hendricks, was a classic "predator" who had been involved in offenses against children over four decades and had consistently reoffended when released from various institutions.

It was this case, *Kansas v. Hendricks,* that was appealed to the Supreme Court and that in 1997 gave the justices the opportunity to rule on the contentious predator legislation. By five votes to four, the Court upheld the Kansas statute, permitting detention past sentence on the basis of a dangerous "abnormality." Coincidentally or not, the decision was announced only a week after the conviction and capital sentencing of Jesse Timmendequas in the murder of Megan Kanka. In an opinion written by Justice Clarence Thomas, the Court agreed with the state's contention that the "predator" hearings were not in fact criminal proceedings and did not therefore threaten double punishment for a single offense, although a dissenting opinion written by Justice Stephen Breyer agreed with the defendant's claim that he was being subjected to double jeopardy imposed by an unconstitutional *ex post facto* law. The implications of the judgment were uncertain. Thomas suggested that the "abnormality" principle justified detaining those whose condition fell short of true mental illness, which could open the way for a vast expansion of semicriminal commitment; other justices warned that future laws would be carefully scrutinized. Whatever the long-term outcome, the reborn sexual psychopath laws had survived their first crucial test.[26]

The collapse of the original sex psychopathy laws in the early 1970s was accelerated by general doubts about the capacity of institutions to do more good than harm. Institutional responses to deviancy revived in popularity during the 1980s, and the sex predator laws reflected the principles that were regaining credence throughout the justice system. The most obvious revival occurred in the prisons and jails. The total number of inmates in the early 1970s stood around 330,000, but the figure soon expanded dramatically; by the mid-1990s it exceeded 1.5 million, by far the highest incarceration rate among the advanced industrial nations.

Although less dramatic, a similar revival of older practices occurred in the mental health arena. In reaction to the excessive use of commitment in the mid-twentieth century, courts and legislatures made it difficult to commit the mentally ill against their consent. It had been hoped that the displaced would now find care in community treatment facilities, but the mentally ill all too often found themselves lacking any kind of care whatsoever. Public concern about an increasingly visible homeless population led many to advocate a return to involuntary commitment, and these demands became strident after one of the well-publicized incidents in which a discharged mental patient committed an act of random violence. Proposals generally followed the precedent established by a law passed in Washington State in 1979, under which involuntary commitment was possible when people were unable to provide for basic needs or would suffer "severe and abnormal mental, emotional, or physical distress" if not hospitalized. The courts upheld the new commitment laws and approved mandatory treatment in limited circumstances. Although not reversing the judicial revolution of the 1970s, the decisions portended a greater sympathy for treatment and institutionalization where justified by urgent public need.[27]

New judicial attitudes permitted the revival of behavior-modification techniques of the sort that had once been strictly regulated, including painful aversion therapy for sex offenders. As in the 1940s, these individuals found themselves in the vanguard of experimental medical means of treating deviancy. While these "treatment" programs were technically voluntary, some institutions made them mandatory for offenders who wanted to be paroled. The most controversial treatments involved forms of castration, reducing the offender's sex drive either by surgery or by chemical means. These questionable programs have met with little public criticism, for their subjects are deeply unpopular and the need to protect children is seen as desperate. Significantly, the most powerful modern criticism of these techniques comes not from a mental heath professional, academic, or journalist but from a novelist, namely, Matthew Stadler, whose fantasy novel *The Sex Offender* was published in 1994.[28]

In advocating therapy, correctional authorities occasionally received the support of sex offenders themselves, who genuinely felt that they needed treatment. In 1984, Connecticut media reported the case of a forty-nine-year-old molester who had been in prisons in various states for most of his adult life and who claimed to have molested as many as one thousand children. He became newsworthy when he actively sought treatment of the sort that had been so controversial in the previous decade, either aversion therapy or chemical suppression of his sex drive by means of the drug

Depo-Provera, and he initiated a lawsuit to require the state to supply the means by which his desires could be controlled. A similar case involved a man in Texas, Larry Don McQuay, who claimed to have molested hundreds of children. Sentenced to prison in 1989, he began a prolonged campaign to prevent his being released when his term was up, warning, "I am doomed to eventually rape then murder my poor little victims to keep them from telling on me." He pleaded that, if his release could not be legally prevented, then he should be castrated.[29]

In the harsher climate of the 1990s, the need to control sex offenders acquired added urgency, and there was a renewed willingness to experiment with solutions once deemed extreme. Sterilization laws of the early twentieth century were recalled by demands for measures mandating that the sexual urges of offenders be reduced or eliminated, and a California law that passed with great fanfare in 1996 required "chemical castration" for repeat sex offenders. Anyone twice convicted of child molestation would be periodically injected with a drug to inhibit sex drive, unless the offender himself agreed to surgical castration, and provisions could be invoked for a first offense if it were sufficiently egregious. Governor Wilson asserted that the goal was "to control the deviant behavior of those who stalk our young," and the bill's sponsor argued that "there is no crime out there more heinous than child molestation." Although courts in other states expressed doubts about the procedure, the public mood made it likely that such proposals could become commonplace.[30]

Pedophiles On-Line

Although legislation enacted in the 1990s revived the debates of the distant past, one of the major areas of controversy concerned a whole new medium undreamed of in earlier panics: the Internet. The image of pedophiles hunting on-line originated as early as 1983, when the NAMBLA inquiry suggested that abusers were using computers to circulate details of potential victims in addition to pornographic images and fantasies. In 1986, the Meese Commission on Pornography placed special emphasis on the need to control the exchange of child pornography through computer networks.[31]

Beginning in the late 1980s, media reports told of molesters using the Internet to seduce children by adopting the personae of young people in the anonymous chat rooms that were so popular a feature of the networks. It was charged that "on-line pedophiles" were conducting sexually oriented conversations with children and teenagers, with a view to arranging encounters or abductions: as one on-line guide for parents warned, "Pedophiles have a new playground on which to attract children—the Internet." Fears were aroused by the facelessness of the medium, which permitted no visual clues about the true identity of a message's sender. The threat-potential was enhanced by the symbolic associations of the phrases *the Net* and *the Web*—both devices used to hunt, entrap, and confine. And these images predated the explosion of home computing: as far back as 1977, those warning of a national menace of organized pedophilia had spoken of "spider webs strung out all over the nation," while ritual abuse was called "the devil's web."[32]

A spate of "cyberstalking" incidents highlighted pedophiles using computers to approach lonely latchkey children. A 1989 case involved two Virginia men accused of using a computer to arrange a meeting with a boy in order to molest him and possibly to kill him in a snuff film, an attempt exposed when the men unwittingly contacted a police officer on-line. Federal investigations were galvanized by an alleged link between Internet usage among pedophiles and the 1993 disappearance of a Maryland boy, and child protectors now went on-line to seek out molesters. Police reported efforts to expose pedophile-oriented Bulletin Board Services, or BBSs, and the vigilante Guardian Angels now formed their CyberAngels. A police officer in San Jose, California, claimed, "It really doesn't take us long to connect with a pedophile, usually only two or three minutes. . . . They are out there waiting to prey on these children." Articles appeared in *Newsweek* and *USA Today*, and the *Washington Post* ran a headline that alerted readers to an innovation: "molesting children by computer."[33]

Media reports of on-line pedophilia peaked during 1995, when a Georgian was charged with "surfing the Internet in search of children to molest" and a Florida man seduced and raped a fifteen-year-old Maryland girl whom he had met through electronic conversations. The *New York Times* devoted a front-page story to an imprisoned pedophile who used a computer system within the penal institution to maintain detailed files on a number of children living in nearby communities in Minnesota. In one case, two Texas men were accused of assaulting boys encountered through a "computerized sex ring," a striking and increasingly common juxtaposition of words.[34] This technological dimension explains a renewed upsurge of charges concerning organized pedophilia. Between 1986 and 1988, the phrase *pedophile ring* was recorded on just four occasions in the media outlets surveyed by Lexis-Nexis, while the combined figure for the four years 1989–92 was nine; but thereafter the frequency rose, from eighteen references in 1993 alone to thirty in 1994 and twenty-nine in 1995.

Concerns about "cyberstalking" soon merged with those about "cyberporn," or the transmission of pornographic imagery through computer networks, although there was some confusion about what cyperporn entailed. Discussions of child pornography on the Internet usually touched on two quite distinct problems, namely, the portrayal of sexual acts involving children and also the exposure of children to adult material. At the height of censorship controversies during 1995, advocates of restriction enjoyed much success in portraying the whole issue as a subset of child pornography, offering the chance to regulate the Internet by the lower legal standards prevailing in that area and also to control merely indecent as well as overtly obscene material. As in previous debates, the amount of child pornography available was vastly exaggerated and portrayed as more central to the broader sex market than was actually the case. Also, pornographic materials were regarded as inextricably linked with actual molestation, so that stalking and obscenity were seen as two sides of one coin. Although the two activities are connected in some cases, it is not certain that sexual fantasy and actual behavior are so inevitably connected.

Much of the controversy concerned the Usenet, a collection of thousands of on-line discussion groups devoted to every conceivable aspect of popular culture, hobbies, politics, and science. Although sexually oriented groups represented a small proportion of the Usenet, they permitted the transmission of any type of text, story, or fantasy, while binary technology allowed the transfer of visual images. Sexual materials became widely available with the expansion of Web access during 1994 and 1995, the vast majority of images showing adult participants engaged in acts no different from those found in any sex magazine, but Internet pornography raised multiple concerns about the creation of a whole environment outside the control of governments, laws, and codes of decency.

The media now warned of the danger posed to public safety and decency. One article from the *Spectator* was read in its entirety into the Senate record by Charles E. Grassley, Republican of Iowa, who had a long record of activism against obscenity and organized pedophilia.[35] Denouncing "an electronic sink of depravity," the *Spectator* piece described stories encountered in specialized Internet groups. One story, by "Blackwind," describes "a six-year-old boy named Christopher, who, among other indignities, suffers a castration—reported in loving detail—before being shot. The other is a girl named Karen, who is seven years old and is raped repeatedly by no fewer than nine men, before having her nipples cut off and her throat slashed." According to this account, Netnews groups regularly featured "tales of fathers sodomizing their three-year-old daughters, or of mothers performing fellatio on their pre-pubescent sons, or of girls coupling with horses, or of the giving of enemas to child virgins." "Alt.sex.intergen," the "intergenerational" group, was described as the "pedophile bulletin board."

On-line services like America On-Line (AOL) and CompuServe came under fire for however unwittingly transmitting extreme and perhaps illegal pornographic materials. In 1993, forty people in fourteen states were arrested for circulating child pornography on-line in a federal investigation named Operation Longarm. U.S. customs agents raided the alleged headquarters of a "worldwide computerized child porn ring," and the federal government declared that computers represented the key front in the war on child pornography. In 1995, one hundred individuals were arrested in the Cincinnati area for downloading child pornography via AOL, and the service was being cited in embarrassing contexts. The services became conscious of the need to act visibly in warding off restrictive regulation, and AOL and the other major networks cooperated with the NCMEC in sponsoring warnings about keeping children safe on the Information Highway.[36]

Virtual Panic

By early 1995, the issue of cyberporn was gaining political force, invigorated by authentic cases of sexual predators who had entered the electronic age. The major legislative endeavor was launched by Senator James Exon of Nebraska, a conservative Democrat who had cooperated with Charles Grassley over fiscal matters.[37] Exon proposed to amend the existing Communications Decency Act (CDA) to regulate "indecent" or offensive material on the Net, imposing fines and prison terms on anyone who knowingly made material available to those under eighteen years of age. For many reasons, the Exon bill was felt to be excessively punitive and a threat to the whole emerging technology. If passed, the law would open to prosecution material that was merely offensive to some, and the moral standards applied could be those of the most conservative and offense-prone communities. This would limit the discussion of virtually any sexual or controversial issue on the Internet and criminalize speech normally subject to First Amendment protections. The measure also treated the Internet as a species of broadcasting, so that anyone transmitting a message judged offensive or indecent would be as liable as a television station would be. Internet advocates argued that a better analogy was provided by the publishing world, in which free speech was well protected, or perhaps of the telephone service, which transmitted information impartially without being held liable for its content or consequences.

In the spring of 1995 the Exon proposal appeared to be doomed, but it not only survived in amended form but was actually voted into law at the end of the year. This turnabout was achieved by a powerful alliance of moral activists in Congress and the executive branch, whose summer-long campaign against cyberporn made moderates reluctant to be seen as opposing a measure to defend children. A turning point came when Exon presented to his Senate colleagues a blue book of extreme pornographic images supposedly downloaded from the Internet. Antipornography activists drew the legislators' attention to similar pictures depicting bondage, bestiality, and pedophilia. As *Time* noted, "few Senators wanted to cast a nationally televised vote that might later be characterized as pro-pornography," and the bill passed handily, eighty-four votes to sixteen.[38]

This movement drew strength from an article in which a student from Carnegie-Mellon University reported that a large proportion of observed Internet usage involved extreme pornographic materials. Examining Usenet groups, Martin Rimm argued that there was "an unprecedented availability and demand of material like sadomasochism, bestiality, vaginal and rectal fisting, eroticized urination, . . . and pedophilia." Ralph Reed, the leader of the Christian Coalition, stressed that "this is bestiality, pedophilia, child molestation." The study became a major news event, with *Time* magazine publishing a lengthy article under the title "On a Screen Near You: Cyberporn," a piece that Grassley promptly read into the Senate record.[39] Reporting on "the first survey of on-line erotica," the magazine remarked that "it's popular, pervasive and surprisingly perverse," citing Rimm's finding that "on those Usenet newsgroups where digitized images are stored, 83.5 percent of the pictures were pornographic." The images portrayed not just conventional nudity and heterosexual intercourse but also "pedophilia (nude photos of children), hebephilia (youths) and what the researchers call paraphilia—a grab bag of 'deviant' material that includes images of bondage, sadomasochism, urination, defecation, and sex acts with a barnyard full of animals." *Time* used the Rimm study as the basis for an account of alleged computer threats to children, reporting that a ten-year-old boy who frequented one chat room received "E-mail from a stranger that contained a mysterious file with instructions for how to download it. . . . The computer screen filled with 10 thumbnail-size pictures showing couples engaged in various acts of sodomy, heterosexual intercourse and lesbian sex." *Newsweek* contextualized the pornography issue with cyberstalking: "Most disturbing of all are the tales of sexual predators using the Internet and commercial on-line services to spirit children away from their keyboards. Until now parents have believed that no physical harm could possibly result when their progeny were huddled safely in the bedroom or den, tapping on the family computer. But then came news of cases like the thirteen-year-old Kentucky girl found in Los Angeles after supposedly being lured by a grown-up cyberpal."[40]

For all the initial furor, the Rimm study soon fell into disfavor. Although both *Time* and Grassley cited its credentials as "the Carnegie-Mellon study," it did not stem from a research team with any official standing but was the work of one undergraduate student. Its clandestine surveillance of computer usage was a possible violation of scholarly protocols governing research on human subjects, and other media sources also showed that its figures were misleading.[41] Most of the images surveyed were taken not from the Internet as a whole but from certain pay-for-service adult BBSs, which cater to a specific market of those who choose to receive pornographic materials; there was in fact little danger that the images might have been accidentally picked up by unsuspecting teenagers. Overall, the volume of pornography on the Internet was perhaps a fraction of 1 percent, rather than the huge proportion alleged. These objections soon led to caution about Rimm's study, and the Senate Judiciary Committee withdrew an invitation for him to appear as the star witness on the proposed legislation.

But the news coverage given to Rimm's work nevertheless enabled campaigners to employ the supposed datum—that more than 80 percent of Internet traffic involved smut—a figure that acquired the status of social fact. By July, the stage was set for hearings to proceed in an atmosphere that was far more sympathetic than might have been likely a few months earlier. Without Rimm, the main witness on threats to youth became Barry Crimmins, a "children's rights and safety activist, . . . also an adult survivor of childhood sexual abuse."[42] Crimmins claimed that AOL offered "numerous atrocious rooms" devoted to incest, pedophilia, and perversion. He argued: "There is a major crime wave taking place on America's computers. The proliferation of child pornography trafficking has created an anonymous 'Pedophile Superstore.' As a result, the *de facto* decriminalization of child pornography is taking place. The demand for child pornography is also a demand for innocent children to be abused. . . . The on-line service America OnLine has become an integral link in a network of child pornography traffickers." Self-regulation had failed: "AOL is the key link in a network of child pornography traffickers that has grown exponentially over the last several months." Crimmins called for urgent punitive legislation: "The pedophiles have a huge head start. People need to see their neighbors (who have participated in these criminal acts) taken away, jailed, and stigmatized as 'perverts.' If this is done in a public, no-nonsense manner, it should seriously reverse the crisis that is destroying countless innocent children. This crackdown must also include serious punitive measures against companies like AOL."

Crimmins's strategy was apparently taken seriously by the federal government. That September, AOL users were the target of a major sting operation, Innocent Images, which culminated in fifteen arrests and 120 searches of homes and offices around the nation, the charges involving both child pornography and the sexual solicitation of children on-line; media coverage portrayed the arrests and raids as a decisive crackdown on child exploitation and on pedophile rings. Similar interventions took place during the next year, when federal agents left baited messages in attempts to detect or entrap potential pedophiles on-line.[43] Although the AOL investigation had been in progress for two years, it is striking that the denouement of these federal actions should have come so shortly after the congressional furor over cyberporn. In keeping with the Clinton administration's policy on child protection, Innocent Images showed that the executive branch yielded nothing to the legislative in its zeal in this area.

The federal government had a vested interest in the regulation of the Internet, above and beyond the more obvious politics of morality. Following the Oklahoma City bombing of April 1995, investigations showed that the Internet was freely used by extremist groups to circulate radical and racist propaganda as well as techniques for waging guerrilla warfare and making bombs. This led liberal legislators to advocate the surveillance or suppression of communications designed to incite violence, an argument identical to the Exon demand for the regulation of Net materials promoting illegal acts. Moreover, the Justice Department was at this time vociferously demanding legal restrictions on the use of encryption technologies that could prevent federal agents from intercepting electronic messages relating to drug trafficking, espionage, or organized crime. It was thus in the interests of the administration to oppose overly strict interpretations of the First Amendment in the context of electronic communications and to exploit concern over child pornography for other ends. At the height of the encryption controversy, media stories declared that international rings of pedophiles and child pornographers were using the same encryption program then being targeted by the Justice Department.[44]

Whatever the reason, a concatenation of congressional and Justice Department action fundamentally changed the nature of the debate and opened the way for the success of the Exon bill. As part of an extensive revision of telecommunications regulation, President Clinton signed a law making it illegal for a company to knowingly transmit sexually explicit material to minors over computers; it would be a serious criminal offense to post indecent or "patently offensive" sexual material that could be viewed by those under eighteen years of age.

The CDA immediately met legal challenges, and crucial components of the law were struck down by a panel of federal judges, who found it "profoundly repugnant" to First Amendment principles. In 1997, the U.S. Supreme Court agreed unanimously that the Internet was entitled to the highest standards of constitutional protection, and thus the CDA's provisions were resoundingly defeated. Under the act, the term *indecency* could apply to artistic works or academic discussions dealing with topics that were sexual or controversial in nature, including "discussions about prison rape or safe sexual practices, artistic images that include nude subjects, and arguably the card catalogue of the Carnegie Library." The potential consequences were frightening: "In order to deny minors access to potentially harmful speech, the CDA effectively suppresses a large amount of speech that adults have a constitutional right to receive and to address to one another." The justices were eager to limit the popular tendency to use the ideology of child protection as an endlessly adaptable excuse to encroach on freedom of speech: "Regardless of the strength of the government's interest" in protecting children, "the level of discourse reaching a mailbox simply cannot be limited to that which would be suitable for a sandbox."[45]

Shortly after the execution of Westley Alan Dodd, a study of his case concluded with a threatening passage: "Until such time that predators like

Dodd can be effectively removed from our midst, society *must* remain aware that there are other Westley Alan Dodds out there at this very moment, lurking in the shadows and waiting for just the right moment to strike." However hyperbolic in tone, this sentiment was more or less accepted as truth by millions concerned about the threat posed by itinerant pedophiles, just as it would have instantly struck a chord with observers half a century ago. What was remarkable was how sharply this view differed from the emphasis of the child-protection movement in 1985, when abuse was widely blamed not on unknown monsters who wandered from "state to state, town to town," but on the familiar men in the next room.[46]

The change was still more marked in the debate about cyberporn, which was founded on an image of the ethereal pedophile insinuating himself into the family home, that fortress of safety, innocence, and domesticity: teaching us whom we should fear also implies whom we should trust. To paraphrase *Newsweek,* what physical harm could possibly result when our offspring are huddled safely in their bedroom or the den?[47] Little more than a decade earlier, feminist writers were arguing that the bedroom and the den were precisely the settings for most sexual abuse and that the perpetrators were often the victims' fathers and brothers. In the 1990s, this perception almost went the way of older notions like that of the passive, nonaggressive pedophile, as ideas about the sexual menace to children underwent yet another sea change.

A Cycle of Panic

We are of all people, not excepting the Germans, preeminently addicted to the habit of standardizing by law, the lives and morals of our citizens. . . . We like to pass laws compelling the individual to do what we think he ought to do for his own good.

— RAYMOND B. FOSDICK

The sex psychopath laws, moreover, are based on the common American misconception that mere passage of a law will solve a social problem.

— MORRIS PLOSCOWE

It is easy to understand why groups or individuals who perceived children as being endangered should have been so active in trying to protect them and to pursue and condemn their exploiters. But activists in child-protection movements, however sincere in their efforts to assist the vulnerable, have all gained in various ways by drawing attention to the problem of molestation, and the same professional groups and ideological strands can be identified in each successive campaign. Even so, this continuity of activism has not reflected any stability in how the issue has been conceived at different times. Concern has fluctuated wildly over the past century, both in the degree of fear apparent at any given time and in the direction from which the threats were believed to come: the nature of sexual threats to children was perceived quite differently in 1915 than in 1930, and the child abuse issue was framed quite differently in 1984 than in 1994. Constructions of the molester have been equally fluid. Interpretations have sometimes favored a fairly benign model (the passive, rather pathetic figure of the 1960s), at other times a model diametrically opposed to the first (the sex fiend of the 1950s or the serial pedophile of the 1990s).

Why has the public been so fickle in its fears? And why have the claims made by different activists gained more or less public support at different times? The lesson seems to be the one so often found in studies of social problems: that claims about danger are rather like commodities in a competitive marketplace, items that gain or lose a following depending on how well retailers strike a chord among the consumers whom they wish to attract.[1] The products themselves, although they may be packaged with greater or less sophistication, remain fairly constant: their success in gaining market share depends on the composition and tastes of the consumers, which change over time. Problems rise and fall, evolve and mutate, depending on such intertwined factors as demographic changes, shifting gender expectations, economic strains, and racial conflicts as well as the social, political, and religious ideologies built upon these underlying realities. Any given concept of childhood or of the dangers that children face cannot be understood without reference to these shifting foundations.

Some interest groups have been perennially active in child-protection movements over the years. In each period we generally find energetic advocacy by child welfare societies, social workers, psychiatrists and therapists, women's groups, prosecutors, law-enforcement bureaucrats, and members of the mass media. For each of these respective groups, part of the motivation for defending children was surely tied to deeply embedded social and religious ideologies, convictions harking back to biblical views of social action as protecting the widow and orphan. Since the early nineteenth century, efforts at social reform have usually concentrated on improving the lot of children, on the assumption that this is the best way of curing problems like crime and poverty. Originally organized through voluntary societies like the New York Society for the Prevention of Cruelty of Children, welfare work became professionalized during the Progressive Era, laying the foundation for the modern system of government-run social work agencies. Welfare expenditures by federal and state authorities rose dramatically during the years when the child abuse issue was being discovered nationally, from less than 12 percent of the Gross National Product in 1965 to more than 20 percent a decade later. Social welfare groups, private and public, have taken the lead in sounding the alarm to sexual threats to children, both in the early twentieth century and from the late 1970s, and they gained increased resources in the process. The number of clinical social workers in the United States grew from 25,000 in 1975 to 80,000 in 1990, and many of them dealt with children's issues and concerns.[2]

Feminists represented another enduring constituency. In the 1880s as in the 1980s, publicizing threats to children enabled feminists to draw attention to pervasive male violence and exploitation and thus identify problems that could be resolved only by structural changes in gender relations.[3] Emphasizing child victimization had a valuable rhetorical effect in other campaigns, too—in countering the long-established idea, for example, that women who were raped or battered were at least partly to blame for their suffering. Both rape and battery had often been portrayed, however absurdly, as mutual and consensual transactions between adults, but moving the focus of sympathy to vulnerable children greatly reduced the tendency to blame the victim. Feminists also had an interest in directing attention to abuse within the family, and this aspect of the problem came to the fore at times when women were politically organized, both during the Progressive Era and in the 1970s and 1980s. The weakness of organization in the 1940s and early 1950s may explain the ideological shape of the sex crime issue in these years, when the focus was entirely on strangers and sex fiends who preyed on the idealized family, and the incest issue went deep underground for forty years after the Goldbergs' study in 1935. But even in eras lacking an explicitly political feminist movement, women often emerged as leaders in campaigns to control sexual crime and delinquency, from the child-protection societies of the late nineteenth century through the citizens' ad hoc committees of the late 1940s. In the second half of the twentieth century, feminist ideology has largely defined its worldview in terms of struggles against sexual victimization and the underlying "rape culture."

For psychiatrists and therapists, the area of sexual deviance offered unparalleled opportunities for demonstrating their expertise. The movement against sex psychopaths helped to consolidate the wartime gains of the psychiatric profession, and by the 1950s therapeutic assumptions had become part of the commonplaces of educated society. This contributed to a widespread tendency to medicalize social problems, be they violence, substance dependency, or educational failings. In the 1980s, therapists benefited once more from their expanding role in the investigation of child abuse, as both preschool cases and recovered memory offered a whole area of jurisprudence that would have been inconceivable without the methodologies of this profession. The child abuse issue validated and encouraged the growing prestige of the therapeutic professions: from 1970 to 1993, the ranks of the American Psychological Association more than doubled, from 30,839 to 75,000 members, and those of the American Psychiatric Association swelled from 18,407 to 38,000 members. By the late 1980s, more than 250,000 psychologists were employed in various capacities in the United States.[4]

In each era also, vigorous reaction to "crime waves" promoted the interests of officials and politicians espousing law-and-order causes. Determined action against sex offenders will generally win favorable publicity and bureaucratic rewards for law-enforcement agencies, and J. Edgar Hoover's sterling example was often emulated by his bureau successors. Police chiefs and prosecutors are usually eager to show that they can fight crime and protect the most vulnerable members of the community, and the successful prosecution of an egregious abuse case gives visibility to the official responsible and may even smooth the path of political advancement. In terms of conventional political divisions, the issue appeals both to conservatives (enforcement of law and morality) and liberals (defending women and children). This dimension has grown in importance since the late 1970s, when a feminist constituency originating on the Left campaigned against sexual offenses that had traditionally concerned those on the moralistic Right: pornography and sex crime thus became the perfect political issue. Politicians at local and national levels benefited from conspicuous vigilance in this area, as illustrated by the Senate campaigns of Arlen Specter and Paul Simon in the mid-1980s and of James Exon and Charles Grassley a decade later.

Religious and moralistic groups have long employed child-protection rhetoric to promote their goals, for raising public awareness in this sensitive area offered the potential bonus of drawing attention to other associated issues. Throughout successive debates over sex crimes, an antihomosexual agenda has rarely been far below the surface of the rhetoric, most markedly in the early 1950s and in 1977 and, to a lesser extent, in 1993–94. In the area of controlling obscenity, the modern emphasis on child pornography has permitted authorities to obtain public support that was not forthcoming where adult material was concerned, justifying the expansion of agencies and task forces that would not have been tolerated if they were seen as interfering with the private, consensual pleasures of grown-ups.

Alongside these core groups were others that became more active in particular periods, as when the general expansion of civil litigation in the 1980s brought the legal profession into the child-protection cause. A whole new branch of the profession developed on the strength of lawsuits undertaken on behalf of victims against parents or against institutions like schools and churches accused of being negligent in failing to prevent abuse.[5]

Of course, enumerating so many interest groups should not suggest that their interpretations of the child-protection issue were identical or even compatible, and there were powerful natural contradictions between the underlying assumptions of the respective groups. Although feminists, social workers, moral traditionalists, therapists, and others all stood to gain from drawing attention to threats to children, each needed to emphasize certain aspects of the problem rather than others. In the 1980s, for example, both feminists and evangelical groups generally demanded credence for claims concerning ritual abuse, although they differed widely in their analyses of the origins of the problem. For religious activists, SRA was a weapon for attacking secularism and the abandonment of children to day care, while an explicit analogy was drawn between the alleged frequency of child sacrifice and public tolerance of legal abortion: all these approaches were of course anathema to feminists. Similarly, psychiatrists and therapists have often allied with law-enforcement interests in emphasizing the scale and virulence of the threat from sex offenders, although the policy lessons that each side drew from the problem differed enormously. In each era of intense concern over sexual dangers to children, the tactical alliances between the various segments of the child-protection movement were often tenuous and sometimes strained.

Despite their occasionally fractious relationships, this impressive range of interest groups stood to benefit from claims about threats to children, and the number of beneficiaries increased as each crisis developed. A particular campaign might begin with allegations by police and decency groups in one locality, and reports of the charges are subsequently taken up by the media and disseminated over the whole nation, with the clear message being that these alleged events are a manifestation of a major sex crime problem.[6] Such reporting allows the media to adopt a crusading stance, in which official activism is praised while a lack of vigor is denounced as neglect of victims. More and more agencies are goaded into action, and often new agencies are created with the specific function of rooting out child exploitation, on the lines of the anticruelty and antivice societies of the Progressive Era or the Child Protective Service agencies founded during the 1970s. Police agencies receive enhanced powers and resources, as exemplified by the growth of the antipornography squads in the modern Customs Service and the Postal Service. These bureaucratic entities have a vested interest in justifying their "crusade" by the constant production of statistics indicating the rising frequency of abuse and molestation, while federal agencies are especially keen to stress the interstate and international dimensions of the problem and its conspiratorial aspects. As official actions intensify, so do the number of instances of misbehavior detected and prosecuted, which in turn increases still further the sense of a spreading epidemic. Statistics and research findings gain credibility to the extent that they fit public expectations, and they are often simplified or even distorted into some easily remembered format that is repeated until it becomes a truism: "between 500,000 and 1 million children are involved in prostitution and pornography in this country"; "one in four girls is an incest victim"; "80 percent of Internet traffic involves perverse sex."

After a few years, the perception of a problem becomes so well entrenched that its reality and significance seem not to brook questioning, and at this stage the emphasis of the original issue changes subtly to reflect slightly different concerns. In the mid-1970s, for instance, the upsurge of books on rape proved the importance of the issue and the degree of public concern, but the literature soon exhausted the obvious points that could be made. Authors and researchers had to pursue more specialized aspects of the problem or other directions that seemed to lead naturally from it, so the next decade was marked by the discovery of rape as it affected particular populations (the very young or old, ethnic minorities) or occurred in particular situations (date and acquaintance rape, marital rape, rape in institutional settings). In turn, some topics developed their own independent lives and generated further work on peripheral aspects of those problems. Thus examinations of child sexual abuse led to studies of abuse by authority figures like clergy, abuse in school and day care settings, or the victimization of boys. Problem construction is a cumulative, incremental process in which each issue is to some extent built upon its predecessors, in the context of a steadily developing fund of socially available knowledge.

Explaining Complacence

Problems evolve, but they also decline, and the question of why that happens presents its own puzzles. If child protection is such an invaluable ideological weapon, why should it ever be discarded or lose its force? One might think that the upward spiral of claims would never diminish, and that once under way, a panic like that of the late 1940s would have continued unchecked to the present day, as of course it did not. From our present-day vantage point, we find it easy to see why societies should be intensely concerned about saving children, but why do some communities *not* share this concern? And why do societies shift with apparent swiftness from one set of priorities to another, radically different set? Put another way, what requires explanation is not that the sex crime panics of the 1910s or 1940s or 1980s should have occurred but that the issue was treated with such relative indifference during the intervening decades.

Linked to this is the question of why panics erupt when they do. An attractive explanation is that latent fears about threats of sexual violence are mobilized by sensational reporting of particular notorious crimes. The formulation of the sex offender issue during 1936–37 owed much to the reporting on the Albert Fish case, just as the child abuse threat of the early 1980s was conditioned by reporting on incidents like the Atlanta child murders, and the recent alarm about sexual predators was shaped by the horrific careers of Earl Shriner and Westley Dodd. The flaw with this explanation is that comparable events at other times did not ignite similar reactions, suggesting that although the spark was lit, the tinder was not available. In the late 1920s, the twenty or so child murders committed by Gordon Stewart Northcott in southern California attracted national attention but conspicuously failed to set off any general panic over sex offenders; nor did the equally sensational murders committed by Ed Gein in 1957, the crimes that inspired the film *Psycho*. In 1973, the roughly thirty sex murders attributed to Dean Corll achieved worldwide notoriety, but there was no attempt to contextualize the Texas incident with other instances of molestation or sex crimes elsewhere or to legislate accordingly: Houston authorities dismissed the victims not as boys but as hustlers and "male whores."[7] This affair actually coincided with an extensive liberalization of the laws affecting sexual deviance and had no impact whatsoever on sidetracking or slowing that process. Grotesque cases can be widely reported, but they can be successfully contextualized as examples of a particular problem only when they are presented in a way that makes sense to a mass public.

Nor does it appear that upsurges of concern are a natural or rational response to new social scientific findings like the abundant evidence that suddenly became available in the late 1970s for the prevalence of child sexual abuse and incest. Victimization surveys certainly contributed to the child abuse revolution, but they were neither the only nor the necessary cause of this transformation. After all, in 1935 the scale of the abuse problem was laid out in remarkably modern-sounding terms by the Goldbergs, who took full account of both stranger assault and incest and who presented their harrowing case studies in sensitive and memorable terms, while in 1953 Kinsey's study suggested that these experiences befell about one-quarter of all American girls. Still, the idea of widespread molestation by intimates and neighbors was all but ignored because it could not be fitted into prevailing social ideologies, and the Goldbergs' work was little noticed until the 1970s.[8] Nor did neglect of the Kinsey findings arise from well-founded doubts about the validity of his samples, as no such qualms prevented immediate acceptance of his estimates for the prevalence of male homosexual behavior. In the mid-1960s, similarly, books seeking to prove an "epidemic" of rape and sexual violence made no impact on policymakers because the works did not meet the needs or expectations of their audience. Significantly, these claims failed to win influence despite the recent example provided by the Boston strangler case and despite clamorous FBI propaganda.

Similar events and discoveries provoke panic responses in one era but not in another, and actions and arguments that win widespread support in one decade fall out of favor in another, when the child-protection ideology can find itself at odds with other competing attitudes and value systems. Throughout the twentieth century, child defense rhetoric has had an instant and powerful appeal, based on concepts like safeguarding innocence, protecting the future of the nation, resisting predators, and so on. At the same time, actions taken to achieve these admirable goals can in one year be praised and at another time be roundly condemned. Those working for an agency that prosecutes sexually active teenagers might be stigmatized as being puritans, busybodies, killjoys, or witch-hunters; therapeutic intervention in cases of minor sexual deviance can be attacked, in the language of *1984*, as brainwashing or psychiatric tyranny. Depending on the prevailing ideological environment, the pursuit of sex rings can be regarded as either a laudable campaign against sinister perverts or a diversion of valuable resources against harmless hedonists.

Thus the rhetoric of child protection can enjoy great success, but only as long as it is not challenged or displaced by countervailing ideologies of libertarianism, sexual freedom and experimentation, and distrust of the state and its agencies. Such rival values are often implied in the narratives told in order to represent the "sex crime problem." In the 1990s, the characteristic story might be that of dedicated postal inspectors who, while seeking to root out illegal child pornography, track down a pedophile in time to prevent him from abusing yet another young victim. In another era, the story may be utterly different in theme and emphasis: perhaps the main character is a man confined for many years as a sex psychopath after he has been found guilty of a consensual homosexual encounter, or perhaps he is a southern black man falsely accused of interfering with a white child and then lynched by a bigoted mob. These rival narratives gain their greatest importance when they contribute to shaping judicial attitudes toward sex crime, which, as we have seen, have changed spectacularly over the past one hundred years or so.

The Shifting Market for Claims

In trying to explain why one set of values prevails rather than another, we find that demographic factors always play a role. Indeed, the history of American sex offender laws is closely related to the shifting demographic balance of the population in terms of age and ethnicity. At the turn of the century, mass immigration on a scale unprecedented in world history contributed to the mushroom growth of cities like New York and Chicago, and the high fertility of the mainly young migrants portended a transformation of the American population. In the first two decades of the twentieth century, American birth rates were a remarkable thirty or so per thousand (almost double the current figure), and the national population grew at a faster rate between 1890 and 1915 than in any subsequent era. Fears of a shifting ethnic balance galvanized old-stock Americans, who launched a social reform movement intended to civilize this new and mainly urban class by "saving" their teeming young, and also boosted eugenic notions. The end of mass immigration in 1924 was followed by a sharp decline in birth rates and the proportion of children in the total population, a fall accelerated by the economic catastrophe of the early 1930s. By 1935, the birth rate was under nineteen per thousand, and the median age of the population rose from twenty-five years in 1920 to twenty-nine years in 1940.

Demographic history since then has been dominated by the vast cohort of the baby boom generation: birth rates between 1946 and 1957 were usually around twenty-five per thousand, and the proportion of children in the national population reached a higher level than for many years before or since. Parental concerns led to demands for laws to protect this group from molestation, so that the emphasis of the sex menace moved away from attacks against women and toward the threat to young children. But as those children came of age, their demands for personal and sexual freedom placed intolerable burdens on sexually restrictive laws and specifically on the age of sexual consent, creating the relaxed attitudes of the 1960s and 1970s. When these teenagers became parents and grandparents in the following decades, the median age of the population rose sharply, from twenty-eight years in 1970 to thirty-three in 1990. Compared to their parents' generation, many adult boomers found that they had less domestic stability and less direct supervision over their own children. These trends created the potential for the new abuse panics of the 1980s and 1990s. Meanwhile, youngsters themselves had less of a voice: Americans from fourteen through seventeen years of age represented almost 8 percent of the population in 1970 but only 5.3 percent in 1990. In each epoch, the audience for claims was substantially different, and problems were conceived differently.[9]

The demographic cycle described here has wider relevance. Concern about sex crimes was at its lowest during periods of relatively high tolerance for sexual experimentation, including the 1920s and especially the sexual revolution under way by the early 1960s. (Although influenced by new reproductive technologies like the contraceptive pill, the second movement was strongly correlated to the sexual maturing of the baby boom generation.) The sexual revolution was in retreat by the early 1980s, under the assault of diseases like herpes and later AIDS, and a new conservatism became evident. The cycle also helps to explain why waves of concern about social dangers like drug addiction are often correlated with fears about sex crimes: drug scares similarly peaked in the critical year 1914, when the federal government effectively prohibited cocaine and opiate drugs, and in 1936–37, the time of the national regulation of marijuana. Later, the baby boom generation was as sympathetic to illicit drugs as to sexual experimentation, and drug use enjoyed broad middle-class acceptability from the late 1960s through the early 1980s. Tolerance for drugs endured a little longer than did easygoing attitudes to underage sex, but here, too, the Reagan era marked a sudden and violent transition.[10] In 1982, the Justice Department declared a war on drugs that was quite as uncompromising as the contemporary campaign against child abuse, and both zero-

large cities.[13] The predator threat assisted in reimposing family discipline and curbing the sexual activities of the young. Emphasizing the uniquely horrible character of illegal sexual acts against children and teenagers reinforced the fundamental message that the age of consent was sacrosanct and should not be transgressed, whether forcibly or voluntarily.

Explanations offered for sex crime in the various eras usually by implication contain a recipe for "correct" child rearing, family structure, gender roles, and personal conduct. In the decade after 1945, children received a conservative message from a culture that believed straying from appropriate roles presaged later deviancy or psychopathy. Effeminacy was a particular danger: the boy who failed to play sports today, or even played with dolls, might become the lurking molester of ten or twenty years hence.[14] The threat of molestation or murder played its role in reinforcing family structures and buttressing narrow concepts of masculinity. Pamphlets and lectures warned that safety was to be found only within the home and family and that the outside world was a dangerous place where the young ventured at their peril and where they could survive only by taking constant precautions: "Never talk to strangers" became enshrined in the credo of postwar domestic ideology.

The strict emphasis on masculinity and the patriarchal family was not exactly replicated in later warnings, but there, too, the sexual threat from outsiders was used to circumscribe the behavior of the young. The movement against child pornography reinforced sexual boundaries that had been crumbling dramatically since the previous decade and also reimposed an ideology of social discipline. This found expression in the emerging definition of child pornography as the depiction of persons under sixteen (later eighteen) years of age; the implication was that youngsters had no business being involved or portrayed in any sexual context. Defining adolescents as children implied that they were or should be subject to appropriate parental and social discipline, especially in sexual matters. This corpus of law has succeeded beyond the wildest dreams of decency campaigners in creating a perilous environment in which eroticism involving a person under eighteen is automatically criminal. A girl of sixteen may marry and bear children in many states, but if her husband takes a revealing photograph of her, he is creating child pornography.

The rhetoric of abuse has also expanded medicalized and deviant labels to include juvenile sexual behaviors that until very recently were commonly regarded as harmless play. Since the late 1980s, a school of therapists has popularized the idea of the danger from "children who molest children," pubescent or younger children identified as abusers on the grounds of their sexual behaviors with their peers. That these acts might be mild by most standards is suggested by the case of the nine-year-old boy whose career of crime involved looking up girls' skirts and sexually touching his sister, but mandatory abuse reporting demands that such behavior be delated to authorities. Schools were also hypersensitive to cases that could lead to expensive litigation, and some attracted media derision when they imposed severe penalties on small children whose depredations extended to kissing classmates. An increasing number of youngsters found themselves before juvenile courts as sex offenders or "sexualized children" requiring lengthy and expensive behavioral therapy: several hundred programs now offer treatment for offenders under the age of twelve, and one critic describes the nascent "problem" as "the next satanic ritual abuse."[15] Therapeutic trends have been reinforced by conservative moralist demands that schools teach total abstinence as the only acceptable form of juvenile sexuality. The whole phenomenon recalls midcentury accounts, by Doshay and others, of young sex delinquents who were guilty of nothing more than intimate experimentation; it also recalls, more distantly, the nineteenth-century doctors who made careers out of advising families how to stop their children from masturbating. In each instance, the ideal of childhood wholly excluded a sexual dimension: the only good child was a non-"sexualized" one.

Shifting gender expectations were as important as issues of generational control in conditioning receptivity to claims. Protecting and nurturing children had always been a central component of the traditional role of women, so if children were being exposed to abuse, this implied that women had failed in their responsibilities and should move proactively to defend their young. Activists promoted concern for political or moralistic reasons, but their dramatic success shows that they were able to build upon existing and ill-defined feelings of malaise and guilt among women who worried that they were not fulfilling their obligations. This nagging sense that all was not right at home would be all the greater when women's movement into the workplace not only occurred quite suddenly but involved a reversal of long-standing roles, as was the case in the 1940s or 1970s. In the decade after 1945, psychiatric experts portrayed sexual deviancy as the result of departures from the ideal of the nuclear family, in which both genders knew and respected their appropriate roles and mothers did not "dominer" over others in the home. The return to postwar "normality" demanded swift restoration of the gender hierarchy.[16] Nor could women abandon their children to day care as they had in the war years, some said, as a child lacking proper role models could grow up to become a pervert or psychopath. The psychopath provided a vital rationale for the assertion that a woman's place was in the home and not in the no-woman's-land of the streets.

The indices gauging women's independence accelerated once again during the early 1970s, and this goes far toward explaining the rediscovery of sex crime, which occurred shortly afterward. The proportion of women working outside the home now increased as rapidly as it had in World War II: in 1970, about 43 percent of women aged sixteen and older were in the labor force, a figure that grew to 52 percent by 1980 and approached 60 percent in the early 1990s. A new independence coincided with the aspirations inspired by the feminist movement, and these factors contributed to the upsurge of divorce from the early 1970s. In 1958, there were roughly four marriages for every divorce in the United States; by 1970, the ratio was three to one, and by 1976, it reached the level of about two to one, where it stayed for the next two decades. Married couples with children represented more than 40 percent of all American households in 1970 but only 26 percent by 1990.[17] In child rearing, day care was much more commonly used, and for younger children; but with all the rhetoric of independence, a confusion of cultural messages ensured that many women felt ambivalent about "abandoning" their children to the kindness of strangers. This offered fertile ground for the new panics, which closely echoed the concern of the previous generation. In the 1980s, the public was all too ready to accept the reality of threats emanating from abductors and child pornographers lurking in caregiver settings like playschools and churches.

The cyberpanics are informative here for the impact of changing social and technological environments. In both ritual abuse and cyberstalking, sexual dangers focused ill-defined fears about children falling outside the control of their parents. The two problems had much else in common, including a quasi-religious or even demonic vision of the child predator. At first glance, the cyberpanic seems quite different from the cult scare, as abusers based their operations upon the most sophisticated technology. However, demonic imagery was if anything even more explicit here, with the vision of children conversing with faceless beings whom they mistook for fellow innocents but who were in reality tempting them to corruption or physical destruction: as *Newsweek* declared, the young might be "spirited . . . away from their keyboards."[18] As with the ritual abuse gangs, the notion would have been instantly comprehensible to the residents of seventeenth-century Massachusetts. Defending against external predators demanded both a firm restoration of parental supervision in the home, and a vigorous response by law enforcement.

Globalization

Any explanations advanced for the success or failure of claims about child exploitation must take account of an international dimension. If we can talk of a "market" for claims, then, in social policy as in commerce and industry, the twentieth century witnessed the advance of globalization on an unprecedented scale. The process was under way in Victorian times, when Americans imported scholarship from Europe in order to create their own disciplines of sociology, psychology, and criminology and when early concern over child sexual exploitation was in large measure a response to English moral activists, especially Josephine Butler and W. T. Stead. Ironically, though, as early as 1901, Stead himself prophesied that "the Americanization of the world" (the title of one of his books) would be "the trend of the twentieth century," and since that time the United States has dominated the export of ideas. Subject to local cultural, legal, and political differences, most advanced countries have demonstrated a sensitivity to child-protection issues quite akin to what was occurring in the United States, and they have often done so under direct American influence. This was suggested by the dissemination of the sex psychopath idea during the 1940s; Canada, for example, acquired a Criminal Sexual Psychopath law in 1948. Between 1948 and 1954, the American panic over the pernicious sexual effects of horror comics was emulated in several other nations, including Britain, France, Australia, New Zealand, and Canada, where American experts like Fredric Wertham were much in demand to testify before investigative commissions.[19]

This influence became much more powerful when concerns revived during the mid-1970s. In Great Britain, a radical transformation of attitudes was evident in the key year 1977, when a campaign against child pornography flourished and the British Pedophile Information Exchange was crushed and demonized. In 1986, new surveys about the extent of child sexual abuse contributed to placing this issue at the center of social debate, and the country soon followed the United States in producing a far-reaching series of panics over mass abuse, incest, pedophile rings, and even satanic and ritual crime.[20] At every stage, British thought was shaped by American emissaries bringing the latest transatlantic insights on these matters. With somewhat different chronologies, similar patterns can be discerned in all English-speaking countries and in nations culturally influenced by the United States, such as Israel.

Australia illustrates the same pattern. In the late 1970s, the spectacular case of a serial pederast led to furious concern and an attack on homosexuality, which was seen as being linked to child molestation. In 1984, the state of New South Wales began a crusade against child abuse that subsequently spread through the whole nation. The Child Protection Council was established, new resources were provided to social service departments, strict mandatory reporting laws were passed, and a major public information campaign was undertaken. Reported cases of sexual abuse predictably soared. As in Britain and other countries, Australia followed the American trend in shifting the emphasis from incest to sexual attacks by strangers, and by 1995, the federal parliament began investigating "organized criminal pedophile activity," examining "pedophile networks" and other covert groups and their involvement in child pornography and sex tours. The study made heavy use of American authorities, citing congressional hearings, FBI documents, and experts like Kenneth Lanning.[21]

Following a harrowing sex murder scandal in Belgium in 1996, public opinion in several European countries began linking pedophilia to abduction and serial violence and soon began demanding stern countermeasures, including a crackdown on indecency on the Internet. In South Africa, a series of child murders, possibly ritualistic in nature, sparked national alarm about the abuse threat and led to calls for a national register of sex offenders against children. Fears about satanic and ritualistic abuse provide another striking index of the dissemination of American ideas in Canada, Australia, New Zealand, South Africa, and the Netherlands. By the early 1990s, the emerging American focus on abuse by clergy was being emulated in these nations as well as Britain, Ireland, and Austria. The independent Canadian discovery of "pedophile priests" shows that panics were partly a response to local conditions, but emerging perceptions of local problems were shaped and interpreted by American experts and delegations, American academic journals and professional texts, and omnipresent American popular culture. Japan and other countries that were slow or reluctant to accept imported American norms in these matters were increasingly subjected to intense international pressure.[22]

The dissemination of ideas from the United States reflected the overwhelming power of the nation's media and the vast scale of its academic establishment, but American views would not have been so influential had they not resonated with constituencies in other nations. These ideas about the sexual abuse of children spread because they appealed to local audiences, which had been conditioned by social circumstances very similar to those in the United States. These included similar demographic cycles, dramatic increases in the status and economic independence of women, declines in two-parent nuclear families, the growth of political feminism, and heightened sensitivity to sexual violence. These other countries had also had their wartime social disruption, followed by their respective baby booms, and had their own not dissimilar recollections of radicalism during the 1960s and 1970s.

The Permanent Problem?

To speak of waves or cycles of American concern about sex crime implies a regular and even predictable process, and at first glance this model seems to work well. Peaks of interest appear to occur about every thirty-five years: the demand for legislation to control or punish molesters and perverts is most evident in roughly 1915, 1950, and 1985; troughs of interest follow in the late 1920s and again in the early 1960s. But there the pattern breaks down. Far from marking a new era of indifference, the year 1995 was characterized by the furor over sex predator statutes and the fear of cyberstalkers. The cycle has been broken in the modern era, when child abuse has become part of our enduring cultural landscape, a metanarrative with the potential for explaining all social and personal ills.

The durable quality of modern concepts about child abuse is linked to irreversible social changes that have brought unprecedented numbers of women into the economy and into public life (and not merely, as in the 1940s, for the duration of a national emergency). A growing literature is examining the many-sided effects of the feminization of American culture and politics. Women voters are increasingly seen as the key constituency in national elections, and women consumers are the powerful market that retailers and advertisers have in mind when they design their products. Because a similar trend affects perceptions of social problems, society in the 1990s has become far more sensitive to sexual violence and exploitation, including not only rape, incest, and child abuse but also sexual harassment in the workplace, which only twenty years ago was trivialized as a source of humor. In this context, the sexual threat to children will likely remain a central social issue, however reconceived; even in 1993–94, when the recovered memory movement was being denounced, the response was not to abandon the abuse threat but to redirect attention to the stranger predator. When journalists and other commentators attacked errant therapists, they usually did so by stressing the harm done to women retractors and their families, inviting a largely female audience to sympathize with these "victims of memory." Any movement that can survive a fiasco as total as the ritual abuse affair must be all but indestructible.

Social change has been reinforced by the institutionalization of the child-protection idea in many aspects of social life, not least in the expanded social welfare agencies. Although these might come under attack for occasional abuses of power, it is unthinkable that any federal or state government in the foreseeable future might trim the child-protection machinery back to the levels of the 1950s or 1960s, as this would attract politically lethal charges of being soft on child molestation. Another focus can be found in the academic world, where themes of incest and abuse are a mainstay of scholarship in departments of social and behavioral science but are also in different ways found in the humanities, especially the fields of literature, social theory, cultural studies, and women's studies.

Another factor has been the vast expansion of the health care industry over the past two decades; therapeutic care and counseling have been among the swiftest growing forms of employment in the contemporary economy. Myriad clinics and treatment programs exist to deal with all manner of personal problems that would once have been regarded as moral or legal issues, including drug abuse, alcoholism, eating disorders, and, of course, child abuse. Whereas analysis and counseling were once reserved for those of private means, a democratization of therapy has followed the extension of insurance coverage throughout the middle class. Moral issues have been medicalized and institutionalized, producing a huge constituency with an overwhelming interest in keeping these issues at the center of public concern. The psychiatric establishment has a powerful interest not only in ensuring that "their" problems continue to be viewed as serious, threatening, and likely to respond only to the medical solutions that they market but also in continuing to bring other issues into their orbit. This does much to explain the constant generation of new syndromes and diagnoses, from recovered memory and multiple personalities to "sexualized children."

The current child-protection movement also differs from its predecessors in being the first to emphasize the experience of victims (beyond merely using the images of faceless children to excite pathos). Since the rape movement of the 1970s, victims of sexual assault have responded enthusiastically to calls for self-assertion and mobilization in successive survivor movements, a trend that reached its height with the incest survivors of the early 1990s. For the first time in history, perhaps millions of people, mainly but not exclusively women, have constructed their self-identity in terms of the experience of sexual victimization. Networks of survivors became a powerful interest group, protesting any weakening in society's vigilance against abuse and launching virulent attacks on therapists or writers who dared to speak of "false memory." The mass media accorded survivor groups the respect and authority due to anyone who had passed through a traumatic ordeal; it became difficult to contest their views without seeming callous or naive. Support from survivor movements has immeasurably strengthened the claims of therapists and counselors, with whom they have formed a solid front.

Several recent developments have made it likely that contemporary formulations of the child abuse problem will not diminish in the near future. One is the expansion of provisions whereby insurance companies or health maintenance organizations pay all or part of the cost of mental health services used by their clients; a 1996 law required employers to be as generous in setting spending caps for mental health coverage as they were for physical health benefits. Enhanced coverage would give therapists and institutions a financial incentive to undertake more searching and wide-ranging investigations of patients' complaints and perhaps also to hospitalize those who would have been treated as outpatients before.[23] The prospects for developing such a market are vast, as the new law would affect some 23 million Americans. Expanded psychiatric intervention would also occur in a new legal environment, as a 1996 Supreme Court decision has extended to therapists and other mental health professionals a confidentiality privilege similar to that held by lawyers and clergy. This would make it more difficult to defend against a child abuse prosecution by demanding video or audio tapes of therapy sessions, which might show that incriminating material had been produced by improper means. More prosecutions could be based on testimony produced during therapy sessions, while at the same time it would be harder to defend against such suits. Despite current media attitudes, abuse suits arising from memory therapy might conceivably gain a second wind.

Another recent trend has been to sex laws as tools to reduce public liability for welfare, which in fact revives an old principle: the American colonies used bastardy prosecutions to avoid the financial burden that would otherwise fall upon them if the charge of supporting illegitimate children could not be "sworn to" a particular man. In the 1990s, concern over welfare costs led to a renewed use of legal sanctions for reducing the burden on the public purse (for example, by pursuing and prosecuting "deadbeat dads" who fail to pay child support), and the rhetoric of child protection and the enforcement of family obligations have encouraged jurisdictions to attempt to deter teenage pregnancies through the criminal law.

This idea gained momentum from studies purporting to show that an astonishing number of pregnancies resulted from liaisons between young girls and older men; because such liaisons should be considered a form of child abuse, they should be punishable under criminal law. In reality, the situation was far less harrowing than the statistics initially suggested, for many of the teenage pregnancies recorded involved girls of eighteen or nineteen, who in many cases were married to men a little older than themselves. Moreover, most of the babies born to fifteen- or sixteen-year-old girls were fathered by boys of comparable ages. Even so, the image of teen mothers as the "abused prey of older men" swiftly established itself in the public consciousness: statutory rape prosecutions have proliferated in Connecticut, Washington, and Florida and are likely to become far more commonplace than at any time in the past half century. Governor William Weld of Massachusetts has asserted, in reference to girls under sixteen years of age: "Statutory rape is not a victimless crime. Little girls pushed by grown men into sex and motherhood—experiences for which they are not in any sense ready—are the victims of crime. They should be defended with the full force of the law."

Sometimes the fiscal goals of these policies are explicit: in Connecticut, for instance, proposed legislation would deny welfare to a mother who refused to assist in the prosecution of her child's father. A sense of déjà vu surrounds the current debate about whether a man in such cases should be imprisoned or compelled to marry the young mother. One Idaho county harks back still further to the earlier recesses of morality law by reintroducing prosecutions for fornication, a decision that has gained national publicity.[24] As in the case of child pornography, framing an issue in terms of the moral protection of children serves to revive legal concepts that quite recently stood on the brink of extinction.

It remains to be seen whether policies designed for a small number of sex offenders may have a much wider impact on policies toward other criminals, juvenile delinquents, and the mentally ill. Treatment programs for sex offenders represent a foothold of the extreme positivist ideal in the prisons and conceivably a model that could be extended more widely. This could soon be a matter of pressing urgency: current demographic trends (the baby boomerang) mean that within a decade or so, the United States will experience a major expansion in the number of people ages fifteen through twenty-five, and this will presumably be accompanied by the worst upsurge of violent crime since the early 1980s. At that point, there will be calls for stern measures to ensure public safety, and if the courts permit the arsenal of techniques now proposed for sexual predators, these might well be extended to "normal" violent criminals. The temptation will be all the greater if forms of behavior modification are seen as the only means of disciplining the inmates of already crowded correctional institutions. Official responses to sex offenders provide glaring exceptions to customary constitutional protections, but exceptions that may yet expand beyond their current scope.

Predators in Perspective

Although a belief that children are vulnerable to dangerous sex offenders has been firmly established as a basic component of social ideology, there is no consensus about who the perpetrators of that threat are or what motivates them, and thus there is no consensus about the best means of prevention. We again encounter a long-familiar paradox: although much evidence suggests that abuse is most likely to occur in the domestic or neighborhood setting, with family or neighbors as culprits, concepts of the problem place the blame on outside forces—on fiends and psychopaths, pedophiles and predators. And of all the possible responses to the issue— psychological, educational, social, or welfare-oriented—official action will inevitably take the form of penal sanctions imposed by the criminal-justice system on these outsider figures.

Americans favor the "justice solution" not because of any national tendency toward being punitive but because it is so much easier to identify a problem as the work of an individual or a group who can be subjected to some form of official sanction. Identifying the root causes of a problem is difficult, as is undertaking the substantial changes in law or social policy necessary to make a real difference. In fact, simply persuading a mass audience that problems are serious can be hard unless the issues can be personalized or contextualized in some way that will make them comprehensible. The late 1980s offer a potent analogy here. While the ritual abuse panic was in full spate and the media were in furious pursuit of nonexistent satanic gangs, a quite authentic crime wave of astonishing proportions was being revealed in the form of the savings and loan debacle, in which corporate crooks stole sums amounting to hundreds of billions of dollars, crippling the economies of whole cities and states and wreaking financial havoc that would not be resolved for decades. The sums are inconceivable, and that is precisely the problem. An audience overawed by bank robberies of a few million dollars had little grasp of the moneys taken from the thrifts, and still less did the ordinary public (or most journalists) ever understand the technical chicanery employed. Advocates wishing to draw attention to the disaster had to do so by placing it in a context that a lay audience would find both understandable and morally wrong. This meant drawing every possible connection with known and stereotyped criminals like organized criminals, rogue intelligence agents, and drug dealers, and a crash among Nebraska thrifts became a "real" crime only when it could be linked with the fashionable bogey of satanic sex rings. The S. and L. issue made little headway with the national audience until corporate criminality found a face (literally) in the form of Charles Keating and the senators whose support he allegedly bought; Keating promptly became the nationally identifiable scapegoat for the whole catastrophe.

A similar incomprehension met contemporaneous claims that 40 or 50 million Americans were victims of child sexual abuse. Even if doubts about survey techniques reduced that number by a factor of ten or twenty, the underlying lessons were still literally unimaginable until the problem found faces in the shape of the McMartin preschool teachers and later of the sex predators, the killers of Polly Klaas and Megan Kanka. In the familiar anthropomorphic process that shapes our response to other problems, the issue of sex offenses is personalized, and once identified, monsters can be defeated, captured, and killed. To quote Matthew Stadler, this "asserts a vision of crime that lawmakers fervently want to believe: a place where sexual violence can be isolated and treated, where the evil lurking in the land can be corralled and eliminated. The predator has become nothing less than that—a symbol of the deepest evil."[25] Given concrete form, the problem can be met by means that legislatures understand, namely, passing ever more stringent laws and beginning a demagogic bidding war to impose the harshest penalties for the behavior. In the 1980s the goal was to produce specific and concrete measures that could be proudly cited to the media and the electors, preferably with resonant titles announcing the goal of defending and avenging children. Who could vote against something called Megan's Law? In this environment, there were even dividends in proposing laws so extreme that the courts would find them unconstitutional, as judges could then be left with the stigma of having failed to defend children.

Unfortunately, the solutions proposed did not necessarily have anything to do with the original abuse issue and were based on a false understanding of the nature of sex crimes against children. Legislatures tended to accept the myth of prevention long ago propounded by the *New York Times:* "moral degenerates are easily discoverable without waiting until acts of violence put them in the category of criminals."[26] And as the revival of statutory rape laws illustrates, the measures imply a dubious faith in the possibility of deterrence. Not only are predator laws and their ilk ineffective, but they foreclose discussion on other possible avenues of approach to child abuse. In the mid-1990s, the federal lawmakers most enthusiastic for predator statutes and Internet regulation showed themselves equally determined to cut social welfare programs in ways that would increase the poverty of children and families, despite the predictable effects on juvenile crime, substance abuse, and domestic violence. After all, had Congress not already dealt with the problem of "real" child abuse?

Predators, psychopaths, and pedophiles represent a very minor component of the real sexual issues faced by children, while even sexual threats must be considered alongside many other dangers arising from physical violence, environmental damage, and the myriad effects of pervasive poverty. During the twentieth century, however, such dangerous outsiders have attracted a vastly disproportionate share of official attention, precisely because they represent the easiest targets for anyone wishing, however sincerely, to protect children.

Abbreviations

AJO	*American Journal of Orthopsychiatry*
AJP	*American Journal of Psychiatry*
BG	*Boston Globe*
CAN	*Child Abuse and Neglect*
JAICLC	*Journal of the American Institute of Criminal Law and Criminology*
JH	*Journal of Homosexuality*
JSH	*Journal of Social Hygiene*
LAT	*Los Angeles Times*
NCAVC	National Center for the Analysis of Violent Crime
NCMEC	National Center for Missing and Exploited Children

NYT	*New York Times*
SFC	*San Francisco Chronicle*
WP	*Washington Post*
WSJ	*Wall Street Journal*
WWW	World Wide Web

Notes

CHAPTER 1: CREATING FACTS

1. Peter Berger and Thomas Luckmann, *The Social Construction of Reality* (New York: Doubleday Anchor, 1967).

2. E. Olafson, D. L. Corwin, and Roland C. Summit, "Modern History of Child Sexual Abuse Awareness: Cycles of Discovery and Suppression," *CAN* 17 (1993): 7–24; compare David Finkelhor, "Sexual Abuse: A Sociological Perspective," *CAN* 6 (1982): 95–102.

3. Joel Best, ed., *Images of Issues*, 2d ed. (Hawthorne, N.Y.: Aldine de Gruyter, 1995); Thomas J. Bernard, *The Cycle of Juvenile Justice* (New York: Oxford University Press, 1992); James B. Gilbert, *A Cycle of Outrage* (New York: Oxford University Press, 1986); Joseph Gusfield, *The Culture of Public Problems* (Chicago: University of Chicago Press, 1981).

4. Best, *Images of Issues*, p. 6.

5. Edwin Sutherland, "The Diffusion of Sex Psychopath Laws," *American Journal of*

Sociology 56 (1950): 142–48, and "The Sexual Psychopath Laws," *Journal of Criminal Law and Criminology* 40 (1950): 534–54; Nicholas N. Kittrie, *The Right to Be Different* (Baltimore: Johns Hopkins University Press, 1971); George Chauncey, "The Postwar Sex Crime Panic," in William Graebner, ed., *True Stories from the American Past* (New York: McGraw-Hill, 1993), pp. 160–78; John D'Emilio, "The Homosexual Menace," in Kathy Peiss, Christina Simmons, and Robert A. Padgug, eds., *Passion and Power: Sexuality in History* (Philadelphia: Temple University Press, 1989), pp. 226–40; Estelle B. Freedman, "Uncontrolled Desires," *Journal of American History* 74 (1987): 83–106. Compare Erich Goode and Nachman Ben-Yehuda, *Moral Panics* (Oxford: Blackwell, 1994), pp. 18–19; Kenneth Plummer, *Sexual Stigma* (London: Routledge Kegan Paul, 1975); David Finkelhor, *Child Sexual Abuse* (New York: Free Press, 1984), p. 3; Paula S. Fass, *Kidnapped: Child Abduction in America* (New York: Oxford University Press, 1997).

6. Although see Chauncey, "The Postwar Sex Crime Panic," p. 175. For constructionist studies, see Joel Best, *Threatened Children* (Chicago: University of Chicago Press, 1990); Debbie Nathan and Michael Snedeker, *Satan's Silence* (New York: Basic, 1995); Martin L. Forst and Martha-Elin Blomquist, *Missing Children: Rhetoric and Reality* (Toronto: Lexington, 1991); Lela Costin, Howard Krager, and David Stoesz, *The Politics of Child Abuse in America* (New York: Oxford University Press, 1996).

7. Stan Cohen, *Folk Devils and Moral Panics* (Oxford: Blackwell, 1972); Goode and Ben-Yehuda, *Moral Panics;* the quotation is from Stuart Hall et al., *Policing the Crisis* (London: Macmillan, 1978), p. 16.

8. Philip Schlesinger and Howard Tumber, *Reporting Crime* (Oxford: Clarendon, 1994); Helen Benedict, *Virgin or Vamp* (New York: Oxford University Press, 1992); Keith Soothill and Sylvia Walby, *Sex Crime in the News* (London: Routledge, 1991); Stanley Cohen and Jock Young, eds., *The Manufacture of News* (London: Constable, 1973).

9. M. Ames and D. Houston, "Legal, Social, and Biological Definitions of Pedophilia," *Archives of Sexual Behavior* 19:4 (1990): 333–42; Gene Abel, Judith Becker, and Jerry Cunningham-Rathner, "Complications, Consent, and Cognitions in Sex Between Children and Adults," *International Journal of Law and Psychiatry* 7 (1984): 89–103; *DSM-IV: A Diagnostic and Statistical Manual of Mental Disorders,* 4th ed. (Washington, D.C.: American Psychiatric Association, 1994), pp. 527–28; James R. Kincaid, *Child-Loving* (New York: Routledge, 1993). For the word *pederast,* for instance, see Mark Vane, "Pederast with AIDS Virus Sentenced to 98–295 Years," *Washington Times,* November 15, 1990; Arlo Wagner, "Pederast Priest Sentenced to Eight Years," *Washington Times,* October 9, 1991.

10. *Uniform Crime Reports* 1994, pp. 287–88; Costin, Krager, and Stoesz, *Politics of Child Abuse;* Robert Hanley, "Study Says Megan Slaying Fits Pattern for Such Cases," *NYT,* June 23, 1997.

11. James O. Finckenauer, *Scared Straight! and the Panacea Phenomenon* (Englewood Cliffs, N.J.: Prentice-Hall, 1982).

12. Compare Patricia Healy Wasyliw, *Martyrdom, Murder, and Magic* (New York: Peter Lang, 1996); R. Po-chia Hsia, *The Myth of Ritual Murder* (New Haven: Yale University Press, 1988).

13. Louise Armstrong, *Rocking the Cradle of Sexual Politics* (Reading, Mass.: Addison Wesley, 1994).

14. Richard A. Posner and Katharine B. Silbaugh, *A Guide to America's Sex Laws* (Chicago: University of Chicago Press, 1996).

15. Jay R. Feierman, ed., *Pedophilia: Biosocial Dimensions* (New York: Springer Verlag, 1990); William Kraemer, ed., *The Forbidden Love* (London: Sheldon Press, 1976). For concern about genital mutilation, see Celia W. Dugger, "Tug of Taboos," *NYT,* December 28, 1996.

16. For the historical context, Sander J. Breiner, *Slaughter of the Innocents* (New York: Plenum, 1990); Jack McIver Weatherford, *Porn Row* (New York: Arbor House, 1986), pp. 161–76; Lloyd De Mause, *The History of Childhood* (New York: Psychohistory Press, 1974). Louis XIII's early years are discussed in Philippe Aries, *Centuries of Childhood* (London: Penguin, 1973), pp. 98–100.

17. Jan Hoffman, "Of Lust, Liaisons, and Laws," *NYT,* October 23, 1994.

18. Charles G. Chaddock, "Sex Crimes," in Allan McLane Hamilton and Lawrence Godkin, eds., *A System of Legal Medicine,* vol. 2 (New York: E. B. Treat, 1894), p. 543.

CHAPTER 2: CONSTRUCTING SEX CRIME, 1890–1934

1. Benjamin Karpman, *Case-Studies in the Psychopathology of Crime,* vol. 2 (Washington, D.C.: Medical Science Press, 1947–48), pp. 517–635.

2. Group for the Advancement of Psychiatry, Committee on Psychiatry and Law, *Psychiatry and Sex Psychopath Legislation* (New York, 1977), pp. 847–48; Louis Crompton, "Homosexuals and the Death Penalty in Colonial America," *JH* 1 (1976): 277–93.

3. Robert F. Oaks, "Things Fearful to Name," in Charles O. Jackson, ed., *The Other Americans* (Westport, Conn.: Praeger, 1996), pp. 24–36; Anthony E. Simpson, "Vulnerability and the Age of Female Consent," in G. S. Rousseau and Roy Porter, eds., *Sexual Underworlds of the Enlightenment* (Chapel Hill: University of North Carolina Press, 1988), pp. 181–206; Lawrence R. Murphy, "Defining the Crime Against Nature," *JH* 19 (1990): 49–66; Martin Killias, "The Historic Origins of Penal Statutes Concerning Sexual Activities Involving Children and Adolescents," *JH* 20 (1991): 41–46; Jonathan Ned Katz, *Gay/Lesbian Almanac* (New York: Harper Colophon, 1983), pp. 42–49, 78–83. The word *abuse* occurs in the context of sexual assault in the King James Bible of 1611, which contains a passage referring to a woman "abused" by a group of thugs (Judges 19:25).

4. George E. Worthington and Ruth Topping, *Specialized Courts Dealing with Sex Delinquency* (1925; reprint, Montclair, N.J.: Patterson Smith, 1969); Morris Ploscowe, *Sex and the Law* (New York: Prentice-Hall, 1951), pp. 149, 201–2; Murphy, "Defining the Crime Against Nature"; Morris L. Ernst and David Loth, *American Sexual Behavior and the Kinsey Report* (New York: Educational Books, 1948), pp. 128–31.

5. Joseph Wortis, "Sex Taboos, Sex Offenders, and the Law," *AJO* 9 (1939): 555–64. For Massachusetts statistics, see the Wickersham Commission, *The National Commission on Law Observance and Enforcement* (Washington, D.C.: GPO, 1931), no. 13, p. 295. The quotation about carnal abuse is from Albert Ellis and Ralph Brancale, *The Psychology of Sex Offenders* (Springfield, Ill.: Charles Thomas, 1956), p. 14.

6. David J. Pivar, *Purity Crusade: Sexual Morality and Social Control, 1868–1900* (Westport, Conn.: Greenwood Press, 1973), pp. 139–46; Lynne Kocen and Josephine Bulkley, "Analysis of Criminal Child Sex Abuse Statutes," and Donna Wulkan and Josephine Bulkley, "Analysis of Incest Statutes," in Josephine Bulkley, ed., *Child Sexual Abuse and the Law* (Washington, D.C.: National Legal Resource Center for Child Advocacy and Protection, 1981), pp. 1–20, 52–66; Charlton Edholm, *Traffic in Girls* (Chicago: Women's Temperance Publishing Association, 1893), pp. 66–67; Martin J. Costello, *Hating the Sin, Loving the Sinner* (New York: Garland, 1991), pp. 1–40; *Report and Analysis of Sex Crimes in the City of New York for the Ten-Year Period 1930–1939* (New York: Mayor's Committee for the Study of Sex Offenses, 1940), p. 22.

7. W. Travis Gibb, "Indecent Assault upon Children," in Allan McLane Hamilton and Lawrence Godkin, eds., *A System of Legal Medicine*, vol. 1 (New York: E. B. Treat, 1894), p. 651; Arthur W. Towne, "Young Girl Marriages in Criminal and Juvenile Courts," *JSH* 8 (1922): 287–305; Ploscowe, *Sex and the Law*, pp. 149, 179, 183; Herbert E. Gernert, "The Age of Consent Laws," *Vigilance* 20:1 (1912): 8–13. For the Tennessee case, see Clyde Thomas Nissen, "Rape—Age of Consent Statute," *JAICLC* 25 (1934–35): 777–78.

8. Michelle Oberman, "Turning Girls into Women," *Journal of Criminal Law and Criminology* 85 (1994): 15–79; Michelle Oberman, "Statutory Rape Laws," *ABA Journal* 82 (August 1996): 86–87.

9. Towne, "Young Girl Marriages"; Ploscowe, *Sex and the Law,* pp. 150, 182; the 1961 case is in Costello, *Hating the Sin, Loving the Sinner,* p. 58.

10. John D'Emilio and Estelle B. Freedman, *Intimate Matters* (New York: Harper and Row, 1988), pp. 216–21; Margaret Werner Cahalan and Lee Anne Parsons, *Historical Corrections Statistics in the United States* (Rockville, Md.: Bureau of Justice Statistics, 1986), pp. 10–11.

11. Michel Foucault, introduction to *The History of Sexuality,* vol. 1 (New York: Pantheon Books, 1978); Katz, *Gay/Lesbian Almanac,* pp. 144–45; David F. Greenberg, *The Construction of Homosexuality* (Chicago: University of Chicago Press, 1988).

12. Bert Hansen, "American Physicians' Discovery of Homosexuals, 1880–1900," in Charles E. Rosenberg and Janet Golden, eds., *Framing Disease: Studies in Cultural History* (New Brunswick, N.J.: Rutgers University Press, 1992), pp. 104–33; George Chauncey, *Gay New York* (New York: Basic, 1994), pp. 37–38, 89–90, 185. The quotations about the Philadelphia, Missouri, and Chicago cases are from Katz, *Gay/Lesbian Almanac*, pp. 179, 233, 367, 423; Jonathan Ned Katz, *Gay American History* (New York: Meridian, 1992), p. 40. The Philadelphia vice investigation is from *The Vice Commission of Philadelphia* (Philadelphia, 1913), p. 23. For the Crane anecdote, see Milton Rugoff, *Purity and Passion* (London: Rupert Hart-Davis, 1972), p. 270.

13. Pivar, *Purity Crusade*, pp. 139–46. The hypothetical court case is from Edholm, *Traffic in Girls*, pp. 68–69; the "human gorillas" remark is on p. 9. The analogies of the leper and the beast are from Benjamin O. Flower, "Wellsprings and Feeders of Immorality," *Arena* 11 (1895): 167, 171. The smallpox comparison is used by Helen H. Gardener in "The Shame of America: A Symposium," *Arena* 11 (1895): 196; Frances E. Willard describes the "frightful indignities" in ibid., p. 200. Compare Helen H. Gardener, *Have Children a Right to Legal Protection?* (Boston: Arena, 1895). Prostitution among children and young teenagers was often mentioned in the antivice exposés at the turn of the century; see, for example, John Regan, *Crimes of the White Slavers* (Chicago, 1912), pp. 33–73.

14. Richard von Krafft-Ebing, *Psychopathia Sexualis*, translated by Charles G. Chaddock (Philadelphia: F. A. Davis, 1893); Richard von Krafft-Ebing, *Psychopathia Sexualis*, translated by Franklin S. Klaf (New York: Scarborough, 1978); Katz, *Gay/Lesbian Almanac*, p. 256; Charles G. Chaddock, "Sex Crimes," in Hamilton and Godkin, *A System of Legal Medicine*, 2:543–47.

15. Lela Costin, Howard Krager, and David Stoesz, *The Politics of Child Abuse in America* (New York: Oxford University Press, 1996), pp. 46–60; Elizabeth H. Pleck, *Domestic Tyranny* (New York: Oxford University Press, 1987), pp. 69–87; Linda Gordon, *Heroes of Their Own Lives* (New York: Viking, 1988); Ruth Rosen, *The Lost Sisterhood* (Baltimore: Johns Hopkins University Press, 1982); Steven M. Schlossman, *Love and the Delinquent* (Chicago: University of Chicago Press, 1977); Anthony M. Platt, *The Child Savers*, 2d ed. (Chicago: University of Chicago Press, 1977). The remark about the "horrible abuses" of young girls appears in Christian Carl Carstens, "The Development in the Work of Children's Protection," *Survey*, November 12, 1910, p. 256; Gibb's conclusion is in Gibb, "Indecent Assault," p. 656.

16. Gibb, "Indecent Assault," pp. 649–52; compare Terry L. Chapman, "Inquiring Minds Want to Know," in Russell Smandych et al., eds., *Dimensions of Childhood* (Winnipeg: University of Manitoba Press, 1991), pp. 183–204.

17. Henry M. Boies, *Prisoners and Paupers* (New York: G. P. Putnam's, 1893), p. 99. The remark about "defilement" is in Ernest K. Coulter, *The Children in the Shadow* (New York: McBride and Nast, 1913); compare Louise De Koven Bowen, *Safe-*

guards for City Youth at Work and Play (New York: Macmillan, 1914), pp. 131, 137. The observation about "lodgers coming in tipsy," is from Albion Fellows Bacon, *Beauty for Ashes* (New York: Dodd Mead, 1914); see also O. F. Lewis, "Crime and Congestion," *Survey,* March 25, 1911, p. 1062. The Massachusetts report is quoted in Henry Pratt Fairchild, "Preventing Cruelty to Children," *American Journal of Sociology* 18 (1912–13): 569.

18. Threats to children were discussed at length in the publications of the American Purity Alliance (later renamed the American Vigilance Association), with its journals *The Philanthropist* and *Vigilance,* and the publications of the American Federation for Sex Hygiene. In 1914, these activist groups merged into the new American Social Hygiene Association, with its journal *Social Hygiene* (later *JSH*).

On sexually transmitted diseases among children, see Allan M. Brandt, *No Magic Bullet* (New York: Oxford University Press, 1985); W. P. Lucas, "Venereal Contagious Diseases in Children," *National Conference of Charities and Corrections: Proceedings* (1912), pp. 293–97. The American Purity Alliance quote is from O. Edward Janney, "Teaching of Sex Hygiene," *Vigilance* 23:6 (1910): 10. The St. Louis material is from Frederick J. Taussig, "The Contagion of Gonorrhoea Among Little Girls," *Social Hygiene* 1 (1914–15): 416. Bowen, *Safeguards,* p. 227, discusses the Chicago hospital, drawing from the Chicago Vice Commission, *The Social Evil in Chicago* (Chicago, 1911), p. 241. The New York survey is found in "Survey of Gonorrheal Vaginitis in Children," *JSH* 13 (1927): 144–49. See also Karen Taylor, "Venereal Disease in Nineteenth-Century Children," *Journal of Psychohistory* 12 (1985): 431–63.

19. Gordon, *Heroes of Their Own Lives,* pp. 204–49.

20. Ruth M. Alexander, *The "Girl Problem"* (Ithaca: Cornell University Press, 1995); Regina G. Kunzel, *Fallen Women, Problem Girls* (New Haven: Yale University Press, 1993); Mary E. Odem, *Delinquent Daughters* (Chapel Hill: University of North Carolina Press, 1995), pp. 8–37, 62–81; Steven Schlossman and Stephanie Wallach, "The Crime of Precocious Sexuality," *Harvard Educational Review* 48 (1978): 65–94; Gordon, *Heroes of Their Own Lives,* pp. 219, 227–49; Worthington and Topping, *Specialized Courts;* "Survey of Gonorrheal Vaginitis," p. 146. The 1931 case appears in Louis A. Schwartz, "Scientific Treatment of Juvenile Delinquency," *JAICLC* 3 (1932): 461–67.

21. Sophonisba B. Breckinridge and Edith Abbott, *The Delinquent Child and the Home* (New York: Charities Publication Committee, 1912), pp. 102–3, 315–25; June Purcell-Guild, "Study of 131 Delinquent Girls Held at the Juvenile Detention Home in Chicago, 1917," *JAICLC* 10 (1919–20): 443–44; Anne T. Bingham, "Determinants of Sex Delinquency in Adolescent Girls Based on Intensive Studies of Five Hundred Cases," *JAICLC* 13 (1922–23): 528–32; "Venereal Diseases in Private Practice," *JSH* 10 (1924): 267–77; William Isaac Thomas, *The Unadjusted Girl* (1923; reprint, Montclair, N.J.: Patterson Smith, 1969), pp. 98–102; Jane Addams,

A New Conscience and an Ancient Evil (New York: Macmillan, 1913), p. 109. For a prostitute's recollection of her childhood molestation by an uncle, probably in the mid-1890s, see Ruth Rosen, ed., *The Maimie Papers* (New York: Feminist Press, 1977), p. 193. The children's court study is from Lewis J. Doshay, *The Boy Sex Offender and His Later Career* (1943; reprint, Montclair, N.J.: Patterson Smith, 1969), pp. 75, 80.

22. The New York reform is described by Gibb, "Indecent Assault," p. 649; Gail S. Goodman, "Children's Testimony in Historical Perspective," *Journal of Social Issues* 40 (1984): 13; Christian Carl Carstens, "The Rural Community and Prostitution," *Social Hygiene* 1 (1914–15): 539–42. The quotation is from Carstens, "The Development in the Work of Children's Protection," p. 256.

23. Gail S. Goodman, ed., "The Child Witness," special issue of *Journal of Social Issues* 40:2 (1984); John Henry Wigmore, *Principles of Judicial Proof* (Boston: Little, Brown, 1913), pp. 332–39; Robert W. Millar, "John Henry Wigmore," in Hermann Mannheim, ed., *Pioneers in Criminology* (Montclair, N.J.: Patterson Smith, 1972), pp. 411–20; L. Bienen, "A Question of Credibility," *California Western Law Review* 19 (1983): 235–68. John Henry Wigmore's *Principles of Judicial Proof* is quoted in E. Olafson, D. L. Corwin, and Roland C. Summit, "Modern History of Child Sexual Abuse Awareness: Cycles of Discovery and Suppression," *CAN* 17 (1993): 8.

24. William Healy, *The Individual Delinquent* (Boston: Little, Brown, 1915), pp. 736–40; William Healy and Mary Tenney Healy, *Pathological Lying, Accusation, and Swindling* (1915; reprint, Montclair, N.J.: Patterson Smith, 1969), pp. 172–97, 225–32.

25. Chaddock, "Sex Crimes," p. 572; see also pp. 561–64.

26. Jay Robert Nash, *Bloodletters and Badmen* (New York: M. Evans, 1973); Jay Robert Nash, *Murder America* (New York: Simon and Schuster, 1980); *Life of Jesse H. Pomeroy, the Boy Fiend* (Taunton, Mass.: Taunton Publishing, 1875). "The most remarkable case" is from E. Luscomb Haskell, *Life of Jesse Harding Pomeroy* (Boston: n.p., 1892). For the Philadelphia case, see Roger Lane, *Violent Death in the City* (Cambridge: Harvard University Press, 1979), pp. 85–86.

27. Allan W. Eckert, *The Scarlet Mansion* (New York: Bantam, 1986); Harold Schechter, *Depraved* (New York: Pocket, 1994); compare Caleb Carr, *The Alienist* (London: Little, Brown, 1994); Philip Jenkins, *Using Murder* (Hawthorne, N.Y.: Aldine de Gruyter, 1994).

28. Nicole Hahn Rafter, *Creating Born Criminals* (Urbana: University of Illinois Press, 1997); Ysabel F. Rennie, *The Search for Criminal Man* (Lexington, Mass.: Lexington, 1978); August Drähms, *The Criminal* (1900; reprint, Montclair, N.J.: Patterson Smith, 1971); Arthur MacDonald, *Criminology* (New York: Funk and Wagnalls, 1893); Chaddock, "Sex Crimes," p. 561; Henry M. Boies, *The Science of Penology* (New York: G. P. Putnam's, 1901).

29. Jenkins, *Using Murder;* Nancy Maclean, "Gender, Sexuality, and the Politics of

Lynching," in W. Fitzhugh Brundage, ed., *Under Sentence of Death* (Chapel Hill: University of North Carolina Press, 1997), pp. 158–88; Leonard Dinnerstein, *Anti-Semitism in America* (New York: Oxford University Press, 1994), pp. 181–84; Philip Jenkins, "Serial Murder in the United States, 1900–1940," *Journal of Criminal Justice* 17 (1989): 377–92; Robert Seitz Frey, *The Silent and the Damned* (Lanham, Md.: Madison, 1988).

30. *NYT*, March 20–30, May 4–18, 1915; "Little Girl Found Murdered in Hall," ibid., March 20, 1915; "Boy Murdered by East Side Ripper," ibid., May 4, 1915; "Thought Prisoner a Ripper," ibid., May 18, 1915; "Mob Seeks to Avenge Girl," ibid., May 16, 1915; "Beat Suspected Ripper," ibid., May 10, 1915; "The City Mother's Load of Terror," ibid., March 27, 1915. See also Michael Newton, *Hunting Humans* (Port Townsend, Wash.: Loompanics, 1990), p. 172.

31. For Hickey, see *NYT*, December 6, 17–26, 1912; "Thought Prisoner a Ripper."

32. Compare Gordon, *Heroes of Their Own Lives*, pp. 221–25. The Chicago account is from Chicago Vice Commission, *Social Evil in Chicago*, p. 240.

33. Seymour Halleck, "American Psychiatry and the Criminal," *AJP* 121, supplement (1965): i–xxi; Gregory Zilboorg, "Legal Aspects of Psychiatry," in J. K. Hall, ed., *One Hundred Years of American Psychiatry* (New York: Columbia University Press, 1944), pp. 507–84; Walter Bromberg, *Crime and the Mind* (Philadelphia: J. B. Lippincott, 1948), p. 36; B. Sachs, "Insanity and Crime," in Hamilton and Godkin, *A System of Legal Medicine*, 2:200–202.

34. See Worthington and Topping, *Specialized Courts*, pp. 198, 395, for prostitutes as psychopathic "sex offenders"; compare Vincenzo Pascale, "Study of the Services for the Control of Venereal Diseases Among Sex Offenders in New York City," *JSH* 19 (1933): 111–42.

35. Rafter, *Creating Born Criminals*, pp. 112–18; James W. Trent, *Inventing the Feeble Mind* (Berkeley: University of California Press, 1994); Stephen Jay Gould, *The Mismeasure of Man* (New York: Norton, 1981); Morris Ploscowe, "Some Causative Factors in Criminality," in the Wickersham Commission, *National Commission on Law Observance and Enforcement*, pp. 37–61; Fernald, quoted in Mark H. Haller, *Eugenics* (New Brunswick, N.J.: Rutgers University Press, 1963), p. 45; Arthur MacDonald, "Criminological Literature," *American Journal of Psychology* 3 (1890): 237.

36. Philip Jenkins, "*Erewhon*: A Manifesto of the Rehabilitative Ideal," *Journal of Criminal Justice* 11 (1983): 35–46; Ferri, quoted in Nicholas N. Kittrie, *The Right to Be Different* (Baltimore: Johns Hopkins University Press, 1971), p. 174. The "quarantine" quotation is from David J. Rothman, *Conscience and Convenience* (Boston: Little, Brown, 1980), p. 201.

37. Boies's *Prisoners and Paupers* and MacDonald's *Criminology* both appeared in 1893. Compare Boies, *Science of Penology*; Piers Beirne, *Inventing Criminology* (Albany: State University of New York Press, 1993); Rafter, *Creating Born Crimi-*

nals; Rennie, *Search for Criminal Man;* Platt, *Child Savers;* Millar, "John Henry Wigmore."

38. Philip Jenkins, "A Progressive Revolution?" *Criminal Justice History* 6 (1985): 177–99; Rothman, *Conscience and Convenience;* Winfred Overholser, "Two Years' Experience with the Briggs Law of Massachusetts," *JAICLC* 23 (1932): 415–26, and "The Briggs Law of Massachusetts," *JAICLC* 24 (1935): 859–83; *Report of the Commission to Investigate the Question of the Increase of Criminals, Mental Defectives, Epileptics, and Degenerates* (Boston: Wright and Potter, 1911); Kittrie, *Right to Be Different,* p. 178; David Abrahamsen, *Crime and the Human Mind* (New York: Columbia University Press, 1944), P. 187.

39. "Ripper Murders," editorial in *NYT,* March 22, 1915; Fred Cohen, ed., *The Law of Deprivation of Liberty* (St. Paul, Minn.: West, 1980), pp. 730–31; Rothman, *Conscience and Convenience,* pp. 198–200; Louis N. Robinson, "Institutions for Defective Delinquents," *JAICLC* 24 (1933): 352–99; Rafter, *Creating Born Criminals.*

40. The quotation about "worm-eaten fruit" is in Boies, *Prisoners and Paupers.* Dr. Daniel is quoted in Katz, *Gay/Lesbian Almanac,* pp. 241–43; compare Boies, *Science of Penology,* pp. 92, 123, and "The City Mother's Load of Terror." See also Trent, *Inventing the Feeble Mind.*

41. Edward J. Larson, *Sex, Race, and Science* (Baltimore: Johns Hopkins University Press, 1995); Trent, *Inventing the Feeble Mind,* pp. 175–224; Paul B. Popenoe and E. S. Gosney, *Twenty-Eight Years of Sterilization in California* (Pasadena, Calif.: Human Betterment Foundation, 1938); Abraham Myerson et al., *Eugenical Sterilization* (New York: Macmillan, 1936), pp. 5–21; J. H. Landman, "Human Sterilization," *JAICLC* 24 (1933): 404–5; Harry H. Laughlin, "Eugenical Sterilization in the United States," *Social Hygiene* 6 (1920): 499–532; William A. White, "Sterilization of Criminals," *JAICLC* 8 (1917–18): 499–501; Charles A. Boston, "A Protest Against Laws Authorizing the Sterilization of Criminals and Imbeciles," *JAICLC* 4 (1913–14): 327. The quotation about "insufficient scientific knowledge" is in Manfred S. Guttmacher, *Sex Offenses* (New York: Norton, 1951), pp. 120–21; for Iowa, see Joel D. Hunter, "Sterilization of Criminals," *JAICLC* 3 (1914–15): 515; for homosexuals, see Katz, *Gay American History,* pp. 143–55.

42. Chester G. Vernier and Elmer A. Wilcox, "Judicial Decisions on Criminal Law," *JAICLC* 3 (1914–15): 419–25; Cohen, *Law of Deprivation of Liberty,* p. 535.

43. Jenkins, "A Progressive Revolution?"

44. Nathan G. Hale, *Freud and the Americans* (New York: Oxford University Press, 1971), and *The Rise and Crisis of Psychoanalysis in the United States* (New York: Oxford University Press, 1995); Rothman, *Conscience and Convenience,* pp. 302–38.

45. Gordon, *Heroes of Their Own Lives;* David J. Langum, *Crossing over the Line* (Chicago: University of Chicago Press, 1994); Mark Thomas Connelly, *The Response to Prostitution in the Progressive Era* (Chapel Hill: University of North Car-

olina Press, 1980); W. T. Sumner, "Child Protection and the Social Evil," *National Education Association* (1911): 1110–16; Edholm, *Traffic in Girls*, p. 9.

46. Ernest K. Alix, *Ransom Kidnapping in America, 1874–1974* (Carbondale: Southern Illinois University Press, 1978).

47. For Health Department observations, see Walter Clarke, "Syphilis and Gonococcal Infections in Children," *JSH* 25 (1939): 7–15; Jacob A. Goldberg and Rosamond W. Goldberg, *Girls on City Streets* (New York: American Social Hygiene Association, 1935). For continuing recognition of sexual abuse, see Gordon, *Heroes of Their Own Lives;* Sheldon Glueck and Eleanor Glueck, *Five Hundred Delinquent Women* (New York: Knopf, 1934), pp. 90–100; Ella Oppenheimer and Ray H. Everett, "School Exclusions for Gonorrheal Infections in Washington, D.C.," *JSH* 20 (1934): 129–38; "Survey of Gonorrheal Vaginitis." For "the cruelty," see Costin, Krager, and Stoesz, *Politics of Child Abuse*, pp. 82–106; Jeanne M. Giovannoni and Rosina M. Beccera, *Defining Child Abuse* (New York: Free Press, 1979), pp. 47–53.

48. David E. Ruth, *Inventing the Public Enemy* (Chicago: University of Chicago Press, 1996); Chauncey, *Gay New York;* Paula S. Fass, *The Damned and the Beautiful* (New York: Oxford University Press, 1977); Wickersham Commission, *National Commission on Law Observance and Enforcement*, p. 373.

49. Ploscowe, "Some Causative Factors in Criminality," pp. 1–161.

50. Franz G. Alexander and William Healy, *Roots of Crime* (New York: Knopf, 1935).

51. Estelle B. Freedman, "Uncontrolled Desires," *Journal of American History* 74 (1987): 83–106; Rafter, *Creating Born Criminals*, pp. 167–87; Ploscowe, "Some Causative Factors in Criminality," pp. 52–53; Maureen McKernan, *The Amazing Crime and Trial of Leopold and Loeb* (New York: Signet, 1957); William A. White, *Crimes and Criminals* (New York: Farrar and Rinehart, 1933). The quotation about White is in the dedication of Karpman, *Case-Studies*.

52. See Karpman, *Case-Studies*, 2:520, for Elton's possibly psychopathic personality.

53. Guttmacher, *Sex Offenses*, pp. 120–21.

CHAPTER 3: THE AGE OF THE SEX PSYCHOPATH, 1935–1957

1. Harold Schechter, *Deranged* (London: Warner, 1992); Mel Heimer, *The Cannibal* (London: Xanadu, 1988); Michael Angelella, *Trail of Blood* (Indianapolis: Bobbs-Merrill, 1979); Fredric Wertham, *The Show of Violence* (Garden City, N.J.: Doubleday, 1949), pp. 65–94; Nicholas N. Kittrie, *The Right to Be Different* (Baltimore: Johns Hopkins University Press, 1971), p. 176.

2. Steven Nickel, *Torso* (Winston-Salem, N.C.: John F. Blair, 1989); Philip Jenkins, *Using Murder* (Hawthorne, N.Y.: Aldine de Gruyter, 1994); Michael Newton, *Hunting Humans* (Port Townsend, Wash.: Loompanics, 1990), p. 280.

3. Charles J. Dutton, "Can We End Sex Crimes?" *Christian Century*, December 22, 1937, pp. 1594–95; Bertram Pollens, *The Sex Criminal* (New York: Macaulay, 1938), p. 170; *NYT*, August 14, 1937, and May 18, 1938. The New York sheriff is de-

scribed in Fredric Wertham, "Psychiatry and the Prevention of Sex Crimes," *JAICLC* 28 (1938): 847. The murders of the three Inglewood girls dominated the Los Angeles media throughout the summer of 1937: see, for example, "Three Girls Found Slain in Hills: Felon Hunted in Fiendish Crime," *LAT,* June 29, 1937; J. Paul De River, *The Sexual Criminal* (Springfield, Ill.: Charles Thomas, 1950), pp. 75–86.

4. Linda Gordon, *Heroes of Their Own Lives* (New York: Viking, 1988), pp. 223–25.

5. The police purge of "degenerates" is described in Jonathan Ned Katz, *Gay/Lesbian Almanac* (New York: Harper Colophon, 1983), pp. 531–32; see also *Literary Digest,* January 2, 1937, p. 34, and April 10, 1937; "Pedophilia," *Time,* August 23, 1937, pp. 42–44; Sheldon Glueck, "Sex Crimes and the Law," *Nation,* September 25, 1937, pp. 318–20; G. Palmer, "Crimes Against Children," *Literary Digest,* October 22, 1937, pp. 14–16; "Sex Criminal," *Christian Century,* November 10, 1937, pp. 1391–93; Dutton, "Can We End Sex Crimes?" The quotation is in Wertham "Psychiatry and the Prevention of Sex Crimes," p. 847.

6. The script of a radio program on sex offenses is found in "Washington, D.C., Considers Sex Offenses," *JSH* 36 (1950): 241–49. See also Charles Harris, "A New Report on Sex Crimes," *Coronet,* October 1947; Clarence A. Bonner, "Who and What are Sexual Psychopaths?" *Focus,* July 1948, pp. 103–5; "Horror Week," *Newsweek,* November 28, 1949, p. 19; "Sex Rampage," *Newsweek,* February 13, 1950; "Unknown Sex Fiend," *Time,* February 13, 1950; J. Crowther, "Answer to Sex Fiends," *American City,* April 1950; I. W. Hewlett, "What Shall We Do About Sex Offenders?" *Parents,* August 1950, pp. 36–38; Albert Deutsch, "Sober Facts About Sex Crimes," *Collier's,* November 25, 1950, pp. 15–16; "Sex Psychopaths," *Newsweek,* March 9, 1953, pp. 50–51. The *Collier's* quotations are in Howard Jay Whitman, *Terror in the Streets* (New York: Dial Press, 1951), pp. x–xi, 7, 26–27, 48. The "shadow" quotation appears in Charles Harris, "Sex Crimes: Their Cause and Cure," *Coronet,* August 1946, p. 4.

7. Quotations are in Whitman, *Terror,* pp. 7–8, 52, 64, 70–73, 392. For abusers in churches and schools, see Bernard Williams, *Jailbait* (New York: Garden City Books, 1951), pp. 35–45, 53–59. See also Earl R. Biggs, *How to Protect Your Child from the Sex Criminal* (Portland, Oreg.: New Science, 1950).

8. Whitman, *Terror,* pp. 45–47.

9. For earlier sensational murders, see Harris, "Sex Crimes," pp. 3–9. For the 1949 cases, see Whitman, *Terror,* pp. 101–38; Edwin Sutherland, "The Diffusion of Sex Psychopath Laws," *American Journal of Sociology* 56 (1950): 142–48; De River, *The Sexual Criminal.*

10. Whitman, *Terror,* pp. 39–41.

11. Whitman, *Terror,* pp. 50–74; George Chauncey, "The Postwar Sex Crime Panic," in William Graebner, ed., *True Stories from the American Past* (New York: McGraw-Hill, 1993), p. 165.

12. Athan Theoharis, *Hoover, Sex, and Crime* (Chicago: Ivan R. Dee, 1995), pp. 65–68;

J. Edgar Hoover, "Organized Protection Against Organized Predatory Crimes," *JAICLC* 24 (1933): 475–82; John C. McWilliams, *The Protectors* (Newark: University of Delaware Press, 1990); David F. Musto, *The American Disease* (New York: Oxford University Press, 1987); Jonathan Simon, *Poor Justice* (Chicago: University of Chicago Press, 1993); Martin Mooney, *The Parole Scandal* (Los Angeles: Lymanhouse, 1939); J. Edgar Hoover, *Persons in Hiding* (Boston: Little, Brown, 1938), pp. 189–90. Hoover's claim that sex fiends are the most loathsome of all criminals is from J. Edgar Hoover, "War on the Sex Criminal," *New York Herald Tribune*, September 26, 1937.

13. J. Edgar Hoover, "How Safe Is Your Daughter?" *American Magazine*, July 1947, pp. 32–33. FBI advice to children is quoted in Kenneth V. Lanning, *Investigator's Guide to Allegations of "Ritual" Child Abuse* (Quantico, Va.: NCAVC, FBI Academy, 1992), p. 3; for later FBI campaigns, see *NYT*, August 31, 1957; ibid., December 7, 1960; ibid., July 3, 1962; M. Hickey, "FBI Reports Sound the Alarm," *Ladies' Home Journal*, April 1960.

14. John McCarty, *Psychos* (New York: St. Martin's Press, 1986).

15. Robert Bloch, *The Scarf* (New York: Dial Press, 1947), pp. 207–8; Charles R. Jackson, *The Outer Edges* (New York: Rinehart, 1948), p. 81.

16. David Wittels, "What Can We Do About Sex Crimes?" *Saturday Evening Post*, December 11, 1948.

17. Pollens, *Sex Criminal*, p. 78; Dolores Kennedy, *William Heirens* (Chicago: Bonus, 1991); Lucy Freeman, *"Before I Kill More"* (New York: Crown, 1955); Williams, *Jailbait*, pp. 64–66; Foster Kennedy, Harry R. Hoffman, and William H. Haines, "A Study of William Heirens," *AJP* 104 (1947): 113.

18. Morris Ploscowe, "Some Causative Factors in Criminality," in the Wickersham Commission, *The National Commission on Law Observance and Enforcement* (Washington, D.C.: GPO, 1931), no. 13:1, pp. 1–161; Benjamin Karpman, *The Individual Criminal* (Washington, D.C.: Nervous and Mental Disease Publishing, 1935); "Symposium: The Challenge of Sex Offenders," special issue, *Mental Hygiene* 22 (1938); Jack Frosch and Walter Bromberg, "The Sex Offender," *AJO* 9 (1939): 761–76; Ira S. Wile, "Sex Offenders Against Young Children," *JSH* 25 (1939): 33–44; C. M. Krinsky and J. J. Michaels, "A Survey of One Hundred Sex Offenders," *Journal of Criminal Psychopathology* 5 (1940): 198–206; A. J. Arieff and D. B. Rotman, "One Hundred Cases of Indecent Exposure," *Journal of Nervous and Mental Diseases* 96 (1942): 523–29; B. Apfelberg, C. Sugar, and A. Z. Pfeffer, "A Psychiatric Study of 250 Sex Offenders," *AJP* 100 (1944): 762–69; W. Norwood East, "Sexual Offenders," *Journal of Nervous and Mental Diseases* 103 (1946): 626–66; William H. Haines, Harry R. Hoffman, and Robert A. Esser, "Commitments Under the Criminal Sexual Psychopath Law in the Criminal Court of Cook County, Illinois," *AJP* 103 (1948): 420–28; George A. Cook, "Problem of the Criminal Sexual Psychopath," *Diseases of the Nervous System* 13 (1949): 137–42; Her-

vey Cleckley, *The Mask of Sanity* (St. Louis: Mosby, 1950); Karl M. Bowman, "The Problem of the Sex Offender," *AJP* 108 (1951): 250–57; Manfred S. Guttmacher and Henry Weihofen, *Psychiatry and the Law* (New York: Norton, 1952). The special number of *Federal Probation* 14:3 (1950) included Philip Q. Roche, "Sexual Deviation," pp. 2–11; R. W. Bowling, "The Sex Offender and the Law," pp. 11–16; Jacob M. Braude, "The Sex Offender and the Court," pp. 17–22; Paul W. Tappan, "Sex Offender Laws and Their Administration," pp. 32–37.

19. The Levin case is from Chauncey, "The Postwar Sex Crime Panic," p. 168; Benjamin Karpman, *The Sexual Offender and His Offenses* (New York: Julian, 1954), p. 490. For New Hampshire, see Manfred S. Guttmacher, *Sex Offenses* (New York: Norton, 1951), pp. 11–12.

20. Karpman, *Sexual Offender*, p. 239; Rothman, *Conscience and Convenience*, p. 200; The *Saturday Evening Post* remark is from Morris Ploscowe, *Sex and the Law* (New York: Prentice-Hall, 1951), p. 228.

21. Sutherland, "The Diffusion of Sex Psychopath Laws," p. 142.

22. Pollens, *Sex Criminal*, pp. 26–27; the Hoover quotation is from Whitman, *Terror*, p. 394.

23. Pollens, *Sex Criminal*, 89; Whitman, *Terror*, p. 62.

24. Karpman, *Sexual Offender*, pp. 4, 45, 63, 77; the final quotation is in ibid., p. 8.

25. Chauncey, "The Postwar Sex Crime Panic," pp. 171–72.

26. Karpman, *Sexual Offender*, pp. 73, 144–65, 296–330, 349, 418, 456; Walter Bromberg, *Crime and the Mind* (Philadelphia: J. B. Lippincott, 1948), p. 91.

27. Johann W. Mohr, Robert E. Turner, and Marian B. Jerry, *Pedophilia and Exhibitionism: A Handbook* (Toronto: University of Toronto Press, 1964), p. 13; Karpman, *Sexual Offender*, p. 44. The *Psychiatric Quarterly* comment is quoted in Hervey Cleckley, *The Caricature of Love* (New York: Ronald Press, 1957), p. 20. See also Bromberg, *Crime and the Mind*, p. 84.

28. John D'Emilio, *Sexual Politics, Sexual Communities* (Chicago: University of Chicago Press, 1983); John D'Emilio, "The Homosexual Menace," in Kathy Peiss, Christina Simmons, and Robert A. Padgug, eds., *Passion and Power: Sexuality in History* (Philadelphia: Temple University Press, 1989), pp. 226–40. The White Legion episode is discussed in Katz, *Gay/Lesbian Almanac*, p. 524. See also John Gerassi, *The Boys of Boise* (New York: Macmillan, 1966), p. ix.

29. Whitman, *Terror*, p. 147.

30. Jonathan Ned Katz, *Gay American History* (New York: Meridian, 1992), p. 391; a reference to "cults" is quoted in Katz, *Gay/Lesbian Almanac*, p. 335. See also Lewis J. Doshay, *The Boy Sex Offender and His Later Career* (1943; reprint, Montclair, N.J.: Patterson Smith, 1969), pp. 97–98; Whitman, *Terror*, pp. 139–63. Compare Lauretta Bender and Samuel Paster, "Homosexual Trends in Children," *AJO* 11 (1941): 730–43; Raymond Waggoner and David A. Boyd, "Juvenile Aberrant Sexual Behavior," in *AJO* 11 (1941): 275–91.

31. Williams is quoted in De River, *Sexual Criminal,* pp. xi–xii; the psychiatrist is quoted in ibid., p. 87.

32. Ploscowe, *Sex and the Law,* p. 208.

33. The quotation about vice squads is from Harris, "Sex Crimes," p. 6; other quotations are from Whitman, *Terror,* pp. 149–52.

34. Chauncey, "Postwar Sex Crime Panic," p. 177; Katz, *Gay American History,* pp. 91–109; Ploscowe, *Sex and the Law,* pp. 195–96; Theoharis, *Hoover, Sex, and Crime,* pp. 103–15; Karpman, *Sexual Offender,* pp. 466, 473; Karl M. Bowman and Bernice Engle, "The Problem of Homosexuality," *JSH* 31 (1953): 2–16; Allan Berube, *Coming Out Under Fire* (New York: Free Press, 1990), pp. 257–60; Robert J. Corber, *Homosexuality in Cold War America* (Durham, N.C.: Duke University Press, 1997).

35. Williams, *Jailbait,* p. 110; *The Problem of Sex Offenses in New York City* (Citizens' Committee on the Control of Crime in New York, 1939); *Report and Analysis of Sex Crimes in the City of New York for the Ten-Year Period 1930–1939* (New York: Mayor's Committee for the Study of Sex Offenses, 1940), pp. 10, 38.

36. *Sex Crimes in the City of New York for the Ten-Year Period 1930–1939,* p. 21; Ploscowe, *Sex and the Law,* p. 181.

37. Ploscowe, *Sex and the Law,* p. 217; Karpman, *Sexual Offender,* pp. 29, 63, 238.

38. *Sex Crimes in the City of New York for the Ten-Year Period 1930–1939,* pp. 40–41; Ploscowe, *Sex and the Law,* p. 161.

39. *Sex Crimes in the City of New York for the Ten-Year Period 1930–1939,* pp. 90, 11; the comment about the "sporadic" or often one-time nature of sex crimes appears in ibid., p. 93.

40. Doshay, *Boy Sex Offender,* p. 167.

41. Ibid., p. 76.

42. Ibid., pp. 93–95.

43. Karpman, *Sexual Offender,* pp. 22–23; *Sex Offenders: A Report to the General Assembly of the Commonwealth of Pennsylvania* (Harrisburg, Pa.: Joint State Government Commission, 1951).

44. Gilbert Geis and Colin Goff, "Edwin H. Sutherland's *White Collar Crime in America,*" *Criminal Justice History* 7 (1986): 1–31; Edwin Sutherland, "The Diffusion of Sex Psychopath Laws," *American Journal of Sociology* 57 (1950): 142–48, and "The Sexual Psychopath Laws," *Journal of Criminal Law and Criminology* 47 (1950): 534–54; compare Marvin E. Wolfgang, *Patterns in Criminal Homicide* (Philadelphia: University of Pennsylvania Press, 1958); Gladys Shultz, *How Many More Victims?* (Philadelphia: J. B. Lippincott, 1965), p. 33.

45. Compare Paul W. Tappan, "The Sexual Psychopath: A Civic-Social Responsibility" *JSH* 35 (1949): 354–73; Fred Cohen, ed., *The Law of Deprivation of Liberty* (St. Paul, Minn.: West, 1980), p. 669; Paul W. Tappan, *The Habitual Sex Offender* (Trenton, N.J.: Commission on the Habitual Sex Offender, 1950), pp. 13–16; compare

Paul W. Tappan,"Sentences for Sex Criminals," *Journal of Criminal Law and Criminology* 42 (1951): 335–36, and "Some Myths About the Sex Offender," *Federal Probation* 12 (1955); Albert Ellis and Ralph Brancale, *The Psychology of Sex Offenders* (Springfield, Ill.: Charles C. Thomas, 1956).

46. Tappan, *Habitual Sex Offender,* pp. 18–19; compare Alfred C. Kinsey, Wardell B. Pomeroy, and Clyde E. Martin, *Sexual Behavior in the Human Male* (Philadelphia: W. B. Saunders, 1948); James H. Jones, *Alfred C. Kinsey* (New York: Norton, 1997); Ploscowe, *Sex and the Law,* p. 209; *Sex Offenders,* pp. 11–12; Karpman, *Sexual Offender,* pp. 6, 63, 512.

47. *Report of the Governor's Study Commission on the Deviated Criminal Sex Offender* (Lansing, Mich., 1951).

48. Elaine Tyler May, *Homeward Bound* (New York: Basic, 1988); Susan M. Hartmann, *The Home Front and Beyond* (Boston: Twayne, 1982); Karen Anderson, *Wartime Women* (Westport, Conn.: Greenwood Press, 1981). See also Chapter 10 of this book.

49. D. Diamond and F. Tenenbaum, "To Protect Your Child from Sex Offenders," *Better Homes and Gardens,* May 1953, pp. 160–62; E. M. Stern, "Facts on Sex Offenders Against Children," *Parents,* October 1954, pp. 42–43; M. Holmes, "How to Protect Your Children from Sex Offenders," *Better Homes and Gardens,* January 1959, pp. 25–26; Fredric Wertham, "Sex Crimes Can Be Prevented," *Ladies' Home Journal,* August 1961, pp. 46–47. For the upsurge of interest in 1957, see M. Hickey, "Parents and Teachers Can Help," *Ladies' Home Journal,* April 1957, pp. 31–33; "Protecting Children Against Sex Offenders: Omaha, Nebraska," *Ladies' Home Journal,* April 1957, p. 31; R. Brancale and F. L. Bixby, "How to Treat Sex Offenders," *Nation,* April 6, 1957, pp. 293–95; M. Van De Water, "Sex Criminal Not a Fiend," *Science News Letter,* July 13, 1957, pp. 26–27; F. Anderson, "Background for Sex Crimes," *America,* July 6, 1957, pp. 377–78; "Picture of the Sex Criminal," *Science Digest,* September 1957, pp. 22–23; B. Goody-Koontz, T. P. Krush, and N. L. Dorner, "Ten-Point Program Against Molesters," *National Parent Teacher,* October 1957, pp. 7–10. See also Leon Radzinowicz, *Sex Crimes* (London: Macmillan, 1957); James Melvin Reinhardt, *Sex Perversions and Sex Crimes* (Springfield, Ill.: Charles C. Thomas, 1957); Cleckley, *Caricature of Love.*

50. Quoted in Elizabeth H. Pleck, *Domestic Tyranny* (New York: Oxford University Press, 1987), p. 121.

51. J. K. Hall, ed., *One Hundred Years of American Psychiatry* (New York: Columbia University Press, 1944), pp. 178–86; Pleck, *Domestic Tyranny,* p. 147; Ellen Herman, *The Romance of American Psychology* (Berkeley: University of California Press, 1995), pp. 2–3; Chauncey, "Postwar Sex Crime Panic," p. 166.

52. Whitman, *Terror,* p. 375; the Michigan commission is quoted in Chauncey, "Postwar Sex Crime Panic," p. 166. De River's *Sexual Criminal* was written as a text for

police agencies wishing to apply psychiatric insights into criminal investigation—almost a pioneering guide to criminal profiling.

CHAPTER 4: THE SEX PSYCHOPATH STATUTES

1. Lewis J. Doshay, *The Boy Sex Offender and His Later Career* (1943; reprint, Montclair, N.J.: Patterson Smith, 1969), pp. 5–6; *Report and Analysis of Sex Crimes in the City of New York for the Ten-Year Period 1930–1939* (New York: Mayor's Committee for the Study of Sex Offenses, 1940), pp. 45–46; compare the Wickersham Commission, *The National Commission on Law Observance and Enforcement* (Washington, D.C.: GPO, 1931), no. 4, pp. 95–100.

2. *Sex Crimes in the City of New York for the Ten-Year Period 1930–1939*, p. 57.

3. Ibid., p. 44; David Abrahamsen, *The Psychology of Crime* (New York: Columbia University Press, 1960), p. 154; Morris Ploscowe, *Sex and the Law* (New York: Prentice-Hall, 1951), pp. 222–23.

4. *Sex Crimes in the City of New York for the Ten-Year Period 1930–1939*, pp. 52–56.

5. For Wigmore, see Elizabeth H. Pleck, *Domestic Tyranny* (New York: Oxford University Press, 1987), p. 156; Alfred C. Kinsey, Wardell B. Pomeroy, and Clyde E. Martin, *Sexual Behavior in the Human Male* (Philadelphia: W. B. Saunders, 1948), pp. 237–38.

6. Howard Jay Whitman, *Terror in the Streets* (New York: Dial Press, 1951), pp. 129, 390.

7. For Fish, see Michael Newton, *Hunting Humans* (Port Townsend, Wash.: Loompanics, 1990); Gladys Shultz, *How Many More Victims?* (Philadelphia: J. B. Lippincott, 1965), pp. 64–72; Fredric Wertham, *The Show of Violence* (Garden City, N.J.: Doubleday, 1949), p. 80; Bertram Pollens, *The Sex Criminal* (New York: Macaulay, 1938), pp. 85–86; the "bogey" quote is from *Sex Crimes in the City of New York for the Ten-Year Period 1930–1939*, p. 92.

8. Pollens, *Sex Criminal*, pp. 93–94; Whitman, *Terror*, pp. 380–81; Jacob H. Conn, "Brief Psychotherapy of the Sex Offender," *Journal of Clinical Psychopathology* 10 (1949): 349–50.

9. *Report on Study of 102 Sex Offenders at Sing Sing Prison* (Albany, N.Y.: Department of Mental Hygiene, 1951); David Abrahamsen, "Study of 102 Sex Offenders at Sing Sing," *Federal Probation* 14:3(1950): 26–32; the New York judge is quoted in Jonathan Ned Katz, *Gay/Lesbian Almanac* (New York: Harper Colophon, 1983), p. 531; Whitman, *Terror*, p. 385.

10. Ploscowe, *Sex and the Law*, pp. 218–19; "Pedophilia," *Time*, August 23, 1937, pp. 42–44; *Sex Crimes in the City of New York for the Ten-Year Period 1930–1939*, p. 9.

11. Pollens, *Sex Criminal*, p. 14; D. Shaskan, "One Hundred Sex Offenders," *AJO* 9 (1939): 565–69.

in the United States, 1850–1984 (Rockville, Md.: Bureau of Justice Statistics, 1986), pp. 10–11.

3. See, for example, Harry Raymond, *Save Willie McGee* (New York: New Century, 1951); Allan Knight Chalmers, *They Shall Be Free* (Garden City, N.J.: Doubleday, 1951); Haywood Patterson and Earl Conrad, *Scottsboro Boy* (Garden City, N.J.: Doubleday, 1950); Eric W. Rise, *The Martinsville Seven* (Charlottesville: University of Virginia Press, 1995).

4. Compare Helen Benedict, *Virgin or Vamp* (New York: Oxford University Press, 1992), pp. 27–39.

5. See various articles from the *NYT:* February 14, 1952; December 10, 1954, p. 56; January 25, 1955, p. 14; February 11, 1955, p. 45; July 23, 1955, p. 33.

6. Caryl Chessman, *Cell 2455, Death Row* (Englewood Cliffs, N.J.: Prentice-Hall, 1960); Caryl Chessman, *Trial by Ordeal* (Englewood Cliffs, N.J.: Prentice-Hall, 1955).

7. *NYT,* January 17, 1960; Harry Elmer Barnes and Negley K. Teeters, *New Horizons in Criminology,* 3d ed. (Englewood Cliffs, N.J.: Prentice-Hall, 1959), p. 99.

8. Edwin Sutherland, "The Diffusion of Sex Psychopath Laws," *American Journal of Sociology* 56 (1950): 143.

9. Morris Ploscowe, *Sex and the Law* (New York: Prentice-Hall, 1951), p. 239; "Pedophilia," *Time,* August 23, 1937, pp. 42–44; Alan P. Bell and Calvin S. Hall, *The Personality of a Child Molester* (Chicago: Aldine Atherton, 1971); Bart Delin, *The Sex Offender* (Boston: Beacon, 1978); Mark Cook and Kevin Howells, eds., *Adult Sexual Interest in Children* (London: Academic Press, 1981); Paul Gebhard et al., *Sex Offenders: An Analysis of Types* (New York: Harper and Row, 1965), p. 74; compare Paul Gebhard and John H. Gagnon, "Male Sex Offenders Against Very Young Children," *AJP* 121 (1964): 576–79; Kurt Freund, "Sex Offenses Against Female Children Perpetrated by Men Who Are Not Pedophiles," *Journal of Sex Research* 28 (1991): 409–23.

10. Richard von Krafft-Ebing, *Psychopathia Sexualis,* translated by Franklin S. Klaf (New York: Scarborough, 1978), pp. 370–74; Ellis, quoted in Johann W. Mohr, Robert E. Turner, and Marian B. Jerry, *Pedophilia and Exhibitionism: A Handbook* (Toronto: University of Toronto Press, 1964), pp. 12–13; William Healy, *The Individual Delinquent* (Boston: Little, Brown, 1915), pp. 210–12; David Abrahamsen, *The Psychology of Crime* (New York: Columbia University Press, 1960), p. 155; Walter Bromberg, *Crime and the Mind* (Philadelphia: J. B. Lippincott, 1948), p. 89. See also John Holland Cassity, "Psychological Considerations of Pedophilia," *Psychoanalytic Review* 14 (1927): 189–99.

11. Mohr et al., *Pedophilia and Exhibitionism,* p. 7; Bernard J. Oliver, *Sexual Deviation in American Society* (New Haven, Conn.: College and University Press, 1967); Samuel Kirson Weinberg, *Incest Behavior* (Secaucus, N.J.: Citadel, 1955); N. K. Rickles, *Exhibitionism* (Philadelphia: J. B. Lippincott, 1950); compare Oskar

Guttmann, "Exhibitionism," *Journal of Clinical and Experimental Psychopathology* 14 (1953): 13–51; Walter Beck, review of *Die Kinderschändung, JAICLC* 25:1(1934): 148.

12. Mohr et al., *Pedophilia and Exhibitionism,* pp. 14–15; J. Paul De River, *The Sexual Criminal* (Springfield, Ill.: Charles Thomas, 1950), p. 265; *DSM-IV: A Diagnostic and Statistical Manual of Mental Disorders,* 4th ed. (Washington, D.C.: American Psychiatric Association, 1994), p. 527.

13. Guttmacher, *Sex Offenses,* pp. 152, 97.

14. The experimental psychotherapy is described in Jacob H. Conn, "Brief Psychotherapy of the Sex Offender," *Journal of Clinical Psychopathology* 10 (1949): 347–72; compare Benjamin Karpman, "A Case of Pedophilia Cured by Psychoanalysis," *Psychoanalytic Review* 37:3 (1950): 235–76; Mohr et al., *Pedophilia and Exhibitionism,* pp. 85, 170.

15. Mohr et al., *Pedophilia and Exhibitionism,* p. 23. A "sadistic pedophile" is described in De River, *Sexual Criminal,* pp. 75–86, but this is a necrophiliac serial child killer.

16. Mohr et al., *Pedophilia and Exhibitionism,* pp. 15, 18; Gebhard et al., *Sex Offenders,* pp. 81–82; Allan M. Brandt, *No Magic Bullet* (New York: Oxford University Press, 1985).

17. *Sex Crimes in the City of New York for the Ten-Year Period 1930–1939,* pp. 67–68; Ploscowe, *Sex and the Law,* p. 217. The most frequently cited work on the impact of child sexual abuse was Lauretta Bender and Abram Blau, "The Reaction of Children to Sexual Relations with Adults," *AJO* 7 (1937): 500–518; Lauretta Bender and Alvin E. Grugett, "A Follow-Up Report on Children Who Had Atypical Sexual Experience," *AJO* 27 (1952): 825–37. Compare Rhoda J. Milliken, "The Sex Offender's Victim," *Federal Probation* 14:3(1950): 22–26; John H. Gagnon, "Female Child Victims of Sex Offenses," *Social Problems* 13 (1965): 176–92.

18. Tappan is quoted in Fred Cohen, ed., *Law of Deprivation of Liberty* (St. Paul, Minn.: West, 1980), pp. 669–70; Alfred C. Kinsey et al., *Sexual Behavior in the Human Female* (Philadelphia: W. B. Saunders, 1953), p. 121.

19. Weinberg, *Incest Behavior,* p. 40; Pomeroy is quoted in Diana E. H. Russell, *The Secret Trauma* (New York: Basic, 1986), pp. 3, 8; the remark about the female being "too fond" is from Benjamin Karpman, *The Sexual Offender and His Offenses* (New York: Julian, 1954), p. 25. Incest also appeared as a powerful theme in other literary works, including Ralph Ellison's *Invisible Man* (1952) and Grace Metalious's *Peyton Place* (1956).

20. Mohr et al., *Pedophilia and Exhibitionism,* pp. 35–37; Larry L. Constantine, "Effects of Early Sexual Experiences," in Larry L. Constantine and F. M. Martinson, eds., *Children and Sex* (Boston: Little, Brown 1981), pp. 217–44; C. A. Tripp, *The Homosexual Matrix* (New York: Signet, 1975), p. 84; R. Ollendorff, *Juvenile Homosexual Experience and Its Effect on Adult Homosexuality* (New York: Julian, 1966).

21. Ruth S. Kempe and C. Henry Kempe, *Child Abuse* (London: Fontana, Open Uni-

versity, 1978), p. 55; Stephen P. McCary and James Leslie McCary, *Human Sexuality*, 3d ed. (Monterey, Calif.: Wadsworth, 1984). The remark about "irrationality" is from John H. Gagnon and William Simon, *Sexual Encounters Between Adults and Children* (New York: Sex Information and Education Council of the United States, 1970), p. 6.

22. Elizabeth H. Pleck, *Domestic Tyranny* (New York: Oxford University Press, 1987), pp. 150–63; *Sex Crimes in the City of New York for the Ten-Year Period 1930–1939*, pp. 70–71; Mohr et al., *Pedophilia and Exhibitionism*, pp. 34–35.

23. David Abrahamsen, *The Psychology of Crime* (New York: Columbia University Press, 1960), p. 161; Karpman, *Sexual Offender*, pp. 72–73. The "widespread problem" quotation is from Bernard Williams, *Jailbait* (New York: Garden City Books, 1951), p. 115; the 1974 textbook is cited in Diana E. H. Russell, *The Secret Trauma* (New York: Basic, 1986), p. 172. See also Tripp, *The Homosexual Matrix*, p. 84, and, for the Australian study, Paul R. Wilson, *The Man They Called a Monster* (North Ryde, N.S.W.: Cassell Australia, 1981).

24. Vladimir V. Nabokov, *Lolita* (Greenwich, Conn.: Fawcett, 1959); Russell Trainer, *The Lolita Complex* (New York: Citadel, 1966). For the new sexual liberalism and relativism, see, for example, John H. Gagnon and William Simon, *Sexual Conduct* (Chicago: Aldine, 1973).

25. Tony Parker, *The Hidden World of Sex Offenders* (Indianapolis: Bobbs-Merrill, 1969).

26. "Chester" would, however, be seen by conservatives as evil rather than satirical: see House Subcommittee on Crime, *Sexual Exploitation of Children: Hearings Before the Subcommittee on Crime of the Committee on the Judiciary* (Washington, D.C.: GPO, 1977), p. 7.

27. Ian R. Taylor, Paul Walton, and Jock Young, *The New Criminology* (London: Routledge and Kegan Paul, 1973); Edwin M. Schur, *Labeling Deviant Behavior* (New York: Harper and Row, 1971); David Matza, *Becoming Deviant* (Englewood Cliffs, N.J.: Prentice-Hall, 1969); Howard S. Becker, *Outsiders* (London: Free Press of Glencoe, 1963); William Chambliss and Milton Mankoff eds., *Whose Law? What Order?* (New York: Wiley, 1976).

28. David F. Musto, *The American Disease* (New York: Oxford University Press, 1987); Edwin M. Schur and Hugo Adam Bedau, *Victimless Crimes* (Englewood Cliffs, N.J.: Prentice-Hall 1974); *The Obscenity Report: The Report to the Task Force on Pornography and Obscenity* (New York: Stein and Day, 1970); Troy S. Duster, *The Legislation of Morality* (New York: Free Press, 1970); Herbert Packer, *The Limits of the Criminal Sanction* (Stanford: Stanford University Press, 1968); Sanford Kadish, "The Crisis of Overcriminalization," *Annals* 374 (1967): 157–70; Edwin M. Schur, *Crimes Without Victims* (Englewood Cliffs, N.J.: Prentice-Hall 1965); Joseph R. Gusfield, *Symbolic Crusade* (Urbana: University of Illinois Press, 1963).

29. Kittrie, *Right to Be Different*, p. 205.

30. *O'Connor v. Donaldson* 1975, in Cohen, *Law of Deprivation of Liberty*, p. 526.

31. Michael Wines, "Mental Institutions May Be as Empty as They'll Ever Be," *NYT,* September 4, 1988; Andrew T. Scull, *Decarceration, Community Treatment, and the Deviant,* 2d ed. (New Brunswick, N.J.: Rutgers University Press, 1984); B. J. Ennis, *Prisoners of Psychiatry* (New York: Harcourt Brace Jovanovich, 1972); David J. Rothman, *The Discovery of the Asylum* (Boston: Little, Brown, 1971); Thomas S. Szasz, *Ideology and Insanity* (Garden City, N.J.: Anchor, 1970), and *Law, Liberty, and Psychiatry* (New York: Macmillan, 1963); Erving Goffman, *Asylums* (Garden City, N.J.: Anchor, 1961).

32. Richard Condon, *The Manchurian Candidate* (New York: New American Library, 1959), filmed 1962; Ken Kesey, *One Flew over the Cuckoo's Nest* (New York: Viking, 1962), filmed 1975; Anthony Burgess, *A Clockwork Orange* (New York: Ballantine, 1963), filmed 1971; Jessica Mitford, *Kind and Usual Punishment* (New York: Knopf, 1973), pp. 137–38; John D. Marks, *The Search for the "Manchurian Candidate"* (New York: Times Books, 1979).

33. American Friends' Service Committee, *Struggle for Justice* (New York: Hill and Wang, 1971); Francis T. Cullen and Karen E. Gilbert, *Reaffirming Rehabilitation* (Cincinnati: Anderson, 1982); Douglas Lipton, Robert Martinson, and Judith Wilks, *The Effectiveness of Correctional Treatments* (New York: Praeger, 1975); Robert Martinson, "What Works?" *Public Interest* 35 (1974): 22–54; Andrew Von Hirsch, *Doing Justice* (New York: Hill and Wang, 1976).

34. Norval Morris and Gordon Hawkins, *The Honest Politician's Guide to Crime Control* (Chicago: University of Chicago, 1970).

35. Cohen, *Law of Deprivation of Liberty,* pp. 365–68, 455.

36. For discussion about the decision by the U.S. Court of Appeals, see Cohen, *Law of Deprivation of Liberty,* pp. 712–15.

37. Ibid., pp. 744–6l; Kittrie, *Right to Be Different,* p. 188.

38. Cohen, *Law of Deprivation of Liberty,* pp. 718–19.

39. Quoted in Philip Jenkins, *Pedophiles and Priests* (New York: Oxford University Press, 1996), p. 84; Cohen, *Law of Deprivation of Liberty,* p. 477.

40. Robert J. Kohlenberg, "Treatment of a Homosexual Pedophiliac Using In Vivo Desensitization," in Irving Jacks and Steven G. Cox, eds., *Psychological Approaches to Crime and Its Correction* (Chicago: Nelson Hall, 1984), pp. 508–14; Richard Speiglman, "Prison Psychiatrists and Drugs," in Tony Platt and Paul Takagi, eds., *Punishment and Penal Discipline* (Berkeley, Calif.: Crime and Social Justice, 1979), pp. 113–28.

41. Cohen, *Law of Deprivation of Liberty,* pp. 540–43; Todd R. Clear and George F. Cole, *American Corrections* (Monterey, Calif.: Brooks Cole, 1986), p. 175.

CHAPTER 6: THE CHILD ABUSE REVOLUTION, 1976–1986

1. Stephen J. Pfohl, "The Discovery of Child Abuse," *Social Problems* 24 (1977): 310–23; C. Henry Kempe et al., "The Battered Child Syndrome," *Journal of the American Medical Association* 181 (1962): 17–24.

2. Barbara J. Nelson, *Making an Issue of Child Abuse* (Chicago: University of Chicago Press, 1984); Dean D. Knudsen, *Child Protective Services* (Springfield, Ill.: Charles Thomas, 1988); John Hagedorn, *Forsaking Our Children* (Chicago: Lake View, 1995). On the increasing number of false accusations, see, for instance, William Glaberson, "Cleared of Child Abuse Five Times, Woman Sues Connecticut for Name of Her Accuser," *NYT*, January 6, 1997.

3. Florence Rush, "The Sexual Abuse of Children," in Noreen Connell and Cassandra Wilson, eds., *Rape: The First Sourcebook for Women* (New York: New American Library, 1974), pp. 65–75; Vincent De Francis, *Protecting the Child Victim of Sex Crimes Committed by Adults* (Denver, Colo.: American Humane Association, Children's Division, 1969), pp. iv, vii; Yvonne M. Tormes, *Child Victims of Incest* (Denver, Colo.: American Humane Association, Children's Division, 1968); Lisa Aversa Richette, *The Throwaway Children* (New York: Dell, 1969), pp. 212–33; compare Lela Costin, Howard Krager, and David Stoesz, *The Politics of Child Abuse in America* (New York: Oxford University Press, 1996).

   For earlier concepts of sexual abuse, see Charles G. Chaddock, "Sex Crimes," in Allan McLane Hamilton and Lawrence Godkin, eds., *A System of Legal Medicine* (New York: E. B. Treat, 1894), 2:525–72; Benjamin Karpman, *The Sexual Offender and His Offenses* (New York: Julian, 1954), p. 345; D. W. Swanson, "Adult Sexual Abuse of Children," *Diseases of the Nervous System* 29 (1968): 677–86.

4. David H. Bennett, *The Party of Fear*, 2d ed. (New York: Vintage, 1995); Ron LaBrecque, *Lost Undercover* (New York: Dell, 1987).

5. Densen-Gerber is quoted in Ernest Volkman and Howard L. Rosenberg, "The Shame of the Nation," *Family Weekly*, June 2, 1985, p. 6. See also D. Kelly Weisberg, *Children of the Night* (Lexington, Mass.: Lexington, 1985); Gitta Sereny, *The Invisible Children* (New York: Knopf, 1985); Robin Lloyd, *For Money or Love* (New York: Vanguard, 1976); Beverley LaBelle, "Snuff," in Laura Lederer, ed., *Take Back the Night* (New York: William Morrow, 1980).

6. Judianne Densen-Gerber, *We Mainline Dreams* (Garden City, N.J.: Doubleday, 1973); Judianne Densen-Gerber and S. F. Hutchinson, "Medical-Legal and Societal Problems Involving Children," in S. M. Smith, ed., *The Maltreatment of Children* (Baltimore: University Park Press, 1978). For the Odyssey House campaign, see *NYT*, January 15 and February 15, 1977.

7. Judianne Densen-Gerber, "What Pornographers Are Doing to Children," *Redbook*, August 1977, p. 86; Gloria Steinem, "Pornography," *Ms.*, August 1977, pp. 43–44; "Child's Garden of Perversity," *Time*, April 4, 1977, pp. 55–56. The NBC report is quoted in Joel Best, *Threatened Children* (Chicago: University of Chicago Press, 1990), p. 98. The *Chicago Tribune* series ran May 15–19, 1977, and is reprinted in extenso in House Committee on the Judiciary, Subcommittee on Crime, *Sexual Exploitation of Children: Hearings Before the Subcommittee on*

Crime of the Committee on the Judiciary (Washington, D.C.: GPO, 1977), pp. 428–41.

8. House Committee, *Sexual Exploitation of Children;* Barbara Ascher, "Crime: Lloyd Martin of the LAPD's Sexually Exploited Child Unit," *People,* October 9, 1978, pp. 99–100; Martin interview in Kathleen Barry, *Female Sexual Slavery* (Englewood Cliffs, N.J.: Prentice-Hall, 1979), pp. 99–102.

9. See, for example, House Committee, *Sexual Exploitation of Children,* pp. 40, 57; E. Weber, "Incest: Sexual Abuse Begins at Home," *Ms.,* April 1977, pp. 64–67.

10. Edward Alwood, *Straight News* (New York: Columbia University Press, 1996); Toby Marotta, *The Politics of Homosexuality* (Boston: Houghton Mifflin, 1981).

11. Anita Bryant and Bob Green, *At Any Cost* (Old Tappan, N.J.: Fleming H. Revell, 1978); Perry Deane Young, *God's Bullies* (New York: Holt Rinehart Winston, 1982), p. 44; John Mitzel, *The Boston Sex Scandal* (Boston: Glad Day, 1980), p. 15.

12. Young, *God's Bullies,* pp. 44–46; House Committee, *Sexual Exploitation of Children,* pp. 75 (Leonard), 433 (*Chicago Tribune*), 205 (Wooden).

13. Enrique Rueda, *The Homosexual Network* (Old Greenwich, Conn.: Devin Adair, 1982).

14. Gladys Shultz, *How Many More Victims?* (Philadelphia: J. B. Lippincott, 1965), pp. 33, 112–19.

15. Joyce E. Williams and Karen A. Holmes, *The Second Assault* (Westport, Conn.: Greenwood Press, 1981); Marian Meyers, *News Coverage of Violence Against Women* (Thousand Oaks, Calif.: Sage, 1997).

16. Susan Griffin, *Rape: The Politics of Consciousness,* 3d ed. (San Francisco: Harper and Row, 1986); Nancy Gager and Cathleen Schurr, *Sexual Assault* (New York: Grosset and Dunlap, 1976); Susan Brownmiller, *Against Our Will* (London: Secker and Warburg, 1975); Andra Medea and Kathleen Thompson, *Against Rape* (New York: Farrar, Straus, and Giroux, 1974); Ann W. Burgess and Lynda L. Holmstrom, *Rape: Victims of Crisis* (Bowie, Md.: R. J. Brady, 1974); Diana E. H. Russell, *The Politics of Rape: The Victim's Perspective* (New York: Stein and Day, 1974); Carol V. Horos, *Rape* (New Canaan, Conn.: Tobey, 1974); Nancy A. Matthews, *Confronting Rape* (London: Routledge, 1994).

17. Peggy Reeves Sanday, *A Woman Scorned* (New York: Doubleday, 1996); John Marshall MacDonald, *Rape: Controversial Issues* (Springfield, Ill.: Charles Thomas, 1995); Linda A. Fairstein, *Sexual Violence* (New York: William Morrow, 1993); Alice Vachss, *Sex Crimes* (New York: Random House, 1993); compare Diana E. H. Russell, *Rape in Marriage* (New York: Macmillan, 1982).

18. Rush, "Sexual Abuse of Children." See also Florence Rush, "The Freudian Cover-Up," *Chrysalis* 1 (1977): 31–45, and *The Best-Kept Secret: Sexual Abuse of Children* (Englewood Cliffs, N.J.: Prentice-Hall, 1980).

19. Judith L. Herman and Lisa Hirschman, *Father-Daughter Incest* (Cambridge: Har-

vard University Press, 1981), p. 4. There is an influential discussion of child sexual abuse in Brownmiller, *Against Our Will,* pp. 271–80.

For the explosion of writing from the late 1970s, see Ann W. Burgess et al., *The Sexual Assault of Children and Adolescents* (Lexington, Mass.: D. C. Heath, 1978); Kee MacFarlane, "Sexual Abuse of Children," in J. R. Chapman and M. Gates, eds., *The Victimization of Women* (Beverly Hills, Calif.: Sage, 1978); David Finkelhor, *Sexually Victimized Children* (New York: Free Press, 1979); Susan Forward and Craig Buck, *Betrayal of Innocence* (New York: Penguin, 1979); Suzanne M. Sgroi, "The Sexual Assault of Children," in *The Sexual Abuse of Children: Implications from the Sexual Trauma Treatment Program of Connecticut* (New York: Community Council of Greater New York, 1979); Christine Courtois, "The Incest Experience and Its Aftermath," *Victimology: An International Journal* 4 (1979): 337–47; LeRoy G. Schultz, ed., *The Sexual Victimology of Youth* (Springfield, Ill.: Charles Thomas, 1980); Rush, *Best-Kept Secret;* Mary De Young, *The Sexual Victimization of Children* (Jefferson, N.C.: McFarland, 1982); David Finkelhor, "Sexual Abuse: A Sociological Perspective," *CAN* 6 (1982): 95–102, and *Child Sexual Abuse* (New York: Free Press, 1984), p. 3; Suzanne S. Ageton, *Sexual Assault Among Adolescents* (Lexington, Mass.: Lexington, 1983); Carol A. Plummer, *Preventing Sexual Abuse* (Holmes Beach, Fla.: Learning Publications, 1984); Ann W. Burgess, ed., *Rape and Sexual Assault* (New York: Garland, 1985); Adele Mayer, *Sexual Abuse* (Holmes Beach, Fla.: Learning Publications, 1985).

For the new literature on the study of the molester, see Nathaniel J. Pallone, *Rehabilitating Criminal Sexual Psychopaths* (New Brunswick, N.J.: Transaction, 1990); Kenneth V. Lanning, *Child Molesters* (Washington, D.C.: NCMEC, 1987); Susan B. McDonald-Doren and Eugene H. Strangman, *Sex Offender Research* (Madison, Wis.: Division of Corrections, Bureau of Clinical Services, 1987); David Finkelhor and S. Araji, "Explanations of Pedophilia," *Journal of Sex Research* 22:2 (1986): 145–61; Ronald M. Holmes, *The Sex Offender and the Criminal Justice System* (Springfield, Ill.: Charles Thomas, 1983); A. N. Groth et al., "The Child Molester," in Jon R. Conte and David A. Shore, eds., *Social Work and Child Sexual Abuse* (New York: Hawthorne, 1982); Gene Abel, Judith Becker, and Linda Skinner, *Treatment of the Violent Sex Offender* (New York: Columbia University Press, 1982).

20. P. Mrazek and C. H. Kempe, *Sexually Abused Children and Their Families* (New York: Pergamon, 1981); Ruth S. Kempe and C. Henry Kempe, *Child Abuse* (London: Fontana, Open University, 1978), and *The Common Secret* (New York: W. H. Freeman, 1984); Diana E. H. Russell, *The Secret Trauma* (New York: Basic, 1986), p. 38.

21. Richard A. Roth, *Child Sexual Abuse, Incest, Assault, and Sexual Exploitation* (Washington, D.C.: U.S. Department of Health, Education, and Welfare, 1979); Charles M. Sennott, *Broken Covenant* (New York: Pinnacle, 1994), pp. 257–59;

U.S. Department of Justice, *Protecting Our Children: The Fight Against Molestation,* National Symposium on Child Molestation, October 1–4, 1984 (Washington, D.C.: U.S. Department of Justice, 1985).

22. F. Berlin, H. M. Malin, and S. Dean, "Effects of Statutes Requiring Psychiatrists to Report Suspected Sexual Abuse of Children," *AJP* 148:4 (1991): 449–53; Susan Diesenhouse, "Child Sex Abuse Cases Rising in Massachusetts," *NYT,* January 31, 1988; Antoinette A. Coleman, *Child Abuse Reporting* (New York: Garland, 1995); John Crewdson, *By Silence Betrayed* (New York: Little, Brown, 1988); Tamar Lewin, "Charges of Parent Sex Abuse and a Family in Tatters," *NYT,* November 14, 1987; Finkelhor, *Child Sexual Abuse,* p. 1.

23. The Children's Defense Fund reference is from Derrick Z. Jackson, "America Lags in Its Treatment of Children," *BG* column reprinted in State College (Pa.) *Centre Daily Times,* July 5, 1994 (emphasis mine); Christopher J. Dodd, "For Children's Sake, Help Families Before It's Too Late," State College (Pa.) *Centre Daily Times,* May 1, 1993; Child Welfare League of America advertisement, *NYT,* February 7, 1990.

24. Weber, "Incest"; Finkelhor, *Sexually Victimized Children;* Chrystine Oksana, *Safe Passage to Healing* (New York: Harper Perennial, 1994), p. xxvii. The quotation from the Parents League of the United States appears in Best, *Threatened Children,* p. 72; Blume is quoted in Philip Jenkins, *Pedophiles and Priests* (New York: Oxford University Press, 1996), p. 87.

25. Douglas J. Besharov, *Recognizing Child Abuse* (New York: Free Press, 1990); Ellen Bass and Laura Davis, *The Courage to Heal* (New York: Harper and Row, 1988), p. 21.

26. Carol Tavris, "The Truth About Sexual Abuse," *Vogue,* May 1986, p. 164; Diana E. H. Russell, *Sexual Exploitation* (Beverly Hills, Calif.: Sage, 1984), pp. 172–81. See also Russell, *Secret Trauma.*

27. Rosaria Champagne, *The Politics of Survivorship* (New York: New York University Press, 1996), p. 14; NCMEC pamphlet, no title or date, c. 1990.

28. Philip Jenkins, *Using Murder* (Hawthorne, N.Y.: Aldine de Gruyter, 1994); Volkman and Rosenberg, "Shame of the Nation," p. 4; Best, *Threatened Children,* p. 134.

29. Paula Hawkins, *Children at Risk* (Bethesda, Md.: Adler and Adler, 1986); Kenneth Wooden, *Weeping in the Playtime of Others* (New York: McGraw-Hill, 1976), and *The Children of Jonestown* (New York: McGraw-Hill, 1981); House Committee, *Sexual Exploitation of Children,* pp. 202–7; John Walsh with Susan Schindehette, *Tears of Rage* (New York: Pocket Books, 1997).

30. Philip Jenkins, *Using Murder* (Hawthorne, N.Y.: Aldine de Gruyter, 1994); Senate Committee on the Judiciary, Subcommittee on Juvenile Justice, *Serial Murders: Hearings Before the Subcommittee on Juvenile Justice of the Committee on the Judiciary* (Washington, D.C.: GPO, 1984); NCAVC (Quantico, Va.: Behavioral Sciences Services, FBI Academy, 1986).

31. Attorney General's Commission on Pornography, *Final Report* (Washington, D.C.: U.S. Department of Justice, 1986); Martin L. Forst and Martha-Elin Blomquist, *Missing Children: Rhetoric and Reality* (Toronto: Lexington, 1991); Best, *Threatened Children;* Kenneth V. Lanning, *Investigator's Guide to Allegations of "Ritual" Child Abuse* (Quantico, Va.: NCAVC, FBI Academy, 1992), p. 5.

32. Paul Gebhard et al., *Sex Offenders: An Analysis of Types* (New York: Harper and Row, 1965), p. 71; Johann W. Mohr, Robert E. Turner, and Marian B. Jerry, *Pedophilia and Exhibitionism: A Handbook* (Toronto: University of Toronto Press, 1964), p. 29; Karpman, *Sexual Offender,* p. 66; De Francis, *Protecting the Child Victim.*

33. Carol Poston, "A Survivor of Incest," *New Woman,* March 1989, pp. 112–19; James B. Twitchell, *Forbidden Partners* (New York: Columbia University Press, 1987); Brenda J. Vander Mey and Ronald L. Neff, *Incest as Child Abuse* (New York: Praeger, 1986); Russell, *Secret Trauma;* E. Ward, *Father-Daughter Rape* (New York: Grove, 1985); Mary De Young, *Incest: An Annotated Bibliography* (Jefferson, N.C.: McFarland, 1985); George Thorman, *Incestuous Families* (Springfield, Ill.: Charles Thomas, 1983); Domeena C. Renshaw, *Incest* (Boston: Little, Brown, 1982); Herman and Hirschman, *Father-Daughter Incest;* Robert L. Geiser, *Hidden Victims* (Boston: Beacon, 1979); Blair Justice and Rita Justice, *The Broken Taboo* (New York: Human Sciences Press, 1979); Sandra Butler, *Conspiracy of Silence* (San Francisco: New Glide, 1978); Karin C. Meiselman, *Incest* (San Francisco: Jossey-Bass, 1978); Susan Forward and Craig Buck, "The Family Crime Nobody Talks About," *Ladies' Home Journal,* November 1978, p. 33; Weber, "Incest." For Brady's congressional appearance, see Senate Committee on the Judiciary, Subcommittee on Juvenile Justice, *Effects of Pornography on Women and Children: Hearings Before the Subcommittee on Juvenile Justice of the Committee on the Judiciary* (Washington, D.C.: GPO, 1985), p. 65.

34. Louise Armstrong, *Kiss Daddy Goodnight* (New York: Hawthorne, 1978); Cristina Crawford, *Mommie Dearest* (New York: William Morrow, 1978); Jennifer Barr, *Within a Dark Wood* (Garden City, N.J.: Doubleday, 1979); Katherine Brady, *Father's Days* (New York: Dell, 1979); Ellen Bass and Louise Thornton, eds., *I Never Told Anyone* (New York: Harper and Row, 1983). Compare the fictionalized treatments in Maya Angelou, *I Know Why the Caged Bird Sings* (New York: Bantam, 1971), and Toni Morrison, *Bluest Eye* (New York: Pocket, 1972). See also Charlotte V. Allen, *Daddy's Girl* (New York: Wyndham, 1980); Toni A. H. McNaron and Yarrow Morgan, eds., *Voices in the Night* (Minneapolis, Minn.: Cleis, 1982); Louise Armstrong, *The Home Front: Notes from the Family War Zone* (New York: McGraw-Hill, 1983); Sheila Sisk and Charlotte Foster Hoffman, *Inside Scars* (Gainesville, Fla.: Pandora, 1987); Elly Danica, *A Woman's Word* (San Francisco: Cleis, 1988); Shelley Sessions and Peter Meyer, *Dark Obsession* (New York: G. P. Putnam's Sons, 1990); Betsy Petersen, *Dancing with Daddy* (New York: Bantam,

1991); Jacqueline Woodson, *I Hadn't Meant to Tell You This* (New York: Delacorte, 1994); Martha Ramsey, *Where I Stopped* (New York: G. P. Putnam's Sons, 1995); Linda Catherine Cutting, *Memory Slips* (New York: HarperCollins, 1997); Caroline Malone, Linda Farthing, and Lorraine Marce, eds., *The Memory Bird* (Philadelphia: Temple University Press, 1997). A startlingly different view of incest is in Kathryn Harrison, *The Kiss* (New York: Random House, 1997), a disturbing memoir of the author's consensual sexual relationship with her father.

35. Christine Courtois, *Healing the Incest Wound* (New York: Norton, 1988); Alice Miller, *Thou Shalt Not Be Aware* (New York: New American Library, 1986); L. Sanford, *The Silent Children* (New York: Doubleday, 1980).

36. A. N. Groth, *Men Who Rape* (New York: Plenum, 1979). Compare Whitman, *Terror,* p. 189; Russell, *Sexual Exploitation,* pp. 289–90; Russell, *Secret Trauma,* p. 392.

37. Anne L. Horton, ed., *The Incest Perpetrator* (Newbury Park, Calif.: Sage, 1990); Daniel Goleman, "New Studies Map the Mind of the Rapist," *NYT,* December 10, 1991. Compare David Gelman et al., "The Mind of the Rapist," *Newsweek,* July 23, 1990, pp. 46–53; Shirley J. O'Brien, *Why They Did It* (Springfield, Ill.: C. C. Thomas, 1986), p. ix.

For Abel's remark, see Patrick Boyle, *Scout's Honor* (Rocklin, Calif.: Prima, 1994), p. 31; compare Gene Abel, "The Child Molester: How Can You Spot Him?" *Redbook,* August 1987, p. 99; G. Fuller, "Child Molestation and Pedophilia," *Journal of the American Medical Association* 261 (1989): 602–6.

38. Anna C. Salter, *Transforming Trauma* (Thousand Oaks, Calif.: Sage, 1995); Gail Elizabeth Wyatt and Gloria Johnson Powell, eds., *Lasting Effects of Child Sexual Abuse* (Newbury Park, Calif.: Sage, 1988); De Francis, *Protecting the Child Victim,* pp. 4–8.

39. Michael Ryan, *Secret Life* (New York: Vintage, 1996); Richard Berendzen and Laura Palmer, *Come Here* (New York: Villard, 1993); Kurt Freund, R. Watson, and R. Dickey, "Does Sexual Abuse in Childhood Cause Pedophilia?" *Archives of Sexual Behavior* 19 (1990): 557–68; Kurt Freund, "The Basis of the Abused Abuser Theory of Pedophilia," *Archives of Sexual Behavior* 23 (1994): 553–63.

40. Senate Committee, *Effects of Pornography on Women and Children.*

41. Crewdson, *By Silence Betrayed,* p. ix.

42. R. Watson, "A Hidden Epidemic," *Newsweek,* May 14, 1984, pp. 30–36; C. O'-Connor, "The Chilling Facts About Sexual Abuse," *Glamour,* June 1984, p. 265; M. Beck, "An Epidemic of Child Abuse," *Newsweek,* August 20, 1984, p. 44; R. Watson, "Child Molesting: The Sad New Facts of Life," *Reader's Digest,* September 1984, pp. 148–52; C. McCall, "The Cruelest Crime," *Life,* December 1984, pp. 35–42.

43. Carolyn M. Byerly, *The Mother's Book* (Dubuque, Iowa: Kendall/Hunt, 1992); Caren Adams and Jennifer Fay, *No More Secrets* (San Luis Obispo, Calif.: Impact, 1981); Ellen Bass, *I Like You to Make Jokes with Me but I Don't Want You to Touch*

Me (Chapel Hill, N.C.: Lollipop Power, 1981); Lory Freeman, *It's MY Body* (Seattle: Parenting Press, 1986); Amy C. Bahr, *It's OK to Say No* (New York: Grosset and Dunlap, 1986); Kristin Baird, *My Body Belongs to Me* (Circle Pines, Minn.: American Guidance Service, 1986); "Jessie," *Please Tell!* (Center City, Minn.: Hazelden, 1991). Compare Jennifer Sowle Aho and John W. Petras, *Learning About Sexual Abuse* (Hillside, N.J.: Enslow, 1985); Roderick Townley, *Safe and Sound* (New York: Simon and Schuster, 1985); Kenneth Wooden, *Child Lures* (Arlington, Tex.: Summit, 1995); Best, *Threatened Children,* pp. 152–60.

44. Maria Laurino, "Custody Wars," *Ms.,* December 1988, pp. 88–95; "Don't Touch My Child," CBS's *48 Hours,* January 4, 1990; Jonathan Groner, *Hilary's Trial* (New York: Simon and Schuster, 1991); Marianne Szegedy-Maszak, "Who's to Judge?" *NYT Magazine,* May 21, 1989, pp. 26–27; Lewin, "Charges of Parent Sex Abuse"; Mary C. Bounds, "Driven by Guilt," *Redbook,* February 1993, pp. 82–85; Alexis Jetter, "Faye's Crusade," *Vogue,* July 1991, pp. 148–51; Tom Junod, "The Last Angry Woman," *Life,* April 1991, pp. 64–76.

45. Jay C. Howell, *Selected State Legislation,* 2d ed. (Washington, D.C.: NCMEC, 1989); Gail S. Goodman, "Children's Testimony in Historical Perspective," *Journal of Social Issues* 40:2 (1984): 9–32; Gail S. Goodman, Christine Aman, and Jodi Hirschman, "Child Sexual and Physical Abuse," in S. J. Ceci, M. P. Toglia, and D. F. Ross, eds., *Children's Eyewitness Memory* (New York: Springer-Verlag, 1987), pp. 1–23; Maria S. Zaragosa et al., *Memory and Testimony in the Child Witness* (Thousand Oaks, Calif.: Sage, 1994); Lucy S. McGough, *Child Witnesses: Fragile Voices in the American Legal System* (New Haven: Yale University Press, 1994); Ellen Gray, *Unequal Justice* (New York: Free Press, 1993); Billie Wright Dziech and C. B. Schudson, *On Trial,* 2d ed. (Boston: Beacon, 1991); Ross Eatman and Josephine Bulkley, *Protecting Child Victim/Witnesses* (Washington, D.C.: National Legal Resource Center for Child Advocacy and Protection, 1986); E. R. Shipp, "The Jeopardy of Children on the Stand," *NYT,* September 23, 1984.

46. Nancy Walker Perry and Lawrence W. Wrightsman, *The Child Witness* (Newbury Park, Calif.: Sage, 1991); Lucy Berliner and Mary Kay Barbieri, "The Testimony of the Child Victim of Sexual Assault," *Journal of Social Issues* 40:2 (1984): 125–38; American Journal of Nursing, Educational Services Division, *Child Sexual Abuse,* 1985, videocassette.

47. Debra Whitcomb, *Prosecution of Child Sexual Abuse,* U.S. Department of Justice, National Institute of Justice (Washington, D.C.: GPO, 1985); Debra Whitcomb, Elizabeth R. Shapiro, and Lindsey D. Stellwagen, *When the Victim Is a Child,* U.S. Department of Justice, National Institute of Justice (Washington, D.C.: GPO, 1985).

48. Ruth Marcus, "Law Allowing Children to Testify Behind Screens Is Nullified," *WP Weekly Edition,* June 30, 1988; Linda Greenhouse, "Child Abuse Trials Can Shield Witnesses," *NYT,* June 28, 1990; Ebrahim Kermani, "Child Sexual Abuse Revisited

by the Supreme Court," *Journal of the Academy of Child and Adolescent Psychiatry* 32:5 (1992): 971–74.

CHAPTER 7: CHILD PORNOGRAPHY AND PEDOPHILE RINGS

1. Shirley J. O'Brien, *Child Pornography* (Dubuque, Iowa: Kendall Hunt, 1983), and "The Child Molester: Porn Plays a Major Role in Life," *National Federation for Decency Journal*, May–June 1987, pp. 9–11; LeRoy G. Schultz, *"Kiddie Porn": A Social Policy Analysis* (Morgantown, W.Va.: School of Social Work, West Virginia University, 1977).

2. Patrick Boyle, *Scout's Honor* (Rocklin, Calif.: Prima, 1994). The content of 1970s child porn is described in House Committee on the Judiciary, Subcommittee on Crime, *Sexual Exploitation of Children: Hearings Before the Subcommittee on Crime of the Committee on the Judiciary* (Washington, D.C.: GPO, 1977), pp. 419–44.

3. House Committee, *Sexual Exploitation of Children,* pp. 39–42, 45–46, 437–38.

4. Ernest Volkman and Howard L. Rosenberg, "The Shame of the Nation," *Family Weekly*, June 2, 1985, p. 4. The Wildmon quote is from Joel Best, *Threatened Children* (Chicago: University of Chicago Press, 1990), p. 47. See also advertisement for National Pornography Awareness Week, State College (Pa.) *Centre Daily Times*, October 11, 1988; Ellen Bass and Laura Davis, *The Courage to Heal* (New York: Harper and Row, 1988), p. 21; Mark Clayton, "Prostitution Circuit Takes Girls Across North America," "Sex Trade Lures Kids from 'Burbs," and "New Laws Fail to Curb Demand for Child Sex," all in *The Child Sex Trade*, series reprint from the *Christian Science Monitor* (1996): 5–11. The continuing tabloid interest in this topic was also suggested by television documentaries like the program "The Child Sex Trade," shown on A&E's *Investigative Reports*, October 11, 1997.

5. Jack McIver Weatherford, *Porn Row* (New York: Arbor House, 1986), pp. 161–75; Kenneth V. Lanning, *Investigator's Guide to Allegations of "Ritual" Child Abuse* (Quantico, Va.: NCAVC, FBI Academy, 1992), p. 3.

6. Attorney General's Commission on Pornography, *Final Report* (Washington, D.C.: U.S. Department of Justice, 1986), pp. 405–18; advertisements in State College (Pa.) *Centre Daily Times*, October 1990; Charles M. Sennott, *Broken Covenant* (New York: Pinnacle, 1994), pp. 257–64. Ritter himself was later discredited following a sex scandal involving teenage boys.

7. Lawrence A. Stanley, "The Child-Pornography Myth," *Playboy*, September 1988, pp. 41–44; Joyce Karlin, "Child Pornography" (letter to the editor), *Playboy*, January 1989, pp. 60–62; Donald A. Downs, *The New Politics of Pornography* (Chicago: University of Chicago Press, 1989).

8. Ralph W. Bennett, "The Relationship Between Pornography and Extrafamilial Child Sexual Abuse," *Police Chief*, February 1991, pp. 14–20; Bill Thompson, *Soft*

Core (London: Cassell, 1994); Catherine A. MacKinnon, *Only Words* (Cambridge: Harvard University Press, 1996), pp. 35–36.

9. Howard A. Davidson and Gregory A. Loken, *Child Pornography and Prostitution* (Washington, D.C.: NCMEC, 1987); Senate Committee on the Judiciary, Subcommittee on Juvenile Justice, *Child Pornography: Hearings Before the Subcommittee on Juvenile Justice of the Committee on the Judiciary* (Washington, D.C.: GPO, 1983), and *Effects of Pornography on Women and Children: Hearings Before the Subcommittee on Juvenile Justice of the Committee on the Judiciary* (Washington, D.C.: GPO, 1985); Committee on Governmental Affairs, *Child Pornography and Pedophilia: Hearings Before the Permanent Subcommittee on Investigations of the Committee on Governmental Affairs* (Washington, D.C.: GPO, 1985), and *Child Pornography and Pedophilia: Report Made by the Permanent Subcommittee on Investigations of the Committee on Governmental Affairs* (Washington, D.C.: GPO, 1986); Senate Committee on the Judiciary, *Child Protection and Obscenity Enforcement Act and Pornography Victims Protection Act of 1987: Hearing Before the Committee on the Judiciary* (Washington, D.C.: GPO, 1988); House Committee on the Judiciary, Subcommittee on Crime, *Child Protection and Obscenity Enforcement Act of 1988: Hearings Before the Subcommittee on Crime of the Committee on the Judiciary* (Washington, D.C.: GPO, 1989); "Senate Supports Tougher Child Pornography Law," *Jet,* October 17, 1988, p. 14; Best, *Threatened Children,* 75; Phyllis Schlafly, ed., *Pornography's Victims* (Alton, Ill.: Pere Marquette Press, 1987); Attorney General's Commission on Pornography, *Final Report;* Pat Califia, *Public Sex* (Pittsburgh and San Francisco: Cleis, 1994), pp. 107–47; Bill Andriette, "Are You a Child Pornographer?" *Playboy,* September 1991, p. 56.

10. "Buyer of Child Pornography Is Convicted Under N.Y. Law," *BG,* February 21, 1990; John Quigley, "Child Pornography and the Right to Privacy," *Florida Law Review* 43:2 (1991): 347–69; Lisa S. Smith, "Private Possession of Child Pornography," *Annual Survey of American Law* 4 (1991): 1011–45; "Private Possession of Expressive Material-Child Pornography," *Harvard Law Review* 104 (1990): 237–47; Stephen Wermiel, "High Court's Child-Pornography Ruling Is Watched for Effect on Adult Privacy," *WSJ,* April 23, 1990.

11. Joan Biskupic, "Court Backs Child Pornography Law," *WP,* November 30, 1994; Tracy Thompson, "Parts of Child Pornography Law Struck Down," *WP,* May 17, 1989; Robert R. Strang, "'She Was Just Seventeen . . . and the Way She Looked Was Way Beyond (Her Years)': Child Pornography and Overbreadth," *Columbia Law Review* 90:6 (1990): 1779–1803; Kim Murphy, "Lords Video Agent Convicted on Child Porno Charges," *LAT,* June 16, 1989; Arthur S. Hayes, "Child Pornography Law Is Dealt Blow by Appeals Court," *WSJ,* December 17, 1992; Linda Greenhouse, "Supreme Court Upholds Government's Ambiguously Written Child Pornography Law," *NYT,* November 30, 1994.

A few observers continue to raise fundamental questions about the entire conceptual basis of the movement against sexualized depictions of the young. See, for example, Camille Paglia, *Sexual Personae* (New Haven: Yale University Press, 1990); James R. Kincaid, *Child-Loving* (New York: Routledge, 1993); Califia, *Public Sex.*

12. Laura U. Marks, "Child Pornography and the Legislation of Morality," *Afterimage* 18:4 (November 1990): 12–16; Dick Polman, "Snap Judgments," *Philadelphia Inquirer Magazine,* January 6, 1991, pp. 19–23; Lawrence A. Stanley, "Art and 'Perversion': Censoring Images of Nude Children," *Art Journal* 50:4 (Winter 1991): 20–27; "French Vintner Censors Labels Bound for U.S.," A.P. story reprinted in State College (Pa.) *Centre Daily Times,* December 13, 1996; "Clinton Seeks Redefinition of Child Pornography," *WSJ,* November 12, 1993; Marjorie Garber, "Maximum Exposure," *NYT,* December 4, 1993; "104 in Congress Petition to Argue Child Pornography Case in Court," *NYT,* December 28, 1993; Doug Payne, "Man Held over Photos of Girl, 13, in Lingerie," *Atlanta Journal and Constitution,* April 20, 1996.

13. Michael Bamberger, general counsel for the Media Coalition, 1996, at the Bookweb web site, http://www.bookweb.org.

14. U.S. Customs Service, Child Pornography and Protection Unit, *The Child Pornography Enforcement Program* (Washington, D.C.: Treasury Department, 1987); Mary Thornton, "U.S. Customs: Crusaders in the Child Pornography War," *WP Weekly Edition,* September 8, 1986; June Stephenson, *Men Are Not Cost-Effective* (New York: HarperPerennial, 1995), pp. 310–14; U.S. Postal Inspection Service web site, "Child Pornography, Obscenity, and Sexual Oriented Advertisements," WWW 1996.

15. Stanley, "The Child-Pornography Myth"; Tim Bryant, "Child-Pornography Buyer Entrapped, Court Finds," *St. Louis Post-Dispatch,* January 13, 1990; Ruth Marcus, "Fair Sting or Foul Trap? Child Pornography Investigation Challenged," *WP,* November 6, 1991; Linda P. Campbell, "Court Uses Child-Porn Case to Place Limits on Stings," *Chicago Tribune,* April 7, 1992; "Entrapment Out of Control," *NYT,* April 8, 1992; Cynthia Perez, "*U.S. v. Jacobson:* Are Child Pornography Stings Creative Law Enforcement or Entrapment?" *University of Miami Law Review* 46:1 (1991): 235–48.

16. The U.S. Senate committee is quoted in John Crewdson, *By Silence Betrayed* (New York: Little, Brown, 1988), p. 260; the remark about the cottage industry is from Matthew Ancona of Odyssey House, quoted in Volkman and Rosenberg, "Shame of the Nation," p. 6. See also Julia Preston, "Acapulco's Smut Ring," *NYT,* August 9, 1996.

17. Tony Perry, "Child Pornography Suspect Pleads Guilty," *LAT,* January 19, 1996; Gerald Hannon, "The Kiddie-Porn Ring That Wasn't," *Globe and Mail* (Toronto), March 11, 1995; Parker Rossman, *Sexual Experience Between Men and Boys: Exploring the Pederast Underground* (New York: Association Press, 1976), pp. 33–42;

David Stout, "Forty-Five Arrested in a Nationwide Child Pornography Ring, U.S. Says," *NYT,* May 10, 1996; Preston, "Acapulco's Smut Ring."

18. O'Brien, *Child Pornography;* Ann W. Burgess and Marieanne Lindqvist Clark, eds., *Child Pornography and Sex Rings* (Lexington, Mass.: Lexington, 1984); Kenneth V. Lanning and Ann W. Burgess, *Child Pornography and Sex Rings* (Washington, D.C.: U.S. Department of Justice, 1984); compare Ann W. Burgess, A. Nicholas Groth, Maureen P. McCausland, "Child Sex Initiation Rings," *AJO,* January 1981, pp. 110–19; Ann W. Burgess and Christine A. Grant, *Children Traumatized in Sex Rings* (Washington, D.C.: NCMEC, 1988); Toby Marotta, Bruce Fisher, Michael Pincus, *Adolescent Male Prostitution, Pornography, and Other Forms of Sexual Exploitation* (San Francisco: Urban and Rural Systems Associates, 1982); House Committee on Education and Labor, Subcommittee on Select Education, *Teenage Prostitution and Child Pornography: Hearings Before the Subcommittee on Select Education of the Committee on Education and Labor* (Washington, D.C.: GPO, 1982); House Committee, *Sexual Exploitation of Children.*

For the view that all underage prostitutes are coerced, see Daniel S. Campagna and Donald L. Poffenberger, *The Sexual Trafficking in Children* (Dover, Mass.: Auburn House, 1988); Clifford Linedecker, *Children in Chains* (New York: Everest House, 1981).

19. House Committee, *Sexual Exploitation of Children,* pp. 429 (*Chicago Tribune*), 58 (Martin), 74–75 (Leonard), 82–90 (camps and churches).

20. For Gunderson, see Maury Terry, *The Ultimate Evil* (New York: Bantam, 1987); Best, *Threatened Children,* pp. 118–22; Ron Handberg, *Savage Justice* (New York: Birch Lane, 1992); Leslie Marmon Silko, *Alamanc of the Dead* (New York: Penguin, 1992).

21. Classical Greek culture distinguished between the benevolently viewed pederast, or boy-lover, and the sinister "corruptor of youth," the *paidophthoros.* See Rossman, *Sexual Experience,* pp. 191–95; Parker Rossman, "The Pederasts," in Erich Goode and Richard R. Troiden, eds., *Sexual Deviance and Sexual Deviants* (New York: Morrow, 1974), pp. 396–409; Edward Brongersma, *Loving Boys* (New York: Global Academic, 1986); Theo Sandfort, *Boys on Their Contacts with Men* (Elmhurst, N.Y.: Global Academic, 1987); Frits Bernard, *Persecuted Minority* (Amsterdam: Southernwood, 1989); Mark Pascal, *Varieties of Man/Boy Love* (New York: Wallace Hamilton, 1992); Mark Blasius and Shane Phelan, *We Are Everywhere* (New York: Routledge, 1997), pp. 459–68; Michael Davidson, *The World, the Flesh, and Myself* (Swaffham, England: Gay Men's Press, 1997); Joseph Geraci, ed., *Dares to Speak: Historical and Contemporary Perspectives on Boy-Love* (New York: Gay Men's Press, 1997).

For the Mattachine Society, see Jonathan Ned Katz, *Gay American History* (New York: Meridian, 1992), pp. 406–20; "Spirit of Stonewall" petition, WWW 1994, http://www.actwin.com/stonewall/handouts; "GLAAD [Gay and Lesbian Alliance Against Defamation] vs. NAMBLA," WWW 1994, http://www.glaad.org. NAMBLA also has a Web presence at http://www.nambla.org.

For European precedents, see Philip Jenkins, *Intimate Enemies* (Hawthorne, N.Y.: Aldine de Gruyter, 1992); Glenn D. Wilson and David N. Cox, *The Child-Lovers* (Boston: Peter Owen, 1983); Tom O'Carroll, *Paedophilia: The Radical Case* (London: Peter Owen, 1980).

22. John Mitzel, *The Boston Sex Scandal* (Boston: Glad Day, 1980), pp. 5, 12.

23. Gerald Hannon, "Men Loving Boys Loving Men," *Body Politic,* November 21, 1977, p. 39; Judy Steed, *Our Little Secret* (Toronto: Vintage Canada, 1995), pp. 57–59; Charles Trueheart, "Toronto Teacher stirs Freedom Debate," *WP,* December 11, 1995.

24. C. Waters, "Twenty-Four Men Indicted for Abuse of Seventy Boys in Boston Hired Sex Ring," *New Times,* January 23, 1978; Mitzel, *Boston Sex Scandal,* p. 28; Frank Rose, "Men and Boys Together," *Village Voice,* February 27, 1978, p. 1.

25. Mitzel, *Boston Sex Scandal,* pp. 125–26; David Thorstad, *A Witchhunt Foiled: The FBI Versus NAMBLA* (New York: North American Man-Boy Love Association, 1985), pp. 9–10; "Spirit of Stonewall"; "GLAAD vs. NAMBLA"; Dudley Cleninden, "Group Promoting Man-Boy Love Is the Focus of Police Inquiry," *NYT,* January 1, 1983.

26. Thorstad, *A Witchhunt Foiled,* pp. 6, 10; Rosalind Wright, "Where Are Our Children?" *Ladies' Home Journal,* March 1994, pp. 118–19; Timothy W. Ryback, "Four Girls Abducted, Raped, Murdered," *NYT Magazine,* February 23, 1997, pp. 42–48; Ted Oliver and Ramsay Smith, *Lambs to the Slaughter* (London: Warner, 1993); Jenkins, *Intimate Enemies.*

27. John Leo, "A New Furor over Pedophilia," *Time,* January 17, 1983, p. 47; compare Cleninden, "Group Promoting Man-Boy"; Thorstad, *A Witchhunt Foiled,* p. 55; Allen Sonnenschein, "Child Molesters and Their Victims," *Penthouse,* April 1983, pp. 60–62, 180–89; Senate Committee, *Effects of Pornography on Women and Children,* pp. 65–90; Crewdson, *By Silence Betrayed,* pp. 94–113; Enrique Rueda, *The Homosexual Network* (Old Greenwich, Conn.: Devin Adair, 1982), pp. 173–79; House Committee, *Sexual Exploitation of Children,* p. 437; Attorney General's Commission on Pornography, *Final Report,* pp. 688–89.

28. Boyle, *Scout's Honor,* pp. 72–73, 129; Volkman and Rosenberg, "Shame of the Nation," p. 4; Andrew Vachss, *Flood* (New York: D. I. Fine, 1985), p. 274. Lanning is quoted in Mike Echols, *Brother Tony's Boys* (Amherst, N.Y.: Prometheus, 1996), pp. 321–74.

29. Crewdson, *By Silence Betrayed;* Judith Reisman and Edward Eichel, *Kinsey, Sex, and Fraud* (Lafayette, La.: Lochinvar-Huntington House, 1990); Rueda, *Homosexual Network.* The influence of groups like NAMBLA is vastly exaggerated in sources like the WWW materials of the American Life League, posted at their Web site in 1996 (http://www.all.org).

30. "Inflammatory Anti-Gay Commercials Debut in Louisville," WWW, March 23, 1995; Chris Bull and John Gallagher, *Perfect Enemies* (New York: Crown, 1996).

31. Scott Lively and Kevin Abrams, *The Pink Swastika* (Keizer, Oreg.: Founders, 1995), p. 155; Alan P. Medinger, "DSM-IV and Pedophilia: What Did the APA Do?" WWW, 1995; Christopher Corbett, "APA, Point of View Clash on Pedophile Definition," WWW, 1995.

32. Echols, *Brother Tony's Boys*, pp. 333–40; Jack Viets, "Pedophile Group at S.F. Library," *SFC,* January 14, 1992; Melinda Henneberger, "How Free Can Teachers' Speech Be?" *NYT,* October 3, 1993; John Leo, "Pedophiles in the Schools," *U.S. News and World Report,* October 11, 1993, p. 37; David Van Biema, "For the Love of Kids," *Time,* November 1, 1993, p. 51; Joseph Scott, "Boy Lover," *New York,* March 28, 1994, pp. 38–39; Beth Landman, "CBS Gets Paglia All Hutton Bothered," *New York,* November 6, 1995, pp. 15–16.

33. Mitzel, *Boston Sex Scandal,* pp. 31–32; David Thorstad, "Man-Boy Love and the American Gay Movement," *JH* 20 (1991): 251–74. The NOW document is found in Blasius and Phelan, *We Are Everywhere,* pp. 468–69. See also Diana E. H. Russell, *The Secret Trauma* (New York: Basic, 1986), p. 82.

34. Gerald P. Jones, "The Study of Intergenerational Intimacy in North America," *JH* 20 (1991): 275–95; Duncan Osborne, "The Trouble with NAMBLA," *Advocate,* December 14, 1993, pp. 40–41, and "Which Side Are We On?" *Village Voice,* February 8, 1994, p. 13; Stephen Holden, "Men Who Love Boys Explain Themselves," *NYT,* July 8, 1994; John Weir, "Mad About the Boys," *Advocate,* August 23, 1994, pp. 32–37; Brent Hartinger, "Separating the Men from the Boys," *Ten Percent,* September 1994, pp. 44–47; "U.N. Suspends Group in Dispute over Pedophilia," *NYT,* September 18, 1994; Jesse Green, "The Men from the Boys," *Out,* September 1994; Harry Hay, "Focusing on NAMBLA Obscures the Issues," *Gay Community News,* Fall 1994, pp. 16, 18; Lively and Abrams, *Pink Swastika,* p. 158.

CHAPTER 8: THE ROAD TO HELL

1. Debbie Nathan and Michael Snedeker, *Satan's Silence* (New York: N.Y.: Basic, 1995).

2. See Paul Eberle and Shirley Eberle, *Abuse of Innocence* (Amherst, N.Y.: Prometheus, 1993). The ten-year-old child is quoted in Philip Jenkins and Daniel Maier-Katkin, "From Salem to Jordan," *Augustus* 9:6 (1986): 14–24. See also Diana E. H. Russell, *The Secret Trauma* (New York: Basic, 1986), p. 81; Attorney General's Commission on Pornography, *Final Report* (Washington, D.C.: U.S. Department of Justice, 1986), p. 688.

3. Lawrence Pazder and Michelle Smith, *Michelle Remembers* (New York: Congdon and Lattes, 1980); Jill Waterman et al., *Behind the Playground Walls* (New York: Guilford, 1993); David Finkelhor, Linda Meyer Williams, and Nanci Burns, *Nursery Crimes* (Newbury Park, Calif.: Sage, 1988).

4. Kee MacFarlane et al., *Sexual Abuse of Young Children* (New York: Guilford, 1986); Roland C. Summit, "The Child Abuse Accommodation Syndrome," *CAN* 7:2 (1983): 177–93.

5. "Brutalized," *Time*, April 2, 1984, p. 21; Robert Lindsey, "Sexual Abuse of Children Draws Experts' Increasing Concern Nationwide," *NYT*, April 4, 1984; S. Strasser, "A Sordid Preschool Game," *Newsweek*, April 9, 1984, p. 38; M. Green, "The Mc-Martins," *People Weekly*, May 21, 1984, pp. 109–12.

6. *60 Minutes* segments broadcast on November 2, 1986, and February 4, 1990; Robert Reinhold, "Long Child Molestation Trial Viewed as System Run Amuck," *NYT*, July 26, 1989; Robert Reinhold, "The McMartin Case: Swept Away in a Vortex of Panic on Child Molestation," *NYT*, January 24, 1990; "The McMartin Nightmare," *People Weekly*, February 5, 1990, pp. 70–80. For continuing belief in the charges, see Alex Constantine, *Psychic Dictatorship in the United States* (Portland, Oreg.: Feral House, 1995); Roland C. Summit, "Digging for the Truth," *Treating Abuse Today* 4:4 (1994): 5–13, and "The Dark Tunnels of McMartin," *Journal of Psychohistory* 21:4 (1994): 397.

7. Philip Jenkins and Daniel Maier-Katkin, "Satanism," *Crime, Law, and Social Change* 17 (1992): 53–75; Philip Jenkins, "Investigating Occult and Ritual Crime," *Police Forum* 2:1 (1992): 1–7; Robert D. Hicks, *In Pursuit of Satan* (New York: Prometheus, 1991); James W. Clark, "Occult Cops," *Law Enforcement News*, November 15, 1988, pp. 5–7; Maury Terry, *The Ultimate Evil* (New York: Bantam, 1987); Larry Kahaner, *Cults That Kill* (New York: Warner, 1988); Carl A. Raschke, *Painted Black* (San Francisco: Harper and Row, 1990).

8. See, for example, Jean S. LaFontaine, *Speak of the Devil* (Cambridge: Cambridge University Press, 1997); Richard Guilliatt, *Talk of the Devil* (Melbourne, Australia: Text, 1996); Judy Steed, *Our Little Secret* (Toronto: Vintage Canada, 1995); Philip Jenkins, *Intimate Enemies* (Hawthorne, N.Y.: Aldine de Gruyter, 1992); Tim Tate, *Children for the Devil* (London: Methuen, 1991); Andrew Boyd, *Blasphemous Rumors* (London: Fount, 1991); Kevin Marron, *Ritual Abuse* (Toronto: Seal, 1988).

9. George A. Fraser, ed., *The Dilemma of Ritual Abuse* (Washington, D.C.: American Psychiatric Press, 1997); Emilie P. Rose, *Reaching for the Light* (Cleveland, Ohio: Pilgrim, 1996); Colin Ross, *Satanic Ritual Abuse* (Toronto: University of Toronto Press, 1995); James R. Noblitt and Pamela Sue Perskin, *Cult and Ritual Abuse* (Westport, Conn.: Praeger, 1995); Linda Blood, *The New Satanists* (New York: Warner, 1994); Dee Brown, *Satanic Ritual Abuse* (Denver, Colo.: Blue Moon, 1994); Margaret Smith, *Ritual Abuse* (San Francisco: Harper, 1993); David K. Sakheim and Susan E. Devine, *Out of Darkness* (San Francisco: Jossey-Bass, 1997); David Ryder, *Breaking the Circle of Ritual Satanic Abuse* (Minneapolis, Minn.: Compcare, 1992); Robert S. Mayer, *Satan's Children* (New York: Avon, 1991).

For survivors' memoirs, see Laura Buchanan, *Satan's Child* (Minneapolis, Minn.: Compcare, 1994); Gail Carr Feldman, *Lessons in Evil, Lessons from the*

Light (New York: Crown, 1993); Torey L. Hayden, *Ghost Girl* (Boston: Little, Brown, 1991); Judith Spencer, *Suffer the Child* (New York: Pocket, 1989); Chrystine Oksana, *Safe Passage to Healing* (New York: Harper Perennial, 1994); Valerie Sinason, ed., *Treating Survivors of Satanist Abuse* (London: Routledge, 1994); Elizabeth S. Rose, "Surviving the Unbelievable: Cult Ritual Abuse Exists," *Ms.,* January 1993, pp. 40–45; Leslie Bennetts, "Nightmares on Main Street," *Vanity Fair,* June 1993, pp. 42–62; Robin D. Perrin and Les Parrott III, "Memories of Satanic Ritual Abuse," *Christianity Today,* June 21, 1993, pp. 18–23; L. N. Driscoll and C. Wright, "Survivors of Childhood Ritual Abuse," *Treating Abuse Today,* 1:4 (1991): pp. 5–13; Cheryl Carey Kent, "Ritual Abuse," in Robert T. Ammerman and Michel Hersen, eds., *Case-Studies in Family Violence* (New York: Plenum, 1991), pp. 187–207.

Compare Bennett G. Braun et al., "Patients Reporting Ritual Abuse in Childhood," *CAN* 15 (1991): 181–94; I. Kirk Weir, "Allegations of Children's Involvement in Ritual Sexual Abuse," *CAN* 19:4 (1995): 491–95; Judith Spencer, *Satan's High Priest* (New York: Pocket Books, 1997).

10. L. J. Stardancer, *Turtleboy and Jet the Wonderpup* (Lakeport, Calif.: n.p., 1993); D. Sanford, *Don't Make Me Go Back, Mommy* (Portland, Oreg.: Multnomah, 1990).

11. Jan Hollingsworth, *Unspeakable Acts* (Chicago, Ill.: Congdon and Weed, 1986). Compare Nathan and Snedeker, *Satan's Silence;* Andrew Vachss, *Sacrifice: A Novel* (London: Macmillan, 1991); Andrew Greeley, *Fall from Grace* (New York: G. P. Putnam's Sons, 1993).

12. Philip Jenkins, "Believe the Children?" *Chronicles,* January 1993, pp. 20–23.

13. Jeffrey M. Masson, *The Assault on Truth* (New York: Farrar, Straus, and Giroux, 1984); Jeffrey M. Masson, ed., *A Dark Science* (New York: Noonday, 1988).

14. Nathan and Snedeker, *Satan's Silence,* p. 5; Margaret Thaler Singer and Janja Lalich, *Cults in Our Midst* (San Francisco: Jossey-Bass, 1995); Kenneth Wooden, *The Children of Jonestown* (New York: McGraw-Hill, 1981); Philip Jenkins, *Using Murder* (Hawthorne, N.Y.: Aldine de Gruyter, 1994); Jerry Johnston, *The Edge of Evil* (Dallas: Word, 1989); Bob Larson, *Satanism* (Nashville: Thomas Nelson, 1989), and *In the Name of Satan* (Nashville: Thomas Nelson, 1996); Ted Schwarz and Duane Empey, *Satanism: Is Your Family Safe?* (Grand Rapids, Mich.: Zondervan, 1988).

15. Catherine Gould and Louis J. Cozolino, "Ritual Abuse, Multiplicity, and Mind Control," *Journal of Psychology and Theology* 20:3 (1992): 194–96; James G. Friesen, *Uncovering the Mystery of MPD* (San Bernadino, Calif.: Here's Life, 1991); Bennett G. Braun, *The Treatment of Multiple Personality Disorder* (Washington, D.C.: American Psychiatric Press, 1986); Craig Lockwood, *Other Alters* (Minneapolis, Minn.: Compcare, 1993); Sally Hill and Jean R. Goodwin, "Demonic Possession as a Consequence of Childhood Trauma," *Journal of Psychohistory* 20:4 (1993): 399–411.

16. Rose, *Reaching for the Light;* Ross, *Satanic Ritual Abuse;* Sinason, *Treating Survivors of Satanist Abuse;* Bennetts, "Nightmares on Main Street"; Sakheim and Devine, *Out of Darkness;* Oksana, *Safe Passage to Healing,* p. xx; Constantine, *Psychic Dictatorship.* Compare Los Angeles County Commission for Women, *Ritual Abuse: Definitions, Glossary, the Use of Mind Control* (Los Angeles: Ritual Abuse Task Force, 1989); Walter H. Bowart, *Operation Mind Control* (New York: Dell, 1978); John D. Marks, *The Search for the "Manchurian Candidate"* (New York: Times Books, 1979).

17. John W. DeCamp, *The Franklin Coverup* (Lincoln, Nebr.: AWT, 1992); "Omaha Tales of Sexual Abuse Ruled False," *NYT,* September 27, 1990; William Robbins, "Omaha Grand Jury Sees Hoax in Lurid Tales," *NYT,* July 29, 1990.

18. Paul Eberle and Shirley Eberle, *The Politics of Child Abuse* (Secaucus, N.J.: Lyle Stuart, 1986); Jenkins and Katkin, "From Salem to Jordan"; James F. Richardson, Joel Best, and David Bromley, eds., *The Satanism Scare* (Hawthorne, N.Y.: Aldine de Gruyter, 1991); Walter Goodman, "Who Programmed Mary? Could It Be Satan?" *NYT,* October 24, 1995. See also several articles by Debbie Nathan: "Are These Women Witches?" *Village Voice,* September 29, 1987, p. 19; "Child Molester?" *Village Voice,* August 2, 1988, p. 31; "What McMartin Started," *Village Voice,* June 12, 1990, pp. 36–38; "Cry Incest," *Playboy,* October 1992, pp. 84–88. Annette's tale is quoted in Ellen Bass and Laura Davis, *The Courage to Heal* (New York: Harper and Row, 1988), p. 417. For "breeders," see Lauren Stratford, *Satan's Underground* (Eugene, Oreg.: Harvest House, 1988).

19. Philip Jenkins and Daniel Maier-Katkin, "Occult Survivors," in Richardson, Best, and Bromley, *The Satanism Scare,* pp. 127–44; Spencer, *Suffer the Child;* Stephen A. Kent, "Deviant Scripturalism and Ritual Satanic Abuse," *Religion* 23:3 (1993): 229–58, and "Possible Masonic, Mormon, Magick, and Pagan Influences," *Religion* 23:4 (1993): 355–73; Feldman, *Lessons in Evil;* David Frankfurter, "Religious Studies and Claims of Satanic Ritual Abuse," *Religion* 24:4 (1994): 353–78; David H. Bennett, *The Party of Fear,* 2d ed. (New York: Vintage, 1995); David Brion Davis, "Some Themes of Counter-Subversion," in *From Homicide to Slavery* (New York: Oxford University Press, 1986), pp. 137–54; Oksana, *Safe Passage to Healing,* pp. 43, 132–33; Alan Dundes, ed., *The Blood Libel Legend* (Madison: University of Wisconsin Press, 1991); R. Po-chia Hsia, *The Myth of Ritual Murder* (New Haven: Yale University Press, 1988).

20. Jenkins, *Intimate Enemies;* Jon Trott and Mike Hertenstein, *Selling Satan* (n.p., 1995); Gretchen Passantino, Bob Passantino, and Jon Trott, "Satan's Sideshow," *Cornerstone* 18 (1989): 23–28.

21. WWW site of the Ontario Center for Religious Tolerance; Anna Quindlen, "Believing the Children," *NYT,* April 29, 1992; Patricia Crowley, *Not My Child* (New York: Doubleday, 1990); Lisa Manshel, *Nap Time* (New York: Zebra, 1990); Kelly Michaels, "Eight Years in Kafkaland," *National Review,* September 6, 1993,

pp. 36–37; Stephen J. Ceci and Maggie Bruck, *Jeopardy in the Courtroom* (Washington, D.C.: American Psychological Association, 1995); Nathan and Snedeker, *Satan's Silence;* Dorothy Rabinowitz, "From the Mouths of Babes to a Jail Cell," *Harper's Magazine,* May 1990, pp. 52–53. Compare David Stout, "Minister Freed Pending Appeal in Child-Abuse Case" *NYT,* July 12, 1996; Dorothy Rabinowitz, "A Darkness in Massachusetts," *WSJ,* January 30, 1995.

22. See the following works by Kenneth V. Lanning: *Child Sex Rings* (Washington, D.C.: NCMEC, 1989); "Satanic, Occult, and Ritualistic Crime," *Police Chief,* October 1989, pp. 62–85; "Ritual Abuse" *CAN* 15 (1991): 171–73; *Investigator's Guide to Allegations of "Ritual" Child Abuse* (Quantico, Va.: NCAVC, FBI Academy, 1992). See also Gail S. Goodman, *Characteristics and Sources of Allegations of Ritualistic Child Abuse* (Washington, D.C.: GPO, 1995); compare LaFontaine, *Speak of the Devil.*

23. Douglas J. Besharov, "Protecting the Innocent," *National Review,* February 19, 1990, p. 44. See also Lawrence Wright, *Remembering Satan* (New York: Knopf, 1994), and "Child-Care Demons," *New Yorker,* October 3, 1994, pp. 5–6; Rabinowitz, "From the Mouths of Babes"; Mark Sauer and Jim Okerblom, "Trial by Therapy," *National Review,* September 6, 1993, pp. 30–39; Bennetts, "Nightmares on Main Street"; William N. Grigg, "Law in Lehi," *Chronicles,* January 1993, pp. 24–27; Perrin and Parrott, "Memories of Satanic Ritual Abuse"; A. S. Ross, "Blame It on the Devil," *Redbook,* June 1994, pp. 86–89; Ethan Watters, "Doors of Memory," *Mother Jones,* January–February 1993, p. 93; Nathan, "What McMartin Started"; "McMartin: Anatomy of a Witch-Hunt," *Playboy,* June 1990, pp. 45–49; Eberle and Eberle, *Abuse of Innocence;* Jeffrey S. Victor, *Satanic Panic* (Chicago: Open Court, 1993); Nathan and Snedeker, *Satan's Silence.* Television investigations included *60 Minutes,* March 15, 1992; *Primetime Live,* January 7, 1993; and a docudrama entitled *Indictment* on HBO, May 1995.

24. Nathan and Snedeker, *Satan's Silence;* Richard A. Gardner, *Sex Abuse Hysteria: Salem Witch Trials Revisited* (Cresskill, N.J.: Creative Therapeutics, 1991); Nat Hentoff, "Once More the Witch Hunt," *WP,* May 23, 1992; CBS's *48 Hours,* May 5, 1993; Michael Granberry, "Is Trial of Church Volunteer Accused of Abusing Children a Witch Hunt?" *LAT,* June 28, 1993; Seth Mydans, "Child-Molesting Case Raises Old Questions in San Diego," *NYT,* September 22, 1993. Compare Jenkins and Katkin, "From Salem to Jordan"; Gilbert Geis and Ivan Bunn, "And a Child Shall Mislead Them," in Robert J. Kelly and Donal MacNamara, eds., *Perspectives on Deviance* (Cincinnati: Anderson, 1991), pp. 31–46.

25. CNN news reports, October 20, 1995, and December 12, 1995; Debbie Nathan, "Justice in Wenatchee," *NYT,* December 19, 1995; Dorothy Rabinowitz, "Wenatchee: A True Story," *WSJ,* three-part series, September 29, October 13, and November 8, 1995; Trevor Armbrister, "Witch-Hunt in Wenatchee," *Reader's Digest,* July 1996, pp. 125–30. Compare William Claiborne, "Child Sex Ring or Witch

Hunt?" *WP*, November 14, 1995; "Back in Wenatchee," editorial in *WSJ*, June 20, 1996; "Free My Family," *48 Hours*, television program broadcast on April 3, 1997.

26. ABC's *Turning Point*, broadcast November 14, 1996; for the original case of the two Bakersfield children, see Crewdson, *By Silence Betrayed*, pp. 120–21; Walter Goodman, "Accusations Too Readily Believed," *NYT*, November 14, 1996.

27. Debra J. Saunders, "After the Witch Hunt, No Remorse," *SFC*, July 9, 1996; Harry N. MacLean, *Once upon a Time* (New York: HarperCollins, 1993).

28. Judith L. Herman, *Trauma and Recovery* (New York: Basic, 1992); Renee Fredrickson, *Repressed Memories* (New York: Simon and Schuster, 1992); E. Sue Blume, *Secret Survivors* (New York: Ballantine, 1991); Lenore Terr, *Too Scared to Cry* (New York: Harper and Row, 1990); Lenore Terr, *Unchained Memories* (New York: Basic, 1994); Judith L. Herman and Emily Schatzow, "Recovery and Verification of Memories of Childhood Sexual Trauma," *Psychoanalytic Psychology* 4:1 (1987): 1–14; Patty Derosier Barnes, *The Woman Inside* (Racine, Wis.: Mother Courage, 1989); Carol Poston, "A Survivor of Incest," *New Woman*, March 1989, pp. 112–19; Sheila Sisk and Charlotte Foster Hoffman, *Inside Scars* (Gainesville, Fla.: Pandora, 1987); Barbara Bolz, "An Interview with Laura Davis," *On the Issues/Choices*, Fall 1991, pp. 17–19; Susan Forward and Craig Buck, *Toxic Parents* (New York: Bantam, 1989); Christine Courtois, *Healing the Incest Wound* (New York: Norton, 1988); Mike Lew, *Victims No Longer* (New York: Perennial Library, 1990). Compare Eleanor Goldstein and Kevin Farmer, *True Stories of False Memories* (Boca Raton, Fla.: SIRS, 1993).

29. Bass and Davis, *Courage to Heal*, pp. 86, 345–47, 417–21.

30. Heidi Vanderbilt, "Incest: A Chilling Report," *Lear's*, February 1992, pp. 49–77; Goldstein and Farmer, *True Stories of False Memories*, pp. 208–14; Rosaria Champagne, *The Politics of Survivorship* (New York: New York University Press, 1996); Kathleen S. Lowney and Joel Best, "Stalking Strangers and Lovers," in Joel Best, ed., *Images of Issues* (Hawthorne, N.Y.: Aldine de Gruyter, 1995), pp. 33–58.

31. Jane Smiley, *A Thousand Acres* (New York: Knopf, 1991). The Franklin case was discussed on *60 Minutes*, October 6, 1991. See also "Daughter with Nightmares Helps to Convict Mother of a Killing," *NYT*, August 7, 1994; "Woman Takes Witness Stand Against Father," AP story in State College (Pa.) *Centre Daily Times*, January 22, 1992; "A Woman's Memories from Childhood Lead to Murder Charges," *NYT*, November 25, 1994; Carol Lynn Mithers, "Incest and the Law," *NYT Magazine*, October 21, 1990, p. 44; Joseph E. Crnich and Kimberly A. Crnich, *Shifting the Burden of Truth* (Lake Oswego, Oreg.: Recollex, 1992); Daniel Goleman, "Childhood Trauma: Memory or Invention?" *NYT*, July 21, 1992.

32. Carol Tavris, "Beware the Incest Survivor Machine," *NYT Book Review*, January 3, 1993, p. 1, and *The Mismeasure of Woman* (New York: Touchstone, 1993), pp. 313–25; Leon Jaroff, "Lies of the Mind," *Time*, November 29, 1993, pp. 52–59. See also the pieces broadcast on *60 Minutes*, April 17, 1994, and November 30, 1997, and on *20/20*, July 22, 1994.

33. Jennifer J. Freyd, *Betrayal Trauma* (Cambridge: Harvard University Press, 1997); Paul S. Appelbaum, Lisa A. Uyehara, and Mark R. Elin, eds., *Trauma and Memory* (New York: Oxford University Press, 1997); Elizabeth A. Waites, *Memory Quest* (New York: Norton, 1997); Reinder Van Til, *Lost Daughters* (Grand Rapids, Mich.: William B. Eerdmans, 1997); Martin A. Conway, ed., *Recovered Memories and False Memories* (New York: Oxford University Press, 1997); Richard A. Gardner, *Psychotherapy with Sex-Abuse Victims* (Creskill, N.J.: Creative Therapeutics, 1996); Nicholas P. Spanos, *Multiple Identities and False Memories* (Washington, D.C.: American Psychological Association, 1996); Kenneth S. Pope and Laura S. Brown, *Recovered Memories of Abuse* (Washington, D.C.: American Psychological Association, 1996); Ian Hacking, *Rewriting the Soul* (Princeton: Princeton University Press, 1995); Claudette Wassil-Grimm, *Diagnosis for Disaster* (Woodstock, N.Y.: Overlook, 1995); Elizabeth Loftus and Katherine Ketcham, *The Myth of Repressed Memory* (New York: St. Martin's, 1994); Richard Ofshe and Ethan Watters, *Making Monsters* (New York: Scribner's, 1994); Michael D. Yapko, *Suggestions of Abuse* (New York: Simon and Schuster, 1994); Mark Pendergrast, *Victims of Memory* (Hinesburg, Vt.: Upper Access, 1995). For Ceci's work, see Ceci and Bruck, *Jeopardy in the Courtroom;* Stephen J. Ceci, D. F. Ross, and M. P. Toglia, *Perspectives on Children's Testimony* (New York: Springer-Verlag, 1989).

    Compare John Doris, ed., *The Suggestibility of Children's Recollections* (Washington, D.C.: American Psychological Association, 1991); Daniel Goleman, "Studies Reveal Suggestibility of Very Young as Witnesses," *NYT,* June 11, 1993; Christopher Scanlan, "Children's Testimony Questioned," *Philadelphia Inquirer,* July 30, 1991; Daniel Goleman, "Doubts Rise on Children as Witnesses," *NYT,* November 6, 1990. See also Susan Chira, "Sex Abuse: The Coil of Truth and Memory," *NYT,* December 5, 1993.

    The story on *20/20* aired on October 22, 1993. The CNN special was broadcast on August 1, 1993.

34. *Forgotten Sins* was shown in March 1996. See also Ofshe and Watters, *Making Monsters;* Wright, *Remembering Satan;* Jenkins, *Pedophiles and Priests.*

35. Jenkins, *Pedophiles and Priests;* Pam Belluck, "Memory Therapy Leads to a Lawsuit and Big Settlement," *NYT,* November 6, 1997; Jane Gross, "Suit Asks, Does Memory Therapy Heal or Harm?" *NYT,* April 8, 1994; Betsy Rubiner, "Retractors Say Therapy Misled Them," *USA Today,* November 29, 1993. See also "Don't Touch My Child," *48 Hours,* broadcast on January 4, 1990; Moira Johnston, *Spectral Evidence* (Boston: Houghton Mifflin, 1997).

36. The other Bikel reports were in the *Frontline* programs "Innocence Lost," broadcast May 1991; "Innocence Lost: The Verdict," July 1993; and "Innocence Lost: The Plea," May 1997. Compare Roland C. Summit, "The Little Rascals Day Care Center Case," *Journal of Child Sexual Abuse* 3:2 (1994): 99–102.

    The 1995 programs were broadcast on April 11 and October 24, 1995. Compare

Walter Goodman, "Who Programmed Mary? Could it be Satan?" *NYT*, October 24, 1995.

37. John Mack, *Abduction* (New York: Scribner's, 1994); C. D. B. Bryan, *Close Encounters of the Fourth Kind* (New York: Knopf, 1995), pp. 138–43; Elaine Showalter, *Hystories* (New York: Columbia University Press, 1997).

38. John E. B. Myers, ed., *The Backlash: Child Protection Under Fire* (Thousand Oaks, Calif.: Sage, 1994). Compare Susan Faludi, *Backlash* (New York: Crown, 1991); David Hechler, *The Battle and the Backlash* (Lexington, Mass.: Lexington, 1988).

For earlier critiques, see Douglas J. Besharov, "Doing Something About Child Abuse," *Harvard Journal of Law and Public Policy* 8 (1985): 539–89; Richard Wexler, "Invasion of the Child Savers," *Progressive,* September 1985, pp. 19–22; Richard Wexler, *Wounded Innocents,* rev. ed. (Buffalo, N.Y.: Prometheus, 1995); Eberle and Eberle, *Politics of Child Abuse;* Lawrence D. Spiegel, *A Question of Innocence* (Parsippany, N.J.: Unicorn, 1986); Mary Pride, *The Child Abuse Industry* (Westchester, Ill.: Crossway, 1986).

For attacks on the "backlash," see Andrew Vachss, "If We Really Want to Protect Children," *Parade Magazine,* November 3, 1996; Randolph Ryan, "Sex Abuse Hysteria Is a Big Lie," *BG,* reprinted in State College (Pa.) *Centre Daily Times,* May 19, 1993; Quindlen, "Believing the Children."

39. Nathan and Snedeker, *Satan's Silence,* pp. 239–43; Goldstein and Farmer, *True Stories of False Memories,* pp. 217–20; Joan Sanchez, "Child Advocate Faces Trial for Child Abuse," A.P. story reprinted in the State College (Pa.) *Centre Daily Times,* April 22, 1992; Peter Applebome, "Child Abuse Rescuer Is Now the Accused," *NYT,* April 27, 1992; Betsy Gleick, "Trial of a Child-Abuse Vigilante," *People Weekly,* May 11, 1992, pp. 101–2.

40. Amy J. Curtis-Webber, "Not Just Another Pretty Victim," *Journal of Popular Culture* 28:4 (1995): 37–47; Ellen L. Hopkins, "Abusing the Rights of Parents," *Newsweek,* October 18, 1993, p. 26; Jane Hamilton, *A Map of the World* (New York: Doubleday, 1994); William Glaberson, "Family Nightmare," *NYT,* December 4, 1990; Evelyn Nieves, "Abuse Case Reversal Called Sign of Trend," *NYT,* April 6, 1993.

41. "Rush to Judgment," *Newsweek,* April 19, 1993. Others remained convinced of the Souzas' guilt: see Bella English, "The Souzas Aren't the Victims in Abuse Case," *BG,* reprinted in State College (Pa.) *Centre Daily Times,* April 18, 1993; Ryan, "Sex Abuse Hysteria Is a Big Lie"; Lela Costin, Howard Krager, and David Stoesz, *The Politics of Child Abuse in America* (New York: Oxford University Press, 1996).

42. Bass and Davis, *Courage to Heal;* Chira, "Sex Abuse: The Coil of Truth and Memory." Compare Champagne, *Politics of Survivorship;* E. Olafson, D. L. Corwin, and Roland C. Summit, "Modern History of Child Sexual Abuse Awareness: Cycles of Discovery and Suppression," *CAN* 17 (1993): 7–24; Andrew Vachss, *False Allegations* (New York: Knopf, 1996).

CHAPTER 9: FULL CIRCLE

1. The first chapter epigraph is from Andrew Vachss, "Sex Predators Can't Be Saved," *NYT,* January 5, 1993. For statistics from the 1980s and 1990s, see "Sex Offender Registration Laws Pit Victims' Rights Against Civil Rights," *NYT,* February 20, 1993; Daniel Goleman, "Therapies Offer Hope for Sex Offenders," *NYT,* April 14, 1992; Lawrence A. Greenfeld, *Sex Offenses and Offenders* (Washington, D.C.: Bureau of Justice Statistics, 1997).

2. Todd S. Purdum, "Clinton Backs Plan to Track Sex Offenders Nationwide," *NYT,* June 23, 1996; Lawrence A. Greenfeld, *Child Victimizers* (Washington, D.C.: Bureau of Justice Statistics, 1996); William Breer, *The Adolescent Molester,* 2d ed. (Springfield, Ill.: Charles C. Thomas, 1996); Douglas W. Pryor, *Unspeakable Acts* (New York: New York University Press, 1996); Dennis Howitt, *Paedophiles and Sexual Offenses Against Children* (New York: Wiley, 1995); Nathaniel J. Pallone, *Rehabilitating Criminal Sexual Psychopaths* (New Brunswick, N.J.: Transaction, 1990); George W. Barnard et al., *The Child Molester* (New York: Brunner-Mazel, 1989); L. Furby, M. R. Weinrott, and L. Blackshaw, "Sex Offender Recidivism: A Review," *Psychological Bulletin* 105:1 (1989): 3–30; Gene Abel et al., "Self-Reported Sex Crimes of Non-Incarcerated Paraphiliacs," *Journal of Interpersonal Violence* 1 (1987): 3–25; Ronald M. Holmes, *Sex Crimes* (Newbury Park, Calif.: Sage, 1991); Howard Hunter, *Man/Child: An Insight into Child Sexual Abuse by a Convicted Molester* (Jefferson, N.C.: McFarland, 1991).

   For "serial" crime, see Doug Smith, "LAPD Assailed for Not Telling Schools About Serial Molester," *LAT,* November 17, 1993; Philip Jenkins, *Using Murder* (Hawthorne, N.Y.: Aldine de Gruyter, 1994). Compare Eric Leberg, *Understanding Child Molesters* (Thousand Oaks, Calif.: Sage, 1997).

3. Jerry Seper, "Pedophile Was Freed Despite Past: Officials Say He Killed Girl, Molested Others," *Washington Times,* June 7, 1989; Jerry Seper, "Mutilation of Boy Prompts Effort to Reform System," *Washington Times,* June 23, 1989; Deeann Glamser, "Rape Victim, 8, to Face Accused," *USA Today,* January 30, 1990; Timothy Egan, "Sex Crimes Against Children: Many Doubt There's a Cure," *NYT,* January 1, 1990.

4. Robb London, "Strategy on Sex Crimes Is Prison, Then Prison," *NYT,* February 8, 1991; F. Berlin and H. M. Malin, "Media Distortion of the Public's Perception of Recidivism and Psychiatric Rehabilitation," *AJP,* 148:11 (1991): 1572–76; "Predators and Politics: A Symposium on Washington's Sexually Violent Predator Statute," *University of Puget Sound Law Review* 15:3 (1992); "Sex Offenders in Washington State Could Get Life in Prison," *Atlanta Journal and Constitution,* November 29, 1989; "Sex Offender Registration Laws Pit Victims' Rights Against Civil Rights." For local Washington precedents, see Robinson A. Williams, *The Washington State Sexual Psychopath Law* (Fort Steilacoom, Wash.: Department of Social and Health Services, Western State Hospital, 1971).

5. London, "Strategy on Sex Crimes."

6. John La Fond, "Predator Laws . . . and Sinister Sex Offenders," *Washington Times,* January 10, 1993, and "Protect Everyone's Rights," *USA Today,* December 8, 1993; Laurie Kellman, "Virginia Studies Tough Washington State Sex Offender Law," *Washington Times,* December 12, 1992.

7. Egan, "Sex Crimes Against Children"; Gary C. King, *Driven to Kill* (New York: Pinnacle, 1993). Compare Lori Steinhorst and John Rose, *When the Monster Comes Out of the Closet* (Salem, Oreg.: Rose, 1994); Vachss, "Sex Predators Can't be Saved," *NYT,* January 5, 1993.

8. Lexis-Nexis search.

9. Jenkins, *Using Murder.* Andrew Vachss's biological speculations are elaborated in his article "If We Really Want to Protect Children," *Parade Magazine,* November 3, 1996; compare Vachss, "Today's Abused Child Could Be Tomorrow's Predator," *WP,* June 3, 1990, and "How We Can Fight Child Abuse," *WP,* August 20, 1989; Jack Olsen, *Predator: Rape, Madness, and Injustice in Seattle* (New York: Delacorte, 1991); Kathleen S. Lowney and Joel Best, "Stalking Strangers and Lovers," in Joel Best, ed., *Images of Issues* (Hawthorne, N.Y.: Aldine de Gruyter, 1995), pp. 33–58.

   For the press's use of predator concept, see, for example, Gil Spencer, "When Protector Becomes Predator, Man the Lifeboats," *Denver Post,* March 31, 1991; Ginny McKibben, "'Predator' Gets Seventy-Five Years in Sex Assaults," *Denver Post,* October 29, 1991; Rick Kogan, "The Doctor as Predator," *Chicago Tribune,* November 12, 1991; Scott Minerbrook, "The Case of the Sexual Predator," *U.S. News and World Report,* April 19, 1993, pp. 31–35; Veronica T. Jennings, "Silver Spring Man Offers a Grim Account of Life as a Sexual Predator," *WP,* April 10, 1994; Maurice Possley, "Predator Gets Life Term Without Parole," *Chicago Tribune,* May 25, 1995; Art Barnum, "Sexual Predator Is Sentenced to Twenty years for Abusing Boys," *Chicago Tribune,* November 23, 1995; Ron French, "Cyberspace Predator Battles Police Chief's Accusations," *Detroit News,* March 6, 1996.

10. Michael DeCourcy Hinds, "More Say They Are Sex-Case Victims," *NYT,* March 31, 1992; "Child Molester Tells of a Rampage in Five States," *NYT,* December 26, 1993; Beverly Lowry, "Should Ellie Nesler Go Free?" *Redbook,* August 1994, pp. 82–85; "Ellie Nesler," *People Magazine,* April 19, 1993, p. 42; Michelle Quinn, "Sympathy for a Mother Accused of Slaying Molester in Revenge," *NYT,* April 12, 1993; James R. Kincaid, "Purity, Pederasty, and a Fallen Heroine," *NYT,* June 1, 1993. Compare Claire Safran "Two Moms Who Saved Their Town from a Child Molester," *Good Housekeeping,* April 1995, p. 82; Shari Geller, *Fatal Convictions* (New York: ReganBooks, 1996).

11. Mike Echols, *I Know My First Name Is Steven* (New York: Pinnacle, 1991); Terry Ganey, *St. Joseph's Children* (New York: Lyle Stuart and Carol, 1989); King, *Driven to Kill;* Don W. Weber and Charles Bosworth, *Secret Lessons* (New York: Onyx, 1994); Mike Echols, *Brother Tony's Boys* (Amherst, N.Y.: Prometheus, 1996);

Philip Jenkins, *Pedophiles and Priests* (New York: Oxford University Press, 1996).

12. "Child Hunter," program on *48 Hours*, August 24, 1994. *48 Hours* returned to the "child hunter" theme in later episodes—in June 1996, for example, and in a segment entitled "A Killer in Friendswood," broadcast May 1, 1997. For lessons in evading abductors, see Raymond Hernandez, "Now, Should They Teach the Potato Famine in Schools?" *NYT*, December 1, 1996. For the renewed emphasis on stranger abduction, see Paula S. Fass, *Kidnapped: Child Abduction in America* (New York: Oxford University Press, 1997), pp. 213–67; Cynthia MacGregor, *Stranger* (New York: PowerKids Books, 1997); Margaret O. Hyde, *Missing and Murdered Children* (New York: Franklin Watts, 1998).

13. Barry Bortnick, *Polly Klaas: The Murder of America's Child* (New York: Pinnacle, 1995); Elizabeth Gleick, "Taken in the Night," *People Weekly*, October 25, 1993, pp. 66–68; Melinda Beck, "The Sad Case of Polly Klaas," *Newsweek*, December 13, 1993, p. 39; Elizabeth Gleick, "'America's Child'," *People Weekly*, December 20, 1993, pp. 84–88; Ernest Van Den Haag, "How to Cut Crime," *National Review*, May 30, 1994, pp. 30–35; "Richard Allen Davis' Life of Crime," *SFC*, August 6, 1996; Elizabeth Gleick, "An Angel named Polly," *People Weekly*, November 28, 1994, pp. 56–59; Jeffrey Toobin, "The Man Who Kept Going Free," *New Yorker*, March 7, 1994, pp. 38–53; "What If . . . ?" ABC's *Primetime Live*, January 27, 1994.

14. Jane Gross, "Crying for Protection," *Saturday Evening Post*, March 1994, pp. 38–39; Polly Klaas Foundation web site, 1995, http://www.pklaas.com; David Shichor and Dale K. Sechrest, *Three Strikes and You're Out* (Thousand Oaks, Calif.: Sage, 1996); "Rape: The Crime That Is Truly Insane," editorial in *LAT*, March 20, 1994; Tom Junod, "America's Most Haunted," *GQ*, September 1997, pp. 342–49.

15. William Glaberson, "'Megan's Law' Sex Offender Defied Efforts at Rehabilitation," *NYT*, May 28, 1996; Jon Nordheimer, "New Look at Jail Unit Housing Sex Offenders," *NYT*, November 2, 1994; Kimberly McLarin, "Fast Assembly Passes Seven Bills on Sex Abuse," *NYT*, August 30, 1994.

16. Peter Davis, "The Sex Offender Next Door," *NYT Magazine*, July 28, 1996, pp. 20–27; Elizabeth Kelley Cierzniak, "There Goes the Neighborhood," *Indiana Law Review* 28:3 (1995): 715–36; House Committee on the Judiciary, *Megan's Law* (Washington: GPO, 1996); McLarin, "Fast Assembly"; Rebecca Goldsmith, "Victim's Advocates Endorse Bills Toughening Penalties," *Philadelphia Inquirer*, May 10, 1996.

17. Robert Hanley, "Federal Appeals Court Rejects Offenders Challenge to Megan's Law," *NYT*, April 13, 1996; Jerry Gray, "House Endorses Bill to Require Notification on Sex Offenders," *NYT*, May 8, 1996; *Megan's Law, Community Notification of Sex Offenders: Report of the Virginia State Crime Commission to the Governor and the General Assembly of Virginia.* (Richmond: Commonwealth of Virginia, 1997).

18. Frank Browning, "From 'Poof' to 'Predator,'" *WP*, March 28, 1993.

19. "What If . . . ?" ABC *Primetime Live*, January 27, 1994; Purdum, "Clinton Backs

Plan"; "Sex Offenders Are Subject of a Registry," *NYT*, August 25, 1996; Democratic campaign commercial, broadcast on ABC television, October 20, 1996.

20. Wallace Turner, "Unusual Sentence Stirs Legal Dispute," *NYT*, August 27, 1987; Jan Hoffman, "Crime and Punishment," *NYT*, January 16, 1997; "Sex Offender Registration Laws Pit Victims' Rights Against Civil Rights"; Robert L. Steinback, "Sexual Predators Should Be Tagged," article from *Miami Herald*, reprinted in State College (Pa.) *Centre Daily Times*, December 8, 1996; CBS's *48 Hours*, "Predators," 1991; Suzanne Fields, "Molesters Should Be Monitored for Life," *Arizona Republic*, April 7, 1997.

21. Don Van Natta, "U.S. Judge Blocks State's Plan to Release Names and Addresses of Sex Offenders," *NYT*, March 8, 1996.

22. Whitman, *Terror*, pp. 383–84; "Sex Offender Registration Laws Pit Victims' Rights Against Civil Rights"; Matthew Stadler, "Stalking the Predator," *NYT*, November 7, 1995.

23. Andy Newman, "New Jersey Court Says 12-Year-Old Must Register as a Sexual Offender," *NYT*, April 12, 1996; Van Natta, "U.S. Judge Blocks State's Plan"; Cathy Young, "Untangling Notification Hysteria," *Philadelphia Inquirer*, May 30, 1996; Monte Williams, "Sex Offenders' Law Prompts Privacy Debate in New York," *NYT*, February 24, 1996.

24. "Commitment Law Faces Constitutional Challenge," WWW page, 1996; Judy Steed, *Our Little Secret* (Toronto: Vintage Canada, 1995), p. 215.

25. Todd S. Purdum, "Registry Laws Tar Sex Crime Convicts with Broad Brush," *NYT*, July 1, 1997; Williams, "Sex Offenders' Law"; Robert Hanley, "Federal Appeals Court Rejects Offenders' Challenge to Megan's Law," *NYT*, April 13, 1996; Lynette Holloway, "Megan's Law Notification Is Barred in Old Convictions," *NYT*, September 26, 1996. On the California situation, see Carey Goldberg, "California Judges Modify Three-Strikes Law," *NYT*, June 21, 1996.

26. The case is *Kansas v. Hendricks*, 95–1649. See Linda Greenhouse, "Likely Repeaters May Stay Confined," *NYT*, June 24, 1997; Aaron Epstein, "Justices Say States Can Keep Sexual Predators Locked Up," *Philadelphia Inquirer*, June 24, 1997; Matthew Purdy, "Wave of New Laws Seeks to Confine Sexual Offenders," *NYT*, June 29, 1997.

27. Andrew T. Scull, *Decarceration, Community Treatment, and the Deviant*, 2d ed. (New Brunswick, N.J.: Rutgers University Press, 1984); Daniel Goleman, "States Move to Ease Law Committing Mentally Ill," *NYT*, December 9, 1986; Robert Pear, "For Mentally Ill, Life on the Streets Is No Boon," *NYT*, January 3, 1987; Linda Greenhouse, "Court Upholds Forced Treatment of Mentally Ill by Prison Officials," *NYT*, February 28, 1990; E. Fuller Torrey, *Out of the Shadows* (New York: Wiley, 1997).

28. Sylvere Lotringer, *Overexposed* (New York: Pantheon, 1988); Joanne G. Greer and Irving R. Stuart, eds., *The Sexual Aggressor* (New York: Van Nostrand Reinhold,

1983); William J. Winslade, "Voluntary Castration for Nonviolent Pedophiles," *Houston Chronicle,* May 16, 1995; Matthew Stadler, *The Sex Offender* (New York: HarperCollins, 1994).

29. The Connecticut case is described in Todd R. Clear and George F. Cole, *American Corrections* (Monterey, Calif.: Brooks Cole, 1986). For McQuay, see Larry Don McQuay and F. Berlin, "The Case for Castration," *Washington Monthly,* May 1994, pp. 26–29; Sam Howe Verhovek, "Molester Seeks Castration: Texas Agrees," *NYT,* April 5, 1996; Sam Howe Verhovek, "Texas Frees Child Molester Who Warned of Backsliding," *NYT,* April 9, 1996.

30. Eli Coleman, Margretta Dwyer, and Nathaniel J. Pallone, eds., *Sex Offender Treatment* (Binghamton, N.Y.: Haworth, 1996); William E. Prendergast, *Treating Sex Offenders in Correctional Institutions and Outpatient Clinics* (New York: Haworth, 1991); Michael A. O'Connell, Eric Leberg, and Craig R. Donaldson, *Working with Sex Offenders* (Thousand Oaks, Calif.: Sage, 1990); Barry M. Maletzky and Kevin B. McGovern, *Treating the Sexual Offender* (Thousand Oaks, Calif.: Sage, 1990); Sean P. Murphy, "Nation Getting Tougher with Its Sex Offenders," *BG,* June 16, 1992; B. Drummond Ayres, "California Bill Would Require 'Chemical Castration' for Repeat Sex Offenders," *NYT,* August 27, 1996.

31. Lynn Walford, "Rooting Out E-vil [*sic*]," *LAT,* February 7, 1996; Dwight Silverman, "Pornography in Cyberspace Poses Dilemma," *Houston Chronicle,* July 21, 1995; John Crewdson, *By Silence Betrayed* (New York: Little, Brown, 1988), pp. 103–5; Attorney General's Commission on Pornography, *Final Report* (Washington, D.C.: U.S. Department of Justice, 1986), pp. 628–29.

32. *How Can Parents Protect Their Children from Pedophiles Roaming the Internet?* on-line brochure, WWW, 1995; Lawrence J. Magid, *Child Safety on the Information Highway,* on-line brochure, produced by the NCMEC and the Interactive Services Association, WWW 1994; House Committee on the Judiciary, Subcommittee on Crime, *Sexual Exploitation of Children: Hearings Before the Subcommittee on Crime of the Committee on the Judiciary* (Washington, D.C.: GPO, 1977), p. 429; Pat Pulling, *The Devil's Web: Who Is Stalking Your Children for Satan?* (Lafayette, La.: Huntington House, 1989).

33. "FBI Says Pair Used Sex Message Service in Plot to Nab a Boy, Kill Him on Film," *Atlanta Journal and Constitution,* August 23, 1989; Robert L. Jackson, "Computer-Crime Sleuths Go Undercover," *LAT,* October 1, 1989; David Armstrong, "Child Molesters Use Computer Talk as Bait," *BG,* March 3, 1994; Julie Morris, "Pasadena Child Molesting Case Takes High-Tech Turn," *Houston Post,* March 4, 1994; Barbara Kantrowitz, "Child Abuse in Cyberspace," *Newsweek,* April 18, 1994, p. 40; John Larrabee, "Cyberspace a New Beat for Police," *USA Today,* April 26, 1994; Sandy Rovner, "Molesting Children by Computer," *WP,* August 2, 1994; Sebastian Rotella, "Computerized Child Porno Ring Broken," *LAT,* September 24, 1994; Laurie J. Flynn, "Guardian Angels Now Patrol the Net," *NYT,* March

16, 1996; "A Twenty-City Search in Child Pornography Inquiry," *NYT,* December 12, 1996.

34. Mark Clayton, "Off-Line Hazards Lie in Web's Links, Lures," in *The Child Sex Trade,* series reprint from the *Christian Science Monitor* (1996): 7; Steven Levy, "No Place for Kids?" *Newsweek,* July 3, 1995, pp. 46–50; Dennis McCafferty, "Georgian Accused of Going On-Line to Find Molestation Victims," *Atlanta Journal and Constitution,* August 4, 1995; "Florida Man Accused of Using Cyberspace to Lure, Rape Teenager," *BG,* August 30, 1995; Steve Olafson, "Jury Picked in Child-Sex Trial of Alvin Man," *Houston Chronicle,* December 5, 1995; Nina Bernstein, "On Prison Computer, Files to Make Parents Shiver," *NYT,* November 18, 1996; "Missing Girl Is Found with Man from Internet," *NYT,* April 18, 1997; "Visits and Vigilance: Sex Offenders Shadowed by Parole Oficers," *NYT,* June 8, 1997.

35. Simon Winchester, "An Electronic Sink of Depravity," *Spectator,* February 4, 1995, pp. 9–11. For Grassley's earlier interest in child protection, see Senate Committee on the Judiciary, Subcommittee on Juvenile Justice, *Effects of Pornography on Women and Children: Hearings Before the Subcommittee on Juvenile Justice of the Committee on the Judiciary* (Washington, D.C.: GPO, 1985).

36. Matt Schwartz, "Computer Child Porn Raid Targets Home in Houston," *Houston Post,* March 5, 1993; Jordana Hart, "Child Pornography via Computer Is Focus of Federal Sweep," *BG,* March 7, 1993; Ronald J. Ostrow, "Fight Against Child Pornography Waged on New Front: Computers," *LAT,* September 1, 1993; Michael Grunwald, "Police Probe America Online–Pornography Link," *BG,* January 18, 1995; Philip Elmer-DeWitt, "On a Screen near You: Cyberporn," *Time,* July 3, 1995, pp. 38–45.

37. Jim Exon, "At Issue: Should the Government Crack Down on Pornography on the Internet?" *CQ Researcher* 5:24 (1995): 577.

38. Elmer-DeWitt, "On a Screen near You"; Edmund L. Andrews, "A Crusader Against Cyberporn Who Was Once Involved in a Sex Scandal," *NYT,* November 27, 1995.

39. Marty Rimm, "Marketing Pornography on the Information Superhighway," *Georgetown Law Journal* 83:5 (June 1995): 1849–73, quoted in Levy, "No Place for Kids?"; Philip Elmer-DeWitt, "On a Screen near You," and "Firestorm on the Computer Nets," *Time,* July 24, 1995, p. 57.

40. Elmer-DeWitt, "On a Screen near You"; Levy, "No Place for Kids?" Compare Stephen Schwartz, "S.F. Man Held, Accused of Enticing Teen On-Line," *SFC,* August 25, 1995.

41. Robert Rossney, "Time's Story on Cyberporn of Questionable Validity," *SFC,* July 13, 1995; G. Bruce Knecht, "*Time* Magazine Notes That Questions Are Raised on Cyberporn Cover Story," *WSJ,* July 17, 1995.

42. Peter H. Lewis, "Computer Pornography Hearing Will Not Include Expert Witness," *NYT,* July 24, 1995; Senate Committee on the Judiciary, *Cyberporn and Children: Hearing Before the Committee on the Judiciary* (Washington, D.C.: GPO,

1995); House Committee on Science, *Cyberporn [and] Protecting Our Children from the Back Alleys of the Internet: Joint Hearing Before the Subcommittee on Basic Research and the Subcommittee on Technology of the Committee on Science* (Washington, D.C.: GPO, 1995); Barry F. Crimmins, "Child Pornography," *BG*, July 29, 1995.

43. Kara Swisher, "On-Line Child Pornography Charged as Twelve Are Arrested," *WP*, September 14, 1995; David Johnston, "Use of Computer Network for Child Sex Sets Off Raids," *NYT*, September 14, 1995; Jared Sandberg, "FBI Crackdown on Child Pornography Opens Hornet's Nest, Stinging America Online," *WSJ*, September 15, 1995; Laura Evenson, "FBI Raid on Cyberporn Heightens Concern About Children On-Line," *SFC*, September 15, 1995; John W. Fountain, "Federal Agents Baited 'Net in Child Pornography Case," *WP*, November 9, 1995.

44. "Pedophiles Use Encoding Devices to Make Secret Use of Internet," *Times* (London), November 21, 1995; CBS evening news, December 15, 1996.

45. Peter H. Lewis, "Judges Turn Back Law Intended to Regulate Internet Decency," *NYT*, June 13, 1996; Linda Greenhouse, "Court, 9–0, Upholds State Laws Prohibiting Assisted Suicide, Protects Speech on Internet," *NYT*, June 27, 1997. The CDA case was *Reno v. American Civil Liberties Union*, 96–511.

46. King, *Driven to Kill*, p. 333; Neil S. Websdale, "Predators: The Social Construction of Stranger-Danger in Washington State a Form of Patriarchal Ideology," *Women and Criminal Justice* 7:2 (1996): 43–68.

47. Levy, "No Place for Kids?" Compare Clayton, "Off-Line Hazards Lie in Web's Links, Lures."

CHAPTER 10: A CYCLE OF PANIC

1. Compare Joel Best, *Threatened Children* (Chicago: University of Chicago Press, 1990), pp. 176–88. For the cooptation of children's rights rhetoric to support various social and political causes, see, for example, Robert Pear, "Washington Kidnaps Dick and Jane," *NYT*, June 15, 1997.

2. Walter I. Trattner, *From Poor Law to Welfare State*, 5th ed. (New York: Free Press, 1994); Linda Gordon, ed., *Women, the State, and Welfare* (Madison: University of Wisconsin Press, 1990); Ellen Herman, *The Romance of American Psychology* (Berkeley: University of California Press, 1995), p. 3.

3. Elizabeth H. Pleck, *Domestic Tyranny* (New York: Oxford University Press, 1987); Linda Gordon, *Heroes of Their Own Lives* (New York: Viking, 1988).

4. Peter Conrad and Joseph W. Schneider, *Deviance and Medicalization* (Philadelphia: Temple University Press, 1992); Herman, *Romance of American Psychology*, pp. 2–3.

5. Peter W. Huber, *Liability* (New York: Basic, 1988); Philip Jenkins, *Pedophiles and Priests* (New York: Oxford University Press, 1996).

6. Richard V. Ericson, *Representing Order* (Toronto: University of Toronto, 1991).

7. Robert H. Gollmar, *Edward Gein* (New York: Pinnacle, 1981); Parker Rossman, *Sexual Experience Between Men and Boys* (New York: Association Press, 1976), pp. 73–75; Jack Olsen, *The Man with the Candy* (New York: Simon and Schuster, 1974).

8. Jacob A. Goldberg and Rosamond W. Goldberg, *Girls on City Streets* (New York: American Social Hygiene Association, 1935); Alfred C. Kinsey et al., *Sexual Behavior in the Human Female* (Philadelphia: W. B. Saunders, 1953).

9. Compare Best, *Threatened Children,* p. 117. On how notions about adolescence have shifted in American history, see Joseph Kett, *Rites of Passage* (New York: Basic, 1977); John Modell, *Into One's Own* (Berkeley: University of California Press, 1989).

10. Paula S. Fass, *The Damned and the Beautiful* (New York: Oxford University Press, 1977); Beth Bailey, *From Front Porch to Back Seat* (Baltimore: Johns Hopkins University Press, 1988); James B. Gilbert, *A Cycle of Outrage* (New York: Oxford University Press, 1986); David F. Musto, *The American Disease* (New York: Oxford University Press, 1987); David Wagner, *The New Temperance* (Boulder, Colo.: Westview, 1997).

11. Anthony M. Platt, *The Child Savers,* 2d ed. (Chicago: University of Chicago, 1977); Steven M. Schlossman, *Love and the Delinquent* (Chicago: University of Chicago Press, 1977); Robert M. Mennel, *Thorns and Thistles* (Hanover, N.H.: University Press of New England, 1973). The word *adolescence* was popularized by G. Stanley Hall's book of that name, published in 1904.

12. Allan Berube, *Coming Out Under Fire* (New York: Free Press, 1990); Karen Anderson, *Wartime Women* (Westport, Conn.: Greenwood Press, 1981).

13. Bernard Williams, *Jailbait* (New York: Garden City Books, 1951), p. 5, also pp. 8–20, 113. Compare John D'Emilio and Estelle B. Freedman, *Intimate Matters* (New York: Harper and Row, 1988), pp. 260–62; Gary Silver, ed., *The Dope Chronicles* (San Francisco: Harper and Row, 1979), p. 280; Gilbert, *Cycle of Outrage,* pp. 25–41.

14. George Chauncey, "The Postwar Sex Crime Panic," in William Graebner, ed., *True Stories from the American Past* (New York: McGraw-Hill, 1993), pp. 173–74; Lewis J. Doshay, *The Boy Sex Offender and His Later Career* (1943; reprint, Montclair, N.J.: Patterson Smith, 1969), pp. 40–46.

15. Felicity Barringer, "Children as Sexual Prey and Predators," *NYT,* May 30, 1989; Carolyn Cunningham and Kee MacFarlane, *When Children Molest Children* (Orwell, Vt.: Safer Society, 1991); Adam Nossiter, "Six-Year-Old's Sex Crime," *NYT,* September 27, 1996; Judith Levine, "A Question of Abuse," *Mother Jones,* July–August, 1996, p. 36; Eliana Gil and Toni Cavanagh Johnson, *Sexualized Children* (Rockville, Md.: Launch, 1993).

16. Stephanie Coontz, *The Way We Never Were* (New York: Basic, 1992). Compare Chauncey, "The Postwar Sex Crime Panic," p. 176; Estelle B. Freedman, "Uncontrolled Desires," *Journal of American History* 74 (1987): 83–106.

17. Peter T. Kilborn, "Shift in Families Reach a Plateau, Study Says," *NYT*, November 27, 1996.

18. Steven Levy, "No Place for Kids?" *Newsweek*, July 3, 1995, pp. 46–50.

19. Arthur MacDonald, "Criminological Literature," *American Journal of Psychology* 3 (1890): 219–40; W. T. Stead, *The Americanization of the World* (New York: H. Markley, 1901).

    See also Augustine Brannigan, "Mystification of the Innocent: Crime Comics and Delinquency in Canada, 1931–1949," *Criminal Justice History* 7 (1986): 111–45; Martin Barker, *A Haunt of Fears* (London, 1984); Fredric Wertham, *Seduction of the Innocent* (London: Museum, 1955).

20. David Connett and Jon Henley, "The Pedlars of Child Abuse," *Observer* (London), August 25, 1996; Ray Wyre and Tim Tate, *The Murder of Childhood* (London: Penguin, 1995); Philip Jenkins, *Intimate Enemies* (Hawthorne, N.Y.: Aldine de Gruyter, 1992).

21. Paul R. Wilson, *The Man They Called a Monster* (North Ryde, N.S.W.: Cassell Australia, 1981), pp. 58–72; Yvonne Roberts, "It Can Happen Here," *New Statesman and Society* (London), July 1, 1988; *Organized Criminal Paedophile Activity: A Report by the Parliamentary Joint Committee on the National Crime Authority* (Canberra, 1995).

22. Marlise Simons, "How Belgium Blinked at Child Killer's Trail," *NYT*, November 4, 1996; Marlise Simons, "Sex Slayings Alarm France on the Peril of Repeat Offenders," *NYT*, February 25, 1997; Edmund L. Andrews, "CompuServe Official Charged in Germany," *NYT*, April 17, 1997; Craig R. Whitney, "French Child Porn Dragnet Is Criticized After Suicides," *NYT*, June 24, 1997; "British Impose a Megan's Law of Their Own," *NYT*, August 12, 1997. For South Africa, see Angella Johnson, "Paedophile's Daughter Defends Her Dad," *Mail and Guardian*, May 20, 1996. For Canada, see W. L. Marshall and Sylvia Barrett, *Criminal Neglect* (Toronto: Seal, 1992); Jenkins, *Intimate Enemies* and *Pedophiles and Priests;* Darcy Henton and David McGann, *Boys Don't Cry* (Toronto: McClelland and Stewart, 1995); Judy Steed, *Our Little Secret* (Toronto: Vintage Canada, 1995). For Japan, see Nicholas D. Kristof, "A Plain School Uniform as the Latest Aphrodisiac," *NYT*, April 2, 1997.

23. Sharon R. King, "Mental Health Ventures May Gain from New Law," *NYT*, October 20, 1996.

24. Steven A. Holmes, "It's Awful! It's Terrible! It's . . . Never Mind," *NYT*, July 6, 1997; Mireya Navarro, "Teenage Mothers Viewed as Abused Prey of Older Men," *NYT*, May 19, 1996; "Connecticut Crackdown on Statutory Rape," *NYT*, June 20, 1996; Ellen Goodman, "In Defense of Adolescent Girls (Jailbait)," *BG*, February 19, 1995. For Massachusetts, see "Statutory Rape Initiative," WWW, 1996. See also "Putting the 'Jail' in Jailbait," *Time*, January 29, 1996, p. 33; B. Drummond Ayres, "Marriage Advised in Some Youth Pregnancies," *NYT*, September 9, 1996; Ellen

Goodman, "This Marriage Begins Broken," State College (Pa.) *Centre Daily Times*, September 17, 1996; James Brooke, "Idaho County Finds Way to Chastize Pregnant Teenagers," *NYT*, October 25, 1996.

25. Matthew Stadler, "Stalking the Predator," *NYT*, November 7, 1995.

26. "Ripper Murders," editorial in *NYT*, March 22, 1915.

Index